10668712

Reason and Passion

Reason and Passion

*Representations of Gender
in a Malay Society*

MICHAEL G. PELETZ

University of California Press

BERKELEY   LOS ANGELES   LONDON

University of California Press
Berkeley and Los Angeles, California

University of California Press, Ltd.
London, England

© 1996 by the Regents of the University of California

Parts of this book were published in earlier versions.
Parts of chapters 1 and 2: *A Share of the Harvest: Kinship, Property,
and Social History among the Malays of Rembau* (Berkeley:
University of California Press, 1988).
Parts of chapter 2: "The Exchange of Men in Nineteenth-Century
Negeri Sembilan (Malaya)," *American Ethnologist* 14, no. 3 (1987).
Reprinted by permission of the American Anthropological
Association. Not for further reproduction.
Parts of chapter 4: "Knowledge, Power, and Personal Misfortune in a
Malay Context," in *Understanding Witchcraft and Sorcery in
Southeast Asia,* edited by C. W. Watson and Roy F. Ellen (Honolulu:
University of Hawaii Press, 1993). Reprinted by permission of the
University of Hawaii Press. "Poisoning, Sorcery, and Healing Rituals
in Negeri Sembilan," *Bijdragen tot de Taal-, Land-, en Volkenkunde*
144, no. 1 (1988). Reprinted by permission of the Koninklijk Instituut
voor Taal-, Land-, en Volkenkunde, Leiden.
Parts of chapter 6: "Neither Reasonable nor Responsible: Contrasting
Representations of Masculinity in a Malay Society," *Cultural
Anthropology* 9, no. 2 (1994). Reprinted by permission of the
American Anthropological Association.

Library of Congress Cataloging-in-Publication Data

Peletz, Michael G.
  Reason and passion : representations of gender in a Malay society /
Michael G. Peletz.
    p.   cm.
  Includes bibliographical references (p.   ) and index.
  ISBN 0-520-20069-1 (alk. paper).—ISBN 0-520-20070-5 (pbk. : alk.
paper)
    1. Malays (Asian people)—Malaysia—Negeri Sembilan—
Kinship.   2. Malays (Asian people)—Malaysia—Negeri Sembilan—
Social conditions.   3. Gender identity—Malaysia—Negeri
Sembilan.   4. Sex role—Malaysia—Negeri Sembilan.   5. Matrilineal
kinship—Malaysia—Negeri Sembilan.   6. Negeri Sembilan—Social
life and customs.   I. Title.
DS595.P45   1996
305.3'09595'1—dc20   94-45698
                                                          CIP

Printed in the United States of America
9 8 7 6 5 4 3 2 1

The paper used in this publication meets the minimum requirements
of American National Standard for Information Sciences—Permanence
of Paper for Printed Library Materials, ANSI Z39.48-1984.

For my parents,
Cyril M. and Shirley G. Peletz

Contents

Illustrations

Figures

Maps

Acknowledgments

In the course of envisioning and carrying out this project, I received intellectual, moral, and material support from many sources. I am indebted to my parents, Cyril M. Peletz and Shirley G. Peletz, for providing a supportive environment in which my aspirations could be pursued. This book is dedicated to them, partly in recognition of their many sacrifices on my behalf, which will always be deeply appreciated. I also remain very much indebted to my mentors—Raymond Kelly, Sherry Ortner, and Aram Yengoyan—both for what they taught me in the seventies and early eighties about anthropology and scholarly inquiry, and for the encouragement and everything else they have given me as colleagues and friends in the years since. I am especially grateful to Aram Yengoyan, who for a full twenty years now has provided an intellectual role model and has also helped impress upon me the inestimable value of having good friendships and a sense of humor.

The material support which made this book possible came from numerous institutions. The first period of field research (1978–80) was sponsored by the National Science Foundation (under Grant No. BNS-7812499) and the University of Michigan (the Center for South and Southeast Asian Studies and the Rackham School of Graduate Studies). The second (1987–88) was underwritten by the Fulbright Scholars Program, the Wenner-Gren Foundation for Anthropological Research, and the Picker Fellowship Program at Colgate University. A 1991–92 Fellowship from the National Endowment for the Humanities provided valuable release time from teaching and related responsibilities, and thus greatly facilitated the writing of this book. My affiliation with the Department of Anthropology and the Southeast Asia Program at Cornell University during the tenure of the latter Fellowship also contributed in important ways to the shaping of the arguments developed here. A 1992–93 Fellowship from the Joint Committee on Southeast Asia of the Social Science Research Council and the American Council of Learned Societies (with funds provided by the Ford Foundation and NEH) was likewise highly beneficial. In addition to thanking these institutions for their support I acknowledge my debt to my former wife, Ellen Peletz, for aiding me during both stints of research. And to my son, Zachary, who was also a key player during the second period of research (although only two and a half years old at the beginning of that fieldwork), many thanks.

A number of friends and colleagues in Malaysia who were acknowledged in *A Share of the Harvest* merit recognition here as well, but I single out only a few. Kala Kovan, project director at the Malaysian-American Commission on Educational Exchange, offered much appreciated assistance and cheer of many kinds; and Siti Shariah binte Haji Shaari was always there with friendship, hospitality, and valuable advice. Shamsul Amri Baharuddin and Wendy Smith provided wonderful camaraderie and hospitality, especially while we stayed in Paroi Jaya (Seremban). To the inhabitants of the community in Negeri Sembilan to which I have given the pseudonym of Bogang, and especially to my adoptive parents (who, like all other villagers mentioned in the text, are given fictitious names, to protect their anonymity), my deepest thanks, again, for accepting me into your lives, sharing with me so many of your thoughts and feelings, and putting up with all of the questions and inconveniences entailed in my research and my extended stays in your community.

I would also like to express my gratitude to Professor Abdul Rashid Haji Ahmad, former chairman of the Department of Malay Studies at the University of Malaya; The Socio-Economic and General Planning Unit of the Malaysian Prime Minister's Department; the Malaysian National Archives (Arkib Negara Malaysia); and the following state- and district-level offices in Negeri Sembilan: the Department of Islamic Religion (Jabatan Agama Islam); the District Office of Rembau (Pejabat Daerah Rembau), and the Office of the Islamic Magistrate of Rembau (Pejabat Kadi Rembau).

Suzanne Brenner, Aihwa Ong, Sherry Ortner, David Pinault, and Nancy Ries read all or part of the book and gave me valuable comments. So, too, did Robert Hefner and Raymond Kelly, whose extremely detailed and comprehensive remarks forced me to sharpen my prose and refine my analyses. Anonymous readers for the University of California Press also provided useful suggestions and other feedback; and Amanda Nathan kindly listened to and evaluated many of the arguments while they were in their formative stages, and in these and other ways contributed to seeing the project through to its completion. James H. Clark, the director of the University of California Press, offered encouragement throughout the project, and I would like to express my appreciation to him once again for his support and his interest in my work. Valeurie Friedman, Steve Gilmartin, Tony Hicks, and other members of the editorial department of the Press were extremely helpful as well. Thanks also to the students who enrolled in one or another version of my course on gender and culture and helped me clarify my thinking on various issues. And many thanks, finally, to Letta Palmer-Holmes and Lisa Todzia for wizardry in editing and word processing.

Note

The Malaysian unit of currency is the *ringgit*. One *ringgit* (M$1) was worth approximately U.S. $0.46 at the time of my 1978–80 fieldwork, and U.S. $0.39 during my 1987–88 fieldwork.

Introduction

This book examines constructions of gender in the Malay world, with particular reference to the "matrilineal" Malay Muslims of Negeri Sembilan, a state in West Malaysia. The specific goals of the book are three. First, to document and analyze cultural constructions of gender, paying close attention to contrasting representations of masculinity and femininity and the different social and cultural contexts with which they are associated. Second, to elucidate the historical, social structural, and other dynamics that help reproduce, challenge, and subvert these representations. And third, to specify the political and other implications of these variegated representations of gender as they are realized in different social and cultural contexts. The broader objectives are to examine the Negeri Sembilan case in comparative perspective, and to address an important set of issues and debates in the theoretical literature concerning systems of exchange and prestige, the loci of male dominance, the relationship between gender and kinship, and the social sources of ambivalence.[1] More generally, the study is meant to enhance our understanding of the political economy of contested symbols and meanings (the ways in which the contestations over symbols and meanings in different societies are informed by, and in turn inform, patterns of political and economic relations among the various groups and classes comprising such societies); the role of ideology in everyday life; and the relationship between ideology and practice—all of which are central concerns in anthropology and in many other areas of the social sciences and the humanities.

My analysis of constructions of gender in Negeri Sembilan has broad significance despite the unique features of the Negeri Sembilan case. Negeri Sembilan is one of many societies in Southeast Asia characterized by the "relatively high status of women" (see Van Esterik 1982; Ong 1989; Atkinson and Errington 1990; cf. Reid 1988). A comparative analysis of Negeri Sembilan material will thus shed light on an important range of Southeast Asian societies and will also help us better understand some of the contrasts between Southeast Asian societies on the one hand, and societies in other parts of Asia as well as Oceania, Africa, and the Americas, on the other. Moreover, the system of marriage and affinity in nineteenth-century Negeri Sembilan centered on the de facto "exchange of men" (transactions over men's labor power and productivity), rather than the "exchange of women," and thus represents a critically important exception to the seminal theories of Claude Lévi-Strauss (see Peletz 1987b). Lévi-Strauss (1949) maintains that the exchange of women occurs in *all* systems of affinal alliance; that it was necessarily entailed in the initial institutionalization of incest taboos that gave rise to (human) kinship and marriage; and that it simultaneously constituted the earliest act of social exchange. Data from Negeri Sembilan illustrate the necessity and value of critically reassessing key features of Lévi-Strauss's arguments (cf. Rubin 1975), central elements of which have been incorporated into standard anthropological accounts of kinship (e.g., Leach 1961; Fox 1967; cf. Goody 1990), have informed recent anthropological studies of the bases of gender and other types of social inequality (e.g., Collier and Rosaldo 1981; Collier 1988), and have been highly influential beyond the discipline as well. These same data (along with data from other societies I discuss) indicate not only that there are some societies in which women exercise far more autonomy and social control than the earlier literature on kinship and social structure would have us believe; but also that gender inequalities in such societies do not derive from institutions of kinship and marriage (e.g., the exchange of women) but are rooted instead in broadly based, cosmologically grounded systems of prestige and virtue that accord greater spiritual power or potency, along with more "reason" and less "passion," to men.

Although men in nineteenth-century Negeri Sembilan were being exchanged by groups of women (not by other men), there is no evidence of an explicit cultural or ideological elaboration of these features of the system. In fact, these elements of the system were culturally distorted or denied, partly through "official" ideologies and Islamic rituals (see Bourdieu 1977:34–38) that portrayed the system of marriage and affinity as focusing on transfers of rights over women. More generally, although women continue to predominate in various contexts of exchange (feasting cycles, agricultural production, etc.), they are effectively denied access to most political offices and various other public arenas for gaining prestige, and are, in addition, more constrained in their everyday movements and activities than men.

The constraints imposed on Negeri Sembilan women (and men) are keyed to a largely implicit ideology of gender. Like gender ideologies in many other parts of Southeast Asia and Oceania (see Van Esterik 1982; Ong 1989; Atkinson and Errington 1990; Strathern 1987), Negeri Sembilan's gender ideology tends, overall, to deemphasize gender and sexuality, and to highlight sameness, equality, and complementarity between the sexes. Such ideologies pose a formidable challenge to analysts, for as Jane Atkinson (1982:257) has pointed out, it is generally much harder to study societies where gender and sexuality are (relatively) muted than "cases where clitoridectomy, foot binding, and homosexual fellatio fairly scream out for ethnographic investigation."

Despite the overall deemphasis of gender and gender differences in Negeri Sembilan, there are certain areas in this society in which gender distinctions are culturally elaborated; for example, women are invariably portrayed as the "spiritually weaker" of the two sexes. Interestingly, key features of Negeri Sembilan's gender ideology also depict women as more deserving and more in need of subsistence guarantees than men, and have long played a significant role in promoting women's effective monopoly in the proprietorship and inheritance of houses and land. This in turn has provided women with an important material base from which to maintain their autonomy and social control in relation to husbands, brothers, and men in other social roles. The social reproduction of this ideology has helped women retain many of their precolonial prerogatives, despite profound changes in Negeri Sembilan society and culture engendered by British colonialism (1874–1957), modern market forces, postcolonial nation-state building, and diverse currents of Islamic nationalism and reform. This situation encourages a critical reassessment of widely held assumptions, underlying the work of Ester Boserup (1970), among others, that economic development and heightened integration into the global economy necessarily entail significant losses for rural women (Peletz 1987a, 1988b; cf. Stoler 1977; Stivens 1985).

My analysis of gender in Negeri Sembilan focuses largely on inconsistencies, contradictions, and paradoxes in the ideology of gender. Inter alia, I explore the symbols and meanings of local concepts such as *akal* and *nafsu*, which denote "reason" ("rationality," "intelligence") and "passion" ("desire," "animality"), respectively. These are key symbols in many domains of Malay culture (and in many domains of other Islamic cultures, e.g., Acehnese, Minangkabau, Javanese, Moroccan, Bedouin) that are frequently invoked in discussions of the similarities and differences between males and females. Villagers in Negeri Sembilan point out that "passion" is present among all of God's creatures, humans and animals alike, and that "reason" is what distinguishes humans from the rest of the animal world. They also contend that "passion" and "reason" are present to one degree or another in all humans, but that "passion" is present in greater concentrations (more pronounced) among women, whereas "reason" is less so. (This, in any case, is the official line.) These are curious, seemingly paradoxical, contentions insofar as villagers also maintain that women are ultimately more responsible and more trustworthy than men, especially in safeguarding and managing cash and other household resources, and in honoring kinship and other social obligations.

Analysis of this apparent paradox reveals that there are contrasting constructions of gender that are associated with different social and cultural contexts. One such context-specific construction promotes an "official" (and "more Islamic") view of men and women which is "explicitly codified in . . . quasi-juridical formalism" (Bourdieu 1977:34) and which serves a number of broadly legitimizing functions. This view, which is keyed to local understandings of biology, sexuality, and reproduction, turns on the idea that, compared to men, women are more lustful and insatiable in sexual matters, and simply more "animalistic." Other context-specific constructions of gender promote a view of men and women which I refer to as "practical" (because it is more thoroughly grounded in the everyday practical situations in which people find themselves and is more explicitly oriented to the practical realities of "getting things done"), focusing on the culturally elaborated belief that men are less responsible and less trustworthy than women, both with regard to managing household resources, and in terms of honoring basic social obligations associated with marriage and kinship as a whole. Central objectives of the book are to explore the contextually variable articulation of these (and other) contrasting representations of gender; to delineate the structural factors that motivate, challenge, and subvert their existence and social reproduction both historically and at present; and more generally, to contribute to the literature bearing on hegemony, which Antonio Gramsci (1971) defines as "the permeation throughout civil society . . . of an entire system of values, attitudes, beliefs, morality, etc. that is in one way or the other supportive of the established order and the class interests that dominate it" (Boggs 1976:39).[2]

I am especially interested in practical views concerning gender, and males in particular. One reason for this focus is that these views are relatively uncommon in the ethnographic literature, though the larger issue is that constructions of masculinity (which should not be confused with masculine or masculinist perspectives) continue to suffer from the "taken-for-granted" syndrome (see Shapiro 1979; Gilmore 1990:1–2).[3] Another reason for this focus has to do with the theoretical implications of such views, especially the implications of their links to the social organization of production, exchange, and prestige. Suffice it to say that in Negeri Sembilan the behavior of married men in relation to their wives is judged largely in terms of the standards that pertain to elder brothers' treatment (nurturance, protection, etc.) of their younger sisters, and that many married men fall short of the "elder brother" ideal due to their inability to produce sufficient wealth and prestige for their wives and their wives' kin. Married men who find that they cannot live up to the expectations of, or otherwise cope with pressures from, their wives and affines frequently abandon (or divorce) their wives, along with any children they might have. This course of action not only feeds into local perceptions that husbands and fathers are unreliable and untrustworthy; it also colors practical views of maleness as a whole. These practical views serve, in turn, to counter and moderate the official view of males, just as they effectively elevate practical views of females.

Negeri Sembilan masculinity, far from being a singular, unitary, or otherwise seamless cultural phenomenon, is thus composed of a number of contradictory representations, many of which are "inveigled in" and therefore best understood as dialectically related to constructions of adult men's kinship roles. In point of fact, the category "male" does not have all that much cultural salience (the same is true of the category "female"), though categories such as "brother," "husband," and "father" (and "sister," "wife," and "mother") clearly do. More broadly, cases such as Negeri Sembilan (and Aceh, which I also discuss) provide an important corrective to the views of Ortner (1981), Ortner and Whitehead (1981a), Chodorow (1978, 1989), and others whose approaches presuppose a rigid dichotomy between structural definitions of males and females. Ortner and Whitehead (1981a:21), for example, point out that, cross-culturally, one or another different female "relational" role—for example, mother, sister, or wife—"tend[s] to dominate the category of 'female' and to color the meanings of all other female relational roles." Ortner and Whitehead go on to claim that there are *no* corresponding patterns in the case of males—in their words, "analogous distinctions among men are *not* critical for masculinity" (Ortner and Whitehead 1981a:21; emphasis added)—because men, unlike women, tend to be defined in terms of "positional" (ostensibly nonrelational) statuses, such as "hunter," "warrior," "chief," and so on.[4] Such claims merit reassessment in light of data from Negeri Sembilan (and Aceh), which indicate that in the practice of everyday life certain male relational roles—for example, elder brother, husband/father—may well dominate the category of "male," and may also inform the meanings of all other male relational (and "positional") roles. These same data illustrate that it is not merely the meanings of "female," or the social position of women, that may be dragged down by the cultural elaboration of relational roles and their relative significance in ideologies of gender. This can also occur with respect to the meanings of "male" and the social position of men, even though males still come out "on top"— at least in official discourses on kinship and gender, and as regards the overall distribution of power and prestige.

In sum, I contend that Negeri Sembilan masculinity is best understood if it is "deconstructed"[5] and analyzed in terms of its constituent elements and their interrelations (the same applies to femininity); and that the deconstruction of Negeri Sembilan masculinity calls for a jettisoning of the "arelational" notion of masculinity enshrined in the comparative and theoretical literature on gender. I also show that practical representations of masculinity simultaneously encode and mask local perspectives on class that are otherwise typically unmarked in discourse concerning gender and social relations; and that the articulation of variables of gender and class has long been informed by state policies as well as nationalist and transnationalist discourse bearing on the Malay social body and the Malaysian body politic.

Analytic concerns with maleness are thus of value not simply because they yield interesting ethnographic data on the contingent, internally dissonant, and ambivalence-laden construction of masculinity while clearly enhancing our understanding of the dialectically related domain of femininity (a central concern of this study as well). These analytic concerns also reveal that Islamic manhood is by no means always shaped by rigid, patriarchal discourses, and that Islam has long allowed a kind of flexibility and precariousness in the construction of masculinity (and femininity), although these features—along with the contradictory imperatives and indeterminances of Islamic masculinities—have not received sufficient attention in Southeast Asia or elsewhere (Ong and Peletz 1995a). More importantly, such concerns help bring into especially sharp focus the merits—indeed, the necessity—of describing and analyzing gender in relation to other forms of difference and inequality (class, race, etc.) which are in a very basic sense both constituting and constitutive of masculinity and femininity alike. One important corollary of this argument is that the compartmentalization of gender as a subject of study "in its own terms" is untenable. The strong version of this position is that gender "in its own terms" is ultimately a "nonsubject" in much the same sense that Schneider (1984) has argued with respect to conventional studies of kinship as an isolable, analytically discrete domain (see also Collier and Yanagisako 1987; Kelly 1993).

Data from Negeri Sembilan are thus highly conducive to a critical evaluation of theoretical debates concerning systems of exchange and prestige, conventional analytic distinctions between kinship and gender, the loci of male dominance, and myriad other issues in the study of gender identities and gender ideologies. These same data afford us an excellent opportunity to examine the political economy of contested symbols and meanings, the scope and force of ambivalence and the contradictory entailments of ideology in everyday life, and the relationship between ideology and practice— all of which, as noted earlier, are central issues not only in anthropology but also in the social sciences and humanities as a whole (see Bourdieu 1977; Foucault 1977; Giddens 1979; Williams 1977; Barnett and Silverman 1979; Taussig 1980; de Certeau 1984; Ortner 1984; Scott 1985, 1990; Dirks, Eley, and Ortner 1994).

As for the organization of this work, the book is composed of seven chapters. Chapter 1 focuses on the ethnographic context of my fieldwork and deals primarily with the research on which the book is based ("how I know what I know"), especially the field research I conducted in Negeri Sembilan from 1978 to 1980 and 1987 to 1988 (though it also presents some basic ethnographic background—on history, economy, polity, etc.— the details of which are fleshed out in subsequent chapters). The main concerns of the chapter are strategies, methods, and dilemmas in fieldwork, my adoption into one of the dominant lineages, and the ways in which changes in my life cycle—moving from bachelor to newlywed status, and ultimately to fatherhood—shaped my social experiences in the field as well as the collection and interpretation of data. I should emphasize, however, that this chapter is not the sole context in which I address fieldwork experiences or issues bearing on the collection or interpretation of data. Rather, I deal with such matters throughout the book; in this and other ways I hope to provide an engaging, reflexive, and humanistic account of the anthropological enterprise.

Chapter 2 is the first of two historical chapters. Here I provide an overview of the systems of prestige, kinship/gender, and political organization in the nineteenth century (especially the period 1830–90), with an eye toward showing how these systems articulated both with one another and with the system of marriage and affinal relations. This is followed by a discussion of the contrasting (indeed, contradictory) representations of marriage and affinal exchange entailed in wedding and funerary rituals, which I analyze by employing a modified version of Pierre Bourdieu's (1977) distinction between "official" and "practical" kinship. This is also the context in which I develop the argument that both in everyday practice and in terms of what I refer to as "practical" representations—though not in official ideology—the system of marriage and affinal relations focused on the "exchange of men." Some of the comparative and theoretical implications of this argument are sketched out toward the end of the chapter; others are dealt with further along.

Chapter 3 concerns themes of continuity and change in kinship, gender, and sexuality from the nineteenth century to the present. The discussion is set in the context of shifts in political, religious, and economic organization, including those induced (directly or otherwise) by British colonialism and Malaysia's postcolonial government. In this and subsequent chapters I draw both on my earlier work (Peletz 1987a, 1987b, 1988b) and on my most recent (1987–88) field research to explain how structural transformations and reproduction in the social organization of production, exchange, and prestige have brought about changes in understandings and attitudes bearing on (hetero)sexual impropriety, but have yet to effect a significant reassessment of traditionally accommodating views on *pondan* or gender crossers (the majority of whom are men)— even though there are strong signals of such in the air. The second half of the chapter is devoted to a description and analysis of a social drama in the form of a shotgun wedding, which provides poignant testimony to themes of continuity and change, especially the allocation of prestige and stigma in contemporary settings.

Beginning with chapter 4, I focus primarily on the present, although all of the data and analyses here and in subsequent chapters are informed by historical perspectives. The main concerns of this chapter—knowledge, power, and personal misfortune—are broached through a discussion of *ilmu*, which refers to mystical knowledge/power, and which, while concentrated among (male) ritual specialists, is also broadly distributed throughout local society, particularly among men. The larger issues here include the gendered dimensions of *ilmu*, the relationship in local culture between knowledge and power, and how knowledge and power figure into accounts of personal misfortune. Also of concern are long-term historical shifts entailing the progressive constriction of women's ritual roles and dealings with the sacred, as well as recent changes in the sources and meanings of marginality, uncertainty, and danger, especially as they relate to gender. Drawing partly on detailed case studies, I argue that it is important to examine poisoning, sorcery, and all major varieties of mystical attack, not simply those involving women who are possessed by spirits that take control of their hosts in highly dramatic, sometimes violent episodes of hysteria. This broader perspective allows for a more complete picture of Malay understandings and representations of gender, and of marginality, uncertainty, and danger—one that differs in significant ways from those in the relevant literature on Malaysia. The case studies presented in the latter sections of the chapter also help substantiate my general arguments that femininity and masculinity can only be understood if they are viewed in relation to one another; that cultural knowledge is contextually grounded and deeply perspectival; and that our ethnographic descriptions and interpretations must therefore attend both to polyvocality (the existence of multiple voices) and to the political economy of contested symbols and meanings. They also make clear that ambivalence, which I define (following Weigert [1991]) as "the experience of commingled contradictory emotions," permeates the local system of social relations and, as such, clearly merits serious analytic attention.

Chapter 5 deals with cultural constructions of the person and the body, with particular reference to the symbols and meanings of "reason," "passion," and "shame," which are core (or key) symbols in many domains of Malay society and culture. The first section of the chapter provides an (ungendered) introduction to local understandings of the person and the body, and examines both the relational nature of personhood (or self) characteristic of Malay culture, as well as the relational views that inform understandings and representations of the body and its most significant constituent elements. The second section of the chapter pursues these issues in the course of a gendered discussion that focuses on conception, pregnancy, and childbirth. The third and fourth sections of the chapter expand the analysis to encompass a broader set of concerns. This involves, on the one hand, describing and analyzing the contextually variable symbols and meanings of "reason," "passion," and "shame," and, on the other, assessing the implications of these data for Sherry Ortner's now classic (1974) argument that women in all societies are held to be "closer to nature" and "further from culture" than men. In my reassessment and reworking of key features of this incisive and controversial argument, I maintain that while it makes insufficient provision for contrasting representations of gender and has various other shortcomings, its central logic helps elucidate important features of Malay society and culture, and of Malay gender in particular.

Chapter 6 builds directly on and is in many respects an extension of chapter 5 in the sense that it too focuses on concepts of "reason," "pas-

sion," and "shame," and on the ways they figure into official or hegemonic discourse on gender. Unlike chapter 5, however, the main concern
here is the ways in which these symbols and their meanings are invoked
in contrasting and at times thoroughly contradictory ways. The bulk of
the chapter is composed of (edited) material obtained from twenty interviews conducted in 1988. The first section of the chapter presents data
collected from ten men I interviewed; the second presents material obtained from ten women. The third section of the chapter analyzes some
of the similarities and differences between men's and women's perspectives on gender, with particular reference to the scope and force of practical, largely counter-hegemonic representations of masculinity on the one
hand, and to the various structural and historical factors that have motivated their (re)production on the other. Among other things, the material
presented here indicates that on a great many issues men and women
are in basic agreement as to the fundamental similarities and differences
between males and females. One important corollary of this is that women
accept much of the official/hegemonic view of gender, including many
features of the hegemony that portray women (and females generally) in
predominantly negative terms. We will also see that many men (and
women) espouse various practical, largely counter-hegemonic views that
portray them (men) in highly negative terms, and that these latter views
simultaneously encode and mask local perspectives on class that are otherwise generally unmarked in discourse concerning gender and social relations. The final section of the chapter deals in more general terms with
some of the variables that serve to constrain the elaboration of oppositional discourses and strategies of resistance.

Chapter 7 provides comparative and theoretical perspectives on Negeri
Sembilan. After a brief overview of the more important ethnographic
findings discussed in earlier chapters, I turn to a comparative analysis of
Negeri Sembilan and Aceh which serves to further substantiate my argument that we need to rethink the "arelational" notion of masculinity enshrined in the comparative and theoretical literature on gender. Inter alia,
I show that the "positional," ostensibly "arelational" notion of masculinity said to prevail in *all* societies has little relevance in these two societies
and, in any case, derives from a dichotomization of Western folkloric notions of masculinity which reflects certain state and other elite biases.
Data from these two societies also illustrate that there is profound ambivalence about official ideologies of gender, and that this ambivalence fuels
the highly elaborated counter-hegemonic discourses found in these societies. Issues bearing on counter-hegemonies and ambivalence are also

taken up in the second section of the chapter, which deals with transformations on Malay-Indonesian and Islamic themes by examining the ways in which "reason" and "passion" figure into contrasting discourses on masculinity among Minangkabau and Javanese, as well as the (Mzeini) Bedouin who inhabit the South Sinai Peninsula (Egypt). The final section of the chapter speaks to more general issues and debates in the literature on ideology, experience, and ambivalence.

1 Ethnographic Context and Fieldwork

Recent debates in anthropology have underscored the importance of attending to issues bearing on ethnographic authority ("how we know—and convey—what we know"), polyvocality (the existence of multiple voices), and the tensions and politics entailed in the collection of ethnographic data and the anthropological enterprise as a whole. This chapter addresses various topics of this sort in the course of a discussion of strategies, methods, and dilemmas of fieldwork, including my relations with local men and women, my adoption by the village headman and his wife, and the ways in which changes in my life cycle—moving from bachelorhood to newlywed status, and ultimately to fatherhood, hence full social adulthood—informed my experiences in the field, including the collection of data. Many of these issues are examined in greater detail in subsequent chapters. So, too, of course, are the brief snippets of basic ethnographic data—on history, social organization, religion, and so on—presented in the short orienting section of the chapter and in the narrative on fieldwork to which most of the chapter is devoted.

LOCATING NEGERI SEMBILAN

Negeri Sembilan is one of eleven states in the Malay Peninsula (see maps 1 and 2).[1] Its population is ethnically diverse (as is true of the Peninsula as a whole), and is usually discussed in terms of three major ethnic categories: "Malays," who make up 48.7 percent of the total; "Chinese," who constitute 34.2 percent; and "Indians," who, along with "Others," account for the remaining 17.1 percent (Government of Malaysia 1991).[2] The Malays of Negeri Sembilan have much in common with Malays elsewhere in the Peninsula, but they also differ in various ways. As for the most basic commonalities, all Malays speak a common language, identify with the Shafi'i branch of Sunni Islam, and order various aspects of their social relations in accordance with a body of cultural codes glossed *adat*. English translations of the term *adat* have included "tradition," "custom," and "customary law," but none of these (or any others that come to mind)

Map 1.   The Malay Peninsula (West Malaysia) and surrounding regions

adequately convey the cultural meanings, moral force, or social relevance of this unifying, broadly hegemonic construct. The scope of this concept can be gleaned from the well-known saying *hidup di kandung adat, mati di kandung tanah,* which proposes that the living are moored and guided in all of their actions by *adat* just as the dead are surrounded and held in place by the earth of the grave.[3] The traditional *adat* concept also subsumed that which is "natural" in the sense of being consistent with the laws of nature; for example, that water runs downhill.[4]

While the *adat* concept is a strongly marked symbol of basic similarities among all Malays, it also symbolizes locally salient (but analytically overdrawn) contrasts, for there are two major variants of *adat* in the Pen-

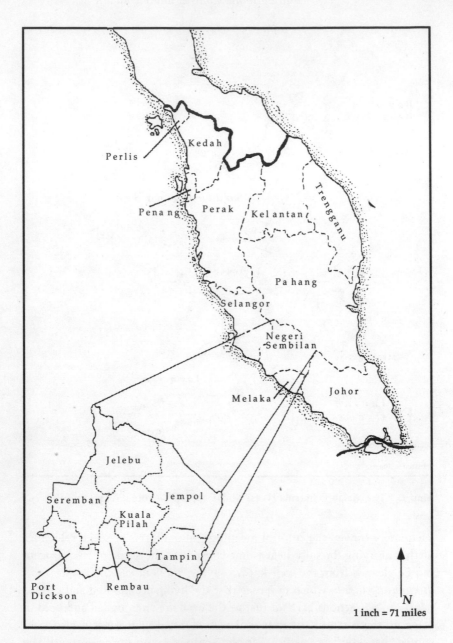

Map 2.   The states of the Malay Peninsula (West Malaysia) and the districts
of the state of Negeri Sembilan

insula. The first, referred to as *adat perpatih*, is predominant in Negeri Sembilan (and in the Naning district of Melaka and a few other enclaves scattered about the Peninsula—see maps 1 and 2). This variant of *adat* has long been associated with a social structure having descent units of matrilineal design, all of which reflects the Minangkabau (West Sumatran) ancestry of the area's earliest permanent settlers, who began immigrating to Negeri Sembilan in the 1500s, and perhaps even earlier. The second, known as *adat temenggong*, prevails in almost all other regions of the Peninsula and has long been linked with a social structure that is usually characterized as "bilateral" (or cognatic). The latter form of *adat* and the Malays who define themselves in relation to it are also assumed to be of Sumatran (perhaps even Minangkabau) origins, and to have evolved from the same ancestral culture as the Malays of Negeri Sembilan; it is also generally agreed that their forebears established permanent settlements in various areas of the Peninsula long before the ancestors of the Malays of Negeri Sembilan began their emigration from Minangkabau areas of Sumatra. (Which of the two *adats* is older is unknown. And no one can say with certainty whether the bilateral variant of social structure predates the matrilineal [or another] variant or vice versa [but see Blust 1980].)

The Malays of Negeri Sembilan are often treated as a special ("matrilineal") case that cannot be accommodated by general statements or models that are meant to apply to the ("bilateral") Malays living in other parts of the Peninsula. Elsewhere I have suggested that this perspective is misguided, and that, matters of convenience aside, we are best advised not to compare and contrast these two variants of Malay society by focusing on their systems of descent ("unilineal" vs. "non-unilineal"—see Peletz 1994a; see also Peletz 1988b). Some of the general conceptual problems with descent-focused comparisons and contrasts have been underscored by Leach ([1961] 1966:3; see also Yanagisako and Collier 1987):

> Ever since Morgan began writing of the Iroquois, it has been customary for anthropologists to distinguish *unilineal* from *non-unilineal* descent systems, and among the former to distinguish *patrilineal* societies from *matrilineal* societies. *These categories now seem to us so rudimentary and obvious that it is extremely difficult to break out of the straightjacket which the categories themselves impose.* (Leach [1961] 1966:3; emphasis added)

Descent-focused comparisons and contrasts of Malay societies tend to gloss over the strong emphases on matrifiliation, matrilaterality, and matrifocality characteristic of all Malay systems of social relations. They also lose sight of the importance of siblingship, which, for all Malays, is a central organizing principle as well as a "core" or "key" symbol in Ortner's (1973:1339–40) sense; that is, it is an object or focus of marked cultural interest and cultural elaboration, which provides both a "source of categories for conceptualizing the order of the world" and a model for human conduct. Comparisons and contrasts of Malay societies that focus on descent also tend to lose sight of basic similarities in all Malay societies with respect to constructions of gender, personhood, and prestige.

For these and other reasons, I prefer to treat both the Malays of Negeri Sembilan and Malays elsewhere in the Peninsula as variations on a single set of Malayan (or Malay-Indonesian) themes, much like the Sumatran (Minangkabau, Acehnese) and Javanese cases I discuss below. In thus locating Negeri Sembilan Malays squarely within the Malayan world, I am also adhering to local practice, for, as explained in greater detail elsewhere (Peletz 1994a), the Malays of Negeri Sembilan view themselves as "thoroughly Malay," and do not regard or refer to themselves as "Minangkabau(s)," or "Minangkabau Malay(s)" (as is frequently suggested in the literature), although in most contexts they do acknowledge and are generally proud of their Minangkabau ancestry.

GENDER, AGE, AND SELF IN THE FIELD: STRATEGIES AND DILEMMAS IN FIELDWORK

Anthropologists are often asked about their fieldwork experiences and about the factors that led to their decisions to settle in the communities which served as the loci for their research. We are also asked, especially by students, how we came to pursue research on the topics on which we eventually focus. Both for these reasons and to provide the reader some sense of how my fieldwork experiences informed my knowledge of Malay society and culture, I devote the rest of this chapter to a discussion of strategies and dilemmas in fieldwork. I introduce the discussion with brief comments on what led me to anthropology and the study of Southeast Asian societies and cultures.

My interest in anthropology dates from my undergraduate years (1969–73) at the University of California, Berkeley. After taking a number of courses in different areas of the social sciences, I was drawn to anthropology, especially social and cultural anthropology, which offered fascinating accounts of radically different cultural alternatives and simultaneously provided what I took to be well-grounded critiques of my own society and culture. Casting about for someone to sponsor an inchoate project on the local Hare Krishna movement, I introduced myself to Professor Herbert Phillips and asked for his support. He was less than receptive to my ill-conceived project but he said he would be willing to sponsor independent research focusing on Southeast Asian Buddhism (which I knew absolutely nothing about). He gave me a lengthy bibliography and sent me on my way. I thus began exploring topics in religion and social structure in Burma and later became interested in Thailand, the Philippines, and other areas of Southeast Asia. The following semester I conducted library research on various issues and debates in the literature on kinship and social structure in Southeast Asia, much of which focused on why Southeast Asian societies have long struck anthropologists and other outside observers as anomalous and "loosely structured" in comparison with Japanese and Chinese societies, and various groups in Africa and beyond. I subsequently decided to pursue graduate work on some of these topics at the University of Michigan.

At the University of Michigan I explored the field of social structure under the guidance of Professors Raymond Kelly and Aram Yengoyan, whose specialties include kinship and social structure, social and cultural theory, and the peoples and cultures of Southeast Asia and Oceania. (Conrad Kottak, Shepard Forman, and Sherry Ortner in particular also provided tremendous intellectual stimulation, but for the most part this came later.) I also began formal language study both in Malay/Indonesian and in Dutch, in anticipation of conducting anthropological fieldwork either in Sumatra or another area of Indonesia (a former Dutch colony), or in the Malay Peninsula. I became especially interested in the social structures of the ethnic groups in West Sumatra, such as the Minangkabau, and the Malay Peninsula, such as the Malays of Negeri Sembilan, who trace their descent from the Minangkabau. These groups have long fascinated outside observers: They are Muslims, yet they have matrilineal clans, and both houses and land tend to be owned and inherited by women. The available literature on these seemingly contradictory features of Minangkabau and Negeri Sembilan was sketchy at best and contained very little information on how Islam and matrilineality were interrelated in local organization, and how they combined in the everyday lives of people in these societies. Much of the literature was also ahistorical, and characterized by a dearth of reliable information on how the precolonial systems of property relations (land tenure, inheritance, etc.) and social structure more generally fared under the impact of colonial rule, modern market forces, and Islamic nationalism and reform. For these and other reasons I decided to focus on such issues in the research that I planned to undertake for my doctoral dissertation.

In the course of preparing proposals to obtain funding for my project, I learned that a project of the sort I wished to pursue might be construed by Indonesian authorities as politically sensitive, and that for this and other reasons the process of obtaining research clearance from the Indonesian government could take well over a year. I therefore decided to pursue my project in Malaysia, among the Malays of Negeri Sembilan. After preparing a number of research proposals that I submitted (in some cases successfully, in others not) to the National Science Foundation, the National Institute of Mental Health, and other granting agencies, I applied to the Malaysian government for a research visa and made other preparations for going to the field. Much to my chagrin, I had to wait a full twelve months for research clearance from the Malaysian government, but since I knew that such a delay was likely, I was able to use this time productively, e.g., by carrying out further language study and making arrangements for institutional affiliation with a Malaysian university.

In September 1978 I left Michigan and went to San Francisco to spend some time with my family and my future wife, Ellen. From there I flew to Hawaii, where I spent a week with an old friend, and on to Japan, where I visited for about ten days with fellow graduate students from Michigan, who were conducting research on organized crime. I then flew on to Singapore, and finally to Malaysia. Arriving in the capital city of Kuala Lumpur, I was met by a Malaysian colleague (Ramli Mohd. Salleh) with whom I had struck up a friendship at the University of Michigan. Ramli was kind enough to help me get settled in a hotel and to provide other assistance during my initial stay in Kuala Lumpur.

In Kuala Lumpur I met with government officials and Malay scholars who directed me to local research efforts of which I had been unaware, and advised me on the best place to carry out the project. Armed with letters of introduction from the president of the University of Michigan and from my local sponsor (Dato Professor Ismail Hussein, then head of the Department of Malay Studies at the University of Malaya), I set out for Seremban, the capital of Negeri Sembilan, where I arranged to meet with government officials who provided additional advice and assistance, including letters of introduction to the administrative heads of the various districts of the state. After a few days in Seremban I traveled to the district of Jelebu, which was the locus of a classic study of Negeri Sembilan society undertaken in the late 1950s, Michael Swift's (1965) *Malay Peasant Society in Jelebu*.

My objectives in going to Jelebu were partly to determine whether or not Jelebu would be the most productive locale for my research, and partly to help give me a sense of regional variations (if any) in the state. To this end I met with local government figures and others, including a leathery, bent old man by the name of Haji Ibrahim, who, upon meeting me for the first time and finding out that I intended to conduct research on local tradition (*adat*), offered to come to the government rest house where I was staying and to share with me his copy of the *Hikayat Jelebu* (Tale of Jelebu). He showed up at the rest house at about 10 o'clock one morning, some fourteen hours after he had agreed to meet with me, and after a bit of small talk he began reciting the tale. That he was familiar with anthropologists and their tool kits was quite obvious from his visible disappointment and frustration that I had no tape recorder to take down his tale. I apologized for being "ill-equipped," at which point he suggested that I find some paper so that I could take notes on the *Hikayat*. I went back into my room and dug up some paper. As soon as I returned he began reciting a very long and difficult to follow myth of origin containing complex genealogical information. It quickly became apparent to both of us that I could not keep up with him, and he became palpably frustrated and annoyed that he had taken the initiative to seek me out, only to find me unprepared to benefit from the encounter! I found Haji Ibrahim rather overbearing, but unfortunately my encounter with him did not serve to impress upon me that my "ethnographic experience" had begun as soon as I stepped off the plane in Kuala Lumpur. Indeed, partly because I initially conceived my study as set within the confines of a village, I did not begin to make systematic notes about my experiences or observations until I settled in a village, some two months later. In fact, most of my first impressions of Malays, and of Malaysia generally, were only set down in writing in letters to Ellen.

Following my brief stay in Jelebu (and a return to Kuala Lumpur to beef up my tool kit) I journeyed to the Rembau district of Negeri Sembilan, where I again made the rounds of government offices, and otherwise endeavored to find a suitable locale for my research. Having been told in Kuala Lumpur, Seremban, and Jelebu that Jelebu or Rembau would be the most suitable locale for my research, my decision boiled down to a choice between Jelebu and Rembau. Partly on aesthetic grounds (Rembau struck me as "much prettier"), I elected to conduct my research in Rembau, and eventually settled on the village of Bogang (a pseudonym) as my field site.

As I have discussed elsewhere, a number of factors influenced my decision to settle in the village of Bogang.[5] I had already decided that I would be best off living by myself, but I wanted to find an empty dwelling close to currently occupied houses. Thanks to the transportation, advice, and other kind assistance of the local parish headman (*penghulu mukim*), who had many relatives and contacts in the community, I was able to locate such a house in Bogang.

My first lesson in Malay kinship and social relations began even before I settled in Bogang in December 1978, largely as a result of my search for someone in the village to hire to cook one or two meals a day and do laundry. Although I had assumed that this would be relatively easy to arrange, I was mistaken. The parish headman, among others, told me that rural Malays were not accustomed, nor did they like, to be paid in cash for the labor and other aid they provided friends and fellow villagers; they would be especially ashamed and embarrassed (*malu*) to accept cash in return for cooking and cleaning, which are usually done free in the context of relationships of reciprocity. At the same time, the parish headman and others observed that Bogang undoubtedly had many households composed of married couples whose children had left home, some of whom would surely welcome me at their afternoon and evening meals. This possibility struck me as ideal, especially since it would present me with many of the research and social benefits of living in a Malay home.

Within a few days of settling in Bogang, I discussed the matter with the wife of the village headman (*ketua kampung*), who was a close relative of the parish headman and one of my immediate neighbors. I asked her if she knew of any households that might like to have the newly arrived anthropologist join them at their afternoon and evening meals in exchange for payment. She replied that most villagers would be reluctant to accept such an arrangement because "people here aren't comfortable with the idea of charging guests for meals." So I decided to upgrade my sparsely provisioned kitchen to allow some improvements on the meals of eggs, bananas, peanuts, and tea that I had been preparing for myself since moving to the village.

In our initial conversations, the headman's wife had plied me with numerous questions about my eating habits in America, the composition of typical American meals, and my experiences with Malay cuisine. Although much of what I told her elicited only puzzlement (about the un-

Figure 1.   Village headman and his wife

fathomable ways of *orang putih,* or "white people"), a fair number of my remarks also met with approving nods and comments such as "my husband likes that too," and "that's just what we eat." It did not occur to me at the time that she was exploring our culinary compatibility or trying to assess my reactions to various Malay dishes, including, especially, her favorites. Nor was I aware, needless to say, that she would soon—and perhaps already did—regard me as her "adopted child" (*anak angkat*).

Within a week of my arrival in the village I realized that I was both welcome and expected to join the headman and his wife for lunch and dinner, and that they had in fact adopted me. Informal adoptions among villagers are extremely common, though the more important point is that our eating together on a regular basis presupposed our having a relationship couched in the symbols and idioms of kinship. The imperatives of this relationship were quite varied but most definitely included the unspoken expectation that I reciprocate the sustenance and care I received from my adoptive parents as village-born children of working age (ideally) acknowledge and repay their obligations to their parents—that is, through periodic gifts of cash and store-bought consumer items such as tobacco, tea, canned or imported fruit, and good cuts of fish and meat.

My adoption by the village headman and his wife proved advantageous in ways I had not anticipated. Soon after being adopted I realized my adoptive father was a healer (*dukun*) specializing in the treatment and cure of people who had been poisoned and/or sorcerized. Since I took my evening meals at the headman's house, and since many of his patients came to his house for treatment in the early evening, I was able to observe many curing sessions and to talk to the headman and his patients about different types of illness, various features of healing rituals, and related matters. I had not originally intended to study such issues, but my adoption afforded me a valuable opportunity to do so, and, in the process, to get a sense of Malay views of the seamier side(s) of human nature. These views comprise the flip side of the idealized picture of human nature, personhood, social relations, and the like that is embedded in the formal ideology of kinship, religion, and community life, and that is frequently (and erroneously) dealt with by outside observers as if it constituted the totality of Malay views bearing on sociality.

My adoption also aligned me with other members of the lineage compound in which the headman and his wife resided, as did the location of my house, which was in the same compound. Consequently, during the early months of fieldwork I became much better acquainted with the members and dynamics of this lineage than with those of other lineages in the village. Although this situation might have posed obstacles to my interacting freely with the members of other segments and factions of the community, fortunately it did not; soon after settling in the village I managed to establish close working relationships with a number of village elders outside my village compound.

During the initial four months of fieldwork, I devoted most of my time to participant observation and to building rapport with my neighbors. I attended numerous ceremonial feasts held in connection with weddings, funerals, and the Islamic ritual calendar, and I spent a great deal of time at village *kedai*, where dry goods and other supplies are sold, but which have the more important (social) function of serving as "coffee shops" where men congregate, relax over cups of coffee or tea, and discuss issues of local interest. Throughout this period I collected data on the content and ideology of bonds among members of households and household clusters, as well as between individuals and groups residing in different parts of the village; the basic characteristics of lineages, clans, affinal ties, kin group alliances, and kinship terminology; and forms of exchange, sharecropping, and tenancy. In addition I began detailed sketches of local political alliances and secular organizations. The material gathered during these early months increased my awareness of local sensitivities with regard to community factionalism and strife (and various national-level political issues); it also helped me organize more structured interviews and design a comprehensive household survey.

My interaction with villagers during the early months of my research was greatly facilitated by my fluency in Malay/Indonesian. The fact that my speech incorporated certain Indonesian (to wit, Jakartan) idioms was, initially, a source of great amusement to adult villagers, some of whom were nonetheless quick to take me aside and instruct me in the more appropriate (local) conventions. Somewhat to my surprise, a fair amount of this instruction—and the ribbing that typically preceded it—came from women over fifty years of age. I soon realized that adult women of, or senior to, the generation of my adoptive mother (aged fifty-one) were just as accessible as, and typically more informative and uninhibited (in their dealings with me, at any rate) than, their male counterparts. Although I did not realize it at the time, I came to understand that women are both permitted and encouraged to be more talkative, outgoing, and "expressive" than men, who are socialized to be more attuned to status and prestige considerations, which require greater verbal and emotional restraints and self-control generally. This pattern, which exists throughout the Malay/Indonesian world (see Siegel 1978; Keeler 1987; Smith-Hefner 1988a,

Figure 2. Village women

1988b), is related to widespread Southeast Asian notions that men have greater spiritual power or "potency" than women, one outward sign of which power is their greater self-control and their tendency to talk less than women (see Atkinson and Errington 1990). Partly because of these unforeseen circumstances, I spent the greater portion of my time—especially during the first three or four months of fieldwork—among middle-aged and elderly women, where I was able to collect extensive data on the dynamics of women's relationships with their natural and classificatory sisters and other kin. These dynamics appeared in especially sharp relief in the context of labor and other exchanges associated with feasting, and in women's appraisals of one another's behavior and motivations.

My observations of interactions among sisters, along with other experiences with villagers of both sexes, confirmed many points emphasized in the literature on Negeri Sembilan: for instance, that ties among adult natural sisters were of central importance in numerous realms of society and culture (see Lewis 1962; Azizah Kassim 1969). At the same time, however, my observations led me to question other published conclusions. The moral force of relationships cloaked in idioms of siblingship, for example, appeared far more compelling than the available literature suggested, yet many such relationships were infused with ambivalence and tension as well. I was similarly struck by the fact that most of the local terms and categories villagers used to describe their ties to their relatives were keyed to concepts of siblingship and only secondarily, if at all, to notions of descent. Initially, I interpreted the relative hegemony of sib-lingship and the profound ambivalences surrounding these and other types of relatedness as indicating the erosion or collapse of an earlier (pre-colonial) system based primarily on principles and idioms of descent. Only much later did I realize that norms and values derived from matrilineal descent were far less pervasive in precolonial times than other observers had assumed, and that principles and idioms of siblingship have long, and perhaps always, been of comparable if not greater significance in myriad domains of society and culture.

A social drama that occurred a few months into my fieldwork illus-trates some of the ambivalences inherent in local siblingship and in local kinship more generally, and also speaks to some of the initial dilemmas I encountered in my fieldwork. The background to this drama is far more complex than can be discussed here, so I will provide only the basic facts.

In certain respects the drama began when Mak Su, my adoptive moth-er's sister, appeared at my house one afternoon announcing that Pakcik Rosli, a knowledgeable *dukun* from a neighboring village, was at her home, and was eager to talk with me and help me with my study.[6] I had already spoken with Pakcik Rosli on a few occasions, and I had been deeply impressed by his knowledge of local myth and history, *adat,* and various kinds of esoteric knowledge (*ilmu*). He was in fact an ideal informant. For these and other reasons I was exhilarated when I heard that Pakcik Rosli had actually taken the initiative to assist me with my study, and I fanta-sized that my experiences with him might prove as productive as Carlos Castaneda's encounters with Don Juan! I eagerly went over to Mak Su's house and drank tea with Pakcik Rosli, Mak Su, and the others who were present. We talked for some time, and it was very productive.

In the weeks that followed Mak Su appeared at my door on other occa-sions, again telling me that Pakcik Rosli was waiting for me at her house. On those and other days I enthusiastically went to her house, though I did so partly for reasons having little to do with my study. I thoroughly enjoyed Mak Su, and I also struck it off rather well with her two daugh-ters—Kakak Zaidah, a thirty-nine-year-old divorcée, and Maimunah, an unmarried and very attractive woman of about twenty-eight. I also en-joyed the company of some of Mak Su's other friends and neighbors, particularly Indok Jaliah, who was an unusually interesting woman and very outspoken and humorous to boot.

Some time later I crossed paths with an old man by the name of Pakcik Hamzah, who stopped me as I was walking, wanting to know why I was

Figure 3.   The author with Maimunah

spending "so much time over at Mak Su's," and wanting to make sure I knew of the dangers of "love magic" (*ilmu pengasih*). I didn't know what to make of his questions and warnings, though they were rather disturbing. On the one hand, I was inclined to discount Pakcik Hamzah's concerns, partly because I knew there was bad blood between his household and Mak Su's. (One of Pakcik Hamzah's relatives had once been engaged to Maimunah. The two of them had apparently been very fond of one another, and all the wedding plans had been finalized; at the last minute, however, Maimunah backed out and refused to go through with the wedding. Among other things, this caused extreme embarrassment to Pakcik Hamzah and his relatives. For these and other reasons he harbored intense bitterness toward Mak Su and her household.) On the other hand, Pakcik Hamzah's questions and warnings made me feel quite uncomfortable and, as time went on, slightly paranoid. I had read a fair amount about Malay poisoning and sorcery, and I had observed many people come to my adoptive father's house seeking alleviation of the pain and suffering they attributed to poisoning and sorcery at the hands of fellow villagers.

Pakcik Hamzah's admonitions were similar to those I had received on many previous occasions. Long before setting foot in Malaysia, I had in fact been warned by my (male) graduate advisors that I would have to be very careful in my dealings with local women; the basic advice, as I recall it, was "stay away from the girls." I was struck by the stereotypical accounts of the faux pas that foreigners, especially Americans, committed in their dealings with local women. I was apprised repeatedly of the dangers of behavior which may appear innocent enough by American standards, but which, in Malay society (and many other Southeast Asian contexts) might seriously alienate village folk, and might even constitute grounds for a forced marriage or expulsion from the community or country. I received similar cautions from the officials at the Immigration Office in Kuala Lumpur.

Interestingly, I was also forewarned about local women on other occasions during my first few weeks in Kuala Lumpur. These warnings were of a different sort than those I had received earlier, and came from young men I encountered in restaurants, hotels, and the like, who were both surprised and impressed by my fluency in Malay, and rather stymied by my statements that I was going to Negeri Sembilan to carry out research on local society and culture. These latter warnings concerned the dangers of women from Negeri Sembilan, who reportedly used powerful "love magic" to get those they were interested in to fall in love with them, or, alternatively, to get back at those who had ignored their advances or otherwise rebuffed them. The dangers of which I was being informed had to do with my presumed ignorance of Malay social dynamics but also, and more importantly, with the active agency of local women.

I continued to receive warnings along these lines after I moved to the village of Bogang. While these admonitions sometimes pertained to other districts than the one from which the speaker hailed (in Rembau, for example, I was advised repeatedly to be especially careful of women from the Jelebu district), they came from women as well as men, and frequently pertained to women who were both neighbors and relatives of the person giving me the warning. (Indeed, some of the most persistent charges along these lines concerned sisters.) This is not to imply that people in Bogang felt that their village was more dangerous in this regard than other villages; rather, they simply felt that since I spent most of my time in Bogang, the greatest dangers to me would "naturally" come from there.

These warnings did not really sink in until my conversation with Pakcik Hamzah, which was followed by a visit to my house by Mak Lang, my adoptive mother's other sister. Mak Lang appeared at my kitchen window one evening and gave me a half-hour-long lecture on how I "better not get married here," that is, to a Malay woman. She did not mention Maimunah by name, but it was clear that she was referring to her. Mak Lang implored me not to forget my fiancée (I had told her and other villagers of my engagement) or the wishes of my parents, who, she assumed, would be devastated if I married a Malay (a Muslim). Mak Lang was visibly shaken at the time, and was pleading and crying intermittently, holding her hands palms up, in prayer position. (Some of Mak Lang's emotional distress may have been due to the fact that her daughter's house in Petaling Jaya had just been robbed. She was in fact on her way to a *dukun* with a reputation for being "very clever" at getting stolen goods returned.) Before leaving, Mak Lang emphasized that she had prayed for me, and for my marriage to Ellen, and that she hoped with all of her heart (more precisely, her liver or *hati*) that her prayers would help.

The situation deteriorated (if only, or especially, in my mind) when Mak Lang's daughter and her husband informed me that a clan leader (Pakcik Abu) with whom I wished to discuss various aspects of *adat* "didn't feel that it was necessary" for us to get together, especially since I "had already learned about many features of *adat* from another clan leader" (who happened to be one of his principal rivals). Mak Lang's daughter suggested that the real reason Pakcik Abu might not want to talk to me had to do with the fact that I was spending "too much" of my time at Mak Su's house—going there for tea in the afternoon and stopping by after dinner as well. Pakcik Abu didn't feel that this behavior was appropriate: Maimunah, after all, was single, and Kakak Zaidah was a divorcée. I was deeply distressed to hear this, particularly since Mak Lang's daughter and her husband also informed me that some other village elders did not approve of this type of behavior either; indeed, some of them were reported to have been less than enthusiastic about having me join them on the verandah at a recent feast, as I had been encouraged to do up until that time.

I felt thoroughly misunderstood, defending myself with the unimpressive argument that I had never gone to Maimunah's house when she was alone; in fact, whenever I had gone to the house, her older sister and mother had been there, along with her disabled (and largely deaf and lame) father, and frequently other villagers as well. It was true, however, that a few weeks earlier I had gone to the beach (some forty miles away) with Maimunah, her sister's adolescent daughter, and a young man from a neighboring community. We had left the village before dawn so that no one would see us, but unfortunately it got light while we were waiting by the side of the road for our ride, and we were thus observed by a few villagers. Making matters worse, we had been "spotted" at the beach by a young school teacher from Bogang, who proceeded to broadcast news of what he had seen to everyone in the village!

Mak Lang's daughter and her husband explained that if I was really interested in Maimunah I should go about things "the right way," and not as I had done. I explained that I was not romantically interested in Maimunah, and that I considered her "family," just as I considered Mak Lang, Pak Lang, and other members of the lineage compound "family," as well.

Much of the anger that Mak Lang's daughter and her husband expressed in the course of our conversation was directed at Mak Su and the other members of Mak Su's household, who, they were sure, had made a concerted effort to "snare" me. They asked me rhetorically why everyone over there was so kind to me—treating me like one of their own—much nicer in fact than they treated Mak Su's husband, Pak Su. "Look at the way poor Pak Su is sometimes left to fend for himself at meal time; there are times when he is not fed or properly cared for because Mak Su and the others are 'too busy with other things.'"

Mak Lang's daughter and her husband also expressed concern that someone "over there" would "charm" me, and in this connection they brought up Pakcik Rosli's frequent visits to Mak Su's house. "Why do you think he is over there all the time? He is a *dukun*, after all, and if he hasn't done so already, he would certainly be willing to concoct some sort of love potion and put a spell on you." They went on to point out that while some such potions are only effective if they are consumed repeatedly, and are very slow acting (taking a number of days "to work"), others are effective after a single exposure and work almost immediately. "Since you go there all the time, you are at grave risk." In good Frazerian fashion they also told me not to leave my clothes outdoors, lest someone from "over there" get hold of them and work magic on them. I, in turn, recalled that they had asked me for photographs of myself, and that I had given them one or more pictures that contained my image.

I was devastated by the conversation and the various warnings and accusations it entailed. And I was certain that everyone in the village was upset with me and that I had thus jeopardized my entire research project. Though I tried to convince myself that I didn't really believe in magic, sorcery, and the like, I knew full well that virtually everyone in the village—and many highly educated, urban Malays I had met, as well—was thoroughly convinced of the phenomenal reality of such things. I was the only person in a community of nearly five hundred people who was skeptical of such matters: They obviously knew something I didn't.

A few days after my conversation with Mak Lang's daughter and her husband I discussed all this with my adoptive mother, who reassured me somewhat by telling me (falsely, perhaps) that she had not heard any complaints about my behavior. She explained that Pakcik Abu's reluctance to talk to me might well have nothing to do with me, or with anything I had or had not done. "He mixes very little with other villagers, doesn't let many people come to his house, dislikes most of the people in the lineage with which I am associated, and hardly speaks to his own brother." My adoptive mother added that her sister Mak Lang was an inveterate gossip, an alarmist, and a worrier, and didn't even get along with her own sisters. She was probably envious or jealous of her sisters because I spent far more of my time at their houses than at her house.

There was still the question of Maimunah, however. I wondered what people would think if I went home, as I had planned, and didn't get married after all. (The status of our wedding was by this point very much in question, largely because of the uncertainties attendant upon our six-month separation, but also because all of the arrangements for the wedding had to be handled by Ellen, who understandably felt burdened by having to shoulder them all herself.) People would surely think that the "love magic" had "worked" and that I had "fallen for" Maimunah. My adoptive mother's sound advice: If you go home and don't get married, and thus come back to the village alone, you simply tell people here that you got married but weren't able to bring your wife back with you; that will put an end to the rumors!

This helped calm me even though I later had serious doubts about the veracity of my adoptive mother's reassurances that she hadn't heard any complaints about my behavior. As I walked out of the village to catch the bus for Kuala Lumpur, I found myself obsessed with the idea that it would be a disaster if I returned to the village unmarried.

The next few days in Kuala Lumpur were disorienting and distressing. The King of Malaysia had died, many shops and offices were closed down, and the streets were largely empty—all of which intensified my feelings of alienation. And I got word of the meltdown at Three Mile Island, the initial reports of which suggested a cataclysmic disaster.

When I returned to the village a few days later, I was extremely anxious and apprehensive, even though I sensed that many of the problems associated with my apparently excessive contact with members of Mak Su's household might quickly dissipate, particularly since I would soon be heading back to the United States for a month to six weeks. I had never had an ulcer and had no clear sense of the symptoms of such, but I felt certain that this was "ulcer material," and that I would soon get one if I didn't have one already. Much to my dismay, I also had to admit that many of the problems that I encountered were largely of my own making, and that, having achieved a certain level of familiarity with Malay society and culture, I had gotten complacent, had let down my guard, and had begun taking too much for granted. At the same time, I realized that many of the dynamics described here indicated that sibling ties, especially among sisters (e.g., my adoptive mother and her two sisters), are suffused with far-reaching tension and ambivalence, and are in fact more conducive to the realization of ambivalence than virtually any other social ties in local society and culture. More generally, I realized that kinship, laden as it is with heavy moral entailments, cuts both ways, and that for these and other reasons the most difficult aspects of my fieldwork were likely to be interpersonal and emotional rather than intellectual.

In mid-April 1979 I left the village for approximately six weeks, which I spent largely in Kuala Lumpur, Singapore, and the United States. Ellen and I got married in mid-May, and in late May I returned to Bogang with her, after which time I no longer ate regularly at the headman's house. With a few exceptions (members of Mak Su's household), Ellen's presence in the village was greeted with considerable enthusiasm even though she spoke no Malay at the outset and had to devote much of her first few months in the village to informal language study. Her commitment to learning Malay and to exploring the experiences of Malay women and children were especially rewarding to her and enriched my own understanding of women, gender, socialization, and other issues.

It is also true that Ellen's presence in the village altered some of my relationships in a fundamental way. Members of Mak Su's household were now rather standoffish to me, and were certainly very cool to Ellen. Maimunah, for that matter, had moved out of the village and was residing with one of her sisters in Seremban. My relationship with Pakcik Rosli grew cold; and some of the young boys that had hung around my house in the months when I lived there alone no longer did so, since they were *malu* ("embarrassed," "ashamed") to spend time there now that I was married. On the positive side, I developed deeper relationships with my adoptive mother and other adult female members of her lineage, particularly since these women (and our next-door neighbors especially) expressed strong interest in spending time with Ellen and me (if only because I was needed as a translator), and in helping Ellen learn to speak Malay and carry out the chores and responsibilities of a Malay woman. I also developed new perspectives on the interactional styles of male elders, realizing, for example, that they were sometimes rather uncomfortable in Ellen's presence and, more generally, that they did not have much experience interacting with women to whom they were unrelated. This was markedly different from the interactional styles of female elders, who exhibited no such discomfort when dealing with unrelated males. In addition, I learned much about the sexual segregation enjoined upon newlyweds and all married couples; for while we had been accustomed to spending much time together in the United States—walking arm-in-arm on occasion, and the like—we quickly realized that in Malay society such behavior is not simply frowned upon, but is largely beyond the pale. This was rather frustrating, all the more so since we were on our honeymoon.

During the next few months I buried myself in my work. By September 1979 I had finished much of the informal, open-ended interviewing pertaining to kinship, property relations, and local history, as well as the survey questionnaire that I administered from October 1979 through January 1980 to each of Bogang's 106 households. The questionnaire focused on basic census issues: the residential and marital histories of household members and their formerly resident children; the acquisition, utilization, and future conveyance of various categories of rights over houses and land; tenancy relations and labor exchanges; and income sources, living standards, and participation in various Islamic rituals and other religious activities. The scope of the questionnaire was, in retrospect, overly broad, but it did yield a wealth of valuable information that lent itself to quantification, diachronic analysis, and a fairly precise delineation of continuity and change in numerous realms of village society and culture. The questionnaire was also extremely helpful in that it began to sensitize me to the differential distribution of knowledge pertaining to Islamic inheritance codes and other aspects of Islam, and to the distribution of cultural knowledge more generally.

In January of 1980 I began a month-long study of all District Land Office records for the village of Bogang (from 1888, when land titles were first recorded in writing, through 1980), to augment the household survey data and elucidate continuity and change in property and inheritance relationships from the late nineteenth century to the present. I was aided in this endeavor by two young men from the village who I had hired as research assistants. Their assistance proved invaluable, as did that of others I hired to help with the transcription of tape-recorded interviews.

At about this time Ellen began teaching at the local elementary school, partly because of her interest in teaching (she has a certificate in elementary education), but also to help repay villagers for their kindnesses in assisting me with my study. The subjects she taught included arithmetic, geography, drama, and English; all of the instruction was in Malay, for by this time Ellen was quite conversant (though not yet fluent) in the language. Her experiences at the school and her informal tutoring of young girls at our home in the late afternoon were especially enlightening to her, and to me as well, since they provided considerable insights into socialization processes and the world of children.

The final months of fieldwork (February–May 1980) were devoted primarily to gathering, through open-ended taped interviews, additional information on the substance and local conceptualization of kinship bonds and other social ties. I also collected mythical material on the origins of the universe and human society, the initial settlement of Negeri Sembilan, and the domain of spirits.

In mid-May 1980 Ellen and I completed our fieldwork, left Bogang, and went to Kuala Lumpur to spend four weeks analyzing early British administration reports on Negeri Sembilan and other historical documents deposited at the Malaysian National Archives (Arkib Negara Malaysia). Our departure from the village was rather traumatic for us, for while we were desperately in need of privacy and eager to reestablish old friendships and familiar routines in the United States, we had also developed intimate ties with villagers, such as my adoptive mother, and we knew that we would miss them dearly and might never see some of them again.

We then left Malaysia and spent six weeks in archival study in England, focusing on colonial records housed in the Public Record Office, the British (Museum) Library, and the School of Oriental and African Studies of the University of London. In late July we returned to the United States, and to our respective careers. In my case, this involved preparing a doctoral dissertation on social structure and agrarian change in Negeri Sembilan, and, with that completed, beginning a teaching job at a small liberal arts college (Colgate University) in upstate New York; in Ellen's, it involved returning to work in the field of graphic design.

Over the next few years I completed a book and a number of articles on kinship, property, and social history in Negeri Sembilan, with special reference to the district of Rembau. In the course of preparing both the book and the latter articles in particular, I realized the value of broadening my perspectives by conducting additional research on topics that I had initially, and, in retrospect, mistakenly, viewed as more or less separate and distinct from the domains of kinship and social structure. I realized, for example, that I knew a fair amount about gender roles and the autonomy of women, but that I had a relatively limited understanding of "underlying" issues, such as the way Negeri Sembilan Malays represent or "construct" not only similarities and differences between males and females, but also gender inequality and domination. I also recognized that I needed to gain a better understanding of meaning and experience, of the ways in which different constructions of gender varied according to context, and of the political economy of contested symbols and meanings generally. Similarly, though I was fairly knowledgeable about continuity and change in norms and laws concerning property relations, marriage, divorce, and related matters, I did not know much about the ways individuals deal with property and inheritance issues and various types of disputes in the local Islamic courts and in Malaysia's pluralistic legal system as a whole, or about the ways the state uses the courts to effect social control and sociocultural change.

I subsequently designed a program of research concerning legal procedures in Negeri Sembilan, especially the handling of disputes within the Islamic legal system. The proposed research would enable me to collect data both on the relevant legal and political issues, and on topics of gender, since the Islamic courts constitute one of the principal arenas in which gender differences and inequalities are institutionalized and given formal, state-sanctioned backing. I took a leave of absence from Colgate University during the 1987–88 academic year in order to conduct field research on this project. The study, which extended over a period of nine months, was carried out mostly in the Rembau district of Negeri Sembilan, though I also spent some of my time in the neighboring, predominantly urban, district of Seremban to acquire a broader perspective. In conducting the research I was struck both by the ways in which court officials and liti-gants alike invoked contrasting representations of gender and kinship in their interpretations of the cases in which they were involved, and by the deeply perspectival nature of cultural knowledge (cf. R. Rosaldo 1980). Since an understanding of these latter issues is a prerequisite for a proper analysis of the cultural logic of judicial process, I decided to write up the material on gender and kinship before embarking on a separate mono-graph on the Islamic legal system.

Our return to Bogang in August 1987 was greeted with considerable enthusiasm, and throughout our stay in the village we were accorded the same warmth and hospitality that we received during our previous visit. On August 7 we had taken the train from Kuala Lumpur to Seremban, where we spent the night. On the following day we continued on, via train, to the bustling town of Tampin, where we hailed a taxi and began the roughly eight-mile trip to the village. We were stirred by a rush of pleasant memories as we turned off the main road and followed the dirt road to Bogang, passing stands of rubber trees and the ancestral shrine that houses the village's mythic founders, and, finally, the mosque. As we had done so many times before, we stopped at the *kedai* run by Mak Azza.

Mak Azza and Abang Ariff, along with a villager I did not recognize, were at the *kedai*, and as we got out of the taxi, I said, "Hey, it's me, Michael," to which they responded with exclamations of "Wah, they've arrived!" (I had kept in touch with my adoptive parents and other villag-ers, and had told them that I would be returning in July or August.) Much of the initial excitement focused on our two-and-a-half-year-old son, Zachary. Mak Azza and Abang Ariff wanted to know if he was a boy or a girl, and what his name was. They were especially pleased about his name; in their words, "Wah, Zakri, a Malay name!"

Some of the early conversation concerned who had died, and I learned that Mak Azza's husband had passed away a few years back after a slow, agonizing illness, widely attributed to sorcery, which entailed his turning black and so *gatal* ("itchy") that he could barely stand being alive. A num-ber of other villagers had died, more than a few in automobile accidents (a disturbing index of Malaysia's "modernization"), but many of those

Figure 4.   Mak Azza and grandson

who were among the eldest villagers during our previous stay were still alive, much to our pleasant surprise.

Our initial encounter with our adoptive parents was quite joyous, as was our first interaction with Mak Lang and Pak Lang (my adoptive mother's sister and brother-in-law), all of whom embraced us warmly. From the outset we were asked how long we were going to stay, to which I replied that much depended on housing. If I was able to find a vacant house that would be suitable for us, we might stay as long as eight to nine months. Though I did not want to proceed too quickly with instrumental inquiries concerning housing or anything else, I also wanted to get settled in the village as soon as possible, so I pursued the matter as tactfully as I could.

I learned that Kak Jamilah's house, which I had lived in from 1978 to 1980, had been torn down, the lumber and other materials earmarked for her new home in Melaka. All that remained of the old house was a part of the kitchen, the rest now being an overgrown lot full of weeds and banana trees. So that option was out. Her sister's house, in the back, was available, we were told, and Mak Su, eager to have us live near to her, offered to help clean it up for us, make it *elok* ("pretty"), and fix up the garden as well. Pak Lang, who lived next door, added that this was a desirable option especially since it would be very reassuring to his wife, who didn't like being alone in their house when he was gone.

Later in the day, as we headed out of the village and back to Seremban, we encountered Haji Baharuddin, whose wife had died a few months earlier. As is the custom among men, most of whom live in houses which are owned by their wives and which are situated on residential acreage belonging to their wives, he had moved out of the house (and village) after his wife's death, and was now living with his daughter and her family in the town of Rembau (some seven miles away). When Haji Baharuddin told us of these developments, I made a point of saying that we were looking for a house, to which he replied, "Well, my house is empty." I remembered his house being one of the nicest—and most spacious— houses in the village; since it was also located in the same lineage compound as the one we had lived in earlier, the possibility of renting it struck me as especially attractive.

The following day I returned to Bogang and talked to my (adoptive) parents about the possibility of renting Haji Baharuddin's house.[7] Both of them were very cool to the idea, even though the house was right next to their own home and would thus afford us the opportunity of living in close proximity to them, as we had done during our previous stay.

Mother was the first to express her disapproval of the plan. She did not like Haji Baharuddin or his children and (correctly) assumed that we would have trouble with them if we rented their house. His children were "not good" (*tak baik*): "They argue with him, and send him away. The son, for that matter, is unsettled and volatile, doesn't have steady work, and once assaulted his mother for not giving him money."

We tried to talk our mother into softening her position, and to this end we spoke separately with our father, who agreed to try to "work on her" so that we could live in the house that seemed most desirable. We let the matter drop for the time being, though it came up later in the day when Mak Su pressed us into looking at Kak Jamilah's sister's house. The latter house was especially unappealing, not only because it needed so much cleaning and renovation, but also because of the dozen or so bats that had made it their home and seemed less than enthusiastic about giving it up for us.

A day or two later, as I was walking into the village, I encountered Mak Su, who told me that Mother "wasn't going to let us" live in Haji Baharuddin's house. It was clear from her comments that she, too, disapproved of our plan to live in his house, if only because it meant that we wouldn't be living next door to her, as would have been the case if we had stayed in Kak Jamilah's sister's house. Mak Lang also told us that if we lived there she "wouldn't have the nerve" (*tak berani*), to come visit us. All of this reminded me of the dilemmas of finding a suitable house nearly a decade earlier, and of the personal politics and favoritism that were so pronounced—and taxing—during our previous stay.

There were few attractive options, however, and so we went ahead and rented Haji Baharuddin's house. This decision caused our mother a certain loss of face, particularly since she had voiced her initial objections to the plans in no uncertain terms ("Mother won't let you"); and it no doubt contributed to some of the tension and ambivalence we subsequently experienced in our relationship with her.

Within the village I was struck by the many changes that had occurred since 1980, foremost among them those of an economic and more generally material sort. My parents, for example, had replaced their "traditional" kitchen with a lavish concrete kitchen with glass windows, and were now the proud owners of a color television, a refrigerator, an electric coconut grater, and other modern appliances, as well as a small motorcycle, which my father used to travel to and from his stand of rubber trees, and to make other daily rounds both within and outside the village. Many village homestead plots were also encircled with urban-style fences and

heavy iron gates, and boasted modern mailboxes as well, typically inscribed with the name of the male head of household, despite the fact that
most houses and residential plots in the village are owned by women.
Similarly, a dirt path running through the village had been widened considerably so as to permit automobile traffic, and the dirt road behind the
village had been metalled and now serviced factory busses that picked up
villagers, especially young women, to work on the shop floors of electron-
ics firms in the satellite town of Senawang and elsewhere. Overall, the
village was much less self-contained and self-supporting (rice production
had declined to an all-time low and had been abandoned by many villagers
altogether)—and much noisier—than it had been during our previous
stay.

Other dramatic changes in the village were associated with Malaysia's
Islamic resurgence, which is known as the *dakwa* movement. (The term
dakwa, from the Arabic *da'a*, means "to call," or to respond to the call,
hence missionary work, including, most notably, making Muslims better
Muslims.) Before addressing these changes—the most visible of which
involved the more modest attire of girls and young women—it will be
helpful to provide some basic background information on what the resurgence is and how and why it has swept over the national landscape in
recent years.

Malaysia's Islamic resurgence is generally said to date from the late
1960s or early 1970s, even though it is most appropriately viewed as an
outgrowth of earlier developments in Islamic nationalism and reform,
such as those associated with the Kaum Muda ("Young Group") movement of the 1920s and 1930s (see Roff 1967). The Kaum Muda movement
was in many respects thoroughly home-grown, but was nonetheless animated and sustained in part by the activities and organizations of Muslims
in Indonesia, Singapore, Pakistan, Egypt, and elsewhere in the Islamic
world. The same is true of *dakwa*, which most scholars approach as a
response—indeed, a form of resistance—to one or more of the following
analytically related and culturally interlocked sets of developments: First,
the postcolonial state's Western-oriented development policies, which entail a heavily interventionist role for the state with respect to economic
planning, distribution, and capitalist processes as a whole. These policies
are widely seen as contributing both to Malaysia's (over)dependence
on foreign (particularly Western) capital, and to the economic successes of Chinese and Indians, who make up about half of the country's
total population. They are also viewed as responsible for having facilitated
upper-class corruption and engendering both deracination and moral and

spiritual bankruptcy throughout the Malay community. Second, the simultaneous shifting and hardening of class interests and animosities, especially the development of a new middle class and the attendant jockeying for power and privilege between its members and members of the entrenched (aristocratic) ruling class. And third, the shifting and/or tightening of ethnic boundaries, particularly those separating Malays and Chinese. These boundaries have become increasingly salient in recent decades due in no small measure to the New Economic Policy (NEP), implemented in 1971, which was geared toward helping Malays "catch up" economically with Chinese and Indians, and which thus placed tremendous emphasis on "race"—being a Malay or a non-Malay—as a criterion figuring into the allocation of scarce and highly prized government resources (scholarships and loans, contractors' licenses, business permits, openings for students and faculty in universities, etc.). The NEP is commonly regarded as having encouraged a certain cultural assertiveness—some would say chauvinism—among Malays (see Chandra Muzaffar 1987; Zainah Anwar 1987). This cultural assertiveness is quite pronounced as regards Islam, which—along with speaking the Malay language and observing Malay "custom" (*adat*)—is a defining feature, and increasingly *the* key symbol, of Malayness. In sum, whatever else the *dakwa* movement is or aspires to be, it is generally viewed by scholars as (though not usually reduced to) a powerful vehicle for the articulation of moral opposition to government development policies, traditional as well as emergent class structures, and ethnic groups such as Chinese and Indians, or some combination of the above.

The movement's organizations are highly diverse and their objectives are in certain respects mutually incompatible, but they all share an overriding concern to revitalize or "reactualize" (local) Islam and the (local) Muslim community by encouraging greater awareness of and stronger commitment to the teachings of the Koran and the Hadith, and in these and other ways effecting a more Islamic way of life (*din*). The movement's primary supporters, for their part, tend to come from the urban middle class.[8] They are especially visible in university settings, and are rather easily identified in such contexts by virtue of the distinctive dress that many of them wear (long, loose-fitting robes [*hijab*] as well as veils and other headgear in the case of women; long, flowing robes [*jubah*] and in some instances turbans in the case of men), as well as their active participation in religious study groups (*usrah*). Their overall numbers, however, are rather difficult to gauge. Some observers have estimated that roughly 60 to 70 percent of university women don the costume of *dakwa* adherents and otherwise ally themselves with the resurgence, and that the figure for university men is comparable (Chandra Muzaffar 1987:3; Zainah Anwar 1987:33; Nash 1991:710). These figures may be too high, or too low. The more relevant and uncontested point is that *dakwa* supporters actually constitute a *minority*—though certainly a vociferous, powerful, and otherwise significant minority—of urban Malays as a whole (see Karim 1992).[9]

Having thus provided some basic background, I should note that evidence of the resurgence, including women donning *dakwa* garb, had been much in evidence during my earlier research, but was largely confined to university settings and other predominantly urban environments (but see McAllister 1987). Indeed, I do not recall ever seeing women in Rembau wearing such outfits during the initial period of fieldwork. In 1987, however, many village girls in Bogang and other areas of Rembau were sporting the attire of the Islamic resurgents, and the uniforms of even the youngest schoolgirls were far more modest as well. While this change in dress did not necessarily signal a greater commitment to the ideals of the Islamic resurgents, it certainly marked a sharp contrast to the late 1970s and early 1980s. It also indicates that local symbols and idioms of gender—and village notions of "taste" as a whole (Bourdieu 1984)—are the product of a dialogue between local traditions and sensibilities on the one hand, and extralocal developments on the other. More generally, circumstances such as these help remind us that gender is most profitably analyzed in relation to broad, extralocal systems of political economy, religion, and prestige.

Another village-level change that struck me was less tangible but no less real. It had to do with the air of negativity and cynicism in the village, particularly on the part of my mother. How much of this had to do with the changing political climate in Malaysia—the trend toward repression; the worsening economic situation; the Islamic resurgence and the heightened politicization of so many things legal, economic, linguistic, and the like—is unclear. Some of my mother's negativity might well have been related to changes in her own life, such as her aging, her husband having relinquished the role of village headman and his—and her—subsequent decline in status, and the fact that her youngest son (following the footsteps of her older children) had left home and was now residing in Kuala Lumpur.

Additionally, it is quite possible that our mother was distressed by the changes that had occurred in our relationship with her, particularly that we were now far more autonomous and independent of her—and spent much less time interacting with her and her husband—than was the case ten years earlier. Part of the reason we spent less time with her was that most of my research in the courts took me out of the village on a regular basis, and thus precluded, or at least made more difficult, the constancy and closeness of the relationship that she and I had once had. Also, the second period of research entailed far less of a shotgun approach—in which virtually all "data" are of interest—and was far more focused on issues relating to gender and law. Consequently, I found myself impatient at times with conversations of the sort I frequently had with my mother that, rightly or wrongly, I regarded as only tangentially related to the main areas of investigation. For these and other reasons (see below), I had a much less satisfying relationship with her than had been the case a decade earlier, even though we remained deeply involved in one another's lives.

Another reason why Ellen and I spent less time with my mother is that we developed new friendships, some of which clearly offended her. Mother was especially disapproving of the relationship we developed with Kak Suzaini, a thirty-seven-year-old divorcée with three children, whom we liked very much and eventually hired to help us with cooking and other chores. Kak Suzaini was a member of a low-status clan, was of mixed Malay-Javanese ancestry, and was from a very poor family. Making matters worse was that, by our mother's standards—and those of the community more generally—Kak Suzaini had had a rather checkered marital history and was of dubious morality: She had been married three times and divorced twice, and two of the three marriages had required hastily arranged weddings since she had gotten caught in compromising circumstances with married men and was forced to wed them. The fact that Kak Suzaini had been involved as the second wife in two polygynous unions caused other women (and presumably men as well) to view her as a "husband-stealer" and troublemaker generally. Two other factors contributed to her questionable morality so far as our mother and other villagers were concerned. First, Kak Suzaini had worked for a spell at a local factory (female factory workers are widely assumed to have lax sexual standards [see Ong 1987]); and second, she was frequently seen flirting, hence assumed to be "involved," with a young Javanese man who had been adopted by our mother's brother-in-law and had taken up residence in Bogang, but who was assumed to be shiftless and transient ("like all [local] Javanese").

Our relationship with Kak Suzaini proved to be one of the highlights of our second period of research, particularly since we thoroughly enjoyed her company and her acerbic sense of humor especially, and learned much from her perspectives on village life and the world at large. Partly because of her marginal position in the community social structure, she was unusually outspoken on many topics of direct interest to me (e.g., local views of men as husbands). Kak Suzaini also provided a perspective on village life that differed radically from the ones we encountered in the course of our interactions with our parents and other members of the local elite, and thus helped impress upon me that with respect to a good many issues villagers neither speak in a single voice nor passively accept the ways in which they (and their worlds) are defined by the powers that be (see Scott 1985, 1990). She was, moreover, much more upbeat and not nearly so negative and cynical as our mother. An added plus was that Kak Suzaini had three small children of whom our son Zachary was very fond, and vice versa.

Other relationships that made the second period of fieldwork memorable—and simultaneously annoyed our mother and helped make up for the disappointment we encountered in our relationship with her—were the friendships that we developed with two of our next door neighbors: Pakcik Hamid, a sixty-year-old pensioner who had served for some twenty-five years as a policeman in Singapore, and his wife, Mak Shamsiah, a fifty-three-year-old woman who was in the same lineage branch as our mother and was very good friends with Kak Suzaini. Pakcik Hamid and his wife were exceedingly kind to us, and we spent a great deal of time in their company. Their household was all the more interesting since they shared their home with Mak Shamsiah's mother, Wan, who was the eldest living member of the lineage and, as such (though also by dint of her strong personality), a force to be reckoned with, despite her advanced senility (see chap. 4, below; cf. Peletz 1988b). Pakcik Hamid and his wife did, moreover, take an instant liking to Zachary (and vice versa), and they were forever treating him to various kinds of fruits, fried cakes, and other delicacies. (Because Zachary was highly verbal in relation to Malay children his own age, and because he rather quickly picked up enough basic Malay to communicate with youngsters and to understand some of what adults said to him, they also thought he was a genius, as did many others!) Zachary clearly enjoyed and benefited from the love and attention they lavished on him. Their many kindnesses toward him also made Ellen's and my job as parents much easier, especially as we had been rather apprehensive about taking a two-and-a-half-year-old child to the field and subjecting him to a physical and cultural environment that differed radically from the one to which he had become accustomed in upstate New York.

More generally, their behavior toward him opened up worlds that would have been closed to us had we not had a child with us in the field.

During the initial months of the second period of research, I spent much of my time at the Office of the Islamic Magistrate (*Pejabat Kadi*) in Rembau, sitting in on hearings, discussing the details of cases with the Islamic judge and various members of his staff, and studying marriage, divorce, and other court records going back to the early 1960s. Most of these cases concerned civil matters relating to marriage and divorce (such as men's failure to support their wives and children) though I encountered some criminal cases as well. I also observed court hearings at the District Office (*Pejabat Daerah*), which handles matters of inheritance and other types of property transactions. Finally, I attended hearings at the Magistrate's Court (*Mahkamah Majistret*), which deals with most civil and criminal offenses (traffic violations, theft, assault, and the like), in accordance with the specifications of national (statutory) law.

By sitting in on formal court sessions and on the informal processes of mediation, especially those run by the Islamic magistrate and his staff, I was able to acquire important insights into Malaysia's legal system and various other issues on which I sought additional information. These activities proved to be helpful in shedding light on conflict and contradiction both in marriages and other types of relationships, and in terms of gender relations more generally. The courts, after all, are one of the few contexts in which Malays are inclined to air their grievances openly and directly. Though procedures for doing so are in theory laid out in *adat*, these are not the quiet, consensus-oriented affairs about which Clifford Geertz (1983) has written in his discussions of legal sensibilities in the Malay-Indonesian world. I was in fact struck repeatedly by the strident nature of some of these disagreements, having been conditioned by the rounds of village life, where restricted speech codes are "pressed into service to affirm the social order" (Douglas 1970:22), to view Malays as thoroughly averse to conflict and litigation.

One of my objectives in observing court hearings and counseling sessions was to try to determine the extent to which the cultural understandings that Islamic magistrates and their staff brought to bear on the disputes that came before them were comparable to those of the disputants themselves. I was particularly interested in ascertaining whether court officials' notions of equity, justice, and due process, as well as their notions of personhood and gender, were similar to, or at variance with, those of villagers who appeared before the court. I also wanted to find out if

Figure 5.   Zachary

court officials' understandings of the dynamics and tensions of marriage, and of the patterns and causes of divorce, corresponded with villagers' understandings of these phenomena, and with my own understandings of these matters, as laid out in arguments I developed after leaving the field in 1980 (Peletz 1988b). Finally, I wanted to see if men and women used and experienced law and legal knowledge—as both a resource and a constraint—in broadly similar or different ways.

Data on marriage, divorce, and gender that I obtained from the study of court sessions and records of past cases were supplemented by data collected in the course of a household survey conducted by my research assistant—a twenty-five-year-old man who had helped me during my previous study—at all of Bogang's houses (which numbered 115 in 1987). This survey was intended to update the similar survey I conducted in 1979, and thus covered many of the topics dealt with earlier, though it was far more limited in scope. One of the advantages of having my research assistant conduct the survey, which was very time-consuming, was that it allowed me to spend my time on other tasks. One of the disadvantages was that much of the information that my assistant collected, but may not have written down due to his viewing it as irrelevant, was lost. Another, less concrete, disadvantage was that it reduced my social field in ways that probably offended villagers whose houses I never visited during the second period of research.

A more narrowly focused research instrument was the questionnaire on gender that I administered to twenty individuals (ten male, ten female) in February and March of 1988, the main purpose of which was to help me assess the degree of convergence in male and female views and understandings of gender. The questionnaire contained relatively straightforward questions which built on my field experience and which were designed to explore issues that frequently came up in conversation. (For example, "In your view, are males and females essentially similar or different?"; "Are these similarities and differences the result of learning and experience, or are they inborn?"; "Why do females appear to be more susceptible to spirit possession and *latah* ["pathomimetic behavior"] than men?"; and so on.) Although questions and questionnaires of this sort have obvious limitations, mine proved very helpful, particularly in light of the other information on gender roles and gender ideologies that I had collected. They were especially useful in my efforts to understand (1) the content and the silences of the dominant/hegemonic ideology of gender to which males and females subscribe; (2) the precise extent to which one can legitimately speak of alternative hegemonies; and (3) the frequently paradoxical and contradictory ways in which particular individuals experience, understand, and represent masculinity and femininity alike. The questionnaire also yielded valuable information on the contexts in which contrasting representations of gender are realized, and on how their implications are dealt with in local society and culture; as such, it clearly enhanced my understanding of various aspects of ideology, experience, and ambivalence.

Data obtained through the questionnaire were also supplemented by life history material and other information that Ellen collected from local women, much of which focused on pregnancy, delivery, postpartum restrictions and experiences, midwifery, and child rearing. Ellen pursued this research both because of her own interest in these topics, and in her capacity as a co-investigator on the project. Though she may write up some of this material in the future, she has generously allowed me to make full use of it in the present book.

As we began wrapping up the fieldwork phase of the project and making public the specifics of our plans to leave Bogang, friends and neighbors in the village hastened to lay claims to the furniture and other consumer items and provisions we had purchased earlier in the year to help make our house more habitable.[10] The staking of such claims also occurred prior to our departure from the field in 1980 and is in fact a common occurrence in fieldwork (see, e.g., Rabinow 1977). A good number of these demands put us into double binds, especially since our parents wanted—and clearly felt morally entitled to—many of our possessions, yet were relatively well off and thus had far less need for these things than some of our closest friends, who were quite poor by village standards. The compromise we decided upon (after discussing the issue with Malay anthropologists and other urban-dwelling friends) entailed distributing a few small items and sums of money as we saw fit, and selling most of our furniture and other "big ticket" items back to the Chinese merchant from whom we had bought them. Though some of our friends were undoubtedly annoyed by this course of action, everyone seemed to recognize—and more than a few people commented—that it solved the problem of competing claims and loyalties.

In the day or so preceding our departure, many of our closest friends shared with us their most cherished secrets and their deepest hostilities. Simmel ([1908] 1971:145) has written incisively about this remarkable phenomenon, noting, for example, that the "stranger" who moves on "receives the most surprising revelations and confidences, at times reminiscent of a confessional, about matters which are kept carefully hidden from everybody with whom one is close." One effect of this "opening up" (confessional venting) was to underscore to us that we had been accepted by the community in important ways, but that such acceptance was nonetheless highly conditional or contingent, based as it was on the tacit recognition that both our time within the village and the ways in which we touched people's lives (and vice versa) were ultimately quite limited. As with the rather mercenary fashion in which some villagers had laid claims to our possessions, these experiences left us feeling rather ambivalent both about the naked instrumentality at the base of fieldwork, and about anthropology generally.

Taking leave from the village (March 1988) was a bittersweet experience, much as our earlier departure (in 1980) had been. On the one hand, we were very sad to say good-bye to dear friends and neighbors, some of whom (e.g., the very elderly) we knew we would never see again. On the other hand, we felt that we had accomplished just about all that we could within the confines of the village and at the district court; and we were eager to spend time in Seremban, where we would have more privacy, more freedom to move about, and more interactions with urban friends and local scholars. Further enhancing the appeal of the move to Seremban was the fact that it was in some ways the beginning of our journey back home.

Overall, the second period of fieldwork was far more trying than the first, which was the most enjoyable period in our lives. Some of the difficulties were related to the fact that during the second period (unlike the first) we had a young child with us, and, as such, had to contend with a host of problems associated with logistics, diet, heat, poisonous insects and snakes, and so on, many of which were basically nonissues during the first research. Others were due to the deteriorating political climate (especially the more pronounced repression), the Islamic resurgence, and the heightened politicization of myriad religious, legal, linguistic, and other phenomena. Especially relevant were political and religious factors: While a non-Muslim anthropologist can relatively easily pursue matters of kinship, social organization, and *adat,* as I did during my initial study, such a researcher is more than likely to run up against suspicions if his or her project focuses to one or another degree on Islamic law or other aspects of Islam, as was the case during my second fieldwork.

I have discussed some of these tensions and suspicions elsewhere (Peletz 1993b). I will simply remark here that most of the difficulties I experienced had to do with treading too closely to the line separating Muslims from non-Muslims, and that the majority of them surfaced in my encounters with bureaucrats and other officials *outside* the village; *within* the village, most of my relations were highly amicable, and people were, as noted earlier, quite hospitable and warm. As a non-Muslim stranger, the dangers I presented to the social order during my second period of fieldwork were more directly related to the threats to the larger Muslim community of believers (*umat*), and less directly to local women, as had been an issue during my first fieldwork. In both cases, however, we see a concern with locally salient boundaries. That I was perceived in the first instance as a potential threat to local sexual mores and the various boundaries associated with them, and only indirectly, if at all, as a threat to the integrity of the Muslim community and the boundaries between Muslims and infidels (*kafir*), may well reflect my identity, at least initially, as an unmarried male, which in some ways overrode my identity as a non-Muslim. During the second period of fieldwork, however, I was both a husband and a father, and thus in many respects a full social adult; hence the issue of possible sexual transgression was much less of a concern, and people's mixed feelings toward me focused on other aspects of my role and behavior. The changing political climate helped guarantee that my status as a non-Muslim would be central here.

The second period of fieldwork was also more challenging and difficult because of changes that had occurred in the 1980s in the field of anthropology and in the human sciences generally—changes which made me more self-conscious and ambivalent about my role as anthropologist, and which also resulted both in shifts in the nature of my research interests and in the investigation of somewhat more vexing issues. During the seventies and eighties the field of anthropology had become more "politicized," and many of the long-taken-for-granted issues in fieldwork were thrown open for debate, especially those bearing on asymmetries between fieldworker and people studied, the uses of anthropological knowledge, and its benefits to local people and host governments. While I cannot claim to have resolved all of these issues to my own satisfaction (or that of others), debates bearing on such issues did have a sobering effect on me and clearly resulted in my being quite self-conscious at times about behavior of mine that might have been construed as intrusive or violative of people's privacy. Thus I was quite reluctant to tape conversations, though I had done so on many occasions during the first fieldwork, and was reticent as well to walk about with a notebook and pencil, or even to write down what people said as they spoke (except in the courts and in interviews focusing on gender). More generally, I was often quite ambivalent about steering conversations along paths that fit my agenda(s), particu-

larly since the issues that I sought to explore were at times of little immediate interest to villagers. Indeed, in many instances I made no effort to
do so, even though this meant spending a tremendous amount of time in
conversations and encounters that were socially and emotionally gratify-
ing but of little if any direct value with respect to the realization of my
research objectives.

In addition to becoming more "politicized," the anthropology of the
eighties was in the throes of paradigm crises, which have been discussed
by Ortner (1984), Marcus and Fischer (1986), Clifford and Marcus (1986),
Sangren (1988), Wolf (1992), and others. These crises have entailed a
questioning of received wisdom and "essentialist," "totalizing" visions
characteristic of much earlier work (including some of my own), and have
led some practitioners and outside observers to wonder whether anthropology in any form is either doable or worth doing at all. (I obviously
think it is both.) It is too soon to assess the long-term consequences of
these developments, but their positive effects to date certainly include
making many of us more self-conscious if not reflexive, and underscoring
the importance of attending to issues bearing on ethnographic authority,
polyvocality, and the tensions and politics involved in the collection of
ethnographic data and the anthropological enterprise as a whole. In planning, executing, and writing up this research, I wanted to make sure that
I addressed some of the more relevant issues foregrounded in the current
debates and crises, and that I captured at least some of the dissonance and
contestation that is characteristic of local understandings and experiences
of gender and kinship both in Negeri Sembilan and in much of the rest of
the world. Commitments such as these made the research and writing for
this book rather difficult but have, I hope, resulted in a book that is richer
than might otherwise be the case.

PART 1

GENDER IN HISTORICAL PERSPECTIVE

2 Gender, Prestige, and Political Economy in the Nineteenth Century

Malays have a high sense of personal honour; and as in the interior the necessary weapons for avenging an insult are always carried about their persons, the outward deportment of natives to each other is remarkably punctilious and courteous. Europeans, particularly sailors, not aware of this sensitiveness, were formerly in the habit of trespassing upon it by practical jokes, but soon found that inexperienced persons playing with edged tools are liable to have their fingers cut. . . . To wipe out a stain on his honour by shedding the blood of an offender, even if assassination be the means employed, is accounted as little disgraceful by him as the practice of duelling by others in civilized Europe.

> T. J. Newbold, *Political and Statistical Accounts of the British Settlements in the Straits of Malacca* (1839)

The approach developed in this and subsequent chapters is informed by recent work on gender and prestige. In particular, it builds on Ortner and Whitehead's (1981a) demonstration that cultural constructions of gender and sexuality are most profitably analyzed as comprising hierarchies or systems of prestige or status (social honor, social value); and that the logic and social and cultural entailments of gender systems are keyed to—and in important ways determined by—the workings of the most encompassing systems of prestige in the societies in which they are found (see also Collier 1988; Atkinson and Errington 1990; Kelly 1993).[1] The first section of the chapter provides an overview of prestige, kinship, and political organization in nineteenth-century Negeri Sembilan. Of primary interest here are data bearing on the criteria for allocating prestige, and the prestige considerations of the political elite, especially their concerns with what I refer to, following Errington (1990), as spiritual power or "potency." Of broader analytic relevance are the links between the systems of prestige, kinship, and political organization on the one hand, and the structure of marriage and affinal relations on the other, and the ways

53

in which (untitled) in-marrying males were pressed into the service of generating property rights, wealth, and prestige for their wives' kin. The second section of the chapter deals with contrasting representations of marriage and affinal exchange, which I analyze by employing a modified version of Bourdieu's (1977) distinction between "official" and "practical" kinship. I demonstrate that while official representations of the system of marriage and affinal exchange portrayed the system as focusing on men's exchange of rights over women, practical representations depicted the system as focusing on women's exchange of rights over men. In the third and final section of the chapter, I argue that the practical system of representations was more in keeping with everyday practice in the nineteenth century. I also address some of the comparative and theoretical implications of the system, including the importance of reassessing the widely held position that institutions of kinship and marriage (e.g., the "exchange of women") constitute the ultimate locus of women's secondary "status" vis-à-vis men. I suggest that prestige differentials between men and women were rooted in cosmological views that accorded men more spiritual power and potency than women, and that these broadly grounded views—rather than institutions of kinship and marriage—lay at the heart of women's secondary "status."

Before turning to a discussion of nineteenth-century Negeri Sembilan, two caveats are in order, the first of which is that my references to "the nineteenth century" pertain specifically to the period 1830–80. Many aspects of the reconstruction presented in the following pages are applicable to Negeri Sembilan during the post-1880 era, and are probably relevant as well to the decades immediately prior to 1830. My decision to focus on the period 1830–80 is based partly on the limited availability of sources on the pre-1830 era; it also reflects a concern to avoid delineating the impact of British colonialism (which was introduced into some areas of Negeri Sembilan as early as 1874) in the initial sections of the chapter. The local effects of colonial rule are discussed in subsequent chapters and elsewhere (Peletz 1987b, 1988b).

The second caveat is more in the form of a warning to the nonspecialist about the language employed in this chapter and some of the conceptual and analytic issues addressed here. This chapter is the most technically daunting in the volume as a whole, and my treatment of various issues (bearing on "official" and "practical" kinship, marriage and affinal relations, the exchange of men, and the like) will undoubtedly strike some nonspecialist readers as highly detailed, rather abstract, or both. Suffice it to say that the technical material is deeply important since it provides the basis on which we can evaluate and challenge some of the most widely held theoretical views on women, kinship, and marriage; that many of these views are packaged abstractly; and that engaging them and laying the foundations for new theoretical orientations thus requires descriptions and analyses that incorporate some degree of technical and abstract discussion. Uninitiated readers who proceed with patience are likely to find their efforts rewarded, and will, in any case, see that subsequent chapters focus more directly on case studies and other discussions of real people and are for these and other reasons more accessible.

PRESTIGE, KINSHIP, AND POLITICAL ORGANIZATION

Malays and other Southeast Asians are intensely concerned with prestige and status.[2] The intensity of prestige and status concerns in Southeast Asia is well documented in Leach's (1954) work on the highlands of Burma and Volkman's (1985) study of the Toraja (Sulawesi), though it is perhaps best illustrated in Geertz's (1973) analysis of the Balinese cockfight. The Balinese cockfight is a ritual dramatization and "celebration of status rivalry" which underscores that "prestige is the central driving force in society" (1973:43, 60), and that status relationships are matters of life and death. Cockfights, and the gambling associated with them, are by no means confined to Bali. They have long occurred throughout the Malay Peninsula (Newbold 1839 II:179, 183; Gullick 1987:330–32, 344–45) and other parts of Southeast Asia, as have myriad other contests and amusements which, at least in times past, frequently ended in the shedding of human blood (Reid 1988:143, 183–91).

The Malay terms that most closely approximate the meanings of the English terms "prestige" and "status" are *pangkat* and *taraff. Pangkat* denotes rank, degree, standing, position; rank or grade in a career. (*Sepangkat* refers to being of the same rank, social position, grade, degree, or age; *berpangkat* to having a rank, position, or grade; being noble, distinguished.) *Taraff* denotes social rank or standing, status, position in a society, standard of living. The two terms are frequently employed as synonyms, though *pangkat* is, at least at present, the more commonly used of the two terms.

In the nineteenth century there were various criteria that were used to allocate and claim prestige: descent, age, birth order, religious knowledge and experience, spiritual power or potency, and wealth were the most common. Each of these criteria may be seen as the axis within a particular system of prestige, though it is important to note that these systems were not equally valorized. Some were more significant than others in the sense of being more encompassing and hegemonic. This is clear from the following observations of Newbold (1839 II:124), which pertain specifically to Malays in the Rembau district of Negeri Sembilan, but which are relevant to Malays elsewhere as well.

> Although the Malays, like the Greeks and Romans, entertain the highest veneration for old age, still the *claims of descent supersede those conferred by years*, particularly with regard to the heads of tribes [i.e., clans], who take precedence in the councils of the state, conformably to the rank of the . . . [clan] they represent. (emphasis added)

Newbold (1839 II:124) goes on to describe a ceremony he observed in 1833 that involved

> a boy, whose dress and weapons betokened some rank, and to whom a considerable degree of deference was shewn by the natives. On inquiry I found him to be the . . . [leader] of the principal . . . [clan]; and that, although a younger brother, he had been elected . . . to that dignity, in consideration of his elder brother's imbecility. This boy affixed his name, or rather his mark (for neither he nor any of his seven compeers could write) immediately after the Penghulu [District Chief] of Rumbowe, before the rest of the . . . [clan leaders], some of whom were venerable old men, and grown grey in office.

The most encompassing and hegemonic system of prestige in nineteenth-century Negeri Sembilan was the system of hereditary ranking or descent (*keturunan*) which was encoded in the political system, and which operated through the kinship system. The kinship system was composed of matrilineally constituted descent units, such as dispersed and localized clans (both referred to as *suku*), lineages (*perut*) and lineage branches (*pangkal*).[3] Clans and lineages were ranked relative to one another and had their own political leaders, who, along with the District Chief (variously referred to as *Undang, Penghulu,* or *Penghulu Undang*), constituted the formal leadership of the (political) system. The relative status of these leaders was, in theory, fixed, and depended largely on the relative status of the kinship and territorial units over which they presided. The heads of dispersed clans, for example, were ranked in relation to one another on the basis of the ranking of their respective dispersed clans, each of which was defined, partly through mythic charters, either as a "gentry" or "commoner" clan, or as a "dependent" (satellite) clan of one or another gentry group. In practice, however, the relative status of political leaders also depended on how well they worked the system of political patronage to attract supporters and dependents and otherwise build up their *nama* ("names," "reputations").

As in other parts of the Malay world and Southeast Asia as a whole, building a name for oneself presupposed the accumulation and display of invisible spiritual power or "potency" (*kesaktian, kekayaan, ilmu, kuasa*),[4] outward signs of which were large numbers of followers and substantial wealth (see Skeat [1900] 1967:81; Milner 1982:130 n.5; Gullick 1987:48; Anderson 1972; Wolters 1982; Reid 1988:120, 125–27; Errington 1990). Political leaders at all levels of the hierarchy sought to bolster their claims to spiritual potency and thus build their names primarily by gaining control over human resources (only secondarily by acquiring land). They amassed supporters and dependents in a number of ways: through military campaigns; through various forms of "adoption"; and by attempting to use their female relatives—especially their sisters and their sisters' daughters—as "bait" (to use Ortner's [1981:371] term) to attract and gain control over men, who, as in-marrying males, would ideally add property rights, wealth, and prestige to the kinship and territorial groups over which political leaders presided. My reference to women as "bait" is not meant to suggest that women were pawns in the status games of men; as I discuss further along, it is arguably more appropriate (assuming we can speak of pawns) to suggest that untitled men, not women, played this role.

Political leaders were typically males, but one should not conclude from this fact—or from the existence of a gendered division of labor—that there were radical prestige differentials or other pronounced inequalities between men and women. As in the nineteenth-century Malay world generally, women were not really viewed (or treated) as inferior to men (Gullick 1987:210), though for reasons noted below they were accorded somewhat less prestige and were likewise regarded as more vulnerable than men. Men's and women's roles and activities were viewed in terms of complementarity rather than hierarchy, as is clearly the case at present. Thus, men were accorded the primary role in matters of statecraft, formal politics, diplomacy and warfare, and in extralocal trade; they also assumed the major role in the production of metals used for tools and weapons, and thus effectively monopolized production of the means of violence. In addition, men performed much of the labor involved in household construction as well as the heavy labor of clearing forest and other land for residential and agricultural purposes. Women, for their part, engaged in fishing and surface mining (as did men), performed most of the tasks associated with rice production, and were primarily responsible for making cloth, for processing foodstuffs, and for everyday cooking as well as the preparation of food for ritual feasts. Women also predominated in childcare and in the exchange of rights over children (informal child transfers). In these and other ways they exercised considerable autonomy and social control, acquired prestige, facilitated the acquisition of prestige on the part of their male kin, and helped maintain and reproduce households and the larger kin groupings and social units of which these households were a part.

The spheres in which men moved were more extensive and inclusive in a physical or territorial sense than the spheres of women and did in fact encompass women's spheres, though it should be noted that women were not subject to strict seclusion or segregation and did not wear veils (Newbold 1839 I:246). Whether men's activities were for this reason alone viewed as more directly related to universalistic concerns or "the social good"[5] is difficult to say (there are no data on the subject), though this is arguably the case at present. What is clear is that Western notions of the universality of "public" and "private" domains—and the attendant universalistic assumption linking men with the public domain and women with the private—do not fit comfortably with the situation in nineteenth-century Negeri Sembilan. True, women were more directly associated with matters of the household than were men, but their activities clearly transcended the domains of household, as well as those of lineage and clan. Women's predominance in rice production was clearly seen as a public and not simply a private activity; so, too, was their centrality in marriage and affinal exchange, funerary ceremonies, and spirit cults.

It merits remark as well that women could and did assume the roles of midwife (*bidan*) and healer (*dukun*). They could also become shamanic specialists (*pawang*) and thus find themselves in the critically significant position of being responsible for mediating relations of metaphoric kinship between the realm of humans and the worlds of nature and spirits. In some parts of Negeri Sembilan, moreover, women held political office (Lister 1887:88; cf. Lewis 1962:44–45). Women's abilities to assume important ritual and political roles had counterparts elsewhere in the Malay world and in other parts of Southeast Asia both in the 1800s and in earlier times (Reid 1988), as was undoubtedly well known in nineteenth-century Negeri Sembilan. More generally, women's involvement in the public domains of communal ritual and formal politics served to mute the cultural elaboration of prestige differentials between men and women (and males and females on the whole).

The situation described here should not obscure the fact that women's involvement in ritual and political activities during the nineteenth century was far more constricted than it had been in earlier times. During the early part of the period 1450–1680, women had been extremely active in communal rituals throughout much of Southeast Asia due in large part to the fact that their reproductive and regenerative capacities gave them "magical and ritual powers which it was difficult for men to match" (Reid 1988:146; Andaya and Ishii 1992:555–56). This had changed by the latter part of this period, however, due to the development in Southeast Asia of Islam and other "Great Religions" (especially Buddhism and Christianity), none of which "provide any textual basis for female participation in religious rituals at the highest levels" (Andaya and Ishii 1992:555). More generally, the highest ritual positions of the dominant faiths came to be reserved for males, who thus presided over communal rituals. Women's public ritual roles became progressively less apparent, and they were increasingly "relegated to the domains of shamanism and spirit propitiation. In the process, the status of the shaman, both female and transvestite, declined . . . , and women became the principal practitioners of 'village' as opposed to 'court' magic" (Andaya and Ishii 1992:555–56). In the Malay case, and throughout much of Southeast Asia, this gendered skewing of ritual (and political) activities was usually rationalized in terms of beliefs relating to spiritual (and/or intellectual) power or potency—that men's was greater or stronger than women's—as discussed later (see also Andaya and Ishii 1992:556–57).

> Alam beraja
> Negeri/Luak berpenghulu
> Suku bertua
> Anak buah beribubapa
> Orang semenda bertempat semenda
> Dagang bertapatan, perahu bertambatan
>
> The realm/empire has a raja,
> The district has a district chief,
> The clan has an elder/clan chief,
> People of the clan have clan sub-chiefs,
> People who marry into a clan have relatives through marriage,
> The stranger finds a place as the boat an anchorage.

Customary sayings or aphorisms (*perbilangan*) such as the one reproduced here (which is cited by Hale 1898:53–54; Parr and Mackray 1910:98; other colonial scholar-officials; and contemporary villagers) provide a suc-

cinct overview of political relations in nineteenth-century Negeri Sembilan. These relations were organized at the district (*negeri/luak*) level, and
were overseen by district chiefs. Some of these chiefs formed an unprecedented but largely ineffectual politico-military union in the 1770s, the
titular head of which was styled *Yang diPertuan Besar* (He Who is Made
Lord), though he was sometimes referred to as *Raja* (King). The *Yang
diPertuan Besar* served in some respects like the sultans of other Malay
states, one principal difference being that he had no real authority within
districts in which there were *Undang*.[6]

The *Undang* sat at the apex of the (district-level) political hierarchy
and was regarded by his subjects as God's Caliph or Vice-Regent (*berkhalifah*) and as sacrosanct (*berdaulat*). He served as the supreme arbiter and
final court of appeals for disputes that could not be settled by lower ranking political figures, and he was vested with the right to invoke capital
punishment (stabbing below the collar bone with a *keris* or dagger). The
Undang also enjoyed the right to conscript (male) villagers for defense
purposes, to make periodic demands on household labor and food resources, and to claim all illegitimate children born in the district (Parr and
Mackray 1910:52). In addition, he was entitled to collect annual payments
in kind from the proprietors of certain categories of land. The resources
which he commanded in these and other ways were used partly to sponsor
lavish feasts held in connection with coronation rituals, marriage, circumcision, and death, as well as Islamic holidays (e.g., the Prophet's birthday),
all of which testified to the *Undang*'s grandeur and largesse. Other resources were deployed in support of the *Undang*'s military campaigns,
many of which were geared toward acquiring or maintaining control over
river traffic and other extralocal trade routes, and thus generating the
wealth and followers that were outward signs of his spiritual potency. In
these and other ways (e.g., through the public display of ritual paraphernalia and certain styles of clothing forbidden on pain of death to all others), the *Undang* legitimated his claims to *berkhalifah* and *berdaulat*.

The *Undang* was the only person in the district who could legitimately
maintain that he was God's Vice-Regent or Caliph, and that he had royal
power, sanctity, or majesty (*daulat*); but he was by no means the only
person who could legitimately claim to have spiritual potency. Indeed, one
of the central tensions in the system was that while the *Undang* could
legitimately contend that he possessed *qualitatively* superior forms or
concentrations of spiritual potency (manifested in *daulat*), others (i.e.,
pretenders and other detractors) could counter with some justification that
the *Undang*'s spiritual powers were at best *quantitatively* superior forms

of the mystical knowledge cum power (*sakti, kesaktian, ilmu*) which was concentrated among certain classes of ritual specialists (shamans, healers, midwives), and which was at the same time broadly distributed (albeit in less concentrated or potent forms) throughout the population, especially among men. Moreover, since the external signs of invisible spiritual power were large numbers of followers and substantial wealth, pretenders and other adversaries needed only amass followers and wealth comparable to or greater than the *Undang* to render concrete their claims to have comparable or superior forms (or concentrations) of *sakti/ilmu*. And if they succeeded, through trickery or force of arms, in capturing the regalia or *kebesaran* (literally, things or symbols of greatness) of an incumbent *Undang*, they were all the more likely to prevail over him, particularly since the paraphernalia of office were suffused with the same sanctity that permeated the body of the ruler (Skeat [1900] 1967:36; cf. Andaya and Ishii 1992:547). Such was a dangerous undertaking, however, and could entail *kena daulat*, which Skeat ([1900] 1967:23–24) described as being "struck dead by a quasi-electric discharge of that Divine Power which Malays suppose to reside in the king's person . . . , [and which] is believed to communicate itself to his regalia, and to slay those who break the royal taboos" (cf. Newbold 1839 I:223, II:193; Gullick 1958:44–45, 1987:35).

Compounding the dilemmas both for the *Undang* and for leaders at all levels of the political hierarchy was the fact that extensive involvement in the affairs of their subjects was inimical to the accumulation and display of the spiritual potency that was a sine qua non for any political office and for being a "big man" (*orang besar*) or "man of renown" generally. Spiritual potency presupposed and had as one of its outward signs a high degree of refinement, detachment, and studied restraint—immobility was a sign of divinity (Gullick 1958:45)—all of which indexed not simply the predominance of "reason" over "passion" but also the divinely inspired cultivation of "reason" in the pursuit of the highest forms of knowledge and enlightenment (see Milner 1982). Concerns with the accumulation and display of spiritual power were thus partly responsible for the highly decentralized regulation of local affairs (and the attendant frequency of challenges to the authority of the *Undang* and other political leaders). Put differently, such concerns help explain why Malay political institutions did not entail "an exceptional concentration of administrative authority" and did not "consist in exercise of pre-eminent power" (Gullick 1958:44). Such concerns were, at the same time, one of the reasons much of the regulation of such affairs fell to women; for women were held to be less preoccupied than men with the accumulation and display of spiritual potency, and, in any event, were assumed to have less developed spiritual capacities.

More broadly, the myriad restrictions on the *Undang* meddling in the affairs of his subjects without their express request for his intervention (see Parr and Mackray 1910:48, 58) were not merely "checks and balances" that helped ensure the autonomy of lower-ranking officials and the untitled majority. They also helped secure the *Undang*'s spiritual potency. More importantly, given the explicit links between the spiritual and general health of the ruler on the one hand, and the welfare of his subjects and the world as a whole on the other, these same restrictions helped guarantee the balance and well-being of the universe and all of its constituent elements (Skeat [1900] 1967:36; cf. Anderson 1972; Jordaan and de Josselin de Jong 1985).

Clan chiefs (*lembaga*) occupied the next highest rung on the political ladder, and presided over dispersed clans (or territorially defined segments of them). Like the *Undang*, they were entitled to collect taxes of various kinds and to call upon the labor resources of the households within their jurisdiction. Similarly, they helped settle disputes among their kin, for which they received certain fees. Clan chiefs also enjoyed the rights to wear certain styles and colors of clothing that were denied to both lower-ranking figures and the untitled majority. These and other ritual prerogatives were highly valued, as was clan chiefs' knowledge of *adat* and *ilmu*, which was manifested in their eloquence, oratorical skills, and overall abilities to attract followers.

There were relatively few clan chiefs for any given (dispersed) clan. Partly for this reason, but also because of the indigenous construction of power, responsibilities for regulating a broad range of political affairs typically devolved on the immediate subordinates of clan chiefs, who were referred to as *buapak* or *ibuapak*, which I gloss "clan subchief(s)." These individuals exercised authority over the compounds of a localized clan (Lister 1887:45–46) and concurrently served to link village residents with extralocal political figures. Clan subchiefs also helped guarantee that the members of their communities received equitable treatment at the hands of clan chiefs, in much the same fashion as the latter effected a check on the activities of the *Undang* (see Parr and Mackray 1910:36–39).

Titled individuals occupying the lowest rung of the political hierarchy were also charged with promoting justice in accordance with *adat* and with increasing the likelihood that their immediate superiors did right by their relatives. These "big people among the kin" (*orang besar dalam anak buah*) helped ensure that capricious, partisan, or extortionary behavior

Figure 6.   Clan chief

Figure 7.   Male elder

on the part of subchiefs either did not occur, or, if it did occur, that it resulted in the appropriate punishment (Parr and Mackray 1910:34). In the latter instances, portions of the fine paid by a guilty subchief to the clan head were shared with the lineage heads, and apparently fines constituted the main source of income associated with the office. Lineage heads also received direct remuneration in the form of percentages of the fees paid by male clan members in the village who were involved in "irregular marriages" (e.g., marriage by storm or abduction), although they were prohibited by *adat* from levying fines on their own accord.

Though I have spoken of "big people among the kin" as occupying the lowest rank of the political hierarchy, the customary saying cited earlier refers to yet another relationship of hierarchy or asymmetry: that between *tempat semenda* ([the place of] the wives' kin) and *orang semenda* (the people who marry in). This was clearly a *political* relationship; it was, moreover, the focus of considerable cultural elaboration. Some of the entailments of this relationship were encoded in the following *perbilangan* (cited in Hale 1898:57 and Caldecott 1918:36–37; cf. Parr and Mackray 1910:87, 116–17):

> Orang semenda bertempat semenda.
> Jika cherdik, teman berunding;
> Jika bodoh, disuroh diarah,
> Tinggi banir, tempat berlindong
> Rimbun daun, tempat bernaung.
>
> Orang semenda pergi karna suroh,
> Berhenti karna tegah.
> Jikalau kita menerima orang semenda;
> Jikalau kuat dibubohkan dipangkal kayu;
> Jikalau bingong disuroh arah,
> Menyemput nan jauh, mengampongkan nan dekat;
> Jikalau ia cherdik, hendakkan rundingan;
> Jikalau maalim, hendakkan doanya;
> Jikalau kaya, hendakkan emas;
> Jikalau patah, penghalau ayam;
> Jikalau buta, penghembus lesong;
> Jikalau pekak, pembakar bedil.
>
> Masok ka-kandang kerbau menguak;
> Masok ka-kandang kambing membebak,
> Bagaimana adat tempat semenda dipakai;
> Bila bumi dipijak, langit dijunjong,
> Bagaimana adat negeri itu dipakai.
> Orang semenda dengan tempat semenda,
> Bagi mentimun dengan durian,
> Menggolek pun luka, kena golek pun luka.

> The married man is guided by [moored/subservient to] his wife's kin:
> If he is clever, they seek his counsel,
> If he is stupid, they see that he works;
> Like the buttress of a big tree, he shelters them,
> Like the thick foliage, he shades them.

The married man must go, when he is bid,
and halt, when he is forbid.
When we receive a man as bridegroom,
If he is strong, he shall be our champion;
If a fool, he will be ordered about
To invite guests distant and collect guests near;
Clever, and we'll invite his counsel;
Learned, and we'll ask his prayers;
Rich, and we'll use his gold.
If lame, he shall scare chicken,
If blind, he shall pound the mortar;
If deaf, he shall fire our salutes.

If you enter a byre, low;
If you enter a goat's pen, bleat;
Follow the customs of your wife's family.
When you tread the soil of a country and live beneath its sky,
Follow the customs of that country.
A bridegroom among his bride's relations
Is like a cucumber among durian fruit;
If he rolls against them, he is hurt;
And he is hurt, if they roll against him.

One might ask here, Which of the "bride's relations" would be most likely to "roll against" a bridegroom on a day-to-day basis? More generally, assuming in-marrying males experienced difficulties living up to the expectations of, or otherwise dealing with, their affines, were the difficulties they experienced primarily in the context of the relationships with their wives' *male* kin, their *female* kin, or some combination of the two? I am inclined to think that in-marrying males experienced most difficulty with their wives' female kin. This is largely because, at the local level, a man's female affines enjoyed considerable autonomy and social control. Let me sketch out the reasons for this.

A married man lived in or near his wife's natal compound, and thus with his wife's closest female kin, other in-marrying males, and unwed individuals associated by birth with his wife's descent and residential unit. Even though a married man fell under the formal jurisdiction of his wife's clan spokesmen, they did not live with him in the same lineage compound or even (necessarily) in the same hamlet or village; in a community settled primarily by a single exogamous clan, for example, they would reside in a separate village, as would his wife's brothers (and mother's brothers). Circumstances of this nature clearly limited the extent to which out-marrying men could exercise direct or indirect control over their sisters and their sisters' children and spouses, or even take part in relatively im-

Figure 8. Female elder

portant decisions bearing on resource allocation and the imposition of informal sanctions within the lineage or its households (as did, of course,
temporary out-migration or *merantau* [see below]). This despite the fact
that as adult male consanguines their role in the judiciary affairs of their
lineage and its residential domain was theoretically preeminent.

A central issue here is that clans, lineages, and their component segments differed from the residential clusters of households representing
them, and that women (especially female elders) exercised considerable
autonomy and social control over the affairs of their natal households and
compounds. This meant that the female elders of a lineage branch probably emerged as the de facto loci of authority (as clearly occurs at present),
particularly since genealogical groupings below the level of lineage were
not political units in the sense of having representative spokesmen assuming permanent titled offices. The implications of these facts are discussed
elsewhere (Peletz 1987a, 1988b; see also chap. 3, below). Here I might
simply point out that it was undoubtedly the activities and expectations
of such women (rather than their male counterparts) that engendered
many of the tensions experienced by in-marrying men owing to affinal
demands on their loyalties and productivity.

In this connection it is especially significant that some of the customary
sayings cited previously have been translated by early colonial-era scholar-
officials as referring specifically to a married man's relationship with his
mother-in-law, even though she represented but one of his in-laws or
tempat semenda (see, e.g., Hale 1898:57; cf. Parr and Mackray 1910:87,
116–17). Such translations may well have been informed by scholar-
officials' first-hand familiarity with the realities of local practice. This
seems quite likely since individuals such as Abraham Hale, who served
as the District Officer (Collector of Land Revenue and Chief Magistrate)
for the administrative district of Tampin (which included Rembau), had
many opportunities, and were in fact required, to gain first-hand knowledge of the workings of the local system. Be that as it may, Hale's
(1898:57) commentary on the first of the texts cited above merits note.

> One can imagine the satisfaction a Malay mother derives from thinking
> over this saying, and reciting it to her cronies and her daughter when she
> has made up her mind to receive a son-in-law into her family; be he sharp
> or slow, clever or stupid, either way she cannot be a loser. Her daughter's
> house will be built behind her own; if the man is clever he will get enough
> money to build the house by easy means; if he is stupid, she will so bully
> him that the poor man will be glad to labour with his hands at her bid-
> ding; it would seem to the anxious mother that she and her daughter can-
> not but be the gainers by this contract; perhaps they forget for the time
> that there is another side to the question, namely that they may have to
> pay his gambling debts.

Hale's remarks raise a number of issues worthy of further analysis,
particularly since they might give the reader the erroneous impression

that we are dealing with a "matriarchal" society. I address such issues in subsequent sections of the chapter, which focus on various aspects of the system of marriage and affinal relations. Before turning to a detailed analysis of marriage and affinity, however, we need to consider a few other entailments of the political system, such as how one attained political office, and how competition among political leaders and "big men" generally informed local understandings and representations of femininity.

How Did One Get to Be a Political Leader?

Succession to political office was determined partly by ascriptive criteria in the sense that it was confined largely to males, and depended partly on being born into an appropriate kin group. Achieved status was also important, however, as we will see.

Rights to political offices were defined as the "ancestral property" (*harta pesaka*)[7] of kin units associated with specific territorial domains. Succession to office rotated in theory among the units defined (through mythic charters) as eligible to furnish candidates for the office. For example, rights to the title of *Dato Perba* (the head of the Lelahmaharaja clan) rotated in theory between the four "founding" villages deemed eligible to provide candidates for this office. When the *Dato Perba* from village A died or relinquished his title, it was village B's turn to provide a candidate; next was village C's turn, then D's, then back to A, and so on.

The scheme of rotation was actually more complex than this, for in theory the different lineages comprising the Lelahmaharaja clan in village A took their turns in supplying candidates whenever it was their village's turn to provide someone for office. The same for villages B, C, and D.

There were no circuits beyond this, however, and there were no rules of primo- or ultimogeniture (or anything of the sort commonly reported for conical clans) specifying which male within a sibling set, lineage branch, or lineage merited preferential treatment when their kin group had its turn at providing a candidate for office. (This despite the importance attached to birth order in most other contexts.) Brothers and other males belonging to the same lineage thus competed with one another for the privilege of holding office, thereby giving rise to invidious intralineage cleavages in the very units they sought to represent. That many such competitions were fierce and frequently bloody is a common theme in the literature on the nineteenth century. More generally, the literature is replete with accounts of armed aggression and full-scale warfare between men, kin groups, and larger territorial groupings linked to one another through siblingship (see Peletz 1988b).

Men thus competed with one another to attract supporters and dependents and otherwise build up their names. As noted earlier, this entailed developing and displaying spiritual potency, knowledge of *adat*, expertise in the recitation of the Koran and other religious texts—and eloquence and oratorical skills generally—as well as competence in economic activities (e.g., the collection and trade of forest products). Bear in mind, too, that the proceeds of economic activities were in many cases used to sponsor feasts that would not only impress supporters and potential supporters alike, but also enable them both to bask in the sponsor's majesty and to revel in the blessings of the various local spirits that were attracted to and pleased by such feasts.

Where did men seek followers? Men sought supporters both among their own kin and among affinal relations. Support from their own kin was necessary since, in theory, a man's succession to (and continued tenure in) office presupposed consensus on the part of his kin (male and female alike) that he was the most appropriate candidate for the office. Support from affines, especially male affines, was also highly advantageous. For the sake of convenience, male affines may be divided into two categories. The first (and for present purposes less important of the two) consisted of the wife's brothers and her other male matrikin. A man could seek political support and various types of assistance from such individuals, but he was constrained in doing so by the fact that he was ultimately beholden to them since he stood as their *orang semenda* (they were his *tempat semenda*). The second (and for present purposes more important) of the two categories consisted of the men married to a man's sisters and sisters' daughters. The men married to a man's sisters and sisters' daughters were, both in theory and in practice, beholden to him since he was their *tempat semenda* (to whom they stood as *orang semenda*). Of comparable if not greater significance, the labor power and productivity of such men helped create property rights, wealth, and prestige for the households and lineage into which they married and thus enhanced the names of all such groupings and members thereof. These, in short, were the male affines who were of greatest strategic importance to a man with political aspirations.

Let us assume, then, that men with political aspirations used their sisters and their sisters' daughters as "bait" to attract men who, as in-marrying males, would create property rights, wealth, and prestige for their kin groups. In what sense did they do this? First, they helped ensure that their sisters and their sisters' daughters had at least respectable (and ideally, impressive) holdings of land and other property to bring to their marriages. And second, they guarded the virginity and moral standing of these women so as to enhance the likelihood that they commanded impressive marriage payments and were otherwise able to be matched as wives with men who not only had comparable or higher status, but also clear potential for contributing to their stores of property and wealth. In these ways they could ally themselves with prestigious clans or segments thereof. Some "beautification" rituals such as teeth filing may also be interpreted in a similar light (i.e., as attracting men) even though many such rituals did not occur until after marriage ceremonies were well under way.

Note, though, that men did not appropriate the labor power of their sisters or their sisters' daughters. Nor, for the most part, were they in a position to appropriate the labor power of the men married to these women. Not only did women retain control over the fruits of their agricultural and other labor; they also exercised important control over the labor power of in-marrying males. In short, we are not dealing with what Collier and Rosaldo (1981) refer to as a "brideservice society" (see also Collier 1988), or a situation in which, in the words of Lévi-Strauss (1949:115), "men exchange[d] other men by means of women."

Some Relational Features of Femininity

There is very little precise information on the ways in which femininity and female sexuality were experienced, understood, or represented in nineteenth-century Negeri Sembilan. However, certain broad inferences can be drawn from the system of prestige outlined in the preceding pages. If we accept the proposition that the prestige considerations of the political elite were instrumental in motivating understandings and representations of femininity, then it seems reasonable to assume that, in relational terms, the category of "female" was dominated by understandings and representations of women in their roles as sisters and sisters' daughters, as opposed to, say, mothers and/or wives. To the extent that this was true, the gender system of nineteenth-century Negeri Sembilan is similar to the gender systems of Polynesia, as described by Ortner (1981), and significantly different from the gender systems found in most other areas (e.g., Buddhist, Mediterranean, Catholic, and many Middle Eastern Islamic societies). In most societies, the category "female" is defined by female relational roles such as mother and wife, which serve to emphasize women's sexuality, reproductive capacities, and links with "natural functions," and which in these and other ways effectively "pull women down."[8] In Polynesia, however, this does not really occur (or occurs on a much reduced scale), for the simple reason that the category "female" is, as noted earlier, defined primarily by women's roles as sisters and sisters' daughters. This is one of the reasons women in Polynesia enjoy "higher status" than women in most other societies (see Ortner 1981). Women in nineteenth-century Negeri Sembilan, for their part, also enjoyed "high status" relative to women in most other societies, and did so for much the same reason(s) as women in Polynesia.

The situation in nineteenth-century Negeri Sembilan both differed from and is more complex than that of Polynesia, however, for while the systems of kinship, prestige, and political organization in these two areas are in many respects quite similar, Negeri Sembilan has long been a Muslim society, whereas Polynesia has never been Muslim. More to the point, Islamic doctrines and cosmologies (like those of Buddhism, Christianity, and the other Great Religions) tend to focus on women in their roles as wives and mothers, rather than sisters and sisters' daughters. In these and other ways—most notably by emphasizing that women have less "reason" and more "passion" than men—Islam highlights women's sexuality, reproductive capacities, and links with natural functions. The fact that nineteenth-century Negeri Sembilan was a Muslim society means that the "Polynesian features" of the system existed alongside and were in some contexts encompassed within a Muslim framework. (In other contexts, Muslim features of the system were encompassed within a "Polynesian framework.") Many but by no means all elements of these two systems were mutually inconsistent, which is to say that there were structural contradictions in the relations between the systems, and that, in relational terms, femininity was thus constituted of diverse heterogeneous elements whose cultural implications and social entailments were in many respects characterized by relations of structural contradiction as well. As we will see later on, some of these contradictions provided crucial structural precedents for historical changes during the period of British colonial rule (1874–1957).

Broadly similar types of contradictions characterized nineteenth-century constructions of masculinity. To understand the nature and locus of these contradictions—and the attendant challenges of masculinity—we need to look more closely at the ways in which in-marrying males were pressed into the service of generating property rights, wealth, and prestige for their wives' kin.

Marriage, Affinal Relations, and the Challenges of Masculinity: An Introductory Sketch

> A man marrying into another tribe [i.e., clan] becomes a member of it. (Newbold 1839 II:123)

> On marriage a man passes from his mother's [clan] to become a lodger in his wife's home. . . . A married man, by the fact of his marriage, is severed from his own [clan], which has no claims on him and no obligations toward him except in regard to "life and blood," so long as his married life continues. (Parr and Mackray 1910:86, 95)

> A man passes on marriage from the control of his mother's [clan] to that of his wife's, so that a large proportion of the males in the charge of any one [clan] do not belong to that [clan] at all by descent. (Wilkinson 1911:316)

> A man definitely passes into his wife's [clan] and becomes subject to her [clan] chief in all matters affecting her and her family. . . . He remains a member of his own [clan] for certain limited purposes but he is definitely subject to his wife's [clan] chief in all matters affecting her [clan]. . . . *The sole exception is the Undang.* (Taylor 1929, cited in Winstedt 1934:78; emphasis added)

Nineteenth-century observers such as Newbold mistakenly assumed that, upon marriage, men were incorporated into their wives' descent groups. Later observers, such as Wilkinson, had a more accurate understanding of the system. In-marrying males were not actually incorporated into their wives' descent groups in any formal or legal sense; for example, although postmarital residence was uxorilocal, men did not change their descent group affiliation on marriage, and they still owed formal allegiance to their own political leaders. In social and political terms, however, and with respect to their day-to-day experiences, the lives of in-marrying men changed in fundamental ways as a consequence of their marriages. These changes were realized in the kinship terms with which in-marrying men were referred to and addressed. In his natal village, for example, a second-born male would be referred to and addressed by same-generation juniors as *bang ngah* or simply *ngah* ("elder brother, second born," or "second born," respectively). If he married a woman who was first-born, however, same-generation juniors in his wife's village would refer to and address him as *bang lung* or simply *lung* ("elder brother, first born," or simply "first-born," respectively), thus reinforcing the change in his social identity. More generally, he would be defined as *orang semenda* in his wife's village, and thus subject to all the constraints entailed in the relationship between *orang semenda* and *tempat semenda*. Some of these constraints were expressed in customary sayings noted earlier, which suggest that the labor power and material resources of in-marrying males were of critical concern to their wives' kin.

These and other data (presented below) indicate that a man's economic competence and social status and prestige within his wife's community were defined largely in relation to how well he provided for his wife and children. A "good provider" built a house for his wife and children on land that was part of (or adjacent to) his wife's natal compound, and he worked with his wife to expand her agricultural (wet-rice) holdings; he also provided his wife and children with cash and commercial items (cloth, jewelry, etc.) acquired through the rearing and sale of livestock and the collection and sale of forest products. Property rights thus created were defined as "conjugal earnings" (*carian laki-bini*), but the bulk of these rights would pass to the man's wife and children in the event of the dissolution of his marriage through divorce or his death. (They would devolve upon the children and the wife's matrilineal survivors in the event that she predeceased her husband.) These features of the property and inheritance system highlight the structurally important role that married men played in the creation and initial transmission of property rights that would ultimately pass only among their wives' matrilineally related kin; more generally, they illustrate that in-marrying males played a crucial role in the reproduction of the material base of descent units and the larger systems of kinship, politics, and prestige of which they were a part.

We do not know how affinal relations were experienced by in-marrying men, but if the present is any indication of the past, married men often found that they could not live up to the prestige-driven expectations and demands of their affines, and otherwise found these situations both rather oppressive and out of keeping with Islamic ideals, which recognize no such political asymmetries or parochial distinctions (see below). One solution to a married man's dilemma would be to divorce or simply abandon his wife, along with any children he might have. This was but a temporary solution, for divorced (like widowed) men would not necessarily be welcome in their mothers' or sisters' homes for extended periods. Nor was living alone (in a local prayer house or mosque, or in a home by oneself) a viable alternative; for socialization and the sexual division of labor left men with little direct knowledge or experience concerning the domestic tasks necessary to maintain themselves, and houses were defined as female property. Avoiding marriage altogether was not feasible either, for marriage, along with fathering (or adopting) children, was a sine qua non for adult male personhood.

Another possible and more long-term solution to the predicaments experienced by in-marrying males was to attain political office (alternatively, to become a healer or a shaman). This would enable a married man to establish a separate base of political support and thus partly offset his dependence on, and subordination to, his affines. It would also provide a separate basis for social identity and self-esteem arguably more in keeping with Islamic ideals emphasizing the seamless brotherhood and equality obtaining among all members of the Muslim community (*umat*).

This solution to the dilemmas encountered by in-marrying males indicates that there was a critically important but largely "hidden" prerogative of political office: Compared to untitled males, political leaders were not nearly as dependent on the cooperation and goodwill of their wives' kin, and were relatively autonomous in relation to them. In their roles as in-marrying males, in other words, political leaders were relatively unconstrained by the political and economic entailments of the system of marriage and affinal relations. This was especially true in the case of the *Undang,* who, as noted earlier, is singled out by Taylor (1929) as "the sole exception" to the rule that "a man definitely passes into his wife's [clan] and becomes subject to her [clan] chief in all matters affecting her and her family." I suspect it was also true, though less pronounced, for clan chiefs, though there is no direct evidence for this other than clan chiefs' exemption from the ritual fetching of the groom and his kin during certain stages of wedding ceremonies. In any event, *Undangs'* freedom from the constraints of the system enabled them both to exert critical leverage toward social and cultural change in the latter part of the nineteenth century (and throughout the colonial era in general), and to confer legitimacy on myriad departures from tradition (see Peletz 1988b).

One should bear in mind, however, that there were not all that many political (or ritual) offices to go around, and that most men were therefore unable to claim roles as political leaders or ritual specialists, or otherwise define themselves in "positional" terms. Rather, most men were defined simply as kinsmen: husbands, fathers, brothers. In light of the material presented earlier, it seems reasonable to assume that they were defined first and foremost as in-marrying males, and as *husbands* and *fathers* in particular.

Nineteenth-century Negeri Sembilan is by no means the only society in which the majority of men, and constructions of masculinity generally, were defined largely in "relational" terms. Such was clearly the case in nineteenth-century Aceh (northern Sumatra), which had systems of kinship, marriage, and prestige that were in many respects quite similar to those in nineteenth-century Negeri Sembilan. Siegel (1969:68) notes, for example, that in nineteenth-century Aceh, "[male] villagers were first of all husbands and fathers." This is to say that men's primary identities and senses of self were defined not by their roles or positions in the political economy, or in terms of citizenship, nationality, or religion, but rather in "relational" terms of the sort that, according to much of the literature on women and gender, are ostensibly reserved for women (see, e.g., de Beauvoir 1949; Ortner 1974; Ortner and Whitehead 1981a; Chodorow 1974, 1989; see also chaps. 6 and 7, below). Of additional interest here is that "even when [Acehnese] men lived up to their material obligations, they had little place in their wives' homes. Women were independent of men, even if they [men] could pay their own way" (Siegel 1969:54). Stated differently, "Although men tried to create a role as husbands and, especially, as fathers, women thought of them as essentially superfluous. They allowed men no part in raising children and tolerated them only so long as they paid their own way and contributed money for goods that a woman could not obtain through her own resources. . . . A man's role as a husband-father in the nineteenth century was small indeed. . . . Men were like 'guests in their own homes' " (Siegel 1969:54). Many and perhaps all of these generalizations pertain to nineteenth-century Negeri Sembilan as well, and are also relevant to contemporary Negeri Sembilan (Siegel 1969:183), as will be discussed later.

Having drawn attention to the pressures and difficulties that many (perhaps most) men experienced in their roles as husbands and fathers (and in-marrying males generally), I should emphasize that some men undoubtedly did succeed in living up to and gaining prestige from these roles. They did this partly by being "good providers," especially by raising and selling livestock and collecting and selling or trading forest products for commercial items and/or cash that could be used to supplement the rice and other agricultural products their wives contributed to the household coffers.

Another way in which men gained prestige was by making the pilgrimage to Mecca (the *haj*). Recall that married men, like the rest of the population, were Muslims and thus bidden to undertake the *haj* should they be financially able. Making the pilgrimage was not merely a way of carrying out one's religious obligations, however; it also brought the pilgrim considerable prestige both as a person of means and as someone who had acquired uncommon and otherwise highly valued religious experience and knowledge. Equally important, the *haj* was apparently widely seen as an "outlet for humiliation" (Gullick 1987:233 n.53, 250; see also Ellen 1983:74) in the sense that its performance enabled individuals to make partial atonement for their social sins and shortcomings.

Not surprisingly, gaining sufficient funds to make the *haj* was a principal objective of men who engaged in cash-cropping in the early years of colonial rule. Even before that time, the sale of forest produce and livestock had been undertaken for this purpose. Thus, in 1892 Lister wrote that the *Yang diPertuan Besar* had informed him that

> The money supply for luxuries had always been obtained from the sale of fruit, vegetables, and orchard produce generally but in a far greater degree from the sale of buffaloes, goats, and poultry reared on these lands. . . . It was also by this industry that the people of the country were able to save up money to accomplish the pilgrimage to Mecca. . . . In former times, prior to the natives having been given facilities in regard to working for wages, this was in most cases the sole source of cash wealth. (quoted in Gullick 1951:48)

We see here the mutual reinforcement of two separate though interrelated criteria for prestige ranking: the one based on the cultural construction of affinal obligations, relatedness, and cleavages keyed ultimately to the system of hereditary ranking and prestige; the other resting on a more transcendent ideology according to which all men are equal before God, but those among them who journey to Mecca enjoy exalted spiritual and social standing. That a man could earn prestige on both accounts through trading activities is, I think, a critical factor in motivating their involvement in trade in the first place, and in encouraging both the colonial-era acquisition of land by males and their involvement in cash-cropping on the whole (see Peletz 1988b).

It would obviously be useful to know something of the effects of the pilgrimage experience on men (and women) from Rembau and other parts of Negeri Sembilan. Unfortunately, there is very little information on such matters, or even on more basic issues such as how many men (or women) from Negeri Sembilan were making the pilgrimage in the mid- or late nineteenth century. Gullick (1958:141) writes that six of thirty "notables and headmen" assembled in Rembau in 1883 had been to Mecca, though he hastens to add that it is highly improbable that a full 20 percent of the entire population had undertaken the pilgrimage. It is quite likely, in any event, that men from Negeri Sembilan who made the pilgrimage

had experiences similar to those of pilgrims from other parts of the Peninsula and the Malay-Indonesian world generally. These experiences may
well have led to the development of a deeper appreciation of the broader
Muslim community to which they belonged, and the beginnings of a clear
sense of some of the similarities and differences between Malayan (especially Negeri Sembilan) Islam and *adat* on the one hand, and Middle Eastern variants of Islam and "custom" on the other. As such, they might
have entailed a greater awareness of the ways in which their roles as husbands and fathers, and as in-marrying males on the whole, contrasted
with the roles of married men elsewhere in the Muslim world. Regretta-
bly, however, the precise extent to which this greater awareness may have
helped motivate men to effect changes either in their roles as husbands
and in-marrying males, or in the more encompassing system in which
these roles were embedded, is unclear, at least for the period prior to colonial intervention. Unclear, too, is the extent to which developments of the
sort at issue here might have led to the increased salience (in local society
and culture) of the concepts of "reason" and "passion."

CONTRASTING REPRESENTATIONS OF MARRIAGE AND AFFINAL EXCHANGE

Much of what I have described thus far has been couched in the terms and
concepts of the outside observer. We also need to know how the actors
represented their system. For this I turn briefly to marriage and funerary
rituals, which indicate that nineteenth-century representations of marriage and affinal exchange were in many respects quite contradictory. Before addressing such matters it will be useful to provide a few comments
concerning the negotiation of marriage and ideal marriage partners.

Nineteenth-century marriages were arranged, and senior kin, especially females, appear to have played the principal role in spouse selection.
Newbold (1839 I:254), for example, notes that "the [marriage] alliance is
first agreed upon by the friends of both parties, generally the *matrons*"
(emphasis added). Precise information on which female relatives played a
decisive role in arranging marriages would certainly be of interest, but
unfortunately no such information exists. At present, mothers, mothers'
sisters, and other matrilineally related female kin typically play the decisive role in arranging marriages, and this situation has probably always
obtained (cf. Lewis 1962:166–67; Abdul Kahar bin Bador 1963). Situations
such as these, which prevail in other parts of the Malay Peninsula and
elsewhere in Southeast Asia, are part of a larger Southeast Asian pattern

of women's predominance in diplomatic matters, trade, and marketing—
and in managing information and social relationships generally—which
serves both to insulate men from the haggling, negotiation, and compromise that could pose serious threats to their status concerns; and to help
ensure that the latter concerns do not interfere with "good business" (see
Reid 1988:163–72; see also Brenner 1995, and chap. 7, below).

Female preponderance in arranging marriages in nineteenth-century
Negeri Sembilan is noteworthy in light of the fact that men rather than
women were accorded the role of giving, receiving, and otherwise publicly
validating affinal transactions in the formal context of engagement and
marriage ceremonies. This suggests an implicit gendered division of labor—between "practical" and "official" tasks—of the sort which is found
in many other parts of the world (see Bourdieu 1977:33–38), and which is
sometimes keyed to a more encompassing (analytic) distinction between
"practical" and "official" kinship, about which more in a moment.

As for ideal marriage partners, contemporary accounts suggest that, in
the nineteenth century, the ideal groom-to-be was an industrious man
with a demonstrated competence in agriculture and trade, as well as Koranic recitation, *adat* lore, various elocutionary skills, and one or another
domain of ritual knowledge. He was also at least a few years older than
his bride-to-be, of generally comparable status and untainted pedigree,
previously unwed, free of physical disabilities, and neither "insane, lep-
rous, impotent, nor lost to a sense of shame" (Parr and Mackray 1910:80–
81). Corresponding qualities were sought in brides (they should be neither
"insane, nor afflicted with dropsy or hemorrhoids, and should be capable
of consummating the marriage" [Parr and Mackray 1910:80–81]), one
principal difference being that a girl's prior marital status and virginity
were of greater social concern. A girl's competence in cooking, washing,
sewing, and agricultural labor also counted for much more than her mastery of Koranic verse and verbal skills.

There also seems to have been a preference for local (but not necessarily village-level) endogamy, and for marriage within the same relative
generation, even though a "good match" might join a man with a woman
held to be one generation his junior. In addition, marriage with (nonma-
trilineal) relatives (*saudara*) was favored over marriage with non-kin or
strangers (both glossed *orang lain* or "other people"), as described by
present-day villagers and by the accounts of earlier observers (e.g., Lewis
1962:164–65). More precisely, ideal marriage partners were of comparable
status and wealth, and stood related as cross-cousins of the same generation.[9]

Less clear, however, is whether these latter ideals pertained to cross-cousins of the first degree or simply to all individuals related as cross-cousins. It is also difficult to determine the extent to which matrilateral cross-cousins might have been favored, if at all, as potential spouses for eligible bachelors (or their marriageable sisters) (but see de Josselin de Jong 1951:174, 1977:250–51). The data suggest only a general preference for marriage with classificatory cross-cousins on either the maternal or paternal side (Lewis 1962:164; Peletz 1988b:64–70).

Official and Practical Kinship

To help make sense of the contradictory representations of marriage and affinal exchange to which I referred earlier, I draw upon and employ a modified version of Pierre Bourdieu's (1977:33–38) distinction between "official" and "practical" kinship, which I find heuristically valuable, though ultimately somewhat simplistic. Bourdieu develops these terms as part of a larger program designed to help social scientists better appreciate that static, highly abstract formulations and models of formal or "official" rules and principles of social structure (such as those for which Lévi-Strauss is justly famous) do not get us very far in understanding social actors or the myriad contexts in which they organize themselves, relate to one another, avail themselves of resources, or create meaning and order in their lives. Bourdieu argues that if we want to understand these phenomena we need to devote far greater attention to social actors' contextually variable behavioral strategies, especially those everyday practical strategies geared toward the attainment of locally defined value. These strategies are of course informed by "offical" rules and principles, but they are also conditioned by culturally induced but largely implicit (and sometimes unconscious) dispositions as well as material and symbolic interests, and are thus not in any way "mere execution[s] of the model (in the . . . sense of norm . . . [or] scientific construct)" (Bourdieu 1977:29). Of more immediate relevance is that, for Bourdieu, the term "official kinship" refers to "official representations" of kinship and social structure, which "serve the function of ordering the social world and of legitimating that order" (Bourdieu 1977:34). Official kinship is "explicitly codified in . . . quasi-juridical formalism" (Bourdieu 1977:35), and is, at least with respect to kinship as a whole, "hegemonic" in Raymond Williams's (1977) sense of the term. "Practical kinship," on the other hand, denotes the uses and representations of kinship in everyday practical situations, which are more oriented toward "getting things done" than to formal representations of kinship and social structure (though I would emphasize that they, too, have important legitimating functions).[10] In many societies the distinction between official and practical kinship is highlighted in the institution of marriage. As Bourdieu (1977:34–35) notes, "marriage provides a good opportunity for observing what . . . separates official kinship, single and immutable, defined . . . by the norms of genealogical protocol, from practical kinship, whose boundaries and definitions are as many and as varied as its users and the occasions on which it is used." To paraphrase: It is practical kin—"utility men," in Bourdieu's terms—who do much of the actual work in arranging marriages; it is official kin—"leading actors," in Bourdieu's terms—who publicly celebrate and validate them.

Bourdieu's distinction between official and practical kinship is useful for my purposes, but it is insufficiently precise both for Negeri Sembilan and for many (perhaps most) other societies. This is partly because official kinship is rarely if ever "single," with all that is implied in terms of being monolithic, internally undifferentiated, and free of contradiction. It is, moreover, essential to appreciate that in some cases—such as those of the Merina and the Andaman Islanders (see Bloch 1987; Ortner 1989–90, respectively)—there are three or more contrasting sets of representations bearing on the culturally interlocked domain of gender (to which domain the distinction may be applied), not simply the two that are suggested by Bourdieu's terminological and analytic distinction. To this we need add three other important qualifications. First, contrasting representations bearing on kinship, gender, and so on, may be invoked—and contested—in all kinds of different contexts (practical and official alike). Second, the majority of (if not all) such representations may be thoroughly grounded in practice, though differently so (e.g., in different contexts and domains, to different degrees, in different ways, with different effects). And third, all may speak to "partial truths," the more general point being that cultures—or, to be more precise, elements of ideological formations—"get things right" (are truly illuminating) in some contexts, but are "wrong" or "false" (profoundly distorting or mystifying) in others.

Caveats such as these should be borne in mind throughout the ensuing discussion. So, too, should the more basic and in some ways far more important point that distinctions of the sort proposed by Bourdieu, which have deep roots in Marxist contributions to theories of ideology, are not intended to effect "an ontological carving of the world down the middle" (Eagleton 1991:83), but rather to highlight the existence and entailments of the different perspectives, discourses, and registers that invariably constitute any given ideological formation. There are, of course, other con-

Figure 9.   Clan chief at wedding

ceptual and analytic frameworks available for handling the polyvocality and multiplicity at issue, but they, too, have their limitations and need not concern us here.[11]

The modified distinction between official and practical kinship that is proposed here is particularly relevant to an understanding of marriage and funerary rituals in nineteenth-century Negeri Sembilan. These rituals are of interest not only because they shed valuable light on how people represented their systems of kinship and gender. They also illuminate highly significant ("on-the-ground") dynamics of the nineteenth-century systems, the historical reproduction and transformation of which are crucial for an understanding of kinship and gender at present.[12]

In nineteenth-century Negeri Sembilan, official representations of kinship, gender, and affinal exchange were especially evident in the first day of formal wedding ceremonies. This day served as the occasion for lavish feasting as well as the ritual presentation of "marriage gold" (*mas kawin*) from the clan chief of the groom to the clan chief of the bride (Parr and Mackray 1910:36, 94). This ritual not only validated the bond between husband and wife and the linkage between their respective descent units. It also highlighted clan chiefs, and men more generally, as "leading actors," effectively denying the role, in arranging and maintaining marriage and affinal relations, of untitled males and women as a whole.

The same day served as the occasion for the specifically Islamic dimension of the wedding, which also symbolized the official view of kinship and gender. This ritual called for the presence of a local mosque official, the bride's Islamic guardian (or *wali*),[13] the groom, and a few male onlookers as witnesses. It focused on the mosque official's recitation of the "marriage service" (*khutbah nikah*) and symbolized, but did not actually effect, a transfer of legal responsibility and control over the bride from her Islamic guardian—usually her father but conceivably her father's brother or another of her father's close male relatives—to her husband. This ritual represented the system of affinal alliance as composed of descent units linked to one another through exchanges of rights over women. As such, it entailed a *mis*representation of the practice of affinal exchange and social reproduction more generally; for the practice of marriage and affinal exchange did not really center on a father relinquishing rights and obligations with respect to his daughter and doing so in favor of his daughter's husband; rather, it focused on a mother's transfer of claims and responsibilities over her son to the son's wife and the latter's immediate kin.

I will return to this theme (the exchange of men) in due course. Before doing so I might explain the basis of my contention that the mosque official's ritualized recitation of the "marriage service" symbolized but *did not effect a transfer of legal responsibility and control over the bride from her Islamic guardian to her husband.* The bride's Islamic guardian was *not* vested with the control over the bride that was encoded in this feature of the marriage ritual; rather such control was vested in the bride's matrilineal kin. The groom, moreover, did not really acquire full legal responsibility and control over the bride, though he did acquire certain rights in his wife's sexual services, labor services, and property (see below); such control remained with the bride's kin.

Why then did this ritual exist? Put differently, what purposes, if any, did it serve? One could conceivably argue that this ritual was simply integrated into local marriage practices when elements of Islam began to be incorporated into various domains of Malay society and culture subsequent to "the coming of Islam" beginning around the thirteenth century. Such an argument begs the question, however, just as it glosses over the possibility that a structurally similar ritual might have existed in the Malay world before "the coming of Islam." It also says nothing about the purposes such a ritual may have served. We can only speculate on this issue, but it is reasonable to suggest the following: By (mis)representing the system of marriage and affinal relations as composed of groups of men exchanging rights over women, this ritual statement helped disguise and render more palatable to men, especially the untitled majority, the basic social fact that it was the exchange of rights over men, untitled men in particular, which made possible the production and reproduction of the material and social basis of households and lineages, and the larger systems of kinship, politics, and prestige of which they were a part. In this view, the ritual statement at issue was structurally motivated by the prestige considerations of titled males such as the *Undang* (and perhaps clan leaders as well), who clearly had much to gain by the reproduction of the system and were at the same time largely immune to its imperatives and constraints, at least in their roles as husbands and in-marrying males. Prestige considerations of the *Undang* aside, the ritual also resonated deeply both with *Undangs'* experiences as husbands and in-marrying males, and with the prestige differentials which obtained between men and women generally (titled and untitled alike), and which were sanctified and rendered theoretically inviolable by their grounding in a heavily (but by no means thoroughly) Islamicized cosmology.

Most other elements of marriage ritual served to foreground practical representations of marriage and affinal exchange, which were clearly contradictory to their official counterparts insofar as they emphasized not only that men—as opposed to women—were being exchanged, but also that they were being exchanged by groups of women, not by other men. Thus, the second day of wedding festivities witnessed the groom's relatives traveling to the bride's home bearing gifts of food, along with a lavish feast sponsored by the bride's mother. Subsequent to the feast, the groom formally entered the bride's mother's home, bringing gifts of food along with a bundle of clothes and other personal possessions, which symbolized the severance of residential ties with his mother, sisters, and other close kin. Once inside, he was welcomed by his in-laws and formally accepted into their household. Other ritualized introductions typically stretched over the course of the following week or two. One such series of introductions involved visits by the bridal couple to various households inhabited by the groom's kin. Not surprisingly, these were glossed *mengulang jejak*, which refers to the groom's "going over," or "retracing," his footsteps for the very last time.

Many of these same practical representations of marriage and affinal exchange were highlighted in funerary rituals. In the event of the husband's death, for example, the widow financed the burial as well as the principal funerary rituals and feasts (Parr and Mackray 1910:88, 91; Taylor [1929] 1970:123), all of which occurred in her village. Particularly noteworthy is the ritualized exchange which ideally took place during the final feast in the funerary cycle, and which consisted of a pair of pants, a coat, a sleeping mat, and a pillow (Parr and Mackray 1910:88; DeMoubray 1931:149–50); in short, the very same items the husband brought with him when he began living among his wife's relatives and simultaneously severed residential ties with his own kin. It is especially significant that these items passed from the widow to her mother-in-law. The design of the transfer symbolized both the end of the daughter-in-law's relationship with her former husband, and a return to the mother-in-law of the son that she had in effect "given away" in marriage. Moreover, just as this ritual depicted the principal exchanges in the formation of conjugal and affinal bonds as centering on transfers of rights over males, so, too, did it portray such exchanges as entailing transfers between women, who were thus represented as trafficking in men, or in rights over them.

The rituals following the dissolution of the conjugal bond owing to the wife's death conveyed generally similar messages. Suffice it to say that they highlighted the peripheral and "guest" status of the widower among his affines, underscoring that he could only remain among them if his children indicated a desire to have him stay.

Practical representations of marriage and affinal exchange were largely congruent with everyday practice in the nineteenth century. These circumstances help account for the references in the early colonial-era literature to men "becoming members of" their wives' clans upon marriage. They also help clarify the meaning of the customary sayings or aphorisms that I discussed earlier.

THE EXCHANGE OF MEN

The data outlined here suggest that the nineteenth-century nexus of affinity hinged on the exchange among localized descent units of rights over grooms (rather than brides), and that males (rather than females) served as the connective elements in the system of affinal exchange and alliance. To appreciate the point one need only step back from the details of marriage ceremonies and funerary rituals and examine the principal categories of rights transferred at marriage. First, however, we might consider some more general theoretical issues.

The "exchange of women" is a shorthand gloss that has been widely utilized in anthropology ever since the publication in 1949 of Claude Lévi-Strauss's *The Elementary Structures of Kinship*. The concept of the exchange of women is central to Lévi-Strauss's theories of kinship and marriage, human sociality, and the origins of culture itself. Lévi-Strauss has theorized that the exchange (or giving) of women occurs in *all* systems of affinal alliance; that it was necessarily entailed in the initial institutionalization of incest taboos that gave rise to (human) kinship and marriage; and that it simultaneously constituted the earliest act of social exchange. Many other anthropologists (e.g., Leach [1954] 1965, [1961] 1966; Needham 1962, 1971; Fox 1967; Dumont 1970; Rubel and Rosman 1978) have made use of the concept even though they reject certain of the evolutionary, historical, and other assumptions underlying Lévi-Strauss's theoretical edifice. In this regard Gayle Rubin's observations are especially instructive.

> The "exchange of women" is a seductive and powerful concept, . . . an acute, but condensed, apprehension of certain aspects of the social relations of sex and gender. . . . "Exchange of women" is a short-hand for expressing that the social relations of a kinship system specify that men have certain rights in their female kin, and that women do not have the same rights either to themselves or to their male kin. . . . [But it] is . . . debatable that "exchange of women" adequately describes all of the empirical evidence of kinship systems. Some cultures, such as the Lele and the Kuma, exchange women explicitly and overtly. In other cultures, the exchange of women can be inferred. In some—particularly those hunters and gatherers excluded from Lévi-Strauss's sample—the efficacy of the concept becomes altogether questionable. (Rubin 1975:175–77)

Rubin's last point is especially relevant to nineteenth-century Negeri Sembilan. This is because the concept of the exchange of women, which appears in earlier accounts of Negeri Sembilan (e.g., de Josselin de Jong 1951, [1956] 1977), obscures the major transactions inherent in the formation of conjugal and affinal bonds. These transactions centered on rights over males rather than females, which is why I argue that the system is more aptly characterized in terms of the exchange of men.[14]

In the latter connection we might bear in mind Leach's ([1961] 1966:107–8) observation that "the institutions commonly classed as marriage are concerned with the allocation of a number of distinguishable classes of rights," and that marriage usually involves the allocation of rights over brides *and* grooms. Leach is reminding us that systems of affinal alliance focusing on exchanges of women are typically characterized by certain types of transactions over males as well. Perhaps more to the point, when we speak of systems characterized by the exchange of women we are actually referring to systems in which the majority, or the most important, but by no means all, of the rights transacted at marriage entail (legitimate) claims over women.

More recently, Goody (1990) has explored the implications of these and related themes, arguing, among other things, that the concept of the exchange of women is at best a misleading gloss and more often than not a serious impediment to our understanding of the practice of kinship and marriage since it frequently carries the implication of women's "complete incorporation" into the domestic and kinship groups of their husbands, and their "thorough dissimilation" from their natal kin.[15] Goody illustrates that even in the "extremely patrilineal" societies of China, India, and the Islamic world, married women (both as heiresses and in other capacities) have long retained important moral and material rights and obligations with respect to their natal kin (particularly their brothers). More generally, women are "carriers of property as well as of sentiments, ties and relationships" (Goody 1990:480), which may compromise unilineal hegemonies and social arrangements in the direction of bilaterality, but which are nonetheless central to "strategies of heirship" and other "mechanisms of continuity" (domestic reproduction). The idea of the total assimilation of women into their husbands' domestic and kinship groups (like the notion of their complete severance from their natal kin) is thus revealed to be a fiction of Western categories informed by market metaphors of purchase, sale, and exchange, and by other features of economistic thinking. (Goody does emphasize, however, that this idea "may suit the notion of the one-way gift" enshrined in Brahminic writing and other texts of the Great Religions, as well as "the idea of the male receiver," and may serve, in any event, to " 'mystif[y]' rather than represent the actual transactions" [1990:168].) Goody concludes that while gender inequality is quite pervasive in the Asian societies on which he focuses his investigation, "women [in these societies] are never simply the pawns of others but themselves players in the game, especially as heiresses" (1990:68); and that the literal and metaphorical "domestic slavery" that Westerners have long associated with the Orient is a chimera (1990:317, 425).

The implications of these arguments for Negeri Sembilan are quite straightforward, though neither Leach nor Goody would be able to make provision in their theoretical frameworks for a society such as Negeri Sembilan and would thus undoubtedly take issue with the way I draw upon their insights to elucidate Negeri Sembilan data. It follows from Leach's arguments that a society characterized by the exchange of men would be one in which the majority or the most important, but not necessarily all, of the rights transacted at marriage involve (legitimate) claims over men. And it follows from Goody's arguments that the analytic positing of the exchange of men should not be taken to mean that men are completely incorporated into their wives' kin groups or thoroughly dissimilated from their own, or that they are passive objects with no agency.

In the pages that follow I first provide a summary overview of the rights over women that were transferred at marriage. I then proceed to an overview of the rights over men that were transferred at marriage. Finally, I attempt to demonstrate that, in practice, though not necessarily in local (official) ideology, men were being exchanged by women and not by other men.

Rights over Women

The rights over a woman that a man and/or his kin acquired in consequence of the man's marriage may be spoken of in terms of three analytically distinct categories: (a) sexual services, (b) labor services, and (c) property.

(a) Sexual Services A man enjoyed an absolute monopoly on his wife's sexual services. There were no forms of polyandry, and all variants of extramarital and premarital sex were explicitly prohibited and severely sanctioned. (It merits emphasis that a husband's exclusive sexual access to his wife did not entail appreciable rights over offspring of the union or any children adopted by his wife.)

(b) Labor Services A man obtained rights in his wife's labor services, particularly her domestic labor services. (Note though that a man did not enjoy the right to appropriate the proceeds of his wife's agricultural labor.) A man's close female kin (his mother and other women of his lineage branch) were vested with limited rights in the fruits of his wife's nonagricultural labor; for instance, they were entitled to periodic prestations of *dodol* cakes that she prepared.

(c) Property A man acquired use rights in the property (*harta dapatan*; e.g., land) that his wife brought to the union or inherited while married. (Note, however, that neither a man nor his kin could unilaterally alienate, or obtain permanent rights over, any form of *harta dapatan* [Newbold 1839 II:220; Lister 1887:44, 1890:316; Hale 1898:55; Parr and Mackray 1910:87, 92].) A man also obtained rights over roughly one-half of all movables (cash, livestock, etc.) classed as conjugal acquisitions. (Equally

important though, neither a man nor his kin had any permanent rights over conjugal acquisitions in the forms of houses, homestead plots, or agricultural acreage.)

These constituted the major types of rights over a woman that a man and/or his kin obtained as a result of his marriage. Both the alienation and acquisition of such rights were of considerable importance. So, too, of course, were the marriage payments due the wife's kin (such as the "marriage gold"), which helped secure such rights.[16] The larger issue, however, is that exchanges of the sort noted above were of far less social and cultural significance than transactions over the labor, productivity, and reproductive powers of males.

Rights over Men

The rights over a man that a woman and/or her kin acquired in consequence of her marriage were more varied and extensive than the corresponding rights obtained by a man and/or his kin, and are best discussed in terms of five analytically distinct categories: (a) sexual services, (b) offspring, (c) labor services, (d) property, and (e) political control.

(a) Sexual Services A woman enjoyed a "near monopoly" on her husband's sexual services. Although polygyny was permitted in Islam, it was strongly discouraged by *adat* and extremely rare (Hale 1898:45; Parr and Mackray 1910:78–79). As noted above, all variants of extramarital sex were explicitly prohibited and severely sanctioned.

(b) Offspring A woman and her kin were vested with monopolistic control over all offspring produced by her marriage.

(c) Labor Services A woman and her kin acquired extensive rights in her husband's labor services. As indicated, a husband was expected to build a house for his wife (and children), and to add to the residential and agricultural holdings claimed by his wife and her kin. A husband was also expected to add money to the household coffers, to help his wife at certain stages of the agricultural cycle (such as the harvest), and to contribute labor to various feasts and public works projects sponsored by her kin or other members of her village.

(d) Property A woman was accorded use rights in the property (*harta pembawa*; weapons, livestock, cash) that her husband brought to the union or inherited while married. Wife's kin could obtain permanent rights over non-"ancestral" *harta pembawa* if the husband agreed to "pa-

ternal provisioning" by formally designating his children as the rightful heirs to such property. Wife and her kin enjoyed permanent rights over all conjugal acquisitions in the form of houses, homestead plots, and agricultural acreage; they also obtained permanent rights over roughly one-half of all conjugal acquisitions classed as movables (livestock, cash, etc.), and could even end up with rights to all such property.

(e) Political Control Wife's kin enjoyed extensive political control over the husband in that they exercised formal and informal authority over him, commanded his loyalties and labor services, and so on.

One need only compare the rights gained by a woman and/or her kin with the previously noted rights that a man and/or his kin acquired to appreciate that the majority of the rights transferred at marriage entailed claims over males. While wives and husbands obtained roughly equivalent rights in one another's sexual services, wives (and their kin) were accorded extensive rights over their offspring as well as their husbands' labor services, property, and political loyalties, which clearly outweighed the corresponding rights that husbands (and their kin) acquired over their wives. This comparison, along with other data presented above, suggests that "the exchange of men" rather than "the exchange of women" is the appropriate gloss for the nineteenth-century system of marriage and affinity.

Women Exchanging Men

It remains to underscore that, in practice, women were exchanging men (men were *not* exchanging other men by means of women), but were not necessarily doing so in an explicit or overt fashion. This feature of the system was largely implicit and culturally distorted even though various aspects of marriage and funerary rituals provided clear symbolic statements that men were being exchanged by women.

My argument that women were exchanging men is based partly on my assumption that senior women played the principal role in selecting spouses for junior kin deemed eligible for marriage. This assumption is consistent with twentieth-century observations and with the limited (admittedly somewhat ambiguous) references found in the nineteenth century (Newbold 1839 I:254; Hale 1898:57). In Bogang, for example, mothers and other female elders (aunts, grandmothers) play the major role both in gathering and "processing" information pertaining to the eligibility and desirability of potential spouses for their junior kin, and in initiating preliminary discussions and negotiations with their potential in-laws. (This is also true for the neighboring district of Kuala Pilah, as noted by the Malay anthropologist Abdul Kahar bin Bador [1962].) Women's initiatives in these and other areas help ensure that their wishes prevail over those of husbands, brothers, and other males, and testify to the influential roles they have long assumed in selecting spouses for their children and other junior kin.

We should bear in mind, too, that a man's female kin were vested with the majority of the rights that were subsequently relinquished (or compromised) as a consequence of his marriage; and that his female affines derived the greatest benefit from these rights. It may be recalled that female kin derived the most immediate and long-term benefit from an unmarried man's labor services and his contributions to agricultural production, and that an unmarried man's mother and sisters were the most direct beneficiaries of his labor power insofar as they held provisional rights to the agricultural holdings he was enjoined to help maintain and expand. In economic terms, a man's mother and sisters had the most to lose from his marriage and from his obligations as husband and in-marrying male. Of special relevance here, a man's mother and sisters bore the primary (if not sole) responsibility to help him raise the "marriage gold" and other marriage payments due his wife's kin. I might add that their difficulties in meeting this responsibility could lead to—and constituted one of the few legitimate grounds for—the mortgage or sale of the "ancestral" properties to which they held provisional rights (Parr and Mackray 1910:70–75).

We might also consider the origins of the *harta pembawa* property that a man brought to his marriage, and the ways in which a man's female kin could be affected by the subsequent devolution of rights over such property. The *harta pembawa* property typically originated in the conjugal or domestic fund of his mother and/or sisters, and thus provides additional evidence that the resources of a man's mother and sisters could be diminished in consequence of his marriage. So, too, does the fact that through the procedure known as "paternal provisioning" (*tentukan*) a man could formally designate one or more of his children as the rightful heirs to all *harta pembawa* property that was not classified as "ancestral." In circumstances of this latter sort, a deceased man's mother and sisters would be unable to reassert their claims to the (non-"ancestral") *harta pembawa* property they had given him at his wedding, and thus would experience further property loss as a result of his marriage.

One could argue that a man's mother and sisters experienced similar, but far more extensive, property losses owing to conventions specifying that rights over conjugal acquisitions in the form of houses, residential plots, and agricultural acreage were not divided between spouses (or their [matrilineal] survivors) upon the termination of a marriage, but remained instead under the control of the wife or her surviving kin. This argument seems plausible when one considers that, in the absence of such conventions, the rights at issue would have probably devolved upon the man's mother or sisters, in accordance with the gender-based demarcation in property and inheritance, which defined houses, land, and certain other types of property in relation to females. It should also be remembered that a man could formally designate his children as the rightful heirs to those conjugally acquired movables that his mother and sisters could otherwise claim upon his death. These latter conventions provide further evidence that the property losses experienced by a man's kin as a result of his marriage were felt most heavily by his mother and sisters.

What then of the other side of the marriage/affinity equation; namely, the extent to which a man's female affines were accorded, or derived the greatest or most direct benefit from, the rights that were obtained in consequence of his marriage to one of their female kin?

I argue that a man's female affines were informally vested with, and in any event enjoyed, the greatest and most direct benefit from the rights his affinal kin acquired over his sexual services and the offspring produced by his marriage. This argument is based partly on my observation that in twentieth-century Negeri Sembilan, adult women exercise greater control than their male kin over young children and never-married adolescents. For example, informal adoptions or child transfers are extremely common and typically involve a reallocation of rights and responsibilities between women (natural and adoptive mothers) associated with the same lineage branch or lineage. These transactions between women are also initiated by women, who thus assume the major role in transferring and acquiring these rights and responsibilities.

A man's wife (and female affines) also enjoyed extensive rights in, and otherwise derived the greatest benefit from, his children's labor power and productivity. Children of both sexes were expected to help maintain and expand the agricultural and residential acreage held by their mother and mother's sisters, which would ultimately pass to female heirs. Children were also morally bound to provide sustenance and care for their mother in the event that she became incapacitated due to illness or old age. These were perhaps the most sanctified of all social obligations and they clearly outweighed children's responsibilities to their father, mother's brothers, and other male relatives.[17]

The extent to which rights over a married man's labor power and productivity were vested in or exercised by his female (rather than male) affines needs little comment except to recall that upon the dissolution of a man's marriage, rights over all land he helped his wife prepare for agricultural or residential purposes were claimed by either his wife or her matrilineal survivors, and that these rights were earmarked for females. This same generalization applies to rights over the house he may have built for his wife (and offspring), to rights over the "asking ring(s)" (or *cincin tanya*), and to portions of the "marriage gold" as well as the movable property that he conveyed to his children.

My contention that a man's female kin were originally vested with the majority of (and the most important) rights that were subsequently relinquished (or compromised) as a result of his marriage receives little support when one considers the domain of formal political control and the fact that men monopolized most (provisional) rights to political office. However, as should be readily apparent, the formal structure of political authority had relatively little direct bearing on the realities of local practice.

To elaborate, the political obligations imposed on a man by his wife's relatives undoubtedly entailed significant political and prestige losses for his own kin, at least some of which were felt most directly by the titled men (lineage head, clan subchief, clan chief, etc.) who exercised formal political control over him and derived prestige therefrom. In particular, these officials probably found themselves less able to command the labor services and political/military support of untitled male relatives once the untitled men had married and severed residential ties with their matrilineal kin. Equally important though is the previously noted fact that female elders exercised considerable autonomy and social control over the affairs of their natal households and compounds, and probably comprised the de facto loci of authority within lineage branches, especially since genealogical groupings below the level of lineage were not political units in the sense of having representative spokesmen with formal titles or offices. Female elders were thus vested with, and in a position to exercise, extremely important political and other rights over the men residing in their households and lineage branch compounds, many of which rights had to be relinquished in consequence of the men's marriages.

None of this is to suggest, however, that we are dealing with some sort of "matriarchal" society. Recall here that men monopolized rights to most political offices and that political leaders such as the *Undang* (and quite possibly clan leaders or *lembaga* as well) stood in many respects "above" the system of marriage and affinal relations insofar as they were largely immune to the imperatives and constraints the system imposed on husbands and in-marrying males generally. Recall, too, that men clearly monopolized both the means of violence and external exchange, and, as a group, enjoyed more prestige (and freedom of movement) than women.

The fact that men were accorded *more* prestige than women but enjoyed *less* autonomy and social control with respect to marriage and affinal relations—and were in fact exchanged by women—is significant for three reasons. First, it indicates the analytic importance of distinguishing—as the local system clearly (if only implicitly) did—between prestige on the one hand, and autonomy and social control in marriage and affinal relations on the other. Second, it indicates that prestige may be—and in this case clearly was—ascribed on the basis of variables other than autonomy and social control of the sort at issue here. And third, it demonstrates, contra Lévi-Strauss and those who have adopted the general lines of his argument, that men's greater prestige and formal authority was not predicated on, and did not entail as part of its institutional realization, a system focusing on the exchange of women.

Before addressing some of the implications of these last two points, I should emphasize that nineteenth-century Negeri Sembilan is by no means the only society having institutions of marriage and affinal alliance based on the exchange of men. Similar institutions exist among (Sumatran) Minangkabau and Acehnese, among Malays in the state of Pahang, among the commoner stratum of the Punan Bah of Sarawak (East Malaysia), and beyond Southeast Asia as well. Concerning the Minangkabau, for example, Umar Junus (1964), who is himself Minangkabau, implies (but does not develop the argument) that the social systems of certain (but not all) Minangkabau communities can be described in terms that are generally comparable to those I have employed for nineteenth-century Negeri Sembilan. Significantly, he also uses the terms "groom exchange" and "bridegroom exchange" when describing various features of Minangkabau systems of marriage and affinity (Umar Junus 1964:300, 311, 312). Similar conventions appear in Thomas's (1985) work on the Minangkabau and are compatible with material presented in Lando and Thomas (1983); Tanner (1982); and Errington (1984:65–70). Schwimmer (1982:8, 11), moreover, states quite clearly that "the Minangkabau have a system of circulating connubium between *kaum* [localized descent groups] . . . [involving] the exchange among *females* of *male* marriage partners" (emphasis added). Finally, Pak (n.d.) devotes an entire essay to demonstrating the relevance of the concept of the exchange of men to contemporary Minangkabau society, though I should perhaps note that her analysis focuses not on "rights" over men—which she claims are "not clearly present in the social philosophy of the [Minangkabau] region," but on "obligations" and the idea that "men are valued in Minangkabau and exchanged because they are transmitters of 'good blood' " (Pak n.d.:4, 5; see also Pak 1986; Ng 1987; Krier 1994).[18]

Much the same situation has been reported for some of Southeast Asia's putatively "bilateral" societies. Jayawardena (1977b:36), for example, concludes his discussion of women and kinship in Aceh with the remark that "anthropologists [need] to take a second look at such interpretations of marriage rules as constituting the exchange of women by groups of men. . . . The question may well be asked: who is giving what to whom? In Aceh there are no descent groups to exchange women. *Marriage customs can be interpreted as exchanges between two groups of women*, not necessarily defined in terms of descent" (emphasis added). Jayawardena does not go on to state explicitly that women are exchanging men (as opposed to other women), but such seems to have been the case for some time now, judging from the accounts of Snouck Hurgronje (1906), Siegel (1969), and others. A similar case has been made for the Malays of Pahang, as indicated by Massard's (1983:112) comments that various aspects of wedding rituals "symbolically prefigure the passage of a man from one domestic group to another," and, more generally, that women "control . . . the circulation of men." Generalizations of the latter sort are also applicable to the commoner stratum of the Punan Bah in Sarawak (Ida Nicoleisen, personal communication, 1986).

There are occasional references to the exchange of men outside of Southeast Asia as well. In her reassessment of the status and future of matriliny in Africa, for example, Mary Douglas (1971:128) includes a passing reference to the existence of (African) societies "where intermarriage takes the form of the exchange of males."[19] There is, moreover, the case of the Eastern Cherokee discussed some time ago by William Gilbert ([1937] 1955), who mentioned that Eastern Cherokee institutions of marriage and affinity focused on the exchange of men (albeit apparently by men, not women), and who was perhaps the first anthropologist to draw attention to the existence of any such institutions.

The data and interpretations presented in the works cited here indicate that the case of nineteenth-century Negeri Sembilan is less anomalous than might be assumed. They also point up the importance of reassessing various aspects of conventional anthropological wisdom concerning the roles of men and women in marriage and affinal exchange, the autonomy and social control enjoyed by women, and the extent to which women's secondary status vis-à-vis men is invariably grounded in systems of kinship and marriage.

Lévi-Strauss and Leach are among those who are unprepared to accept the possibility that certain systems of affinal exchange focus on transfers of rights over men. It warrants remark, however, that both Lévi-Strauss and Leach make *partial* provision for such scenarios, or at least for their *appearance*. For instance, in a footnote to his often repeated statement that "it is men who exchange women, and not vice versa," Lévi-Strauss ([1949] 1969:115) registers the following caveat:

> Certain tribes of South-east Asia . . . *almost* provide a picture of the inverse situation. . . . This would *not* be to say that in such societies it is the women who exchange the men, but rather that men exchange other men by means of women. (emphasis added)

Similarly, in a subsequent essay, Lévi-Strauss (1956:284) appends the following comments to a discussion of the exchange of women:

> The female reader, who may be shocked to see womankind treated as a commodity submitted to transactions between male operators, can easily find comfort in the assurance that the rules of the game would remain unchanged should it be decided to consider the men as being exchanged by women's groups. As a matter of fact, *some* very few *societies*, of a highly developed matrilineal type, *have to a limited extent attempted to express things that way.* (emphasis added)

This latter view might be interpreted as representing a departure from Lévi-Strauss's earlier position, although I do not regard it as such. Even if one concludes that the 1956 statement reflects a (limited) change in Lévi-Strauss's perspective, the fact remains that the statement is qualified in such a way as to all but rule out the existence of societies in which men "are (or were) being exchanged by women's groups." Note, for example, that Lévi-Strauss's sole concession is that "some . . . societies . . . have to a limited extent attempted to express things that way." This concession is rendered more or less meaningless by the fact that Lévi-Strauss does not assume any necessary correspondence between societal "expressions" and patterns of behavior or social relations (see, e.g., Lévi-Strauss 1953, 1960).

A slightly different version of the 1956 passage quoted above appears in Lévi-Strauss's *The View from Afar* (1985:60). There and elsewhere

(Lévi-Strauss 1960:51) we are reminded that Lévi-Strauss is concerned with the "formal properties of the structure," in which "nothing would be changed" if men were being exchanged instead of women. While this point may be valid so far as Lévi-Strauss is concerned, it also draws attention to one of the major shortcomings of his approach: his preoccupation with *forms* of exchange and his relative neglect of the *contents* and *strategies* of exchange (see Leach [1961] 1966:90; Bourdieu 1977:1–30; Comaroff 1980; Collier and Rosaldo 1981:315–16; Strathern 1984; Goody 1990).

Even among anthropologists who, contra Lévi-Strauss, focus on the contents and strategies of exchange, there is a refusal to acknowledge that certain systems of marriage and affinal alliance focus on the exchange of men. Leach ([1961] 1966:101), for example, allows only that "there are cases [he refers to the Minangkabau of Sumatra] where the wife's group . . . 'buy' the sexual services of the husband from the husband's group." The problem with statements of this sort is that they reflect an extremely limited appreciation of the full range of rights that may be acquired by a woman and her kin in consequence of the woman's marriage. In nineteenth-century Negeri Sembilan, such rights ranged well beyond claims to the husband's sexual services (and monopolistic control over the offspring of the union); as we have seen, they included critically important claims to the husband's labor power and productivity; permanent control over jointly acquired earnings in the form of houses, homestead plots, and agricultural acreage; and extensive social and political control over the husband. Similar generalizations apply to the Minangkabau and Acehnese systems, and to all others involving the exchange of men.

Such cases indicate that there are more than a few societies in which women exercise far more autonomy and social control than the earlier literature on kinship, marriage, and social structure would have us believe. This is a common theme in relatively recent work on "matrilineal" societies (see, e.g., Schlegel 1972; Brown 1975; Weiner 1976, 1992; Smith 1983; Tanner and Thomas 1985; Whalley 1993; Krier 1994), but it is also relevant beyond matrilineal settings. Numerous anthropologists working in "bilateral" (cognatic) and other contexts in Southeast Asia, Africa, and elsewhere have commented upon the relatively high degree of autonomy and social control enjoyed by women in various "traditional" and "modernizing" societies (see Burling 1965; Tanner 1974; Draper 1975; Rogers 1975; Bacdayan 1977; Sacks 1979; Sanday 1981; Van Esterik 1982; Reid 1988; Ong 1989; Atkinson and Errington 1990). They have also demonstrated that an understanding of these (and other) societies requires that we devote sustained analytic scrutiny to the gendered division of labor and exchange, and its relationship to kinship, marriage, and other domains of social life (cf. Siskind 1978; Collier and Rosaldo 1981; Collier 1988). In this same spirit, I suggest that we not only look more closely at the diverse forms, contents, and cultural realization of the gendered division of labor and exchange, but that we also reexamine earlier assumptions about the universality of the exchange of women and the purported nonexistence of institutions predicated on the exchange of men.

In light of the foregoing I should perhaps make explicit that cases of the sort with which I have been concerned also pose a serious challenge to those who follow the general lines of Lévi-Strauss's argument concerning kinship and marriage as the ultimate locus of women's secondary "status" vis-à-vis men (see, e.g., Rubin 1975; Collier and Rosaldo 1981; Collier 1988; see also Chodorow 1978). In nineteenth-century Negeri Sembilan, as we have seen, women were accorded *less* prestige than men, yet they were *not* exchanged by men. Prestige differentials between men and women thus cannot be explained in terms of the system of kinship and marriage. One could conceivably argue that men's greater prestige standing reflected their predominance in arenas of (regional) exchange that encompassed the system of marriage and affinal exchange overseen by women, but this leaves unanswered why this should be so, that is, why men's predominance in such arenas garnered them more prestige. Men's control of the production of the means of violence and their effective monopolization of weapons and tools might also be invoked as an explanation of their superior prestige standing relative to women (see Whitehead 1986, 1987). But this too leaves unanswered why it is that men were accorded more prestige owing to their preeminence in such realms. More generally, as Kelly (1993) makes clear in his incisive analysis of the cosmological grounding of social inequality among the Etoro, all such arguments imply that gender hierarchies are unique in relation to other hierarchies of prestige (based on descent, age, birth order, etc.) insofar as they alone are assumed to rely for their moral force and reproduction on brute strength or force of arms.[20]

Prestige differentials between men and women in nineteenth-century Negeri Sembilan are best seen in relation to—and, in important ways, determined by—the most encompassing system of prestige, which was the system of hereditary ranking or descent. This system, as we have seen, was encoded in the political system, operated through the kinship system, and effectively defined as the ultimate value the accumulation and display of spiritual potency. As has long been the case in much of Southeast Asia, men were assumed to have more spiritual potency than women and were for this reason accorded more prestige (see Reid 1988; Atkinson and Errington 1990; Andaya and Ishii 1992).

The basis for this cultural assumption lay in largely implicit understandings of the fundamental similarities and differences between men's and women's temperaments, personalities, and behavioral inclinations, which, in turn, were grounded in basic understandings concerning the person, the body, and the relationships among the constituent elements of such entities and the universe as a whole. These assumptions and understandings derived much of their force from and were otherwise informed by beliefs concerning "reason" (*akal*) and "passion" (*nafsu*) and their differential distribution among men and women; to wit, that men have more "reason" and less "passion" than women. These (Arabic-origin) concepts (discussed in greater detail later; see, esp., chap. 5) are of central importance in contemporary understandings and representations of gender in Negeri Sembilan, among Malays elsewhere in the Peninsula, and in the Muslim world at large. We cannot presume that the present-day scope and force of these concepts accurately reflect their cultural salience in the nineteenth century, but there is ample evidence to indicate that they did inform experiences, understandings, and representations in various domains of Malay society and culture both in the 1800s and in earlier times.

Malay texts from the early part of the nineteenth century, for instance, cite as negative examples despised political leaders becoming *sombong* (arrogant, haughty), acting unjustly, and otherwise behaving in accordance with their "passion"; and they warn their own not to follow such examples (Milner 1982:43). So, too, do texts dating from the seventeenth century, such as *The Malay Annals* (*Sejarah Melayu*) (Milner 1982:43, 50, 106). Similarly, Islamic modernists of the late nineteenth century objected to spirit possession and exorcistic rituals not simply because they entailed "the worship of false gods," but also because of the "unbridled license—'loss of reason'—which a seance gave to the baser elements of human nature" (Gullick 1987:322, 327 n.31; cf. Swettenham [1895] 1984:208–10). Noteworthy as well is that women have long been more susceptible than men to the culture-bound syndrome known as *latah*, which involves echolalia, echopraxia, and other forms of "pathomimetic" behavior that index a loss of control over speech, gesture, and the person or self generally (Kenny 1990:127–28). For these and other reasons, women have long been viewed as having weaker *semangat* or "life force" than men, and as

otherwise more vulnerable to the afflictions of spirits and human malevolence that (masculine) "reason" and spiritual potency ideally guard
against.

These ideas (along with contrasting discourses on gender that are keyed
to contrasting representations of marriage and affinal exchange) will be
described and analyzed in much greater detail further along. The main
point here is that prestige differentials between men and women were
broadly grounded in cosmology. So, too, of course, was the system of
kinship and marriage, but it was not this system, which focused, in any
event, on the exchange of men not women, which lay at the heart of
women's secondary status.

3   Kinship, Gender, and Sexuality from the Nineteenth Century to the Present

The systems of gender, prestige, and political economy outlined in the preceding chapter existed throughout much of the nineteenth century (and perhaps long before as well). There are, moreover, numerous elements of these systems and their interrelations that have been reproduced more or less intact since the late nineteenth century, though it is also true that many others have been radically transformed. In the first section of this chapter I provide an overview of some of the more salient patterns in nineteenth and twentieth-century social history, briefly examining the ways in which changes in political, economic, and religious organization affected the structure of prestige (including prestige differentials between men and women) and various aspects of kinship, marriage, and sexuality (especially sexual impropriety). Also included here is a discussion of *pondan* (gender-crossers), which emphasizes, on the one hand, that locally defined communities have long been highly accepting of individuals associated with this mediating (once sacred) category; and, on the other, that recent state policies and initiatives bolstered by the Islamic resurgence are geared toward restricting the behavior of such individuals and eliminating the (increasingly contaminating) category altogether. The second and third sections of the chapter are devoted to a description and analysis of a social drama, culminating in a "shotgun" marriage, which occurred in Bogang in 1979. This drama provides poignant testimony to themes of continuity and transformation outlined in the first section of the chapter, particularly since it helps illustrate some of the ways in which prestige and stigma are allocated in a contemporary setting. These themes are also taken up in subsequent chapters, all of which focus on the present.

STRUCTURAL TRANSFORMATION AND REPRODUCTION

Political and Religious Organization and the Structure of Prestige

The indigenous system of political organization experienced unprecedented challenges and stresses during the mid-nineteenth century, largely as a result of the development of Negeri Sembilan's tin-mining industry beginning in the 1830s. The 1830s witnessed the early stages of a massive influx of Chinese labor and capital into many of the tin-rich regions of Negeri Sembilan, which was followed by the infusion of European, especially British, capital into these regions as well. These developments greatly increased the stakes in competition over local and regional trade, and likewise rendered the skirmishes and battles over such resources all the more bloody and costly in terms of human life; indeed, the situation in certain parts of Negeri Sembilan in the mid-1860s was described by some observers as bordering on civil war and anarchy.[1] This situation, in turn, prompted alliances between highly placed Malay political leaders and Chinese, British, and other foreign investors for protection to help secure their investments; it also paved the way for greater British involvement in the region, especially since the British, with their superior firepower, were in an excellent position to help shore up embattled political leaders and ensure that their burgeoning and increasingly transnationally oriented enterprises remained profitable, or at least continued to operate.

For these and other reasons the British were increasingly drawn into local affairs and ultimately established various types of "protectorates" in parts of the Peninsula. Some protectorates were established in portions of Negeri Sembilan as early as the 1870s, though in other areas of the state the British did not get centrally involved until the 1890s.[2]

When the British colonized Negeri Sembilan (and other Malay states), they introduced a colonial bureaucracy and British-style civil and criminal courts whose structure and operations were geared toward the attainment of British political and economic objectives as well as the institutionalization of British notions of propriety and morality. These institutions eviscerated indigenous precolonial polities (and simultaneously transformed and undermined many features of Malay *adat*), though they did not actually abolish the indigenous political system. In fact, they operated through the system and thus strengthened many of its key features even though they effectively stripped most indigenous leaders of any real political or economic power. Ironically, these same policies ensured that Malay leaders would find themselves at considerable remove from the actual corridors of power, despite their retention of traditional titles, royal regalia, and other symbols of authority and prestige. Such policies also encouraged established leaders at the uppermost levels of the indigenous polity to assume increasingly pivotal roles in religious (specifically, Islamic) affairs. This is partly because the domain of Islam (like that of *adat*) was one of the few spheres in which Malays enjoyed a constitutionally guaranteed measure of autonomy vis-à-vis the British. Relevant as well is that modern education and greater contact between local elites and (mostly foreign-born) Muslims in Melaka, Singapore, and other parts of the Malay-Indonesian archipelago enhanced Malay awareness of and dialogue with developments in Egypt, Saudi Arabia, and other regions of the Muslim world. This had the effect, in the Malay world, of galvanizing diverse currents of Islamic nationalism and reform, and of promoting nationalist discourse on the virtues of Islamic rationalization and the necessity of eradicating the "backward" (e.g., pre-Islamic [animist/Hindu-Buddhist]) elements of Malay culture so as to help bring Malays and Malayan Islam into the "modern era." This goal was partly achieved by elite-backed efforts to upgrade the quality of religious instruction and to curtail the performance of largely pre-Islamic rituals. With the same goal in mind, the elite provided much of the impetus for the creation and consolidation of district- and state-level Islamic administrative hierarchies charged with overseeing the affairs of all Muslims. Developments such as these led to the institutionalized differentiation and segregation of *adat* and Islam, about which more in a moment.

The progressive expansion and empowering of state-controlled Islamic administrative hierarchies that began under colonial rule continued after Malaya attained its independence from the British in 1957, and has clearly led to the more centralized and standardized (rationalized) implementation of Islamic religious law. Among other changes, Islamic magistrates (*kadi*) have been accorded authority over many domains of activity that once fell within the jurisdiction of clan leaders and their councils: for example, the formal registration of marriage and divorce, issues of conjugal maintenance and child support, and the payment of religious taxes and tithes. Islamic officials have also acquired far more authority with respect to the distribution of rights over intestate property and the settlement of various types of inheritance and other property disputes, all of which further undermined the prerogatives and social standing of clan spokesmen.

These same developments were partly responsible for the progressive delegitimization and subsequent decline (though not disappearance) of various types of spirit cults and shamanism. I already made brief reference (chap. 2) to late nineteenth-century Islamic modernists who sought to discourage royal and chiefly rituals involving spirit possession and exorcism on the grounds that they entailed "loss of reason" on the part of the practitioners. (Some of these rituals were discouraged for other reasons as well; e.g., for being economically unsound or wasteful, and for being incompatible with modern education and medicine, and "science" and "progress" generally.) Islamic denigration of "unbridled license" was part of an ongoing process which had begun some centuries earlier (and which continues today). As Anthony Reid (1988:81, 86–88, 89, 148–51, 156–57) has noted for Southeast Asia generally during the period 1450–1680, Islam discouraged nakedness, placed greater emphasis on sexual restraint, and suppressed the use of penis pins and balls that were surgically inserted under the skin of the penis to enhance women's sexual pleasure (which were once common throughout much of Southeast Asia and which are still found among non-Muslim regions of the Malay world [see Reid 1988:89, 148–51, 162]). So, too, of course, did the other Great Religions introduced into Southeast Asia.

Even so, the system of prestige outlined in the previous chapter has remained very much intact. This despite the fact that it has clearly lost some of its moral force and other constraining qualities due, on the one hand, to the revalorization of nineteenth-century criteria for prestige, and, on the other, to the emergence and spread of new and cross-cutting criteria that accord prestige to wealth, modern education, and the like, rather than descent. Spiritual potency, for example, is still highly valued; and significantly, there is little if any skepticism among villagers concerning either royal sanctity or majesty (*daulat, berdaulat*) or the efficacy of the mystical knowledge/power that is concentrated among ritual specialists but which is also widely dispersed throughout local society, especially among men (see chap. 4). At present, such knowledge/power is typically referred to by the Arabic-origin term *ilmu*, rather than by the Sanskrit-origin term *sakti*, which seems to have been the most commonly used term in the nineteenth century (and before). This conceptual shift (from *sakti* to *ilmu*) parallels an earlier shift from *sakti* to *daulat* (an Arabic-origin term) which occurred during the period 1500–1800 (Andaya and Ishii 1992:546), and which presumably reflects efforts both to put a more Islamic face on the "divine kingship" of political leaders, and to better distinguish their powers from those of lesser leaders and the untitled majority.

It is nonetheless true that villagers are increasingly ambivalent and nervous about the pre-Islamic features of such knowledge/power. This situation is due for the most part to diverse currents of Islamic national-ism and reform, including in particular the largely urban-based, middle-class *dakwa* movement that dates from the late 1960s and early 1970s. As mentioned earlier, twentieth-century currents of Islamic nationalism and reform have contributed to the delegitimization and subsequent decline (though not the disappearance) of shamanism and spirit cults, and have, at the same time, raised serious doubts among villagers concerning the Islamic validity of *ilmu* and other local traditions. Such matters are dis-cussed at length in chapter 4.

Prestige differentials between males and females, for their part, are still conceptualized and rationalized in terms of spiritual potency: Men are still believed (by men and women alike) to have stronger "life force," or *semangat*, and to be more likely to possess *ilmu*. These phenomena (*semangat* and *ilmu*) are not systematically related in local discourse, however; though, all things being equal, persons with unusual amounts or concentrations of *ilmu* are seen as having unusually strong *semangat* (the latter being a prerequisite [necessary but not sufficient] for the for-mer). It is important to emphasize, in any event, that the gendered con-trasts at issue are most often discussed in terms of the symbols and idioms of "reason" and "passion": Men, according to the official line, have more "reason" and less "passion" than women, all of which is consistent—but never in my experience directly linked in local discourse—with the dogma concerning men's stronger "life force" and greater likelihood of pos-sessing *ilmu*. Such prestige differentials may well have become exagger-ated over the course of the past century, but even if they have (as I sus-pect), this is less a new pattern than a continuation and intensification of trends set in motion many centuries earlier.

The exaggeration of distinctions between men and women seems closely tied to the development of Islam in the region, though the consoli-dation and centralization of state power, which went hand in hand with the development of Islam, is clearly relevant as well. Interestingly, Portu-guese accounts of the sixteenth century reported that Malays were "fond of music and given to love," that "pre-marital sexual relations were re-garded indulgently," and that "virginity at marriage was not expected of either party" (Reid 1988:153). Recall, too, that during this time there were female heads of state in various parts of the Malay-Indonesian world. After about 1700, however, "the Islamic model of male kingship seemed finally to prevail," and few women ruled, partly because, as one (male) observer put it, they were held to be lacking "complete intelligence" (Reid 1988:170; see also Andaya and Ishii 1992:556–57). By the nineteenth century, moreover, by which time Islam had become much more thoroughly integrated into people's lives, virginity at marriage was clearly expected of both parties, especially women; and women were severely chastised for even the appearance of pre- (or extra-)marital dalliance. Bear in mind also that women had been extremely active in communal rituals throughout much of Southeast Asia prior to the period 1500–1800, and that this had changed by the latter part of this period due to the development in Southeast Asia of Islam and other Great Religions, which provide no textual basis for women's active participation in the highest rituals of the land. Women's public roles became progressively less apparent during this period (communal worship came to be dominated by males), and, as we saw in chapter 2, they were "increasingly relegated to the domains of shamanism and spirit propitiation. In the process, the status of the shaman, both female and transvestite, declined . . . , and women became the principal practitioners of 'village' as opposed to 'court' magic" (Andaya and Ishii 1992:555–56). In these and other ways, the development of Islam, bolstered by state strategies discussed below, had the effect of restructuring important aspects of male-female relations and of reconfiguring representations of gender, and of women in particular.

While prestige differentials cast in terms of "reason" and "passion" are a dominant feature of local understandings and representations of gender, men do not always come out "on top" in the local (conceptual) scheme(s) of things. To appreciate why, we need to bear in mind that men are still very much encapsulated within the system of marriage and affinal relations which bestows esteem, honor, and social value in accordance with the property rights, wealth, and prestige that men create for their wives' households. Put differently, a man's prestige still hinges in large measure on the nature of his relations with his affines, who tend to judge him in his capacity as provider and household entrepreneur. Important changes have occurred insofar as the prestige and other benefits engendered by in-marrying males attach to a much smaller range of their affinal kin than used to be the case, especially since affines' jural control over in-marrying males' labor power and productivity has been weakened considerably. Significantly, however, divorce rates are still quite high (though they have declined in recent decades), and men and women alike identify the central problem in marriage and the major cause of divorce as tension in the relationship between men and their wives' female kin, particularly their wives' mothers and sisters. The specific dynamic cited over and over again is that husbands do not provide well enough for wives and children (and that even when they do, their female in-laws place too many demands on their labor power and productivity), and are, more broadly, both rather unreliable and unresponsive when it comes to honoring kinship and other social obligations. This perception informs (men's and women's) understandings and representations of masculinity in its entirety and, not surprisingly, helps motivate the practical/counter-hegemonic view that men are neither reasonable nor responsible and, more generally, have less "reason" and more "passion" than women. Some of the structural factors motivating such views are considered in the following section.

Kinship, Marriage, and Gender

Political and religious changes of the sort outlined in the preceding pages are profitably viewed in relation to state policies that promoted the development of rural capitalism. From the outset these strategies included policies that effected a break with tradition insofar as they encouraged men to take up commercially valued land in their own names, independently of their wives, sisters, and other female kin. One reason for these policies was that the British viewed traditional constraints on male proprietorship and inheritance as part of a larger institutional framework deemed primitive, anachronistic, and overly cumbersome as regards the objectives of colonial rule (see NSAR 1889:2; NSGG 1898 III:151–52). At the same time—and this, I think, is the more critical issue—the British clearly viewed as "unnatural" a system in which provisional rights over land devolved upon females to the exclusion of males. In consequence, women appeared to have a great stake in agriculture and to "cultivate their holdings to the fullest extent," whereas men were said to "rarely help the women in looking after" the land owing to their position that "We shall never get it, so why should we help to improve it?"[3] This situation, aside from suggesting an inversion of the system of gender relations in Victorian England, was believed to foster a lack of interest among males in local events and economic development, and to account for the "considerable majority of women" revealed in Rembau's 1891 census (NSGG 1897 II:4). "Unnatural" imbalances of this sort prompted British officials, in the mid-1890s, to induce Rembau males to acquire parcels of land for coffee cultivation; as a result, men were soon "beginning to have a stake in a country in which almost all landed property is vested in women" (NSAR 1896:4).

State strategies geared toward promoting the development of rural capitalism also involved the introduction of highly individualistic forms of proprietorship and inheritance, which undermined many features of the traditional system of inheritance and property relations as well as various

types of collateral ties, including relationships among (natural and classificatory) siblings. Especially noteworthy is that changes in these areas
undercut the economic dimensions of brothers' ties with their sisters, and,
in the process, helped shift the burden of support for women and children
from brothers to husbands. More broadly, responsibilities for the creation
of property rights, wealth, and prestige for lineages and clans came to fall
increasingly, though not exclusively, on husbands and in-marrying males
generally. I will return to this point in a moment.

The new economic opportunities—cash-cropping, expanded trading activities, and a limited number of civil service jobs—that were made available to men and to rural society at large in the late 1800s were in many
(but not all) respects socially divisive and profoundly disruptive. So, too,
were the effects of other state economic policies that I have discussed elsewhere (Peletz 1987a, 1988b). Suffice it to say that the period since the
late 1800s has witnessed increased household dependence on male cash-
cropping, and declines not only in the predominantly female domain of
subsistence rice production, but also in the viability of traditional reciprocity-based and redistributive economic institutions. The past few decades
in particular have also seen heightened demands for modern household
conveniences and commodities of various kinds (electricity, piped water,
sewing machines, radios, televisions, bicycles, and motorcycles), which are
nowadays widely, albeit unevenly, distributed in rural settings. They
have, at the same time, seen the development of a rather pronounced
degree of class differentiation and stratification based largely on differential access to commercially valued land (most notably land suitable for the
small-scale cultivation of rubber).

These and related changes have undermined many of the political and
economic functions of clans and lineages, and have likewise helped bring
about the partial demise (though certainly not the wholesale destruction)
of the system of divided title and various other aspects of property and
inheritance relations. As in all other areas of social change, however, what
has occurred in the domain of property and inheritance relations is less
the "breakdown of the system" than a series of highly selective social
transformations informed in large measure by structural precedents that
existed in precolonial times. Thus, the fact that sons are in many cases
allowed, or at least given the option, to inherit rights over land, especially
newly alienated land that is not formally classified as "ancestral," is not
so much a breakdown of the system as a recasting of the precolonial practice of "paternal provisioning" by means of which fathers could convey
certain categories of (movable) property to their children.[4] Of perhaps

greater significance is that even though sons do at times inherit "acquired" (as opposed to "ancestral") property from their parents, daughters (and women generally) are still strongly favored in property and inheritance relations. In short, as discussed in considerable detail elsewhere (Peletz 1987b, 1988b; Fett 1983; Stivens 1985, 1987, 1991; McAllister 1987; Azizah Kassim 1988), the system of property and inheritance relations has not witnessed a shift toward patriliny or bilaterality, despite the conjectures and predictions of earlier observers such as de Josselin de Jong (1960:165, 190); Lewis (1962:192–93); Swift (1965:172); and A. Wahab Alwee (1967:40–41).

It is important to emphasize here that in recent decades neither the clan system nor the sanctions linked with it have been instrumental in perpetuating traditions which effectively barred males from inheriting houses and land. In point of fact, quite the opposite has occurred. The question arises, then, as to why most of this property still passes to daughters. Issues of this sort assume considerable significance in the light of villagers' strong identification with Islam—the religious laws of which entitle sons to inheritance shares twice the size or value of those allotted to daughters—as well as twentieth-century forces of Islamic nationalism and reform, which have underscored Koranic perspectives on the privileged position of male heirs in relation to females.

Daughters continue to be favored over sons in inheritance, regardless of the gender of the initial owner, and even when houses and land are not classified as "ancestral"—hence exclusively female—property. This occurs owing largely to the reproduction of practical views of gender. Interestingly, even when all children are designated as heirs to their parents' estate, sons and daughters tend to not be included as co-heirs with respect to any particular plot of land, or other item of property. This strategy of heirship reflects the assumption and concern that sons might well run up debts, through gambling or otherwise, and thus find themselves compelled to mortgage or sell land or other property held in common with their sisters. Circumstances such as these would bespeak an inversion of proper brotherly behavior insofar as they could easily jeopardize their sisters' subsistence guarantees and force them into inappropriate employment, such as prostitution, to support themselves and their children.

More generally, women are believed to require greater subsistence guarantees than men partly because they are held to be less flexible, resourceful, and adaptive than men, who can eke out a living wherever they find themselves, be it in the village in which they were born (or into which they married), or a culturally foreign city such as Kuala Lumpur or Singapore. It is also taken for granted that all women will marry and have children, and that they must have resources to fall back on, especially since they may not always be able to depend on their husbands, who may be involved in temporary out-migration for many months or years at a stretch, or who may simply predecease their wives. There is also the issue of desertion and divorce by husbands, which is a common theme in local society and culture. More to the point, marriage is regarded as a tenuous arrangement, for men's commitments to their wives and children (as well as other kinship and social ties) are seen as provisional, even capricious. In the final analysis, then, women require greater subsistence guarantees than men not only because they are held to be the less flexible, resourceful, and adaptive of the two sexes; but also—and in some ways more relevant—because they must be protected from men, particularly their husbands (but also their brothers and men in other kinship and social roles). In the practical view, men are simply much less reliable and trustworthy than women.

State-sponsored changes fueled the reproduction of practical, largely counter-hegemonic representations of masculinity in a number of ways, two of which merit brief remark. First, because they entailed the highly inequitable distribution of land and other productive resources, these changes are directly implicated in the marked disparities that exist in men's abilities to live up to the expectations and demands of their wives and affines. Relatively wealthy men, who constitute a very small minority of the adult male population, can rather easily meet these expectations and demands, but the overwhelming majority of adult men cannot. The discrepancy between those that can and do on the one hand and those that cannot and do not on the other clearly contributes to the widespread view that most men are "lazy and irresponsible," and typically expect to "eat for free."

A second, less obvious way in which state-sponsored capitalism helped motivate the reproduction of practical representations of masculinity has to do with the colonial-era restructuring of the roles of brother and husband. I noted earlier that since the late 1800s the responsibility for providing for women and children shifted increasingly from brothers to husbands. I need to add here that this shift did not in any way undermine the "elder brother" (abang) norms that seem always to have informed the husband role (i.e., that husbands should support and protect their wives, and otherwise behave toward them much like elder brothers behave toward younger siblings). On the contrary, elder brother norms appear to have become more central to the definition of the husband role. They have, at the same time, become increasingly idealized, particularly since many of the moral and material imperatives of brotherhood are no longer put to the test on a daily basis. It warrants emphasis, too, that the everyday behavior of men in their roles as husbands is judged not in terms of standards derived from the actual behavior of elder brothers but, rather, in relation to an increasingly lofty and heavily mythologized set of ideals which comprise the fantasy of the perfect elder brother.

Now, I would argue, married men have—or at least are perceived to have—a very hard time living up to the "elder brother" ideals informing the husband role. This is largely because married men have heavy—and in some ways mutually incompatible—moral and material obligations to their relatives, especially the females among them—that is, their mothers, sisters, and other female matrikin on the one hand, and their wives and female affines on the other. Most relevant here are the appreciable affinal demands on married men's labor power and productivity, which reflect the critically important role of husbands, and of in-marrying males generally, in producing property, wealth, and prestige for their wives' kin groups, but which frequently exceed married men's productive capacity. These demands, along with the expectations to which they are keyed, can make married life very difficult for men (particularly men with little or no productive land), and they often exacerbate tensions in marriage ties and affinal relations. Married men who find that they cannot deal realistically with expectations and pressures from their wives and affines frequently divorce or simply abandon their wives, along with any children they might have. This course of action not only feeds into practical views that husbands and fathers are unreliable and untrustworthy; it also colors practical views of masculinity as a whole. These latter, practical views serve, in turn, to counter and moderate the official view of males, just as they effectively elevate practical views of females.

A somewhat similar restructuring of femininity has also occurred as a result of state-sponsored changes of the sort that effected the realignment of the constituent elements of masculinity. In the case of femininity, the changes have entailed the historical deemphasis of women's roles as daughters as well as (natural and classificatory) sisters, and sisters' daughters, and a foregrounding of their roles as wives and mothers. The factors responsible for such shifts include the economically and politically engendered erosion of a broadly encompassing clanship, and the attendant weakening and contraction of the siblingship undergirding it; the demise of various forms of predominantly female labor exchange associated with the agricultural cycle, which, in former times, drew heavily on women as sisters; and the resurgence of Islam, the doctrines of which focus on, and are seen locally as focusing on, women's roles as wives and mothers rather than daughters and sisters. In these and other ways Islam highlights women's sexuality, "natural functions," and links with biological reproduction. The involvement of women in factory work in "free trade zones" and elsewhere, has had much the same effect, particularly since images of such women, aside from being exceedingly negative, focus on their sexual promiscuity and dubious morality generally. Ong (1987, 1988) addresses such matters in some detail. Suffice it to say here that many factory women wear Western-style makeup and clothing (blue jeans, t-shirts, etc.) and are for those and other reasons assumed to have the same "loose" dating habits and morals that Malays widely attribute to Western women.

My earlier comment that social change since the late 1800s has involved less a breakdown of the system than a series of highly selective social transformations is especially relevant to sexuality, mate choice, and marriage on the whole. As will be discussed shortly, basic moral tenets concerning "illicit proximity" and the specific classes of individuals who should not be married are still very much intact (i.e., traditional notions of *sumbang* still carry their moral force), though it is nonetheless true that close cousin marriage, local endogamy, and the practice of arranged marriage are much less frequent now than they were in the nineteenth century (see Peletz 1988b).

Most elements of marriage rituals outlined in chapter 2 are likewise still performed, though such rituals are on many occasions streamlined and temporally compressed—some of their "nonessential" features are dispensed with, much to the dismay of elders—so that they can be held within a single day (or two). There has, moreover, been a radical inflation in marriage payments, and an attendant shift toward greatly discrepant payments (as between rich and poor), though this is less a change in the system than an elaboration of one of its central features.

In addition, the groups of kin linked through marriage and affinal exchange are far more narrowly defined than used to be the case, and are, for all intents and purposes, composed only of the members of the households of bride and groom and their immediate relatives. This pattern is partly a consequence of heightened geographic mobility and declines in the incidence of local endogamy, the flip side of which is the increasing prevalence of marriage with individuals who were born outside of Negeri Sembilan and who are thus unfamiliar with, and in some cases hostile to, *adat perpatih* traditions. Another contributing factor is the tendency toward neolocal residence on the part of newlyweds. Due to develop-

Figure 10.   Bride

ments such as these, it is no longer the case that the system of marriage and affinal relations centers on a *jurally* elaborated or recognized exchange of men between groups of women, or otherwise entails the *jurally* elaborated or recognized political subordination of men to their affinal kin. Even so, the system continues in many respects to be both *experienced and*

Figure 11. Bride with sister

Figure 12.   Bride with attendants

Figure 13.   Wedding procession

represented in terms of such exchanges and subordination. This is particularly evident both from the comments of married men (and women) concerning divorce and their marriage experiences generally, and from the ways in which women (and to a lesser extent men) represent maleness or masculinity.

Sexual Impropriety

Continuity and change in the domain of sexual impropriety is perhaps most usefully approached through a discussion of the concept of *sumbang*, which is of central importance in local culture, and which occurs in one or another form in much of the Malay-Indonesian world. The concept of *sumbang* covers a range of offenses and improprieties covered by the English term "incest," but it also has a much broader range of meaning (Needham 1971:26–27; Peletz 1988b:53). As Needham notes for the Malay-Indonesian world generally, *sumbang* refers to improper or repugnant behavior or conditions and, more generally, to phenomena that are deformed, disharmonious, or discordant; for example, a tree (*pokok*) that has been grafted and consequently bears blossoms of two different kinds is a *pokok sumbang*. In social conduct, *sumbang* refers generally to what is offensive because it is "out of place or unseemly, a subversion of propriety," including even adultery and cheating at cards (26–27).

In Negeri Sembilan, various types of moral offenses are included under

Figure 14. Musician at wedding

the heading of *sumbang*. They are elaborated with respect to heterosexuality (rather than homosexuality), and in terms of relations between (real and classificatory) brothers and sisters. I have discussed these types of offenses elsewhere (Peletz 1988b:52–57) and will simply list a few of them here. In the case of an adolescent or adult female, such improprieties include sitting in a secluded or confined area alongside a man other than one's husband, particularly a man with whom *adat* forbade marriage (see below); walking side by side or conversing with such a man; engaging in sexual activity with such a man; and being frequently observed in irregular conduct associated with one or another variant of *sumbang*.

The vast majority of prohibitions pertaining to specifically sexual relationships involve persons interrelated through siblingship. Sexual relations between a brother and sister of the same parent(s) rank as the most reprehensible of all such offenses (comparable to sex involving a parent and child), and are still regarded as a variant of treason (*derhaka*), though they are no longer defined as a capital offense. Sexual transgressions of this sort figure prominently in myths and are in fact enshrined in mythic accounts of the origins of much dreaded, vampire-like spirits (*pelisit*) whose predilection for sucking the blood of pregnant and postpartum women and newborn children entails serious, indeed potentially fatal, threats to their prey. In one such myth that I have recounted in another context (Peletz 1988b:52–53), a brother and sister engaged in sexual relations that resulted in the sister becoming pregnant. When the sister came to term and delivered, the brother went beneath the floor of the house to lap up the discharge that flowed from the woman's vagina. As a consequence of their transgressions, both the brother and sister were turned into *pelisit*, whose very survival is inimical to human reproduction in both the social and biological senses of the term. Such relations have long constituted one of the most fundamental and reprehensible inversions of propriety (comparable to cannibalism). More generally, sexual relations with persons of the same lineage are still viewed as a heinous offense, as in many contexts are sexual relations involving persons belonging to different lineages of the same clan.

The elaboration of sexual restrictions in terms of brother-sister impropriety is best viewed in light of norms of siblingship, especially cross-sex siblingship, and the structure of prestige. Men have always been expected to look after, protect, and help safeguard the virginity and overall moral standing of their sisters. This is particularly so since the moral standing and prestige of lineage branch, lineage, and entire (localized) clan hinge in no small measure on the reputation of their female members, positioned to attract in-marrying males who will ideally produce property rights, wealth, and prestige for these groups. A man's failure to look after his sisters is a serious dereliction of duty, one with potentially broad implications for lineage branch, lineage, and (localized) clan. Sexual intimacy or "illicit proximity" with a sister goes far beyond dereliction of duty, however; it amounts to a wholesale inversion of proper brotherly behavior, the more so since it renders the sister unfit for marriage, taints the broader social groups to which brother and sister belong, and thus threatens social reproduction, particularly since a child born of such a union would be forever heavily stigmatized and thus unable to marry properly.[5]

It merits remark as well that brother-sister impropriety (and *sumbang* generally), in addition to being a sin in the eyes of and thus punishable by God, is believed to entail the automatic triggering of "supernatural" punishment in the form of skin disorders (rashes, blotching, discoloration, and the like). These disorders affect not only the guilty parties but also their descendants (up to seven generations), and are high on the list of traits that define an individual as an undesirable marriage partner. (Their "last minute" or belated discovery could, in former times, constitute legitimate grounds for backing out of a proposed union or even nullifying an extant one.) As such, the transgressions responsible for their surfacing are all the more reprehensible and threatening to social and biological reproduction. Bear in mind, too, that inappropriate sex of the sort at issue here is believed to result in plagues on chickens and other domesticated animals, and other threats to the natural world (cf. Jordaan and de Josselin de Jong 1985).

The theme of brother-sister impropriety also figures prominently, albeit indirectly, in the way villagers conceptualize and talk about prostitution (*pelacuran*). The topic does not come up much in local conversation, though when it does it is often cited as a possible consequence, in a worst-case scenario sort of way, of what might happen to a woman who is not afforded sufficient subsistence guarantees (a house and land) by her parents. The idea here is that if females are not accorded priority over males in inheritance—if, for example, sons are favored over daughters, or even included as co-heirs in the inheritance that might otherwise pass exclusively to daughters—their brothers might run up debts, through gambling or otherwise, and thus force the mortgage or sale of property held in common with them, thereby undermining their subsistence guarantees just enough to force them into prostitution to support themselves and their children. In this scenario, brothers are viewed as rather directly responsible for their sisters' moral decline. More generally, what we see in this scenario is a highly unflattering portrayal of men in their roles as brothers that diverges rather markedly from (indeed inverts) the elder brother ideals that should inform men's behavior toward their sisters. When one considers as well that the scenarios at issue derive much of their moral force from the widely held belief that women are quite likely

to be divorced or simply abandoned by their husbands—who should behave toward them much like elder brothers but more often than not
clearly do not—it becomes even more apparent how inversions of norms
cast in idioms of siblingship thoroughly infuse the culturally interlocked
domains of kinship, marriage, and sexuality.

As mentioned earlier, the concept of *sumbang* involves not merely
what Westerners would regard as sexual activity, but also various types
of "unacceptable closeness" that do not involve physical contact of any
sort; for example, a woman sitting (even standing) in a secluded or confined area with a man with whom *adat* forbids marriage. Nowadays such
offenses are usually referred to under the heading of *khalwat*, an Arabic-
origin term that refers both to "illicit proximity" and to a specific category
of criminal offense in Islamic religious law (cf. Karim 1990:61 n.2). A
colloquial synonym for *khalwat* is *tangkap bassah*, literally, a "wet
catch," which is somewhat like the American expression "caught with
your pants down," though the latter expression implies being caught in
flagrante delicto, whereas "a wet catch" does not necessarily carry any
such connotation. (Alternatively, one might suggest that the main difference between the two expressions lies in the fact that the concept of in
flagrante delicto is more narrowly construed in Western culture than
among Malays.)[6]

Individuals believed to be guilty of *khalwat* are typically forced to
marry one another, assuming that they are not prohibited from doing so
by considerations of social relatedness or prior marital status. If, for example, the individuals are barred from marrying one another by virtue of
common clan membership, or because the woman is already married,[7] the
case may be referred to religious authorities, who pursue the matter as a
criminal offense.

Young boys and girls are sometimes threatened by elders that they will
be arrested and charged with "illicit proximity" if they go into the back
of a provision shop, or venture into other secluded or confined areas, with
children of the opposite sex. But one is more likely to hear mention of
khalwat in connection with stereotypic cautionary tales concerning preda-
tory divorcées' and widows' laying of traps for desirable young men
whom they would like to marry. According to such tales, divorcées and
widows lure young men to their homes when no one else is present (or to
another secluded or confined area), and then hope for the best (or worst):
that someone has reason to suspect they are together and will thus notify
a local mosque official or some other relatively well positioned villager

who will proceed to burst in on them and charge them with *khalwat*. In the normal course of things, this results in their forced marriage.

While *sumbang*, "illicit proximity," "wet catches," and the like, figure prominently in the ways people think about male-female relations and sexuality in general, the theme of rape (*rogol*) does not. The sole case of rape involving a resident of Bogang that came to my attention during my fieldwork involved Maimunah's twenty-two-year-old sister, Zaini, who was raped by a Chinese man from Seremban.[8] The man, who was either Zaini's employer or a co-worker, raped her ostensibly to punish her for slighting him (or a fellow Chinese) at her workplace. He waited for her as she got off the bus and began walking back into the village, and proceeded to force himself on her, telling her in the process that he would kill her if she went to the police or otherwise identified him.

There are undoubtedly other cases of rape involving villagers from Bogang of which I have no knowledge. Noteworthy too is that some cases of rape that are brought to the attention of the Islamic courts and the police are not formally classified as rape, but are treated instead as adultery. As in most if not all other societies, the reported incidence of rape among Malays is unquestionably much lower than its actual occurrence. If only for this reason, cross-cultural comparisons of the frequency of rape that are based on official reports of the incidence of the crime must be viewed with extreme caution.[9]

Interestingly, many of the most blatant sexual improprieties and offenses of which one hears in villages like Bogang do not involve Malays at all but, rather, other ethnic groups, most notably Chinese and Indians. Indians, for example, are said to be given to *main belakang* or "playing in the back/rear," a euphemism for anal sex, which is an illicit form of sexual activity (*zina*) in Islam.[10] Chinese are viewed as similarly unrestrained and volatile (recall that Zaini's rapist was Chinese), much like the Japanese, who are remembered for raping and pillaging during their occupation of Malaya during the Second World War. Compounding villagers' extremely negative views of Chinese sexuality (and Chinese culture generally) were the highly sensationalized reports of a Chinese man who had sexually abused and murdered a young (Chinese) girl, which were widely publicized in the press during the second period of fieldwork.

The sexual practices of "white people" (*orang putih*) are likewise held in extremely low regard, especially since much of what villagers know of Westerners comes from the television shows piped into their homes by the state-controlled Malaysian media (*Charlie's Angels*, *Baretta*, *Kojak*,

Six Million Dollar Man, Bionic Woman, Dallas, Dynasty), which portray Westerners as a rather depraved and wanton lot. A particularly shocking affront to local sensibilities centered around an incident in the late 1970s, widely reported and documented with photographs in the local press, involving Prince Charles and a woman he did not know (indeed had never seen before), who swam up to him and kissed him as he was wading in the sea. On more than one occasion I was called upon to clarify how Westerners could abide such outrageous behavior, which involved among other things a grave affront to the dignity and majesty of royalty. In much the same fashion I was sometimes asked to explain—and justify—the "sexual license" of Catholic priests, who are assumed by some villagers to engage in church-sanctioned sexual activity even though they are prohibited from marrying.

Many other features of sexual impropriety have yet to be considered here, and I have said next to nothing about the other side of the sexual coin—"good sex." Some of these matters are taken up in the following sections of this chapter; others are addressed in chapter 5, which deals with the person and the body and includes discussions of conception, pregnancy, and childbirth, and the various sex-related and other prescriptions and prohibitions associated with these events and processes. Such being the case, I would simply emphasize that press reports, televised serials imported from the West, and other media coverage bearing on non-Malay, especially Western, gender relations and sexuality, have clearly entered into and help shape and animate local discourse on sexual relations and male-female relations generally. This is nowhere more evident than in the recently emergent discourses bearing on the sexuality of female factory workers employed in "free trade zones" and elsewhere, for, as noted earlier, these women frequently wear Western-style makeup and clothing such as jeans and t-shirts, and are, for these and other reasons, widely assumed to be sexually promiscuous and of dubious morality on the whole (see Ong 1987, 1988; Ackerman 1991). Although there are relatively few adolescent or adult women currently residing in Bogang who are engaged in such work, those who do—or have done so in the past—provide excellent negative examples of female sexuality as far as the rest of the village population (male and female alike) is concerned. (This despite the broad recognition that such women often make critically important economic contributions to their parents' households.) In these and other areas we see the importance of viewing local notions of sexuality and morality within the larger context of a rapidly changing political economy. A similar point emerges from my material on gender crossing, to which I now turn.

Pondan

The term *pondan* is used in Malay culture to refer to a variety of different types of behavior and individuals. In my experience the term is used exclusively for males whose dress or behavior constitutes a significant departure from stereotypical male gender roles. (Villagers knew of no female *pondan*, though they suggested that such might be found in Kuala Lumpur.) Thus, it may denote an adolescent or adult male who dresses or otherwise adorns himself like a woman; or it may refer to a male who walks like a woman, behaves sexually like a woman (i.e., has sex with men), or acts like a woman in other ways (e.g., prefers the company of women to men). In keeping with the relative deemphasis of sex and gender in local society and culture, the encompassing nature of the *pondan* concept works against the elaboration of distinctions—found in English and many other languages—between transvestism, transsexualism, hermaphroditism, homosexuality, and effeminate behavior.[11] I should underscore as well that sexual orientation is not a primary marker of the *pondan* category, which is, in any event, a mediating rather than supernumerary category.

There is, overall, both considerable tolerance for and acceptance of *pondan*. The same "relaxed" attitudes toward these phenomena exist among Malays elsewhere in the Peninsula (Raybeck 1986), among Indonesians and Filipinos (Yengoyan 1983), and among Southeast Asians generally (Keyes 1986). As one observer summed up the situation in the 1960s:

> Basically, S. E. Asians are far more tolerant of personality deviation, abnormality and disorder than we are. Homosexuals and transvestites are treated with kindness and an amused tolerance; they are seldom considered a menace to society, blamed for being what they are, or made to feel that they must be kept in separate places from other people, ostracized or confined to institutions. Physical imperfection or mental abnormality are [also] regarded as something bestowed by God, as an act of fate (*adjal* or *nasib*), and accepted as such by kinsmen and the community. (Jaspan 1969:22–23)

Villagers in Bogang often invoke the term *pondan* when discussing people like Razak (age thirty-four) and Kadir (age thirty), both of whom belong to the wealthiest lineage in the community but, like many other young people, males especially, have long since moved out of the village. The term is typically used to indicate that Razak (who is married and frequently returns to the village on weekends) and Kadir (who has never married and rarely returns home) really enjoy spending time with women, and do in fact spend far more time with women than most "normal" men. People sometimes add that Razak and Kadir are effeminate in gesture, speech, and walk; that they are very good cooks; or simply that they are "like women" (*macam perimpuan*). But there is no additional reference to or implication about their sexual orientation; in most contexts this simply does not come up. Sexual orientation, as noted earlier, is not a primary marker of the *pondan* category.

While many *pondan* marry and have children, villagers' occasional expressions of (mock?) surprise about *pondan* who marry suggest that, at some level, the concepts of *pondan* and marriage are mutually incompatible. It is sometimes said of *pondan*, especially after someone has commented on how effeminate or otherwise involved in gender crossing they are, "Yes, and can you believe they are married!" Similarly, villagers who heard that a woman who had been married to a village *pondan* (Razak) for eleven months and was, sadly, still a virgin (*anak darah*), were not at all surprised, since, as one woman put it, "He is, after all, a *pondan*." (Razak's uncle told me that Razak and his wife had no children because Razak has a sickness or disease [*penyakit*], but this was not a biologized interpretation of why he is a *pondan*.) On the other hand, when Razak's marriage showed signs of breaking up some months later, few of the comments about the problems involved made mention of Razak being a *pondan* (focusing instead on his poor choice in selecting a wife who couldn't cook, look after a house, etc.). It merits note in any case that when Razak was teased incessantly and directly accused by his mother's sister of being a *pondan* (or *bapo*), he got extremely upset with her, offering in the process, in what was a very unMalay move, to show her that he wasn't (i.e., that he [still?] had a penis and/or testicles).[12]

Kadir's parents seem relatively unconcerned that Kadir is a *pondan*, but they are clearly very upset that he has no apparent interest in getting married, let alone marrying properly. Both his parents were distraught when they learned that the young woman he was spending time with in Kuala Lumpur was half-Chinese and half-Indian. Making matters worse, she knows nothing of cooking or other domestic tasks, and likes to spend money on restaurants and discos. These were the primary regrets Kadir's father mentioned to me on a number of occasions, though he was also saddened by the fact that Kadir rarely returned home anymore. The reason for this, according to his father, was out of embarrassment for having failed in a business enterprise in Kuala Lumpur, for which he had borrowed M$5,000 from his mother, a sum which he is in no position to repay.

There are no specific occupational niches monopolized or favored by, or closed off to, *pondan*. Some *pondan*, however, are bridal attendants, or *mak andam* (as occurs in the Philippines, and elsewhere in the world as well [Yengoyan 1983]); and, generally speaking, there seems to be a conceptual link between *pondan* and *mak andam*. The best known and most skillful *mak andam* in Negeri Sembilan is in fact a *pondan* from Bogang named Zainal, whom I interviewed in January 1988.

I first met Zainal in 1979 or 1980, but it was not until my second period of research that I had the opportunity to talk with him at length. I had run into him at a village wedding, in December 1987, and had taken pictures of the bride he helped make up, which I later sent to him along with an invitation to come to the house for lunch. Zainal arrived sporting eyeliner and toting a large imitation-leather bag of the sort made for slide projectors and accessories, and a bag containing three photo albums of his work. The first bag contained various items of women's jewelry—necklaces, chokers, belts, gold pins, etc.—and a ceremonial dagger (*keris*), the *kain sengkit* that grooms wear around their waists, some colored eggs (*bungga telor*), and miscellaneous items he uses in his professional capacity as *mak andam*. The photo albums, for their part, contained pictures of various brides he had made up, photos and clippings of wedding gifts and bridal chambers that he uses to help people decide what they want to have done for their weddings, and some newspaper and magazine clippings featuring stories about his work.

Among the very first things Zainal mentioned to me as he sat down and began unpacking his things was that he was "very gifted," that he had been aware of this from an early age, and that God had given him his special talents. His father, who eventually became a high-ranking member of the Survey Department, had also been very clever at school, and had in fact been raised by a "white person" from the time he was fifteen or so until he was about seventeen.

Although both his parents are from Rembau, Zainal grew up in various areas of the country (but never in a village) and has traveled widely. His mother (still living) resides within the confines of Bogang, he said, but she really doesn't know anything about "village ways" of making a living. In fact, she never planted rice, tapped rubber, or raised animals because "she never had to do any of these things." By way of rounding out the picture, Zainal added that each and every one of his (six or seven) siblings has high status: One is a lawyer, one has a Ph.D., another is in the army (or married to a high-ranking army officer), and so on.

When Zainal was in school he didn't have to study very hard, and he soon realized that he had a flair for making decorations on special days at school, and for the field of decoration generally. Eventually this led him into the business of *mak andam*, which he began professionally in about 1969. At first he didn't charge the women who asked him to make themselves up, though sometimes they would give him a few *ringgit*. Later he began charging for his services, and at the time of the interview he made a fair amount (he did not specify how much) from this line of business, though his full-time job was at the Survey Department. His fee for a village wedding was usually around M$400 (though he sometimes did them for free), but he charged much more for the weddings of urban Malays, particularly since his fees were structured in part around what people could afford and included the cost of materials used to adorn both the bride and the bridal chamber. One of the most expensive weddings he helped arrange was that of the child of a large housing developer in Seremban. The bridal chamber alone cost more than M$30,000, mostly for the price of an imported Italianate bed.

Zainal's work has taken him throughout the Peninsula and to other countries as well. Much of his overseas travel is in connection with his involvement in a Negeri Sembilan cultural organization, which has sponsored his trips to Singapore, Indonesia, Japan, and Turkey. He has also been to Hong Kong, though that may have been a pleasure trip, courtesy of a British friend (an estate manager), who paid his way. The impression I got was that the estate manager was gay and that he and Zainal were lovers for a while (perhaps before Zainal got married), though Zainal never came out and said this.

Zainal mentioned a few times that he was the only male *mak andam* in all of Negeri Sembilan, and that he was also the best known of all *mak andam* (women included) in the entire state. As for why other males didn't become *mak andam*, Zainal said that they might be embarrassed to do this kind of thing because it was regarded as women's work, but he had no other comments on the subject.

In response to one of my questions, Zainal explained that he recited incantations and prayers to enhance the beauty of the bride, to make her more radiant and attractive, and that he also applied special oils that had been passed down to him for this purpose. The incantations and prayers were nothing elaborate, he assured me, but they did make the bride look

better. Such things were not used on *janda* (widows and divorcées), however, since they were "already old" and "aren't pretty anymore" (*tak can-
tik lagi*).

Zainal also mentioned (this, too, in response to one of my questions on
the subject) that people occasionally asked him for advice on sexual matters. These requests for information typically came from those who
"haven't mixed much," like village girls who had never worked in factories, for they did not usually receive any advice or information about
sex or physical intimacy from their mothers, or from anyone else. As
a consequence, they really didn't know how to behave when they were
approached for the first time by their husbands, and they were understandably scared, he said, adding "we were scared at first too, right?" (*kita
pun takut mula-mula juga, bukan?*). But Zainal didn't usually bring up
sexual matters, because he didn't think it was his place to do so. And he
worried about his reputation: "What would people think of me if I just
started talking to them about sexual matters? They would surely think
that is very inappropriate."

I was not very successful getting Zainal to elaborate on the symbolism
of wedding attire, or various aspects of wedding ceremonies, but he did
raise a few interesting points. He used the expression *raja sehari* (literally,
"king [and/or queen] for a day") when talking of the bride and groom on
the day of their wedding. The notion that bride and groom are like royalty
on their wedding is widespread, but I don't recall anyone using this specific term before (though it appeared in one or more of the clippings Zainal
had with him). Zainal mentioned as well that it was inappropriate if the
bride laughed or even had her mouth open while she and the groom "sit
in state" (*bersanding*). Laughing in particular was a clear sign of losing
control and indicated cheekiness; that is, it brought her morals into question, as is true elsewhere in Southeast Asia as well (Jaspan 1969).

On the symbolism of the eggs (*bungga telor*) that figure prominently
at weddings, Zainal said only that eggs were displayed and given to guests
since "people like them," and since "they feel especially honored and
pleased when they are given them." But he added nothing more. I asked
about the possibility of eggs being symbols of fertility and prosperity, and
he seemed to think this quite plausible. I also went through the gender
interview with Zainal, thinking that he might have a unique perspective.
As indicated by the synopsis of the interview (see chapter 6), he did not.

Prompted perhaps by my questions on gender and sexuality, Zainal
went into considerable detail about genitalia and related matters. When I
asked him about circumcision, for example, he said that this was done

because it was very unbecoming to have a "long penis that just hung down there like that" (he indicated with his finger), adding that it wasn't clean or healthy either, since "all that stuff just collects there." Zainal then related a story about one of his non-Malay friends (the British estate manager), who wasn't circumcised. Zainal chastised him for being uncircumcised, and so he (the friend) ultimately agreed to undergo the surgery while he was back in England. He then proceeded to send Zainal pictures of his newly circumcised penis, one *berdiri* ("standing up") and one *duduk* ("sitting" or "lying down"). This was related with much laughter on Zainal's part, though he was watching my reactions closely to see what I thought of his story. The friend in question was apparently the same man who had invited Zainal to Hong Kong (all expenses paid), and who later asked Zainal to come to Los Angeles and stay with him. Zainal was a bachelor at the time and considered the invitation very seriously. But when he told his mother about the possibility of his going to America, she cried and cried; so he decided not to go, especially since his father was quite ill at the time.

Zainal also told me that he has a "gay friend" (his expression), a Christian, as I recall, who lives in Melaka or Port Dickson and hosted the big New Year's Eve party that Zainal attended. Zainal emphasized that he "loved parties," and that he stayed at this one until about 2 A.M. His response to my question about whether he took his wife to the party was "no," to which he added, "there are some things that you just don't talk about with your wife, right?" At about the same time in the conversation, he said that one of his friends (the gay Christian again?) had lots of pornographic magazines and some pornographic videos as well, one of which showed people at various "nude [night] clubs." Zainal mentioned that he had been concerned about where to keep all the magazines, and that it would have been unfortunate if someone had found them, so he gave them away to friends.

It was, I think, during this part of the conversation that Zainal asked about "free sex" (his expression) in America, but, for better or worse, I didn't provide much information on the subject.[13] I should perhaps add that I never asked Zainal if he considered himself (or realized that others regarded him as) a *pondan*. Nor did I broach any other topics bearing on *pondan*. The main reason for not addressing any such issues is that, at the time, it seemed impolite and otherwise inappropriate to do so.

As the afternoon wore on, I grew tired. Zainal, however, continued to be very animated, though he may have eventually sensed that my energy was waning. Before leaving, he offered to dress Ellen and me in formal wedding attire, promising to make us up very elaborately. He would need a bit of advance notice, however, and the evening would be best. He would dress us in our home, thus making sure that the outfits and decorations fit well with the decor and style of our house. Zainal also insisted that we come up to Seremban and spend the night, and that we would have lots of fun cooking, eating, and talking together. He added that he would be very upset if we went back to America without first saying good-bye.

A number of themes emerge from my interview with Zainal, but I will confine my comments to a few of the more basic issues. Among the things that struck me most forcefully during the interview with Zainal was how articulate and cosmopolitan he was, and how proud he was both of his accomplishments as a *mak andam*, and of his enviable status (both ascribed and achieved) in general. His status concerns were expressed toward the beginning of the interview, when he laid out his genealogy and cultural pedigree, along with his broad travel experiences and the educational attainments and professional accomplishments of his siblings and their spouses. It is significant that Zainal's masculinity and overall status were by no means compromised by the fact that he was a *pondan*; indeed, he derived considerable esteem from the role of *mak andam*, which, especially in the case of male *mak andam*, is clearly linked to the status of *pondan*. This situation contrasts rather markedly with what one finds in Western societies, where gender crossing of any variety typically entails a loss of status (stigma).

Gender crossing in Western societies is invariably viewed (particularly in official discourse) in strongly negative terms, as highly "unnatural," an abominable violation of God's will. It does, moreover, elicit ambivalence, hostility, and, on occasion, violent outbursts from non-gender-crossers, especially males. Such is not the case among Malays, or most other Southeast Asians, who, as noted earlier, display a relatively accepting, accommodating, and "relaxed" attitude toward such phenomena. That Malays and other Southeast Asians do not seem very threatened by gender crossing is probably related to the fact that gender is not all that strongly marked in most domains of Southeast Asian society and culture; and that, as such, behavior which blurs the boundaries of gender categories is less problematic and threatening with respect to the basic (relatively ungendered) structure of the universe. The question of markedness aside, gender categories are not arranged in a strongly asymmetric fashion (male and female are viewed in many contexts as complementary, not hierarchical) and do not constitute the foundation of social hierarchy; hence, gender crossing does not pose a serious challenge to the basic social hierarchy, which is structured in terms of descent, age, birth order, and, in recent times, social class.

Local attitudes toward *pondan* might well be decidedly less accommodating if the majority of *pondan* and other gender crossers were female. They might also be far less accommodating if there were gender crossers living full time in Bogang, especially if such crossers were, in addition, engaged in publicly recognized and acknowledged homosexual liaisons.[14] Inquiries along these lines are certainly worth pursuing, but unfortunately they are beyond the scope of the present discussion.

I mentioned earlier that sexual orientation is not a primary marker of the *pondan* category. I should note, though, that some *pondan* wear their sexuality on their sleeves. Such was clearly the case with Zainal, whom I (and Ellen) assumed from the outset was homosexual, and in any case, was far more interested in talking about sexuality and (male) genitalia than any Malay I have ever encountered. Some of this may well have been related to his being a *pondan*. (Bogang's two other *pondan* are also decidedly "cheeky" by Malay standards.) Also relevant perhaps is that Zainal clearly viewed me as a Westerner and a Christian to boot, someone who was "free," like him, of many sexual and gender constraints, and thus appropriately positioned to discuss sexual matters.

The overall situation I have described here may soon change. For while *pondan* are certainly tolerated and accepted in village society, the past few years have seen concerted efforts by Islamic reformers and various state governments to crack down on and ultimately eliminate transsexuals, transvestites, and all other types of gender crossers—and thus to "clean up" male sexualities and locally defined masculinities alike. These efforts include legislation as well as scholarly conferences, some of which were held at the University of Malaya while I was in the field in 1987. A spokesman at one such conference went on record as saying that transsexualism (being a *mak nyah*) is an act of God, and that transsexuals should be accepted by the Muslim community—"Islam always opens its door to everyone"—particularly since "they don't have any control over their situation."[15]

He added, however, that the Islamic stand on the *mak nyah* question was very clear since Islam divides humans into two categories: male and female; and that problems necessarily arise when a transsexual tries to behave or dress like a woman, or take hormone pills, all of which is forbidden in Islam. Thus, while "these people require guidance, sympathy and fair treatment from all quarters," "efforts should be made to bring them to the right path" (i.e., "they should be convinced that they are men");

"Islam recognizes them as men and hence they should be treated as men." [16]

In addition to sponsoring scholarly conferences focusing on *mak nyah* and *pondan*, the state has introduced legislative measures to help realize its goals in this area. The state of Kelantan recently passed laws making it an offense for Muslim men to dress or act like women in public. The state of Penang was seeking to enact similar laws during the period 1987–88, so as to broaden its ability to act against transvestites. Under existing legislation, authorities in Penang could only act against transvestites caught or suspected of "soliciting." In certain areas of Penang, the Department of Religious Affairs, with the cooperation of the police, conducted one or two raids in the area every month, though this was also an effort to curtail (heterosexual) prostitution.

Legislative changes such as these will probably be introduced in Negeri Sembilan and other states as well. Similarly, it seems reasonable to assume that the next few years will also see an increase in federal regulations aimed at better regulating and perhaps eliminating all types of gender crossing, such as the 1983 ruling that forbade sex-change operations among all Muslims in the country. [17]

Recent legislation and other moves against *pondan* and *mak nyah* are profitably viewed alongside contemporary legislative and other initiatives aimed at exercising greater control over the body, and the bodies of women in particular. Ong (1987, 1988, 1990a, 1990b), among others, provides incisive analyses of some of these issues, so I need not elaborate here. I would simply emphasize a point that is more often than not dealt with implicitly rather than explicitly—or otherwise effectively glossed over—in the literature as a whole: Even if we are concerned primarily with women (as opposed to gender), we need to keep squarely within our analytic view the ways in which state policies and discourses affect (and are likely to affect) the bodies and sexualities of both women *and* men (a theme to which I return in a moment). It is important to bear in mind, too, that the legislative and other recent trends at issue have clear antecedents which date back many centuries. Recall here that while women and transvestites (the majority of whom seem to have been male) were highly regarded as ritual specialists throughout much of Southeast Asia during the early part of the period 1400–1680, they experienced a marked decline in status and prestige during the latter part of this period owing to the development of Islam and other Great Religions. For the most part this decline in status did not entail actual stigma, at least in the case of transvestites and other varieties of gender crossers. It is nonetheless true that at present the sole ritual activity specifically linked with the once sacred role of gender crosser is that of bridal attendant (*mak andam*). Recent legislative and other measures of the sort discussed earlier will probably eliminate this link in the not-too-distant future and thus contribute to a further secularization of the role—one which also involves its redefinition as a contaminating (as opposed to sacred) mediator "perversely muddling and enmiring the [increasingly] polar terms of the classical [gender] system" (Stallybrass and White 1986:110). More generally, it appears likely that such measures will contribute to an increased dichotomization of gender, especially since their central goals clearly include the elimination of all mediating categories such as *pondan* and *mak nyah* and the simultaneous cleansing ("defeminization") of locally defined masculinities.

Recall, finally, my earlier point that our analytic gaze needs to be focused on the ways in which state policies and discourses affect (and are likely to affect) the bodies and sexualities of women *and* men. The more encompassing theme here is two-fold. First, femininity, masculinity, and mediating categories such as *pondan* and *mak nyah* are dialectically related elements of a single system, an understanding of which fully requires us to give due attention to each of its major components. And second, that system is most usefully analyzed in relation to the vicissitudes of political economy and historical change, including, in particular, the reproduction and transformation of the criteria and axes entailed in the allocation of prestige and stigma. For further substantiation of these broad contentions we need only consider the case study presented in the following section.

A SHOTGUN MARRIAGE: THE CASE OF RUBIAH AND NORDIN

The remainder of this chapter is devoted to a description and interpretation of a social drama which occurred in Bogang in September 1979 and which provides poignant testimony to many of the themes of continuity and transformation in local society and culture that were outlined in the preceding discussion. The precipitating events involved a violation of sexual and moral codes on the part of Rubiah, a fifteen-year-old schoolgirl, and Nordin, a twenty-five-year-old man who had grown up in Bogang but was now residing in Singapore. The climax of the social drama was the hastily orchestrated "shotgun wedding" (*bidan terjun*),[18] which, it was hoped, would help put a good face on both the principal actors and their respective households and kin. The wedding, as we shall see, was deeply infused with pathos on account of the palpable humiliation and shame that enveloped the households and relatives of Rubiah and Nordin. More generally, the wedding helps illustrate some of the ways in which prestige and stigma are allocated in a contemporary setting.

Confession and Options

Bogang seemed (deceptively) quiet and calm when we returned after spending a few days in Kuala Lumpur. What we didn't know was that shortly after coming back to the village (on the evening of 12 September 1979), Rubiah, a shapely and otherwise extremely striking fifteen-year-old schoolgirl who was about to sit for her LCE (Lower Certificate Examination), acknowledged that she had had sexual relations with Nordin, the young man who had long lived behind her house but had recently moved to Singapore. This sparked a tremendous crisis and a veritable flurry of activity geared toward finding out what exactly had transpired between Rubiah and Nordin, and what to do next.

Rubiah was forced to acknowledge her transgression as a result of having told her (adoptive) mother,[19] Kakak (R.), that she "didn't want to go to school anymore" and "wanted to get married." Her mother in turn told her own (adoptive) mother-in-law (Rubiah's [adoptive] grandmother), who immediately went over to "shake the whole story out of her." Rubiah confessed to her, adding that the fellow in question was the one who used to live right behind her house. Soon thereafter the grandmother, accompanied by another female elder, went to the young man's house (he happened to be home for the weekend) to see what he had to say. He admitted that he and Rubiah had had sex.

When Rubiah's (adoptive) father, Abang (S.), was informed of all this, he exploded in a rage, enough so to seriously frighten both his wife and (adoptive) mother, among others. He had to be restrained, lest he make good on his threat to "go after Rubiah and kill her," and "do in" the boy as well. His (adoptive) parents tried to calm him down, but their efforts were largely unsuccessful, so they spirited Rubiah away to their house, where she remained for the next day and a half or so. Meanwhile, Abang screamed and fought with his wife, trading accusations with her that Rubiah had not been brought up properly. The intensity of his initial reaction was all the more ominous since Abang had a well-deserved reputation both for being extremely moody and volatile (he was, I think, manic depressive) and for having a taste for liquor,[20] which is widely regarded as inducing uncontrollable behavior. Moreover, everyone knew that Abang's father had killed a man whom he suspected of having sexual relations with his (the father's) wife, a crime for which he had been hung. People tend to assume that patterns of behavior such as these "run in families." And so they do, at least in some cases, for, as is a matter of public record, Abang had once pummeled a local *haji* (my landlord) whom he suspected (rightfully so, apparently) of having had an affair with his wife.[21]

There was no universally acceptable solution to the problems posed by Rubiah and Nordin's transgression, particularly since there was very bad blood between Rubiah's parents and Nordin's relatives. There were, however, three courses of action that emerged as possibilities, each of which received backing from different members of the community.

First, lodge a complaint with the police against the young man and have him thrown in jail, presumably on charges of *zina* (illicit fornication), which is a clearly demarcated and very serious offense both in religious law and in local custom. This was the "harshest" course of action, and the one favored by Abang's (natural) mother, his other (matrilineal) relatives, and apparently Abang as well.

Second, see if Rubiah and Nordin "wanted to get married," and, assuming that they did, make immediate arrangements for a wedding feast sponsored by Rubiah's parents. This was the most "conciliatory" course of action, and the alternative favored by Rubiah's mother, Kakak.

And third, arrange for a simple marriage ceremony at the village mosque and forego the feast. This was a compromise between the first and second options, which would bestow Islamic legitimacy on the union, but would nonetheless render the marriage more or less illegitimate, or at least heavily stigmatized, from the point of view of local custom. This was the alternative favored by Abang's (adoptive) father, Pak Daud, who was also the village headman.

The second option (favored by Rubiah's mother), won out, much to the dismay of Abang, his relatives, and many others. Rubiah and Nordin claimed that they did indeed "want to get married," so preparations began almost immediately for the marriage ceremony and wedding feasts that were to be held on the following day.

I went over to Abang's house to talk with him about what was going on, and found him sitting alone on the verandah, staring off into space and occasionally shaking his head and lighting a cigarette. This was very unlike Abang, who was usually extremely talkative and almost always enjoyed clowning around and playing to a crowd. When I climbed up onto the verandah, Abang greeted me by telling me that he was very distressed, that his body and blood were "hot," and that his head was spinning. His eyes were red and puffy since he had been crying much of the day, and he continued to complain of being extremely hot and uncomfortable on account of his emotional state. He looked more glum than I had ever seen him; far more so in fact than when his father-in-law had died some six months earlier.

Abang told me that all of his (matrilineal) relatives were furious with the way things were being worked out; they did not think a wedding feast was appropriate, and, as noted earlier, they thought that Abang should have simply lodged a complaint with the police and had the boy thrown in jail. Further compounding Abang's grief was the fact that he was short of money, especially since he had used up all his accumulated resources in connection with the recent celebration of Hari Raya Puasa (Aidilfitri).

Abang was obviously not in a particularly talkative mood, though when his (adoptive) aunt wandered onto the verandah, he began talking quite heatedly, saying that he had raised up Rubiah from the time when she was "no bigger than his forearm," had always provided for her and taken care of her schooling, clothes, and food, and "now she did *this*" to him. He added that Nordin used to "bother" (*kacau*) Rubiah at school, but it was not exactly clear what he meant by this, for he also said that whatever occurred between Rubiah and Nordin had happened on more than one occasion, and with Rubiah's consent.

Abang's aunt tried to soothe Abang and calm him down. She instructed him to recite Koranic passages, and she proceeded to do so herself, with the apparent aim of lending a semblance of tranquillity to the situation. But Abang could not sit still for long, so after a while he excused himself, evidently to get a bottle of liquor, which he walked through the house with a few minutes later.

Abang's frail, largely blind, and nearly deaf mother-in-law, who rarely makes her feelings known, was also visibly angry and distressed by the turn of events. Echoing a refrain I heard on many occasions, she lamented that children nowadays were very difficult to raise. The problems were especially acute in this case, she explained, since she was nearly blind, so much so in fact that when people passed by or came into the house, she didn't know who they were or "whether they are people or ghosts." To this she added, "Once Rubiah and Nordin leave the village they might as well stay away forever; this is what they deserve. However they make a living or fare in general is none of my concern; I am not going to worry about them."[22]

Preparations and Wedding

Shotgun weddings, like funerals, usually involve feasts and expenditures for which little if any advance planning is possible. Thus, women who attend feasts associated with shotgun weddings and funerals typically bring as contributions to help defray expenses not only small containers of uncooked rice (which are standard fare in "regular marriages"), but also gifts of coconuts. Some brought only a few, others many more. Coconuts, which are widely used in curing rituals for their "cooling" properties, would seem a significant item to "cool" the event, though this was not something anyone commented upon.

The women were busy cutting up pineapple, washing and otherwise preparing the meat, vegetables, and other items of food, and talking among themselves about the turn of events. One woman informed me that she had played a major role in seeing that justice was done, although the way she expressed it was more on the order of "I caught them." I also learned that Rubiah was three months pregnant. Though she was not yet "showing," this seemed to be one of the reasons why there was little if any talk of postponing the wedding until after she sat for her LCE.

The feast itself began around 8 P.M. I showed up shortly after 7 P.M., having been instructed by Abang to come over then, only to find that no other men (besides Abang) were there, and only a half dozen or so women. Within an hour's time, a few other men appeared and were invited up onto the verandah to eat. The side dishes accompanying the rice included a fair amount of meat and dishes of anchovies, squash, string beans, pickle, and plain hot water as a beverage. There was enough food to go around, but it was clearly an extremely low-budget affair, and obviously little care had gone into the preparation of the food. Thus, there was no tea, the dishes weren't sufficiently spiced—spiciness of dishes being an index of expenditure and prestige—and there were no desserts or garnishings to speak of. No one commented publicly on such things, however, since to have done so would have been highly inappropriate.

Abang's mother and some of the young girls present served the food and watched to see when the plates needed refilling, but this was done in a perfunctory fashion, with very little talk and no joking or lighthearted conversation whatsoever. More generally, the air was thick with gloom and despair, and the overall atmosphere was even more depressing than it had been at the funeral feast for Abang's father-in-law that I had attended there some months earlier. For that matter, Abang's father left right after he finished eating, thus registering his disgust with the whole affair. So, too, did many of the other males who showed up later, although a few of them returned toward the end of the evening, when Nordin, accompanied by his friends, relatives, and representatives appeared at Abang's house for the marriage ceremony.

In addition to doing virtually all of the cooking and other food preparation that made the feast possible, the women present helped make sure that the wedding ceremony would go off as well as possible under the circumstances. Thus, some of them brought items considered essential for any wedding (e.g., a ceremonial box used to hold small containers of betel, areca, and lime; a bag full of makeup and related paraphernalia; and "wedding quilts"). Abang's mother showed off the bridal chamber, pointing out to me and others how she had helped fix it up. Her acerbic comment on the hastily prepared yet not unattractive chamber summed up her sentiments on the wedding as a whole: "It's not much, but it's enough."

The older women ate inside, after a few groups of men had eaten, and although they were a bit livelier, overall, than the men, they were also quite subdued. (So, too, were the young girls present; e.g., Rubiah's sisters and other female age-mates.) After the older women finished eating, they chewed betel and smoked cigarettes, and doted on a grandson, who had just learned to walk. This achievement was greeted with much approval, and a great deal of clucking and cooing, particularly since the young boy was from the wealthiest and most prestigious lineage in the entire village.

As time wore on, people began wondering aloud—and expressing palpable anxiety about—where the *imam* was and whether he had been able to get in touch with Rubiah's elder brother, who lived in Kuala Lumpur and who was to serve as Rubiah's *wali* ("Islamic guardian") in the marriage ceremony. In most cases, the bride's biological father serves as *wali*, but Rubiah's biological father had died some years earlier, thus precluding such a possibility. (Even if Abang had been related by blood to Rubiah, it is not certain that he would have consented to serve as *wali*.) The *imam* had been sent off to Kuala Lumpur earlier in the day to locate the brother, but no one had heard from him since he left, so no one knew what was going on, or even if the wedding would actually take place.

Finally at about 10:30, shortly after the *bilal* (muezzin) had appeared at Abang's house, the *imam* showed up. He was soaking wet and looking very disheveled and undignified on account of having traveled to and from Kuala Lumpur in heavy rain, but much to everyone's relief he had succeeded in finding Rubiah's brother and obtaining the relevant signature. Had the *imam* failed to locate Rubiah's brother, or failed to secure his consent to the wedding, it would have been necessary to postpone the marriage. This, in turn, would have required another feast and additional expenditures, which Abang could ill afford. The elation over the *imam*'s successful mission was short-lived, however, for as soon as he went home to eat, bathe, and prepare himself for the marriage ceremony, an air of gloom and frustration settled over the assembled group.

As for Rubiah, no one had seen her all evening since she had been sequestered at her grandparents' house, where she had spent the past two days. She made a brief appearance at about 10:30, dressed in the same casual clothes she had apparently been wearing earlier that day. It seemed that she had done little if anything to prepare herself for the wedding, which meant that the celebration, such as it was, would go on for another couple of hours at the least.

Finally Rubiah came back and entered the bridal chamber where she was helped into her clothes by a group of women who worked diligently, and as fast as they could, to coif her hair and apply makeup. Despite their best efforts, this was a slow and laborious process, particularly since the electricity had gone out about a half-hour earlier and there were too few kerosene lanterns to go around. Making matters worse, there was no kerosene on hand on account of a local shortage. Due to all of the delays and the poor lighting (many people sat in the dark), at least half of those present had fallen asleep and were lying about on the floor or propped up in one or another corner.

Midnight came and went, and around 12:30 the women present served another round of food. Shortly thereafter there was much noise and commotion owing to the fact that Nordin and his contingent had been sighted coming from the house next door (where they had just eaten). Nordin was dressed in a "Malay shirt" (*baju Melayu*) and loose fitting trousers with an apron the same color as Rubiah's dress, but this hastily arranged outfit included none of the ritual paraphernalia usually donned by grooms (e.g., headgear, *keris*). He was accompanied by an attendant (male), five or ten women, and about forty boys and young men between the ages of fifteen and twenty-five, a good number of whom looked rather unkempt.

As Nordin and his friends took their place on the verandah, there was much noise, but the air of excitement and suspense, not to mention joy, that usually accompanies weddings was clearly lacking. Nordin seated himself with the help of his attendant at the far end of the verandah, near the *imam* and the *bilal*. Rubiah's father (Abang) was at the other end of the verandah, virtually hidden by the horde of young boys who scrambled up to watch the proceedings. Nordin's representatives had to be given cues at virtually every stage of the ceremony; Nordin, moreover, appeared to need to have Rubiah's father pointed out to him, as if he might not know whose hand to shake at the beginning of the proceedings.

Shortly after they had taken their positions on the verandah, the groom's representatives brought out three ten-*ringgit* bills, took them into the inner room, and then came out and gave them to Mak Lang. She counted them and seemed to hand them over to someone. (I do not recall to whom she gave them.) Of this sum, M$20 was the *mas kawin* ("marriage gold"). Under normal circumstances, the other M$10 would have been given to the *adat* leader of the village, but in this case there were no *adat* officials present let alone involved in the ceremony, and I'm not sure what happened to it.

There were no gifts present and there was no talk or display of the larger sums of money (*hantaran, belanja hangus*) that are usually (but in this case were not) given to the bride's relatives by the groom's kin. Similarly, no rings were produced or exchanged, as usually happens in the case of a "regular" marriage. Nor, to my knowledge, did representatives of the two sides share any betel, "long the essence of courtesy and hospitality" among Malays and in much of Southeast Asia generally (Reid 1988:44), though there was some suggestion that betel be shared. And, needless to say, there was no music or dancing of any sort.

The *akad nikah* part of the ceremony involved the groom repeating a formulaic phrase recited by the *imam*, which must be done in one breath in order to make it valid. The *imam* also recited some passages in Arabic, and others prayed shortly thereafter, with their palms in an upward position. Many of the groom's friends did not make even the slightest attempt to pretend they were praying, and, as mentioned earlier, they behaved in a most disrespectful manner throughout the entire ceremony.

After the completion of the *akad nikah*, Rubiah was led out of the bridal chamber by Mak Lang, who had arranged two plain chairs in the interior room for the newlyweds to sit upon. The chairs were of the card table variety and were covered with simple but attractive pieces of batik. Rubiah took her place on the chair, but since the electricity was out both she and her chair were pushed about for roughly ten minutes so that those outside would be able to see her in the light of the pressure lamp that had been borrowed from a neighbor. This commotion was greeted with much nervous and embarrassed laughter.

Finally, after this agonizing delay, Nordin was invited into the room to join Rubiah and take his place at her side. This he did with a great deal of nervousness, looking as if he would burst out crying, or laughing, at any minute. Rubiah and Nordin sat for a few minutes, staring straight ahead, facing the group of women and children who had assembled in the interior room. They were then led into the bridal chamber, where they spent the night, which was, I would guess, rather tense.

Aftermath

A few days after the wedding, Nordin said good-bye to Rubiah and returned to Singapore, where he held a job as a laborer, with the understanding that Rubiah would join him there as soon as her papers were in order. By the time Nordin left for Singapore, talk of the tragedy had died down somewhat, or perhaps it is more accurate to say that the talk shifted to issues other than those directly involving Rubiah and Nordin and their breach of propriety, such as the newly established *besan* (in-law) relationship between the parents of the bride and groom. Much of the talk that I heard was cruel, or at least insensitive, and was frequently accompanied by glints of laughter: for example, "Why is Abang always over at Kakak Nab's watching television, when his *besan* have a TV and live just next door?" Comments such as these were intended to draw attention to the fact that Abang not only had insufficient resources to purchase or rent a television, but also that his relations with his *besan* were seriously strained. In short, what was once a very hush-hush matter and an incredible source of embarrassment, shame, and frustration, had now become the source of gallows humor and a tragicomic lesson about the perils of raising up your children in a careless, unthinking way.

Talk of Rubiah and Nordin was revived briefly when Rubiah received a letter from Nordin that contained no money. This was a source of great disappointment and shame, for support of Rubiah is clearly her husband's responsibility at this point, and not Abang's or anyone else's.

In January 1980 Rubiah gave birth to a healthy girl at the local hospital. Her parents had long since effectively disowned her, but there was apparently a large ruckus at the hospital because Rubiah's mother wanted to "take the baby" even though she wanted nothing to do with Rubiah. This was viewed as very bad form by everyone who heard of it. Rubiah's grandmother in particular thought it quite offensive and embarrassing that there had been such a scene.

We visited Rubiah and her baby once or twice before leaving the field (May 1980); the formal reason for one such visit was so that Ellen could give Rubiah the receiving blanket she had knit for her and her new daughter.

Seven Years Later (1987)

The next time we saw Rubiah was in September 1987. We were awakened by the caretaker of the mosque shortly after 5 A.M., as he began summoning people to prayer. Sometimes his calls to prayer were highly sonorous, rather short, and "to the point"; on other occasions, however, they were anything but melodic and went on and on, seemingly forever. This was one of the latter mornings, and the incredibly raspy voice, off-tune "singing," and erratic stops and starts were really irritating, the more so since all of this went on for about fifteen to twenty minutes, more or less nonstop, at a very loud volume. I thought that in the future it might be better to get up with these calls rather than to try unsuccessfully to sleep through them, all the while getting mad at Zachary for not going back to sleep, being irritated with the mosque official (a warm and charming man who we liked very much), and cursing the mosque's loudspeaker.

I decided that I wanted to spend a bit more time with Zachary than had been possible in the past week or so, so I postponed my trip to the Islamic court, which didn't seem all that worthwhile anyway since there were no cases on the docket and since (being Friday) the entire office closed at midday. Having made this decision, I looked forward to a relatively unstructured day.

I suggested to Ellen that we go visit Rubiah out in the New Hamlet (Kampung Baru), since we hadn't seen her yet and wanted to know how she was doing. So shortly after 9 A.M. I changed from *sarong* into pants, found my umbrella and a few *ringgit*, and we headed out to Rubiah's.

I carried Zachary through much of the village because I didn't want to dawdle in the heat. There were no shade trees along the road leading from the Old Hamlet to the New Hamlet, so even by 9 A.M. it was extremely hot and the sun bounced off the asphalted road, making the heat all the more unbearable. As always, however, the view from the back road was spectacular, even though the water buffalo that usually roamed around in the (by then largely abandoned) *padi* fields were not readily visible. From that vantage point, the village looked much as it did before (1978–80), and one did not see any evidence of the recent changes that had taken place. On the other side, looking toward Mt. Rembau, the hills rose up out of the morning mist, thick with foliage and forest, seemingly resistant to all that occurred below.

We reached the turn-off to the New Hamlet after the short walk along the asphalted road, and noticed that the old *kedai* that had been on the left, on the near side of the turn-off, was no longer there. In its place was a much larger and seemingly new house that looked like no one lived in it yet. As we came to a house on the left side of the road, I asked the young woman there where Rubiah's house was. At first, she didn't seem to know who I was talking about, probably because Rubiah is most commonly known either by her nickname or her birth-order name. I explained that I was referring to Kakak R.'s daughter, and she said, "Oh yes, up there a bit. Take the lane off to the left, before you get to the brightly colored gate." We headed down the lane, wondering if we had it right, and came to an open area that contained a small house which was set off from the ones in front and back, and which had a primitive run-down bathing area in the foreground, along with three cows tethered to stakes and a few goats in a pen. We noticed a young woman bathing and I whispered to Ellen, "Is that Rubiah?" I thought it might be her because she was rather tall and slender by local standards, and because she looked as I remembered her from before. There was a little girl bathing with her, and Rubiah (or whoever it was) appeared to be naked although I couldn't see clearly. Actually I could see into the bathing area pretty well, all things considered, and I thought back to the day long ago when Ellen and I had been walking past Rubiah's mother's house and had seen the mother bathing in the nude, albeit within the confines of her poorly built bathing area. This had startled us since we had never seen that much bare skin in the village. In both cases, the circumstances of these women's poverty precluded their having more substantial bathing areas, and did, as a consequence, expose them to the gazes of passers-by.

The young woman turned around as we said "Is that Rubiah?" Before she answered, we knew it was her, for she displayed the same beautiful features we had remembered. At the same time we were struck, indeed appalled, because the warm smile greeting us revealed that Rubiah, now aged twenty-three, had already lost four of her (upper) front teeth. Our strong reactions undoubtedly reflected our own standards of beauty but also our pity for the circumstances of her present living conditions.

Rubiah was very pleased to see us, but she also seemed embarrassed, perhaps because it was after 9 A.M. and she and her daughter were just now beginning to bathe and start the day. She apologized profusely for being in the middle of her bath and for rising late, and shouted instructions to the children in the house to wake up their father. He wasn't working today, Rubiah told us, and had slept in.

Rubiah and Nordin's house is, by local standards, both small and exceedingly cramped, and adorned with only the barest essentials. There is no electricity or kerosene stove, there are no tables or chairs, and many of the conveniences found in other village houses are altogether absent. The house also rests on the ground, rather than on stilts, and the foundation is built of ill-fitting cinder blocks that look rather hastily slapped together. Nordin may have built the house himself, for he has some experience in construction. In any event, the contrast between Rubiah's home and living standards and those of the wealthiest segment of the community struck us with considerable force as we approached.

Nordin got up as we entered the house and apologized for rising so late, adding that he wasn't working today and that he had been at the prayer house until late the previous evening. He went out to relieve himself and came back and sat down. We talked for a bit and then Rubiah came into the house, wearing a *sarong*, an old t-shirt, and a pair of very stylish glasses that reminded us of her more carefree days as a schoolgirl.

We talked about the seven years that had passed since we had last seen each other, and about their four children (two girls, two boys). The eldest, born shortly before we left the field in 1980, was now seven; the youngest, about two, was born with a hole in his heart and was rather small, frail, and feeble for his age. He had just learned to walk, they told us, and "can't yet run." Nordin bragged that the five-year-old boy was a "hero" (he used the English word), by which he meant "a tough guy"; the daughters, he added proudly, were "heroine" (his word), by which he seems to have meant strong and rugged.

Rubiah's comments about her children were decidedly less upbeat than Nordin's. She mentioned, for example, that one of her daughters (it wasn't clear to us which one she meant) is subject to spirit possession (*kena hantu*) (see chap. 4). Ellen and I were quite taken aback by this, for we had never heard of anyone that young being afflicted by spirits. The daughter's condition was noted in connection with why Rubiah and Nordin had moved from Jelebu after living there for a few months; apparently her (spiritual) health required it.

Rubiah also informed us rather matter-of-factly that she didn't go out of the house much. "Four children are an awful lot of work, and only one of them is in school," which meant that Rubiah was at home with three of them all of the time. Rubiah, who, it will be recalled, dropped out of school when she was fifteen, underscored that she was very upset with the poor quality of English teaching at the local school, and that she really hoped her children would learn English. She also mentioned having bought them a small Malay-English dictionary to help them in their studies.

Nordin, for his part, spent much of his time working as a laborer, though he also tapped rubber. I had seen him riding through the village on his motorcycle, with an imposing chainsaw slung across his legs, and I knew that he felled trees for people who wanted their houseplots cleared of old growth (e.g., coconut trees that were no longer healthy or productive). He also dug trenches and graves, and engaged in the seasonal harvesting of *petai* (a type of large, green bean), which he sold. His earnings from these sources, which constituted the household's total income, came to about M$300 a month.

The receiving blanket that Ellen knitted for Rubiah shortly before the birth of her first child also came up in conversation. Rubiah and Nordin mentioned that they still had it, so we asked to see it and they brought it out. They had obviously taken very good care of it, for it was in excellent shape (save for a small hole). It could well have been one of their prize possessions, along with their imitation-silver tea service, Nordin's motorcycle, and the chainsaw that he either owned or rented.

Our conversation with Rubiah and Nordin was rendered rather difficult because Zachary was not all that enthusiastic about staying indoors, as he made clear to us by his whining. I took him out to play with the other children and tried to distract him with the cows and the goats that were lolling about the yard. Unfortunately, however, the cows frightened him, and he frightened the goats, who ran away from him as he approached. Zachary finally agreed to stay outdoors with the other children, but after about ten minutes of running about, he appeared at the front door whimpering, with a look of horror on his face, and fresh green cowshit covering the entire front of his body. He had slipped on and literally fallen into one of the large puddles of cowshit that dotted the garden area in front of the house, and was thoroughly disgusted and traumatized by the malodorous green goo sticking to his entire front side. As Ellen rushed him off to the well to clean him up, we tried not to think of tetanus and such, or about the effects that this incident might have on someone in an intense phase of toilet training. While Zachary was soon clean enough, he was humiliated, and completely soaked from the buckets of well water that Ellen had used to help wash him off.

It was about this time that Nordin instructed Rubiah to make us some tea. Once I realized she was starting to build a fire to boil water, I emphasized that "it wasn't necessary, that we hadn't come to drink tea." Refusals of reciprocity couched in these terms are acceptable if they come from fellow Malays, so I had started using them whenever they seemed appropriate. I really didn't want to stay for another hour anyway, which is what we would have been expected to do if we had accepted the offer to drink tea. Nordin also asked Rubiah to find out about some cakes (*kueh bulat*) they had, but I insisted that it wasn't necessary, and that the fruit they had shared with us was more than sufficient (and much appreciated).

As we prepared to leave, we impressed upon Rubiah and Nordin that we hoped they would come visit us. Though they promised to do so, I later realized that they most likely never would, for our home was located deep in the heart of "enemy territory" as far as Nordin was concerned. Indeed, it was centrally located in the area of the village associated with the lineage (*perut darat*) which had been feuding with Nordin's lineage (*perut tengah*) since the mid-1960s (see Peletz 1988b, chap. 9). (It was young Nordin's theft of sugar cane from a fellow clansman associated with the *darat* lineage, and the excessive retaliation that followed, that sparked the crisis in the first place.) Nordin's lineage, moreover, was strongly associated with the opposition party (PAS), whereas most members of the *darat* lineage were UMNO stalwarts. Included in the latter category was the former village headman (my adoptive father) who lived right next door. He also happened to be Rubiah's grandfather, and it was his wife, recall, who had shaken the story out of Rubiah in the first place. If only on this account, a visit to this part of the village would undoubtedly revive painful memories for Nordin and Rubiah alike.

Walking back to our house was rather tiring since it had grown very hot and since Zachary needed to be carried most of the way. As we made our way home, we were forcefully struck by the sharp socioeconomic contrasts in the village, which were sometimes easy for us to forget both because they were often muted if not altogether denied by villagers of all socioeconomic backgrounds, and because we lived and spent much of our time in the wealthiest and most prestigious part of the community. In some ways even more striking than such contrasts, however, was the fact that Rubiah and Nordin were still together after seven years of marriage. Divorce is exceedingly common in communities such as Bogang (more than two-thirds of all marriages in the village end in divorce), and it is especially pronounced among the poorer segments of the community. Most unions that end in divorce do so within the first seven years of marriage; yet Rubiah and Nordin had endured this difficult period, despite the tragic circumstances of their wedding and the attendant stresses and tensions associated with them.

I cannot offer a definitive statement as to why Rubiah and Nordin managed to remain married, and thus beat the odds, though their residence in the New Hamlet, far from the potential meddling of Rubiah's in-laws (who lived in the Old Hamlet) certainly helped. All was not rosy, however, for five or six months after our visit to their house I came across documents at the Islamic magistrate's office which indicated that Nordin had repudiated Rubiah, who was by this time eight months pregnant, by pronouncing the standardized divorce formula ("I divorce you with one *talak*" [repudiation]). The written statement provided by Nordin, no doubt with the help of clerks at the magistrate's office, reads as follows:

> I married Rubiah on September 17, 1979. We have four children; the eldest is nine, the youngest is three; and at present my wife is eight months pregnant. On January 13, 1988, after digging a grave, I returned home and took a bath. My wife's sister came over and said that I had slandered her. Because of this we had a misunderstanding, and in a state of anger I repudiated my wife with one *talak*. After doing this, my wife and I still stayed in the same house. We decided to reconcile and register the divorce [and the reconciliation] at the *kadi*'s quickly, but for reasons relating to work we were late. This wasn't intentional.

Like many such accounts, this is undoubtedly an extremely sanitized version of the problems Rubiah and Nordin experienced in their marriage. The local grapevine had it that Nordin and Rubiah fought more than occasionally, and that in the course of these arguments Nordin sometimes struck Rubiah. A day or two before we left the field, moreover, Rubiah's father (Abang) came to the house, ostensibly to say good-bye, and spent most of his time telling me that he and Nordin had just had yet another argument, and that in the heat of the moment, Nordin had unsheathed and brandished his *parang* in a most threatening way. Though Abang had refrained from unsheathing his own *parang* in response, he told me in no uncertain terms that he would not tolerate this type of thing in the future. This was the last conversation I had with Abang, and the last I heard of Rubiah and Nordin.

COMMENTARY

The social drama sparked by Rubiah's confession that she had had sex with Nordin raises a number of issues that warrant detailed analysis, but I will confine my comments here to a few of the more salient themes in this drama and the light they shed on patterns of continuity and change. My main concerns are to explain why the transgression engendered such a crisis, why Rubiah's parents in particular were so distressed by the whole affair, and why Rubiah's father, Abang, was especially stigmatized by the events surrounding the wedding. Before turning to such matters, I provide a brief discussion of the roles played by women in arranging the marriage and overseeing the actual wedding and attendant feast.

The Centrality of Women

Women (especially Rubiah's mother) played a central role both in arranging the marriage in the first place, and in managing the organization of the actual feast and the appropriate ritual activities. Recall that in terms of the initial alternatives that villagers envisioned as "solutions" to the problems created by Rubiah and Nordin (e.g., lodge a complaint against Nordin and have him thrown in jail; arrange for a simple ceremony at the mosque and forego the feast), the one that was settled upon was favored by Rubiah's mother, but was nonetheless opposed both by Rubiah's father and the latter's father, who was not only the village headman and the head of various secular councils which nowadays constitute the principal organs of community government, but also the most respected healer (*dukun*) and repository of *ilmu* in the village. (I have no information concerning the preferences of Nordin's kin, the locally resident members of whom were mostly female, but I suspect they were in favor of the conciliatory solution favored by Rubiah's mother, since the alternatives would have brought them and their son even more shame.) This indicates considerable continuity with times past, as does the fact that women played the decisive role in actually arranging and overseeing the details of the wedding ceremony and feast.

Noteworthy as well, while women assumed the majority of the practical tasks associated with the wedding and feast, they also took over some (but not all) of the official functions at the wedding, such as the handling of the marriage payment. Such payments are almost invariably handled by men (clan leaders), but since clan leaders were so incensed about the turn of events and were, in addition, embroiled in factional feuding discussed elsewhere (Peletz 1988b, chap. 9), they effectively boycotted the marriage and left such matters to women. Significantly, women had no difficulty assuming these tasks and raised no eyebrows in this regard, though their handling of the marriage payment may well have detracted from the legitimacy of an already dubiously legitimate marriage in the eyes of some villagers. These were exceptional circumstances, however, and like all other exceptions, they "prove(d) the rule" that with respect to marriage and affinal relations the implicit gendered division of labor between official and practical tasks that was documented for the nineteenth century (see chap. 2) still exists and continues to be a central feature of the ritual division of labor. In this respect, contemporary weddings, including shotgun weddings, are highly congruent with weddings of the past.

In the latter connection it is significant that the *imam*'s trip to Kuala Lumpur to obtain Rubiah's brother's formal approval for Rubiah's marriage was in many respects a key concern and a focal point of tension and anxiety throughout the evening of the wedding. There was palpable relief when the *imam* returned to the village and made it known that he had been successful both in locating Rubiah's brother and in securing his consent to the union. As with other aspects of the division of labor between official and practical tasks, the primacy accorded to the *imam*'s role served to highlight the centrality of male specialists as leading actors in marriage ceremonies and affinal relations generally, thus denying or at least eclipsing the roles of women and the male majority in marriage, affinal relations, and social reproduction on the whole. Here, too, we see considerable continuity with times past.

Why Did Rubiah and Nordin's Transgression(s) Engender Such a Crisis?

There are a number of reasons why Rubiah's parents (and others) were so upset that Rubiah had sex with the boy next door. I will mention five of them.

First, Rubiah violated fundamental sexual and moral codes. To appreciate the gravity of Rubiah's transgression one needs to bear in mind that premarital and extramarital sex of all varieties are both morally reprehensible and severely sanctioned. So, too, as we have seen, are all forms of "illicit proximity" (*khalwat*). Significantly, those believed guilty of "illicit proximity" are not necessarily assumed to have engaged in any form of physical contact; for, as Durkheim made clear, mere appearance of the violation of a norm is as reprehensible as the actual violation of the norm. The same is true with respect to *tangkap bassah* (literally, "a wet catch," or "being caught wet"), the latter being the term which is often used synonymously with "illicit proximity." Such acts, recall, are so morally offensive that individuals assumed to have engaged in them are generally expected and forced to marry one another, unless they are prohibited from doing so by considerations of social relatedness or prior marital status. Perhaps more to the point, Rubiah and Nordin's untoward behavior (engaging in sexual intercourse) clearly went far beyond "illicit proximity."

Second, Rubiah "ruined her life" by getting pregnant and proceeding to quit school just a few weeks before an important exam (the LCE). Students must pass this exam if·they want to go on to the next grade; more importantly, successful completion of the exam is a prerequisite for most types of urban employment, including factory work. Failing the exam (or not sitting for it, which amounts to the same thing) thus precludes meaningful employment outside the village. This means, among other things, that Rubiah was destined to spend much of the rest of her life in the village (or in another rural setting; e.g., Jelebu), rather than in an urban environment.[23]

Third, Rubiah's actions rendered impossible a proper, let alone a lavish, wedding, and thus prevented her parents from realizing what could well have been one of the most socially significant and joyous occasions of their lives. Recall, too, that Rubiah was Abang and Kakak's only daughter (Kakak had another daughter, but this was by a former marriage), which meant that Rubiah "ruined" what was literally a once-in-a-lifetime opportunity for Abang and Kakak. Most weddings are planned many months, and in some cases years, in advance and are finely orchestrated affairs calculated to bring the maximum status and prestige to the sponsors of the event and their relatives and supporters. The advance planning is necessary both to accumulate the capital to finance the wedding and to ensure that everything "goes off well." Ideally, this involves extensive advice and other assistance from a gifted and esteemed *mak andam* like Zainal and also includes: the staining of the bride's and groom's hands and feet with henna in the ritually prescribed fashion; making sure that the bride and groom are attired in dazzling finery (and that the bride is adorned with an elaborate headdress of gold and silver); and seeing to it that the Indic-origin "sitting in state" (*bersanding*) of the bride and groom and their circumambulation of their respective households in sedan chairs carried by raucous young men bearing royal regalia—all of which symbolizes their ascension to royalty—is carried out with maximum attention to detail, decorum, and dramatic flair. Sadly, however, most such ritual elements were absent from Rubiah and Nordin's wedding, which was clearly a rather "amateur" production, with no *mak andam* to oversee it. Absent, too, were the troupes that provide gong and drum music during various phases of wedding ceremonies, the stylized dancing performed for the bride and groom, and the Islamic chanting (*dikir*) that sometimes occurs during the beginning of wedding ceremonies. Missing as well were all of the modern additions to weddings which are nowadays commonplace, including, most notably, the teen rock bands that are often hired to attract and entertain guests and to impress upon them the sponsors' facility with things "modern" (Western). As noted earlier, Rubiah and Nordin's wedding was a decidedly bare-bones affair.

Moreover, while sponsoring a lavish wedding feast provides an opportunity to advance one's claims to status and prestige, it simultaneously enables villagers to reciprocate the generosity of numerous friends and relatives, whose feasts they have attended in the past. Failure to sponsor an appropriate feast, or an appropriately large and lavish feast, which amounts to much the same thing, thus precludes the fulfillment of reciprocal obligations on the part of sponsors.

Rubiah's marriage was not merely a failure with respect to building up her parents' prestige and social capital; it actually had the opposite effect, of depleting their social capital and incurring stigma. One reason for this is that her parents had to borrow a relatively large sum of money from Abang's parents to sponsor the feast. This put a serious strain on the relationship between Abang and his parents, especially since they had laid out a fair amount of money to help finance the funeral of Abang's father-in-law roughly six months earlier. I don't know whether they ever intended to pay back this money, but having to borrow money is a situation that villagers seek to avoid, if only because it is an obvious sign of a lack of wealth and prestige.

Fourth, both the circumstances leading up to the wedding and the wedding itself brought shame and disgrace to relatives and neighbors alike. This was all the more upsetting since Kakak's other daughter (by a previous marriage) had gotten married in distressingly similar circumstances, such that there has yet to be (and never will be) an acceptable marriage within Kakak's household. To make matters worse, Kakak herself had had a brief liaison with Nordin's mother's brother (she was unmarried at the time, he was married) which, when discovered, necessitated a shotgun marriage much like Rubiah's. This was followed by the mother's brother fleeing with his first wife to Singapore, from whence he has never returned.

And fifth, Nordin was a highly undesirable marriage partner for Rubiah, at least—or especially—as far as her parents were concerned. This was so not only because of the bad blood between the two households and the fact that Rubiah's "choice" of marriage partners threw in sharp relief the indiscretions of her mother. It also had to do with the fact that Nordin, though a member of a gentry clan, came from a low status (because poor) household, and was, in addition, "merely a laborer." That he was of such a lowly and ill-paying occupation meant Rubiah's parents could not expect to attain much, if any, status or prestige from his future earnings, and certainly could not expect to see their own meager house or holdings of land improved or expanded by his labor power or the fruits therefrom. In this respect he differed very little from Rubiah's father, Abang, who was not only a landless laborer, but had also added very little over the years to his wife's holdings. It is thus quite possible that Rubiah's "choice" of marriage partners drove home some of her father's inadequacies as provider and head of household generally.

Abang's Stigma

I have already cited most (but not all) of the factors that contributed to the loss of status and prestige that Abang experienced, and to the stigma he acquired, as a consequence of this sordid affair. The problem for Abang was not simply that he had failed to provide his daughter with a proper upbringing, proper sleeping quarters, proper supervision, and a proper wedding. (All such failures were laid at Kakak's feet as well.) In some ways most embarrassing and stigmatizing was the way he handled himself throughout the whole affair, especially his indulgence of "passion" (*nafsu*) which was manifested in his loss of inner restraint and control. Recall that when Abang first heard of his daughter's transgressions he threatened to kill her and Nordin alike (for having disgraced him, sullied his name as a father and a guardian of his daughter's virginity and virtue, etc.), and that he had to be forcibly restrained (and Rubiah spirited away) lest he make good on his threats. Bear in mind, too, that Abang spent much of the wedding day crying and, apparently, drinking as well; and that he was, more generally, widely regarded as being an extremely unpredictable and volatile character who invariably gave in to his *angin*, or "winds," and whose moods "wax and wane with the cycles of the moon," as his mother sometimes put it. Behavior and temperamental dispositions of this sort are the antithesis of refinement and virtue for men and women alike, but they are extremely inappropriate on the part of men since men are expected to have more "reason" and less "passion" than women. Abang's behavior thus seriously compromised his standing both as a person of moral virtue and as a virtuous adult male in particular.

Interestingly, shortly after Rubiah's wedding Abang pummeled a man who had been "bothering" his adult sister (a divorcée in her forties who lived in Melaka) and was, as a result, temporarily detained by the police. The circumstances surrounding this beating are not altogether clear, but apparently Abang had been told by his sister or another reliable source that a young man had been panhandling in the vicinity of his sister's restaurant, and had threatened or otherwise "hassled" the sister for not responding favorably to his requests for money. Abang's violent reaction may well have involved compensation, displacement, or some such (or have been otherwise "overdetermined"), but it is broadly consistent with the value placed on men serving as protectors and guardians of their female kin, especially their sisters and daughters. It was, at the same time, an excessive (*amok*-like) display of force and an unfortunate example of loss of control, and, as a result, further stigmatized Abang as someone whose actions were guided by "passion" rather than "reason."

Abang's overall temperament and behavioral style are partly responsible for the fact that he has few, if any, allies on whom he can count for support, other than his father (the village headman). He is, more generally, the antithesis of a "big man" (*orang besar*) in the sense that he lacks the oratorical skills and refinement that "big men" display and utilize to "get things done" and draw supporters. As such, but also because he is landless and poor, has been largely unsuccessful in guarding both his daughter's and his wife's virtue (recall that during their marriage his wife had an affair with a local *haji*), and is apparently impotent as well (none of his marriages produced any natural children), he has few if any symbols to draw upon to help validate his sense of maleness either in his own eyes or in the eyes of the community at large. Indeed, the only symbols that are readily available for this purpose are the large, dangerous snakes to which he makes incessant reference whenever he finds himself with a captive audience. His frequently repeated stories of fighting with and hacking up deadly snakes with his ever ready *parang* are legendary, as are his accounts of his bravery in the forest. That women and children, who are usually the audience to whom these tales are directed, are far more fearful of snakes (and the forest as a whole) than adult men adds to the effect of such narratives, even though they are often seen, especially by women, as highly exaggerated if not altogether mendacious.

Rubiah and Nordin at Present

Finally, a brief note on Rubiah and Nordin's marital status and current living situation. They are, as noted earlier, living in that section of the village which is known as the New Hamlet, and which is composed primarily of households whose adult female members live at some distance from their natal households (i.e., such women are residing neolocally, not uxorilocally). While this is the major area in Bogang where there is land available for new houses and houseplots, living there has the added advantage, especially in men's eyes, of enabling residents to go about their daily lives without the everyday intrusions and meddlings of women's natal kin. Even so, the affidavit Nordin filed with the local Islamic magistrate cites as the main reason for his repudiation of Rubiah that he was "slandered by her sister," who lives on the other side of the Old Hamlet. Whether or not this accurately sums up the difficulties he and Rubiah experienced in their marriage, it resonates deeply with the culturally elaborated theme that the primary reason for divorce is tension between men and their wives' female kin. It merits note as well that the tensions men feel in their relations with their in-laws are felt most heavily by poor men such as Nordin, for the simple reason that such men are, by virtue of their meager resources and earning power, the least likely to be able to live up to affinal demands on their labor power and productivity.

In these facts we also see considerable continuity with times past. This despite two important historical shifts. First, Rubiah and Nordin's living situation (residing neolocally) differs both from that of previous generations of villagers and from most contemporary residents of Bogang, who reside in one or another of the Old Hamlet's matrilineally defined compounds. And second, Rubiah finds herself in the unenviable and unusual position (relative to most locally resident women) of having no residential or agricultural acreage to call her own, and little if any likelihood of inheriting land from her (poor, largely landless) parents. As such, her dependence on her husband, economically and otherwise, is quite pronounced, much more so than what one finds among most other adult women. This may well be one of the reasons she has stayed with Nordin for the past seven years, even though staying with him has entailed (at least according to the local grapevine) some degree of verbal and physical abuse.

The case of Rubiah and Nordin, along with the other material presented in this chapter, underscores some broader historical themes, the most fundamental of which is that the nineteenth-century system of prestige outlined in chapter 2 remains very much intact. This is true despite the fact that it has lost some of its moral force due to the emergence of new and cross-cutting criteria that accord prestige to wealth, modern education, and the like, rather than descent. Spiritual potency, for example, is still highly valued; and it continues to be one of the main symbols in terms of which prestige differentials between males and females are both conceptualized and rationalized. Thus, men are still believed (by men and women alike) to have stronger "life force," or *semangat,* and to be more likely to possess mystical knowledge/power (*ilmu*). It is also true, however, that gender differences such as these are increasingly cast in the symbols and idioms of "reason" and "passion" (and "shame"), and are more firmly and asymmetrically entrenched in local society and culture than at any point in times past.

Many of the historical developments discussed here are taken up in greater detail in later chapters. Chapter 5, for example, elaborates on various features of contemporary sexuality and also examines selected aspects of conception and pregnancy in the context of a discussion focusing on the person and the body and the symbols and meanings of "reason," "passion," and "shame." Chapter 6, for its part, is devoted to an analysis of contrasting representations of gender, especially the highly variable ways in which villagers invoke the concepts of "reason," "passion," and "shame" in their representations of masculinity and femininity. Before addressing these topics, however, it will be useful to return to the theme of *ilmu* which was touched upon briefly in the first section of this chapter. The main concerns of chapter 4 are the gendered dimensions of *ilmu* and personal misfortune, along with recent historical shifts in the sources, symbols, and meanings of marginality, uncertainty, and danger, especially as they bear upon gender.

PART 2

GENDER IN CONTEMPORARY SOCIAL AND CULTURAL CONTEXTS

4   Knowledge, Power, and Personal Misfortune

'Ala'u'd-din [the Sultan of Melaka from about 1477 to 1488] died in the prime of life, probably before the age of thirty, and it was soon rumoured among his subjects that he had been poisoned. This was the normal assumption in the Malay world when a man died young. The pious might say that an allotted span in the Book of Life had been rubbed out, but the common man tended to be more concerned with the instrument of fate, and in the absence of *keris* or spear, could only assume poison.

> Paul Wheatley, *Impressions of the Malay Peninsula in Ancient Times* (1964)

A person entering a Malay house is generally presented with a green cocoa-nut and a little coarse sugar. . . . The young cocoa-nut is opened with the ever ready *parang,* always in the presence of the person to whom it is offered, to ensure its juice not having been poisoned or charmed.

> T. J. Newbold, *Political and Statistical Accounts of the British Settlements in the Straits of Malacca* (1839)

A Kedah lady the other day, eulogising the advantage of possessing a familiar spirit [*pelisit*], . . . said that amongst other things it gave her absolute control over her husband and the power of annoying people who offended her. . . . One is not surprised to hear that everyone in Kedah, who is anybody, keeps a *pel[i]sit.*

> Sir Frank Swettenham, *Malay Sketches* (1895)

The native of the [Malay] Peninsula believes that an esoteric knowledge of the origin of any being gives the possessor of that knowledge an extraordinary power. A sorcerer who wishes to force some man or woman to do his will has only to refer to the mysterious elements which go to make up the human embryo; if he wishes to control a demon, he alludes to the theory of its generation from the placenta and other concomitants of childbirth. . . . [More generally,] special forms of knowledge give supernatural power. . . . Knowledge is in itself a power since it enables man to avail himself of the forces of nature or of the unseen world.

> R. J. Wilkinson, *Malay Beliefs* (1906)

Ilmu is a central concept in Malay culture that refers to knowledge, especially esoteric or systematic knowledge, science, higher education, and intelligence. The term is most commonly used to denote esoteric religious knowledge concerning the manipulation of spirits and the unseen forces of the natural world. This chapter deals with the distribution of *ilmu* in local society, its acquisition, the uses to which it is put, and some of the ways one goes about counteracting the *ilmu* of those bent on causing one harm. The larger issues include: the gendered dimensions of *ilmu*; the relationship in local culture between knowledge and power; how knowledge and power figure in accounts of personal misfortune; and recent historical changes in the sources and meanings of marginality, uncertainty, and danger, particularly as they relate to gender. The case studies presented in the latter sections of the chapter also help illustrate my more general arguments that femininity and masculinity can only be understood if they are viewed in relation to one another; that cultural knowledge is contextually grounded and deeply perspectival; and that our ethnographic descriptions and interpretations must therefore attend both to polyvocality and to the political economy of contested symbols and meanings.

KNOWLEDGE AND POWER

The possession of *ilmu* is a virtue (though it is sometimes used in unvirtuous ways), and can in fact be seen as a sort of summarizing virtue or "metavirtue" in the system of moral evaluation as a whole. As might be expected, *ilmu* is concentrated among ritual specialists and religious teachers, but it is also widely distributed throughout society. In its concentrated forms, it occurs most commonly among men, for the majority of ritual experts (e.g., healers and shamanic specialists)—and all local and itinerant Islamic teachers—are men. In Bogang, for example, there were ten male healers and shamanic specialists in 1980, but only one woman. That a woman became a healer, and a very successful one at that, is not so much a violation of a largely implicit conceptual linkage between males and *ilmu* (and the strong *semangat*, or "life force," with which both are associated), as testimony to her having "beaten the odds," to borrow the phrase Atkinson (1990:83) employs to describe a similar situation among the Wana of eastern Indonesia.

I have noted that *ilmu* is also widely distributed throughout local society. Indeed, most men and women over sixty years of age seem to know a bit of *ilmu*, which they have acquired either through study or meditation with a knowledgeable elder, or through dreaming, illness, or trance. This broad relatively ungendered distribution of elementary forms of *ilmu* serves to deemphasize the conceptual link between *ilmu* and maleness (and strong *semangat*). So, too, does the fact that men and women alike deploy *ilmu* against both same-sex and cross-sex individuals toward whom they harbor envy, jealousy, or malice.

The deployment of *ilmu* outside of—and even within—healing rituals is not an easy subject to investigate, for villagers tend not to talk openly or casually about *ilmu* (to do so is, among other things, not only dangerous but also a sign that one does not really have [much of] it). And villagers are understandably sensitive to the charges of extralocal reformers that many local forms of *ilmu* are not grounded in the Koran or other religious texts and are therefore "survivals of pre-Islamic days of ignorance"[1]—the traffic in which is gravely sinful. There are, moreover, deep-rooted and pervasive concerns that those who possess *ilmu* can and frequently do use it not only in socially acceptable ways (to cure illness, to find lost or stolen money or other objects, to help mend strained relations), but also in socially unacceptable ways (to cause illness or death, to make money or other valuables disappear, to engender alienation between spouses and others). As I discuss later on, many of these ambivalences about *ilmu* are, at base, ambivalences about human nature and the local system of social relations. Social constraints on the public airing of such ambivalent sentiments serve as a further constraint on the open or casual discussion of *ilmu*.

In private conversations, people in Bogang are quick to point to kinsmen, neighbors, and other community residents who use *ilmu* to gain control of the affections and loyalties of—or otherwise influence—fellow villagers; but direct accusations of the use of *ilmu* in socially unacceptable ways are extremely rare (and, as I discuss in a moment, villagers do not usually acknowledge that they themselves have ever used *ilmu* in nontherapeutic settings, let alone socially unacceptable ways). A few examples of the use of *ilmu* in non-therapeutic contexts will be useful here, particularly since they will help convey a sense of the local social landscape.

Haji Baharuddin, a wealthy pensioner (former school teacher and headmaster) who is widely despised, has run up enormous debts throughout the village and beyond. Though he is not a ritual specialist, he is widely assumed to use *ilmu* to get people to lend him money and/or extend his credit, and to keep his creditors at bay. That he is always in need of pocket money is also partly a function of *ilmu*, for, as I was told on many occasions, his wife (not a ritual specialist) relied on *ilmu* to help make sure that he turned over his monthly pension to her as soon as it arrived at the local post office. (She also accompanied him to the post office to help guarantee that her will prevailed.)

Lebai Ismail, another male elder, is an extremely successful entrepreneur and a local "big man" (*orang besar*) in the dual sense of being able to "get things done" and enjoying many followers who will do his political and other bidding for him. He is the de facto leader of the opposition party (PAS), and also heads the lineage (*perut tengah*) which has been at odds with the wealthiest and most prestigious lineage in the village (*perut darat*) for quite some time. His successes in attracting and retaining loyal followers are due to his being *pandai cakap*, literally, "clever at talking/ speaking," which, in turn, is a function of his knowledge and deployment of *ilmu*.

Datuk (Haji) Latiff was, until his death in 1981, one of Bogang's oldest and most feared *dukun*. He was widely believed to be responsible for the mystically induced death of Kakak Z's young child. He caused the child's death, it was said, because he was incensed that his request for some of the bananas that one of the child's male relatives carried by his house one day was rejected or simply ignored.

Mak Shamsiah and Maimunah have been subject to spirit possession for decades now. Possession by spirits is due, in Mak Shamsiah's case (at least in the official household and lineage version of her illness) to the *ilmu* of an amorous *dukun* whose advances to her she quickly rebuffed; it is due in Maimunah's case to the use of *ilmu* on the part of a man (not a ritual specialist) she ran out on in the midst of their wedding. Maimunah's mother, for her part, relies on *ilmu* "all the time" to help find a mate for Maimunah, and most certainly did so (so I was told) as part of her overall strategy to get me to marry her (see chap. 1).

Though most villagers disavow the use of *ilmu* in non-therapeutic settings, some villagers do acknowledge the deployment of *ilmu* in such contexts. Thus Mak Lang told me that she used *ilmu* on her husband to help make sure that he would always find her attractive and remain faithful to her. And she confided that she brought *ilmu* to bear on her grandson to help ensure that he would study diligently and do well in school. (In the former instance she was successful; not so in the latter.) Such admissions, though rare, are significant, for men and women alike contend that women are more inclined than men to use *ilmu pengasih*, which is often translated as "love magic" but is more appropriately glossed "affection magic." Women's greater reliance on such magic may be due to their greater insecurity in conjugal and other relationships, though as Lambek

(1988:725) has argued for the somewhat similar situation in Mayotte (Comoro Islands), it is more likely a function of their more pronounced concerns with "maintaining peace and order" within their households and kin groups, "articulating social relations," and "looking after reproduction in both the social and biological senses."

Fears and anxieties relating to being victimized by *ilmu*, and by poisoning and spirit possession more generally, seem to be more or less equally distributed among men and women (though this is difficult to gauge with any degree of precision). So, too, are real and imagined illnesses brought about by manipulation of *ilmu*. These points merit emphasis since much of the recent literature concerning mystical attacks among Malays (e.g., Kessler 1977; Ong 1987, 1988, 1990a) focuses on the prevalence of women as victims of highly dramatic forms of spirit possession and effectively glosses over or ignores the prevalence of men as victims of poisoning and sorcery that do not involve possession by spirits taking control of their hosts in dramatic episodes of hysteria. This focus on women's afflictions to the relative exclusion of men's leads to an unjustifiably dichotomized treatment of the roles and meanings of male and female both in "traditional" Malay culture and in the rapidly changing world of contemporary Malaysia. When one examines the major varieties of mystical attack, and not just spirit possession, one gets a more complete picture of Malay understandings and representations of gender, and of marginality, uncertainty, and danger, one that differs in important ways from those in the literature. I will return to this point later on.

Just as men and women are affected by the malevolent uses of *ilmu* in different ways—with men more likely to experience slow wasting away, and women highly dramatic forms of spirit possession—so, too, is there gender-based variation both in modes of acquisition of *ilmu*, and in its deployment in healing rituals. This will be clear from a brief comparison between Pak Daud, my father, and Mak Ijah, Bogang's only female healer.

Pak Daud and Mak Ijah

Pak Daud is a renowned healer specializing in treating victims of poisoning and sorcery who was fifty-six years old when I first met him (1978). He began curing people around 1946, which is when he moved to Bogang and took up residence with his new bride (a cross-cousin, to whom he is still married), and he served as the village headman (*ketua kampung*) from 1962 to 1987. Pak Daud treated victims of poisoning and sorcery—the majority of whom were male—on almost every night of the more than sixteen months that I spent in Bogang during my first period of research, and I had the good fortune of being able to observe many of the healing rituals he performed.

I have commented on Pak Daud's curing sessions elsewhere (Peletz 1988a, 1993a [see also below]), and will simply note here that they are rather matter-of-fact and thoroughly undramatic; for example, unlike Mak Ijah, he does not light candles or burn incense, don special attire, or go into trance during the rites he performs. The *ilmu* Pak Daud deploys in such sessions derives in large part from his father and his father-in-law, both of whom were ritual specialists in their own right. More generally, Pak Daud's apprenticeship entailed lengthy periods of fasting and prayer, submission to numerous food and other prohibitions, and battling with spirits over whom he was learning to gain a measure of control. In the course of his apprenticeship, Pak Daud refined his powers of concentration and prayer, and otherwise developed control over his inner self, the latter being a goal of all *dukun*, and to a lesser extent of all other Malays as well (cf. Anderson 1972:8–13).

Compared to most other villagers, Pak Daud spends a good deal of time in the forest—hunting game animals of various kinds and harvesting *petai* and other forest products—and is thus associated in many villagers' eyes both with the forest (and the malevolent spirits who live there) and with the forest-dwelling aborigines, who are believed to have extremely dangerous (partly because non-Islamic) forms of *ilmu*. This conceptual link enhances villagers' views of his *ilmu*, as does the fact that Pak Daud was forcibly taken to Thailand by the Japanese during their occupation of the Peninsula from 1942 to 1945, and is believed by some villagers to have acquired at least some of his *ilmu* from his journeys among Thais and others living north of the Malaysian-Thai border.

The majority of Pak Daud's patients are from other villages (as are most of Mak Ijah's), but this is a common pattern both in Bogang and elsewhere in Negeri Sembilan (Swift 1965:164), and among Javanese (Geertz 1960:90) and others. As Obeyesekere (1969:180) suggests, it is probably related to the fact that it "facilitates the performance of the priest role by creating a social distance between priest and audience."

Pak Daud is an extremely charismatic individual, but he seldom speaks and is in this regard quintessentially male. Partly because of his taciturn nature, I was less successful than I would have liked in getting him to talk about *ilmu* and healing rituals, and about most other things. Some of his reluctance to talk about *ilmu* and healing rituals was no doubt related to his concern that I might share his secrets with others, for as another of

Bogang's *dukun* once told me, "This *ilmu* is my capital (*modal*), and I can't afford to spread it around and lose it." Perhaps more relevant, though, is that to talk casually or excessively about *ilmu*—either one's own or someone else's—is a sign that one lacks *ilmu*. More generally, in many contexts talking indexes a lack of rationality (*akal*), and since most men, particularly the ritual specialists among them, go to great lengths to assert their rationality (though obviously not always successfully), they do not usually talk much about *ilmu*—or anything else of substance.

In this connection, Siegel's (1978:20–21) observations concerning the culturally similar Acehnese are especially interesting:

> Men seldom speak. This is not because they value silence, but because they think they should speak only when they have something of significance to say. Their speech expresses their rationality; it must therefore be substantive. The result is that it is usually portentous in tone but banal or absurd in content. Limiting oneself to saying only what is so limits one to the obvious or nearly obvious. Conversations with men tend to be confined to subjects such as what bus passed by, prices of various commodities, and other matters of fact. When they speak to their wives men are freed from the constraints of experience, which does nothing to lighten their tone but rather allows them to utter an order for duck for dinner or to have a child washed up and make it sound highly important.
>
> Women, on the other hand, chatter continuously. Their activities are always filled with sounds, illustrating the [Malay-]Indonesian concept of *ramai*—or noise-making activity. What they say is occasionally outrageous, but they feel, nonetheless, that they can say anything. Unlike men, they feel no constraint to be rational, but neither do they conceive of themselves as irrational. Rather their speech to them has authority which comes from a different source. In their struggle with their husbands they win not simply by subverting men's belief in themselves as rational, but by feeling no hesitation to speak. It is my contention that they find a source analogous to the Koran for the resultant authoritative tone in curing rites and dreams.

The situation described (and clearly oversimplified) for Aceh differs in some important ways from that of Negeri Sembilan—for example, in Aceh all healers are women, whereas in Negeri Sembilan and among Malays generally, most are men; and Acehnese women's culturally elaborated concerns with dreaming have no Malay counterpart. Even so, Siegel's observations help us understand some of the differences between Pak Daud and Mak Ijah (aged sixty-seven), who is Bogang's only female healer, and between (Malay) men and women generally.[2]

Mak Ijah is the granddaughter of a Chinese woman who was born in Singapore and adopted while quite young by the nineteenth-century Hill lineage luminary who became *Undang*. Mak Ijah has been married five times and lives in a house set off from all others in the village. Her parents and collateral ascendants are all dead, and she has neither siblings nor any natural children. For these and other reasons, Mak Ijah views herself as having no kin either within the village or outside. In this regard she is extremely atypical; all the more so since she adopted a former neighbor's daughter and reared her as her own for a number of years.

Unlike Pak Daud, Mak Ijah is very expressive and dramatic, extremely high-strung, and quite marginal in the community. And although she is a very successful *dukun* who is able to cure, as she put it, "everything from injured bones to spirit possession except diabetes, high blood pressure, and heart disease," she is viewed with considerable ambivalence and skepticism by many members of the community. There are at least three reasons for this. First, unlike most (if not all) other healers in Bogang, Mak Ijah goes into trance (*terun-menerun*) in the course of her healing rituals. Trance states brought about by spirit possession were long regarded—and to some extent still are—as legitimate sources of authority, much like dreams; but like dreams, they have come to be increasingly delegitimized as authoritative sources for speech and other behavior due to religious and other (e.g., political) changes of the past century that have encouraged the rationalization of village religion, and in particular the demise of most forms of shamanism and spirit cults. All things—and people—associated with trance states, shamanism, and spirit cults are thus viewed by villagers with ever increasing ambivalence and skepticism.

Second, Mak Ijah financed her pilgrimage to Mecca with money obtained from patients, whom she is widely believed to have exploited. Though concerns that *dukun* exploit their patients are widespread, they are especially pronounced when *dukun* appear to profit handsomely from the ritual services they provide (as Mak Ijah has done).

The third reason Mak Ijah is viewed with much ambivalence and skepticism is that she is anomalous since, as a female, she beat the odds by becoming a *dukun*. The anomaly lies not so much in the fact that females are not supposed to be ritual specialists or repositories of *ilmu*. For until quite recently, midwives, the vast majority of whom were female, drew upon *ilmu* in the course of delivering babies and providing both prenatal and postnatal care, and otherwise plied their trade widely.[3] (One of Bogang's last shamanic specialists [*pawang*], moreover, was a female.) Rather it is that to become a *dukun* or a "big person" (*orang besar*) of any sort presupposes the development and refinement of qualities such as rationality, which are most commonly realized in inner tranquillity/serenity and outward restraint, and which are more strongly associated (at least in official discourse) with males than with females. There is, moreover, the issue of leadership and dependency relations. Traditional leaders' efficacy and spiritual potency were gauged in no small measure by the number of supporters or retainers they could muster, and this is true of contemporary leaders as well. Those who have benefited from a *dukun's* services are his/her *anak ubat* (literally, "medicine children," "children through curing"), and in theory at least they are forever indebted to the *dukun* for restoring their health. The hierarchical/asymmetric component of this relationship is not particularly problematic when the leaders are men; but when they are women and have many male supporters, they are in certain respects out of keeping with the usual state of affairs. This is all the more true now that there are no more traditional midwives and no more female (or male) *pawang*.

Just as Mak Ijah is viewed with more ambivalence and skepticism than Pak Daud, so, too, did she acquire her *ilmu* in more dramatic fashion: she was chanting and fighting off delirium-inducing fever (and perhaps death itself) brought about by her adoptive daughter's attempt to murder her and her husband through sorcery. Mak Ijah's highly charged, near hysterical account of the circumstances leading up to this attack, and of the attack itself—which entailed the mystical injection of needles and stones into their bodies—and its outcome, would easily fill a book. Suffice it to say that her adoptive daughter was furious with her because Mak Ijah refused to agree to transfer some of her land to her, or simply enter the adoptive daughter's name on the back of the land grant so that the land would pass to her when Mak Ijah died. The incensed woman thus contacted both a locally resident Javanese man who (like all other Javanese) is believed to have dangerous forms of *ilmu* ("he has tattoos all over his arms," Mak Ijah confided in me) and local aborigines in the hope that they could provide her with *ilmu* to kill Mak Ijah and her husband. The fee for this service, Mak Ijah told me on a number of occasions, was well over M$700! "How could she do this to me when I raised her as my own for so many years?"

Mak Ijah is far more talkative than other *dukun*, and is in many respects a caricature of female styles of speech and comportment. She talked continuously, and at a feverish pitch; and much of what she said struck me—and my (male) research assistant—as outrageous.[4] She was, nonetheless, an excellent informant, for in our conversations she seemed altogether indifferent to status considerations and to whether or not she appeared rational. Moreover, both she and her husband (who was often present when I spoke with her) were in my experience uncharacteristically forthcoming about the quality of social relations in the village and among Malays in general. In their view, fellow villagers (and most other Malays) know very little about Islam and are consumed by passions of greed, envy, and malice; these, along with obsessive concerns with face and honor, are responsible for the "treachery" (khianat) that suffuses local social relations. Not surprisingly, Mak Ijah's husband would rather have his two acres of rubber trees go untapped than have them worked by someone who might possibly cheat him of his rightful share (50% of the tapper's yield), even though this results in the land lying unworked and hence in a substantially reduced household income. Summing up his experience with tenant tappers in metaphors of food and eating, he said "the [tenant] tapper gets all of the meat, while the owner is left with the sauce" (orang potong dapat daging, orang punya dapat kwa saja). On another occasion he characterized his overall experiences with local reciprocity by saying "you give flowers and get shit in return" (kasih bungga, balas tahi).

These sentiments, shared by Mak Ijah, highlight profound ambivalences concerning human nature and social relations. They also illustrate some of the ways in which breaches of the social order are cast in the imagery of food and eating. When speaking of adultery and of men involved in the offense of sororal polygyny, for example, villagers use expressions indicating that the offender "was given one but ate two" (diberi satu, makan dua). Similarly, villagers liken the crime of incest to cannibalism insofar as they sometimes compare the behavior of individuals involved in incestuous unions with the habits of domesticated chickens who consume scraps of cooked food thrown to them at the end of meals, including the flesh/meat of other chickens with whom they share biogenetic substance (macam ayam makan daging sendiri). We have seen, too, that in local mythology the primordial act of brother-sister incest was followed both by the brother lapping up the discharge that flowed from his sister's vagina as she gave birth, and by brother and sister alike being transformed into pelisit, which, as noted earlier, thrive off the blood they suck from pregnant and postpartum women as well as newborn children. Interestingly, the most detailed version of this myth that I encountered in the field came from Mak Ijah. Of perhaps greater interest is that the concerns realized in the myth (the inversion of proper kin relations, failed biological and social reproduction) are highly congruent with the themes accorded primacy in Mak Ijah's account of her relationship with her adoptive daughter and her acquisition of ilmu more generally.

A brief summary of some of the similarities and differences between Pak Daud and Mak Ijah may be useful here. First the similarities: Pak Daud and Mak Ijah are about the same age, and are associated (albeit in different ways: Pak Daud through marriage, Mak Ijah through adoption and satellite status) both with the same gentry clan (Lelahmaharaja) and with its wealthiest and most powerful and prestigious lineage (*perut darat*). They treat many of the same forms of illness, and both of them acquired their *ilmu* as a result of association with same-sex kin.

As for the differences: Pak Daud acquired his *ilmu* through prayer, observance of food and other prohibitions, and meditation and study with elder kinsmen—all of which required active mastery of Koranic texts (the Word of God) as well as studied control and refinement of his various senses and inner being. Mak Ijah, in contrast, obtained her *ilmu* as a result of near fatal illness (including delirium-inducing fever), trance, and spirit possession brought on by a younger kinswomen's (her adoptive daughter's) attempt to murder her through sorcery—all of which entailed loss of control and lack of agency. Mak Ijah thus calls upon different sources to lend authority to her speech and comportment (trance, possession by spirits, rather than Koranic texts), invokes different intergenerational links in her account of how she acquired *ilmu* (links with the descending, rather than ascending, generation), and is, more generally, more attuned to the future (social and biological reproduction) than the past.

Differences in the quality of—and degree of elaboration concerning —the social relations directly or indirectly implicated in the acquisition of *ilmu* in the two cases are also quite striking: Pak Daud obviously had a high degree of rapport with the male elders from whom he acquired his *ilmu*, though, significantly, he did not comment on this; Mak Ijah's relation with her adoptive daughter, on the other hand, was both treacherous and the subject of extremely detailed, near hysterical elaboration. Some broad inferences can be drawn from these latter differences, but it would be erroneous to conclude that women's relationships are problematic whereas men's are not. The more accurate generalization is that, compared to men, women are more concerned with the tenor of social relations (e.g., maintaining peace and order) within their households and kin groups, and with looking after social and biological reproduction. (Men's moral concerns complement those of women and are, in any event, realized in different contexts. Note, for example, that Pak Daud is able to articulate his moral concerns in his roles as village headman and member of the various village councils that nowadays constitute the principal organs of local government and administration.) Case studies presented in subsequent sections of the chapter illustrate how these concerns are realized in spirit possession and other forms of mystical attack.

Finally, a few comments concerning Mak Ijah and spirit possession among women generally. Mak Ijah's first experience with possession occurred when she was about thirty-five years of age. In this respect (as with many other features of her life) she is highly unusual, for most women who are subject to possession by spirits have their first experience with possession during their late teens or early twenties. This pattern seems always to have obtained. So, too, does the general principle that once a woman is possessed she tends to have recurring bouts of possession throughout her life: "Once possessed, always possessed," as Boddy (1989:177) puts it writing about possession among women in the Sudan. It is difficult to say with certainty why possession should first afflict women during their late teens or early twenties, but I suspect it is because this is when their sexuality and fertility are activated and publicly marked. These developments involve profoundly important psychological and social transformations which serve to impress upon young women both how central they are with respect to the honor, prestige, and reproduction of their households, kin groups, and society at large, and how threatening their activated sexualities, along with their bodily fluids and orifices, can be to themselves and others. The fact that the spirits that possess females are drawn to *fertile* women, and to their activated sexualities, bodily fluids, and orifices in particular, is also relevant here, as is the fact that many of these spirits are believed to be sent by male suitors, who as a group are altogether uninterested in prepubescent (and postmenopausal) females.[5]

The case studies presented below provide a closer look at spirit possession in Bogang. They suggest, among other things, that possession provides women with a morally authoritative source to express and dramatize their most pressing social concerns, and thus serves some of the same purposes as women's curing rites and dreaming among the Acehnese.

SPIRIT POSSESSION OBSERVED: THE CASE OF MAIMUNAH

It was a Friday (February 1979), shortly before noon, and I was participating in a small feast at Mak Rahmah's home. Just after the start of the meal there was a blood-curdling scream from next door. Everyone present seemed to recognize the scream as coming from Mak Rahmah's sister's daughter, Maimunah, who was about twenty-eight years old and worked as a secretary/clerk in a Chinese-run bus company whose offices were located in a small town about eight miles from Bogang. From the very start, Mak Rahmah's son and Maimunah's elder (and only) brother—who had returned home on one of his rare visits—knew that Maimunah was experiencing *kena hantu* (spirit possession). Mak Rahmah and her sister (Maimunah's mother) rushed over to the house, as did most of the others. A few moments later I followed suit.

When I arrived, Maimunah was slouching in a chair in the front room, being restrained by her brother and Mak Rahmah's son. She was struggling with all of her might to be free of their hold, but to little avail; her eyes were glassy and her stare vacant, and she was sweating profusely and weeping as if in great pain. Amidst her sobs Maimunah told Mak Rahmah—whom she dislikes intensely—that she (Mak Rahmah) was *sombong* (arrogant, haughty, conceited, unresponsive to social expectations); Maimunah leveled a similar charge at her elder sister, who was also present. She went on to make a disparaging remark about Mak Rahmah having made the pilgrimage to Mecca, and complained about not having received some cakes she had wanted, which ended up going to someone else close at hand. Neither Mak Rahmah nor the sister seemed upset by these insulting remarks; they claimed it was not Maimunah speaking but the spirit (*pelisit, hantu*) who had temporarily taken control of her.

While Maimunah continued groaning, weeping, and screaming, she was brought into the central room of the house by those who had come to her aid. The latter placed themselves around her and someone fetched some water to be used as the base of a home remedy. Small bits of chili, pepper, and red onion were mixed in with the water, which was then rubbed on her head, arms, feet, chest and legs. Incense was lit and the fumes were blown over her face. Maimunah's sister gathered some of the smoke in her cupped hands and placed her hands firmly over Maimunah's mouth, during which time Maimunah screamed and tried to escape with all her force. Mak Rahmah began reciting Koranic passages and blowing them over Maimunah's body as she rubbed the medicine she had prepared on Maimunah's temple and face, and on other parts of her body.

At this point and for the next ten or fifteen minutes, those present addressed the spirit and asked it how long it had been bothering Maimunah and why it was disturbing her. They screamed at the spirit and commanded it to return whence it had come, adding that it had no right to bother people there, that no one had disturbed it, and so on. This was met with a response, said to be from the spirit, that it had been there "for more than a month." Those present continued to shout at and insult the spirit, calling it stupid (*bodoh*) and stubborn (*degil*) for not leaving Maimunah alone. Maimunah, for her part, complained that her stomach and head hurt, and lapsed into fits of wailing and mournful crying; she was still sweating profusely and looking quite anguished. The reciting of Koranic passages continued for another ten or so minutes, during which time the others laughed at some of Maimunah's (the spirit's) comments, screamed at the spirit to leave Maimunah alone, and made small talk.

It was about this time that someone either asked Maimunah if she wanted the help of a *dukun,* or simply mentioned the name of Pak Daud. I am not certain what was said, but Maimunah (or the spirit) replied that she (it) was frightened of Pak Daud. It was then decided that someone should call Pak Daud to help her through the attack. Pak Daud, who was praying at the mosque, was summoned and soon appeared on the scene.

Pak Daud's arrival was greeted with little ceremony or exchange of information. This is partly because Pak Daud is closely related to Maimunah (he is her adoptive father and mother's sister's husband), and has treated Maimunah for spirit possession on many occasions. Pak Daud was informed that Maimunah was not conscious (*tak sedar*), and he proceeded to recite largely inaudible incantations over a glass of water, which he gave Maimunah to drink. Maimunah drank the water without much difficulty and was later instructed not to eat meat of any variety. Since spirits of the sort afflicting her are thought to like meat, she could encourage the spirit's departure from her body by refraining from consuming its favorite foods.

Pak Daud's other major tack involved the use of a small, thin section of bamboo, about six or eight inches in length, which had a closed safety pin fastened at one end of it. Pak Daud placed the stick between Maimunah's fingers, near where they joined the palm of the hand. With a good deal of force, he then squeezed her fingers together, thus evoking cries of pain from Maimunah (the spirit). This went on for five or ten minutes and was done in the belief that spirits of the sort afflicting Maimunah frequently reside in (or simply linger about) these areas of the body, or in the neck or groin area. The idea is to place strong pressure on such spots so as to make the spirit uncomfortable and therefore much more likely to leave the body of its host.

Pak Daud left Maimunah's house before she regained consciousness, but he did so with the knowledge that the worst of the attack was over. At the same time, he knew that such attacks would most likely recur, partly because Maimunah is notoriously uncooperative when it comes to following his advice concerning food prohibitions and other restrictions. Despite Pak Daud's admonitions not to eat meat, for example, Maimunah proceeded to eat meat the very next day (which she later denied to Pak Daud). Maimunah also refused to have anything to do with the amulet (*tangkal*) that Pak Daud (or another *dukun*) had previously prepared for her, the wearing of which is thought to speed recovery and/or to induce the offending spirit to leave and stay away. More important, though, is that Maimunah is believed to have an especially weak *semangat* and is thus held to be particularly susceptible to spirit possession and emotional breakdown. Owing to her weak *semangat*—this being a condition that is said to prevail to one degree or another among all women (and thus to work against, though not preclude, their attainment of *ilmu*)—Maimunah should not have attended the funeral feast held for her adoptive brother's father-in-law, who died a few days before the attack. She went ahead and attended the feast, however, although (to no one's surprise) she was forced to leave early due to the severity of her headaches, dizziness, and weakness.

Interestingly, Maimunah complained of these same symptoms a few hours before the attack described above, and was taken to one of the local clinics or hospitals for treatment both immediately before the onset of the attack and on the following day. On the latter occasion she was given tranquilizers or sleeping pills and was instructed "not to worry so much." On that same day Maimunah told me that it is "bad" if she gets overly worked up (emotionally). Her mother reiterated the theme when she explained to me that Maimunah's older brother—of whom Maimunah was very fond—had recently returned home on one of his rare visits, and that Maimunah often got very upset on such occasions, since he had never brought his wife (of many years) home to meet his family, and in other ways generally refused to acknowledge his familial ties and obligations. The brother's behavior was a source of considerable pain and embarrassment for Maimunah and other members of her household. So, too, was the fact that shortly after her wedding (which occurred some years before my fieldwork), Maimunah decided that she did not want to have anything to do with the husband who had been chosen for her. Inter alia, this rejection brought great embarrassment and shame to the husband (and his kin), and may well have led him to contemplate or actually engage in sorcery. It is significant, in any case, that the spirit that had repeatedly attacked Maimunah was widely held to be doing the bidding of a rejected suitor, whom no one felt inclined to name.

Before turning to a brief discussion of this case, a few comments of a "follow up" nature may be in order. I saw Maimunah on many occasions in the months following the attack described here, although when Ellen arrived in the village (June 1979) my relationships with Maimunah and other members of her household deteriorated (see chap. 1). (By the time I returned to the field with Ellen, Maimunah had in fact moved out of the village, though she frequently returned for short visits.) In March 1980 Maimunah married a young man (Hamzah) who worked as a warden in the prison in the state capital. Some scandal surrounded the wedding, for before they had gotten married Maimunah and Hamzah had apparently spent some time together unchaperoned, and were thus guilty of *khalwat*. Though not formally regarded as a "shotgun wedding" (*bidan terjun*), Maimunah and Hamzah's wedding was perforce a rather hastily arranged and anxiety laden affair.

When I returned to the field in 1987, I assumed that Maimunah and her husband would have at least two or three children, but this was not their fate, for they experienced fertility problems and had also been unsuccessful in their attempts to adopt a child (see chap. 5). Maimunah, who bore her ill fate rather well, was nonetheless widely pitied on account of her childlessness. She also continued to be plagued by spirits of the sort described above.

Discussion

Viewed from a cross-cultural perspective, the healing ritual outlined here is of interest both for its constituent elements and for what it did not include. Despite the initial, ultimately rather cursory, efforts made to ascertain the identity of the spirit afflicting Maimunah, for example, there was, overall, relatively little interest in identifying the spirit (or its master), or finding out why it had attacked Maimunah. Similarly, no one mentioned any possible transgressions that Maimunah or other members of her household or lineage might have committed in the distant or recent past; and there was little if any stated concern with relationships among her relatives that might have been strained, alienated, or otherwise problematic. And no one paid much attention to the words or other sounds that issued forth from Maimunah (or the spirit); for example, no one seemed to take such words or sounds as signs of how best to deal with Maimunah or the spirit either during the episode of possession or in the future.

Nor, for that matter, was there much concern with Pak Daud's incantations. Recall here that Pak Daud's chanting was barely audible and was altogether unintelligible to everyone present, though it was presumed to derive from or at least to include incantations from the Koran. As I have discussed elsewhere (Peletz 1988a, 1993a), circumstances such as these render analyses of the sort provided by Lévi-Strauss (1963) in his classic study of Cuna Indian cures altogether untenable. Lévi-Strauss argues that the statements made by healers provide a (verbal) language in the form of a myth whose enactment enables the afflicted individual (and others present) to make sense of otherwise meaningless and existentially intolerable illness. This is not the case in Bogang. Rather, in Bogang—and in many other societies, like Tengger (Hefner 1985) and Wana (Atkinson 1987, 1990)—healers typically confirm what patients already know through consultation with relatives and others, though they do of course ritually validate their self-diagnoses and thus vest them with a broader legitimacy and simultaneously help reconstitute and reinvigorate the patients' senses of self, social life, and the cosmos.

In terms of what the ritual did include, it is significant that, prior to Pak Daud's arrival, the females present (Maimunah's sister, mother, and mother's sister) played a far more active role in Maimunah's treatment than did the males present (Maimunah's brother, and her mother's sister's husband and son). This changed dramatically once Pak Daud appeared on the scene, for he is a specialist in the treatment of spirit possession, and everyone present, except of course Maimunah and the spirit afflicting her, deferred to him once he arrived. Indeed, when he arrived he "stole the show," effectively denying or at least eclipsing the role of the women who had been managing Maimunah and her illness before he showed up. In this regard Pak Daud's activities constitute a structural parallel to the roles of titled men who formally officiate at engagements and weddings; for while women do most of the work in arranging and maintaining marriage and affinal relations, it is titled men who monopolize the ritual validation of such ceremonies, thus denying or eclipsing the role of women (and of untitled males) in marriage and affinal relations and in social reproduction as a whole.

The comments made by Maimunah (the spirit) during the episode of possession seem not to have been regarded as particularly significant by those present, but they are of analytic interest nonetheless. Recall that they included criticism of Maimunah's sister and her sister's mother for being *sombong,* as well as disparaging remarks about Mak Rahmah having made the pilgrimage to Mecca, and complaints about not getting a cake that most likely went to another female relative. These remarks might be seen as evidence of status rivalries and competition among female members of the lineage—and among women generally. They might be seen instead—or in addition—as a form of protest against Maimunah's subordinate status vis-à-vis her (female) elders (both her sister and her mother's sister); or, more broadly, as protest against a social system in which elders and males are accorded greater prestige and status than their juniors and females, respectively. In a similar vein, one could perhaps suggest that the struggle between Maimunah (the spirit) and Pak Daud entailed a symbolic protest against Pak Daud—who is not only a renowned healer and the village headman, but also Maimunah's adoptive father and uncle (mother's sister's husband)—and against males overall.

Interpretations along these lines have a long history in the literature on spirit possession (see Lewis [1971] for the locus classicus of such interpretations; see also Lambek [1981:56–69] and Boddy [1989:139–45, 278–79] for well-argued critiques of these views). However plausible they may appear at first glance, they seem to me to be wide of the mark. My understanding of Maimunah's afflictions—and of women's predominance in spirit possession more generally—builds primarily on Siegel's previously cited (1978) work on Aceh, and on recent research on spirit possession in Africa (e.g., Lambek 1981, 1988; Boddy 1989) which suggests that possession is a means of asserting household and kin group identity and one's own relevance in its ongoing reproduction (see also Ong 1987, 1988, 1990a [discussed below]). As Lambek (1988:725–26) argues for Mayotte (Comoro Islands) and beyond, spirit possession "gives women greater scope and authority in activities in which they have always taken an interest: . . . maintaining peace and order" and otherwise "articulating social relations" within their households and kin groups, and "looking after reproduction in both the social and biological senses"; more broadly, through spirit possession women not only "positively articulate kinship ties," but also "exercise their general moral concerns."

Bear in mind here that Maimunah's possession occurred very shortly after two profoundly disconcerting events, both of which served to foreground moral/existential dilemmas inherent in social reproduction and all social relations. The first of these events was the death of her adoptive brother's father-in-law, an event which was very disturbing to Maimunah and other members of her kin group and neighborhood, partly because (like all deaths) it made it painfully clear that one's abilities to control one's own life and others—in short, one's autonomy and social control—are ultimately quite limited. (Recall also that Maimunah had been instructed not to attend the funeral.) More generally, this death (like all others) served as a distressing reminder that total control over others is never really assured since everyone (each and every other) is endowed with some measure of autonomy and ultimately dies, and that there is, therefore, an inherent threat of danger and rejection in all social relations (cf. Weiner 1976).

The second disconcerting event was the apparently unexpected ("surprise") return home of Maimunah's elder brother, who had "married badly," had never introduced his wife and children to his parents or siblings, and, to make matters worse, rarely visited his parents or other relatives. The brother's return home highlighted the fragility of social (most notably familial) relations, particularly since it could not help but focus attention on his inappropriately long absences from his natal household and village which, along with the rest of his behavior, clearly entailed an inversion of the behavior expected of him as a son, brother, and kinsmen more generally. (It might have also sparked remembrance of Maimunah's abortive marriage.) Maimunah's possession might be seen in part as the lodging of a moral claim on her brother, who should have been her moral guardian but obviously abandoned her, especially since, as Maimunah's mother told me (and as her brother undoubtedly knows), "Maimunah gets possessed when she gets extremely upset, and she gets upset whenever her brother comes home." At the same time, whatever the factors "motivating" Maimunah's episode, her possession distracted attention away from her brother's return home, and from his inappropriate behavior as a whole, and thus served both to maintain peace and order within, and to unite (if only temporarily) her household and kin group. If only on this latter account, Maimunah's possession enabled her to assert her relevance with respect to the positive articulation of kinship ties.

Let us now reconsider the comments made by Maimunah (the spirit) during the episode of possession. Rather than view them as evidence of status rivalries among female kin (or women generally), or as a protest against Maimunah's subordinate status vis-à-vis elders and men, I would suggest that they should be interpreted as ritual dramatization of moral concerns with the tenor of social relations within households and lineages, and, more specifically, with the importance within those relations of equality and reciprocity. Maimunah and her mother's sister, of course, belong to the same lineage, and they are next door neighbors linked through co-heirship since the land on which their houses are located was originally a single plot owned by the woman who was the mother both of Maimunah's mother and the latter's sister. Despite the equality and reciprocity that should prevail among members (particularly same-sex individuals) of the same lineage, especially those linked through co-heirship, there are marked disjunctions between the economic and prestige standing of the two households; to wit, Mak Rahmah's household is extremely wealthy and prestigious by any local criteria, whereas Maimunah's is quite poor and enjoys very little prestige. Maimunah and other members of her household have long felt slighted by Mak Rahmah and others of her household, and have felt, more generally, that they are not treated as equals. The critical remarks made by Maimunah (the spirit) during the episode of possession may thus be seen as the lodging of a moral claim on Mak Rahmah's household to toe the line in this regard; and, more broadly, as a moral reminder that Maimunah and her mother (Mak Rahmah's sister) are of the same lineage as Mak Rahmah, and thus share lineage identity. Maimunah's (the spirit's) remark about her elder sister being *sombong* may be interpreted in similar terms; for while they are sisters and therefore equal in many respects, Maimunah's sister is older and consequently enjoys many prerogatives not extended to Maimunah.

Themes of reciprocity and failed reproduction are also evident in the implicit understanding that Maimunah's spirit master is a rejected suitor, which, in turn, can be read as a clear symbolic—and counter-hegemonic—statement that suitors/spouses, and men especially, sow dissension among natal kin, particularly women, despite their obviously being necessary for reproduction in all senses of the term. Such themes also appear both in the beliefs that the type of spirit afflicting Maimunah (the *pelisit*) was born of a primordial incestuous union between brother and sister that entailed a form of cannibalism and failed reproduction (the child born of the union would never have been able to marry or have [legitimate] children), and in the belief that such spirits feed off the blood of, and thus pose potentially fatal threats to, both pregnant and postpartum women as well as newborn children. Similar themes dominate Mak Ijah's narrative of the circumstances leading to her acquisition of *ilmu* (and her comments on local sociality); they also suffuse the contrasting accounts of Mak Shamsiah's illness and misfortune, which I discuss below.

This is not to suggest that only women attend to these matters. Men are involved with such themes as well, though the arenas (and idioms) in which they express them differ. Men are allowed and expected to display their moral concerns in the more universalistic arenas provided by Islam and formal politics, both of which have become increasingly disassociated from spirit possession (cf. Lambek 1988:725–26). Men also exercise such concerns in illness brought about by poisoning and forms of sorcery that do not usually involve dramatic possession of the sort described here, but rather slow wasting away. That men's moral interests are displayed in this way, rather than through possession by spirits which suddenly take control of, talk through, and otherwise merge and identify with them, is undoubtedly related to the fact that gradual wasting away is far less of a threat to their masculinity than is the dramatic loss of control entailed in spirit possession. Also relevant is that the socialization process leaves men with ego and body boundaries that are more rigid and less flexible and permeable than those of women (cf. Chodorow 1978:169). Though villagers do not employ (psychoanalytic) terminology of this sort when discussing gender differences (or anything else), their interpretations of why men are less prone to spirit possession than women do resonate with psychoanalytic perspectives insofar as they place considerable emphasis on the fact that, compared to women, men are less easily "poked," "pierced," "invaded," and "taken over" by spirits; and that they "worry far less" and are "far less easily upset/traumatized" by death, poverty, and other (especially domestic) hardship. The death and household hardship to which villagers refer in these interpretations are not abstractions but actual death and hardship within one's own household, particularly the death of one's own children. This is to say that men are viewed in local culture as (self-)identifying less with their children and with others in their social universe, and with social and biological reproduction as a whole.

Interestingly, these views of the differences between men and women also find expression in villagers' interpretations of *latah*—a behavioral complex involving echolalia, echopraxia, and other forms of "pathomimetic" behavior which is extremely widespread in the Malay-Indonesian world, and which is a cultural elaboration of the startle reflex found among all humans. There is a vast (and rather clichéd) literature on *latah* which need not concern us here.[6] Suffice it to say that *latah* is very common in Bogang and usually involves middle-aged and elderly women who are rather poor, destitute, and marginalized; that it often entails scatological humor that is harnessed to counter-hegemonic critiques of the social order; and that it bears a family resemblance to spirit possession inasmuch as it provides women a means through which they can articulate and dramatize their moral concerns. Most relevant in the present context is that when villagers are queried on the subject of why *latah* occurs primarily among women, they respond that it does so because women are more easily startled, have weaker *semangat*, and are, more generally, more inclined to lose control (give in to their fears and anxieties, indulge their "passions") than men. They also cite circumstances of poverty or the loss of a child as factors which induce *latah* in otherwise non-*latah* women, such as Mak Zuraini, who was never subject to *latah* until she experienced the deaths of two of her children. As my mother put it: "Sometimes *latah* occurs as a result of *keturunan* (one's ancestry), but sometimes it is because of *susah* (worry). Women worry more than men, are more anxious, or at least are quicker to verbalize their worries and anxieties." To help illustrate the broader point about male-female differences, she gave the telling example of her son's upcoming wedding, commenting that while she was extremely anxious about it, her husband wasn't really worried at all. He had confidence that they would have enough money to "pull it off," and that "everything would work out."

Some observers have suggested that *latah* might well have originated during the early years of Malays' experiences of European domination and colonial rule, for the earliest written accounts of the complex come from Europeans who employed Malay servants in their homes and observed the complex among them. Michael Kenny (1990), however, argues convincingly that in all likelihood the *latah* complex is of much greater antiquity. So, too, does Leonard Andaya, who has made the important observation that in various parts of the pre-modern Malay world, *latah* was attributed to possession by spirits (Leonard Andaya, personal communication, 1991; see also Kenny 1990: 132–33). The fact that *latah* is no longer viewed in relation to the world of spirits or anything else bearing on the realm of the sacred is yet another manifestation of the secularization and rationalization process discussed in this and earlier chapters (see also Peletz 1988a, 1988b, 1993a, 1993b).

Many of the themes taken up in the preceding pages are addressed (albeit from different perspectives) in the case studies of Mak Shamsiah and Rashid presented below, which also highlight the fundamental point that we need to attend to female *and* male afflictions if we hope to understand gender among Malays in Negeri Sembilan or other parts of the Peninsula. These case studies are in some ways richer than that of Maimunah, however, for I encountered contrasting interpretations of the illnesses and misfortunes at issue. These contrasting accounts indicate that cultural knowledge is deeply perspectival; that cultural phenomena lend themselves to many different readings; and that, as such, our ethnographic descriptions and interpretations need to make full provision for polyvocality and the political economy of contested symbols and meanings.

MAK SHAMSIAH AND HER DEMONS

Mak Shamsiah was born in Bogang in about 1935 and was thus about forty-three when I first met her in 1978. The youngest of six children, she belongs to one of the village's gentry clans (Lelahmaharaja), and is, like Maimunah, a member of the clan's wealthiest and most prestigious and powerful lineage (*perut darat*, the "upland lineage"). Unlike Maimunah, however, Mak Shamsiah's immediate kin include the former governor of a neighboring state (her mother's brother, now deceased) as well as a highly placed national-level politician (her older brother). Another of Mak Shamsiah's brothers holds the title of clan subchief (*buapak*), and is thus the highest ranking *adat* figure in the village. Mak Shamsiah's sisters, I might add, are also quite wealthy, and both of them have made the pilgrimage to Mecca (one went twice). Mak Shamsiah and her husband, who are very well off as well, were scheduled to make the pilgrimage in 1980, but due to the severity of Mak Shamsiah's illness, her husband felt it best to postpone the trip. They finally went to Mecca in 1985.

During my first fieldwork I saw Mak Shamsiah on many occasions since she lived in the house next door, but I didn't get to know her all that well because she was severely depressed and often seemed extremely disoriented and altogether incapable of any form of verbal communication. One of my main recollections of her from the first fieldwork was seeing her sitting in the corner of her sister's kitchen, looking anxiously about, while a group of lineage sisters and other women prepared food for a feast. I remember, too, being warned by women and others present not to walk or stand behind her lest she get startled and "have an attack." I did get to know her husband, however, who discussed many of his domestic and other concerns with me, including his wife's illness. And I had a number of conversations with Mak Shamsiah's widowed mother (Wan), who lived with Mak Shamsiah and her husband and young son. I also spent a fair amount of time with Mak Shamsiah's nine-year-old son, Hassan, who was my companion and buddy until I got married (at which point he became "too shy" to hang around the house) and her nineteen-year-old son, Kadir (described briefly in the discussion of *pondan* in chap. 3), who had moved to Kuala Lumpur but frequently visited Bogang on weekends. I did, moreover, spend a good deal of time with Mak Shamsiah's brother and two sisters (and their families). During the first fieldwork, then, most of what I knew of Mak Shamsiah came from her relatives and neighbors, and not from Mak Shamsiah herself.

In 1952, when Mak Shamsiah was about seventeen years old, she married a cross-cousin (Pakcik Hamid) from a neighboring village, who was chosen for her by her relatives. Pakcik Hamid worked as a policeman in the predominantly Chinese city of Singapore, and shortly after the marriage Mak Shamsiah joined him there, where they took up residence in the local police barracks. In the years that followed her move to Singapore, Mak Shamsiah gave birth to six children (three boys, three girls), one of whom (a boy) was severely deformed and died shortly after being born. She knew during her pregnancy with this child that something was wrong, for she felt unusually sick, not just dizzy or tired, and her belly quickly grew very large. When the baby was born it made one small noise and just stopped breathing. It had no cranium and its arms and legs were curved inwards at strange angles and could not be straightened out. When the *imam* came to read prayers (*baca doa*) and prepare for the funeral, he told Mak Shamsiah and her husband that they were fortunate that the baby was taken back by God so quickly. Otherwise, he said, life for the family would have been very difficult, as the child never would have had a normal life. He comforted them with words to this effect, reassuring them it was better this way.

After moving to Singapore, Mak Shamsiah became quite ill, though it is not clear when her illness began. By her own account, the onset of her illness dated from shortly after her move to Singapore, though before she had any children, hence sometime around 1953. This was before her husband settled down to the idea of marriage and stopped staying out late at night. He had been very handsome as a young man, Mak Shamsiah told me, and was "dark and good looking, like a Hindustani." He had a roving eye, however, and before their marriage he had seriously considered marrying a Chinese woman, a plan which was foiled by the latter's relatives, who refused to entertain the idea of her converting to Islam. In any event, during my first period of research from 1978 to 1980, Mak Shamsiah was still debilitated, though living back in Bogang with her husband and children. In 1987 she seemed much better, though I was informed that she still experienced bouts of severe illness.

Mak Shamsiah's illness and misfortune have manifested themselves in various ways: the previously noted birth of a deformed child who died immediately after being born; a lack of interest in caring for one of her other children when it was born; her refusal to greet people and perform basic chores and responsibilities seen as central to her role as a married woman (such as cooking rice and washing clothes); and her dancing at night by herself. During the first period of fieldwork, Mak Shamsiah seemed to spend much of the time sleeping, and her husband and mother took over many of her chores. When she did appear outside the house, she seemed extremely disoriented and depressed.

The first and seemingly most widespread account of Mak Shamsiah's problems (the "official" household and lineage version) refers back to the

Figure 15. Mak Shamsiah with Pakcik Hamid

time when she and her husband lived in Singapore. One day while Mak Shamsiah's husband was away at work, a Malay *dukun* from Negeri Sembilan who Mak Shamsiah or her husband had sought out on a previous occasion came to the house and proclaimed his romantic interest in her. Mak Shamsiah reportedly attacked him with a broom and/or slammed the door in his face. The amorous *dukun* was gravely incensed by this rejection, and he cast a spell on her, which affects her to this day: Whenever he thinks of her, for example, she thinks of him; she also hears voices (including the *dukun*'s?) that tell her to dance, not to work or cook rice, and so on.

The second explanation of Mak Shamsiah's personal misfortune comes from Mak Rahmah, a relatively wealthy cousin who belongs to Mak Shamsiah's "lineage branch" (*pangkal*), and who is also one of her immediate neighbors. Though Mak Rahmah knows and apparently believes the story of Mak Shamsiah's encounter with the amorous *dukun* in Singapore, she also holds that Mak Shamsiah's illness is at least partly a result of Mak Shamsiah's throwing her trash over her fence into the vacant lot next door. This disturbs and insults the spirits (*jinn*) residing there, and they have taken their vengeance on her either by helping bring about her illness in the first place or by prolonging it. Mak Rahmah also told me that because Mak Shamsiah does not pray much, she has not gotten better, although she (Mak Rahmah) also realizes that the illness is responsible for her lack of prayer.

The third explanation of Mak Shamsiah's illness comes from Mak Zaini, a relatively poor clan sister who lives on the other side of the village and who belongs to a lineage with which Mak Shamsiah's lineage has been at odds for quite some time. Interestingly, two of the principal actors in the feud involving the two lineages are Mak Shamsiah's older brother—the highest ranked *adat* figure in the village—and Mak Zaini's older brother, who has also held clan titles in the past and is, independently of his titles, a local "big man" with a reputation for "getting things done" and for using *ilmu* to attract followers and supporters and enhance his prestige. The details of the feud need not concern us. What is important here is that Mak Zaini's explanation of Mak Shamsiah's illness focuses on a grave offense against "ancestral property" (*harta pesaka*) and the traditions of the ancestors that was committed, she says, by Mak Shamsiah's mother's brother, Datuk Abdul Ghani. The offense involved a gold *keris* and other gold jewelry or ornaments that one of Mak Zaini's relatives had asked Datuk Abdul Ghani to store in his house for safekeeping. Mak Zaini's ancestors owned this ancestral property, but they were poor and lived in a dilapidated, bamboo-slat house, and they thought it wise to have someone else keep it for them. Datuk Abdul Ghani's crime is that he later turned around and sold it, and kept the proceeds. And this offense is what caused Mak Shamsiah's illness. It was wrong (and dangerous) because the property did not belong to Datuk Abdul Ghani (he had no right to sell it) and because ancestral property like this should not be sold (or mortgaged) since it is sacred and reminds villagers of their parents, grandparents, and great-grandparents. Mak Zaini reassured me that she would never have the courage to sell any such property, even if *adat* allowed her to. She added that those who sell ancestral property are likely to become *gila* (crazy, insane) and even die. It is thus "natural," "only to be expected," Mak Zaini told me in 1980, that Mak Shamsiah cannot get out of bed, sleeps much of the day, and is otherwise unable to function. If Datuk Abdul Ghani escaped unharmed or somehow avoided the repercussions of his actions, his children and other descendants would surely suffer one way or the other.

The fourth explanation of Mak Shamsiah's illness comes from her son, Kadir, who works and lives in the largely Chinese city of Kuala Lumpur, where he has spent most of his time since leaving school. Kadir and I spoke about his mother's situation in 1979, when Kadir was about nineteen years old. He told me that he did not accept the conventional wisdom concerning his mother's disorders, which holds that her problems stem from the amorous *dukun* casting a spell on her. He believes that his mother is simply a very anxious person; she worries too much about her children, Kadir explained, and she fears they will consort with drug addicts and other types of "bad people" (*orang jehat*) in the city. She probably worries that he has a girlfriend, Kadir added, and that the girlfriend is not the "right type." (On this count some of her fears seem well grounded, for as Kadir pointed out, he does have a girlfriend, and she is half-Indian and half-Chinese; the girlfriend enjoys going to discos, as does Kadir, spending money, and having a good time; on top of all this, she doesn't have any interest in cooking and other household chores.) Putting his comments in a larger context, Kadir went on to say that he doesn't believe in ghosts and spirits, and that he views the village's sacred shrines (*keramat*) and the various rituals associated with them—along with ritual feasts at the graveyard—as against the teachings of Islam. All such things are tied up with "superstition," and reflect a lack of formal education and a relatively shallow understanding of Islam.

These, then, are the four different interpretations of Mak Shamsiah's illness that I encountered in Bogang. Despite the underlying structural similarities in these accounts (about which more in a moment) there are important differences. Contrasting features of the four accounts include, most obviously, the types of relationships held to be at the heart of the problem (which involve suitors, spirits, clansmen, and children); the types of emotions assumed to have engendered Mak Shamsiah's illness (unrequited love, feelings of rejection, loss of face); proprietary anger and betrayal (on the part of local spirits and clansmen alike); and parental anxiety.

Other contrasts involve the issue of mystical agency. In the first account, mystical agency manipulated through the *ilmu* of a rejected suitor cum *dukun* is responsible for Mak Shamsiah's afflictions. In the second account, mystical agency is realized in the actions of spirits, who are held to be at least partly responsible for these afflictions. The third account makes reference to mystical agency as well, but does not specify the medium or channel through which this agency comes into play. And in the fourth account there is no reference to mystical agency.

The fourth account, it will be recalled, comes from Mak Shamsiah's son, Kadir, who works and lives in Kuala Lumpur, and is in many ways far less "traditional" than the majority of Bogang's full-time residents. We could perhaps generalize here and conclude that Kadir's disinclination to invoke mystical agency and any type of human malevolence in his account of his mother's illness reflects the experiences and perspectives of Malays in urban areas, and of "modern" Malays in general. There are no solid grounds for this conclusion, however, even though some of Kadir's experiences and comments obviously resonate with the more cosmopolitan orientations found among many urban and "modern" Malays. In fact, as Provencher (1979:48) discovered on the basis of his research among Malays in the Kuala Lumpur area, "most urban Malays who become ill suspect that they have been poisoned"; more importantly, as I discuss below, "the fear of [poisoning and] sorcery is *greater* . . . in urban communities than in rural villages" (emphasis added).

As for the underlying structural similarities, all four accounts interpret Mak Shamsiah's illness both relationally (in terms of Mak Shamsiah's social relations with others) and in a moral framework. These generalizations hold even for Kadir's interpretation of Mak Shamsiah's illness, which focuses on her anxiety concerning her children, the urban, primarily non-Malay, social fields in which they find themselves, and their prospective spouses and mates. In addition, all four accounts speak to social relations that are strained, alienated, or otherwise disordered, and that are fraught with ambivalent and/or contradictory sentiments and behavior (e.g., the suitor who turns on and harms the object of his affection, the normally quiescent spirit who attacks). Other similarities include actual or potential breakdown or failure in reciprocity, reproduction, or both; and loss of autonomy and social control due to actions of people (suitors, relatives, or others) or spirits (or both) who (mis)appropriate power for their own individualistic and otherwise socially divisive ends.

Seven Years Later

During my second period of fieldwork I spent a great deal of time with Mak Shamsiah, for by this time her illness had abated somewhat and she was quite outgoing and communicative, though still very moody and given to episodes of screaming and occasional frenzy. The house we lived in during the second fieldwork was next door to Mak Shamsiah's (as the first had been), and its location was highly conducive to our interaction with her since, unlike our first house, it was not separated from Mak Shamsiah's by a small ravine and wire fences. It wasn't simply the location of our house, however, that led us to seek out Mak Shamsiah (and vice versa); for she was extremely friendly and warm to us (e.g., she took an instant liking to Zachary, and was forever treating him to sweet cakes, fruits, and other local delicacies), and we thoroughly enjoyed her company. Because Mak Shamsiah and Kak Suzaini (the woman who cooked for us and became one of our dearest friends) were so close, we had additional reason to spend time with her.

Though she now was "much better," both she and her husband told me (as did others) that she was not altogether cured. As she put it on one occasion when I asked her if we could discuss various aspects of gender, "Why do you want to ask me all sorts of questions when my mind [still] isn't right?" I do not have any detailed information about the timing of Mak Shamsiah's partial recovery; the only explanation I heard was that the amorous *dukun* in Singapore had died, and that, being dead, he could no longer exert any control over Mak Shamsiah. (I would have liked to know more about the timing of the onset of Mak Shamsiah's mother's senility; e.g., if it helped "jar" her into good health, or, alternatively, served to prolong her illness, but I have no accurate information on this.)

I never asked Mak Shamsiah about the cause(s) of her misfortune(s), for it seemed too delicate a subject, especially since she still experienced bouts of severe illness, and I feared that questions on the topic might conjure up unpleasant and painful associations and thus "set her off." She brought up the subject on a few occasions, however, remarking, for example, that the onset of her illness began before her husband had settled down to the idea of marriage. She mentioned as well that during the early part of her marriage he frequently berated (and sometimes struck) her, and that there were many *pantang* (taboos) that she failed to observe. She also recounted that earlier in her marriage she "worried a lot" about Pakcik Hamid and Kak Suzaini. Kak Suzaini had a habit of coming to the house in the evening with her children, ostensibly to watch television, but she was frequently wearing makeup, along with sleeveless and rather low-cut, revealing blouses. Pakcik Hamid and Kak Suzaini would laugh and laugh until late in the evening—long after Mak Shamsiah had gone to bed—and though she brought her children with her, they often fell asleep on the verandah and thus could not serve as chaperones or obstacles to any form of intimate behavior. Mak Shamsiah informed Pakcik Hamid she didn't like this type of behavior, and he stopped. She also told him, half-jokingly, that while she wouldn't mind if he took another wife after she died (she was convinced that he would outlive her), she would "slit his throat" if he did so while she was still alive.

In other conversations, which focused largely on gender, Mak Shamsiah told me that women are more susceptible to spirit possession than men because, compared to men, women have "less" or "weaker" *semangat*. Similarly, women are more prone to *latah* because they "worry" (*susah hati*) more than men and are more easily "startled" (*runsing*). More generally, whereas women and men have the same "rationality" (*akal*), women's "passion" (*nafsu*) is stronger than men's. God made them this way; and this is why they have a stronger sense of "shame" (*malu*). If they didn't have stronger "shame," their "passion" would be even more obvious than it already is, and they would be more "ferocious" and "wild" (*ganas*) than men are. She mentioned, too, that women are often more "fierce" (*garang*) than their husbands.

While in previous years Mak Shamsiah had obviously been quite anxious about her relationship with her husband—and perhaps especially concerned that difficulties in their marriage could lead to its dissolution and thus call into question her own relevance to the ongoing reproduction of her household and lineage—she was no longer. In fact, one of the more unusual things about her during the second period of fieldwork was how communicative she was about her husband, her positive feelings for him, and her apparent security in the relationship. I remember seeing her wearing her husband's *sarong* on various occasions, and when I asked her if it was his she replied yes and then explained that she "missed him" when he spent much of the day out of the village at his garden (*kebun*), and that wearing the *sarong* helped remind her of him. Such admissions of positive affection and intimacy between husband and wife are, in my experience, relatively unusual. Moreover, she sometimes commented on what a "good man" he was, how kind he had been to her during all the years that she was ill, and that he could have abandoned her, as many of his friends and relatives apparently told him to do, especially since he had a salary/pension, an automobile, and was otherwise highly desirable and thus could have easily found another wife.

Mak Shamsiah's relationship with her husband was no longer a major source of anxiety or concern, but she was very much preoccupied with the circumstances and relational dilemmas of other members of her household, such as her son Kadir, who, as noted earlier, had a non-Malay, "mixed-race" and (by local standards) otherwise extremely inappropriate girlfriend, and expressed no interest in getting married. Her main problem, though, was her eighty-six-year-old mother, Wan, who had become quite senile, and was subject to recurring hallucinations and nightmares. Wan, who was exceedingly thin and commonly refused to eat, spent much of her time hunched over in the compound, picking weeds (and occasionally eating rotten fruit that had fallen from *rambutan* and other fruit trees), but she was also given to wandering around the village in a daze, especially in the late afternoon and early evening hours. During these forays Wan often invited relatives and neighbors to imagined feasts, thus recalling both the grandeur of her healthier days and the time when her husband was still alive. These invitations were received good-naturedly, and Wan was in fact humored in many situations. For the most part, however, Wan was regarded as a terrible nuisance, and was the object of much ridicule and scorn. Some of her closest relatives locked their doors and the gates surrounding their wells when she appeared in their compounds, drove her away, and otherwise treated her "like dirt." This upset Mak Shamsiah tremendously, particularly since, as Mak Shamsiah pointed out to me on numerous occasions, many of these same people had frequently partaken of Wan's generosity when she was still healthy. In some ways more distressing, though, was Mak Shamsiah's fear/premonition that Wan would get run over and killed by the train which passed through the village. Mak Shamsiah had forbade Wan to cross the railroad tracks, but Wan didn't listen—or simply forgot—particularly since she needed to cross the tracks to get to the *kedai* one of her daughters operated, and to attend the mosque.

Wan's behavior created problems in Mak Shamsiah's relationship with her husband. Her hallucinations and nightmares made it extremely difficult for Mak Shamsiah and her husband to get a good night's sleep. And Wan claimed that Pakcik Hamid was "always hitting her" and "wanted to kill her." This was most likely an exaggeration, though on one occasion, when Wan was tearing down clean laundry that had just been hung out to dry, I did see him strike her with a long bamboo pole. More generally, both Mak Shamsiah and her husband mentioned that their lives were not at all "their own" since they had to watch Wan all of the time. They couldn't even go to Singapore to visit their daughter and grandchildren, particularly since doing so would require taking Wan with them (an impossibility) or leaving her behind (also impossible, because "there was no one to care for her" [even though three of her other children lived in the village]).

Wan's behavior also exacerbated tensions in Mak Shamsiah's relations with her brothers and sisters (though the fact that Wan was alive also kept some of these tensions in check [see below]). This was because Mak Shamsiah shouldered virtually all of the responsibility for looking after Wan, even though she was one of six children. When Wan could still cook and work, everyone used to welcome and love her; now that she had "lost her mind" and "reverted to childhood," she couldn't do any of these things anymore, and no one wanted to look after her. To make matters worse, Wan wouldn't let anyone else take care of (even bathe) her, even though she spoke fondly of her son Haji H., claiming (falsely) that he gave her money and other presents, and was otherwise very good to her. But Haji H. wouldn't even come to "look at her face" or visit her, even though he came to this part of the village (e.g., to talk with the anthropologist) now and then. Mak Shamsiah's two sisters (Wan's other daughters), for that matter, didn't do anything except help give her a bath once in a while. Mak Shamsiah went on to say that she didn't want to speak ill of her brothers and sisters (literally: cause them to stink or rot [*busukkan saudara*]), but they just didn't do anything for Wan, even though she was mother to all of them.

Mak Shamsiah frequently told me—and anyone else who cared to listen—that she didn't know what she was going to do if Wan "lives to be one hundred." The problems would only get worse, she lamented, with much frustration—and desperation—in her voice.

Wan's advanced senility, which in many respects (e.g., its debilitating effects) paralleled the earlier (more severe) forms of Mak Shamsiah's illness, brought into painfully sharp focus what many villagers saw as the uncertainties and dangers inherent in aging and social reproduction. To wit, that once they ceased to be (re)productive and thus of value to their kin and society at large, they would be cast aside and otherwise mistreated and abused, and would thus experience rather severe (if not complete) loss of autonomy and social control. Such treatment entailed the most heinous violation of norms informing relationships between children and their parents, yet it was a common theme in the everyday discourse of villagers, particularly women. So, too, was the theme of ambivalence, alienation, and tension among siblings, which also figured into Mak Shamsiah's account of her dilemmas with Wan. Interestingly, however, while Mak Shamsiah cited the problems Wan's behavior created with her (Mak Shamsiah's) siblings, she made no reference to the fact that the problems would most likely become far more pronounced after Wan's death. Such a scenario was highly probable since Wan would no longer be around to mediate petty disputes and everyday tensions and antagonisms—and otherwise articulate social relations—among her children. Nor would she be able to serve as a palpable symbol of their common interests and identities. There was, moreover, the issue of the land and other property owned by Wan that would have to be divided among her children after she died. This was potentially a source of great tension and strain, even though the land (especially residential and rice land) has relatively little monetary value in today's economy.

The concerns—with articulating social relations, preserving peace and order within the family, and looking after reproduction in both the social and biological senses of the term—that surface in Mak Shamsiah's account of her problems with Wan resonate deeply with the common themes underlying the various interpretations of Mak Shamsiah's illness that I discussed earlier. Such concerns are, to reiterate my earlier point, quintessentially (though by no means exclusively) female. Men's concerns with the articulation of social relations, peace, order, and reproduction are in many respects both parallel and complementary to those of women, though they tend to be cast in terms of more expansive social units (lineage, clan, village, religious community, and ethnic/racial grouping) and in different idioms (political, religious, ethnic/racial). They are, moreover, frequently expressed in different, more public arenas (village councils, local political party organizations and activities, prayer houses and mosques) that have long been associated with maleness.

It would be a mistake to overvalorize these contrasts, however. For men no less than women are susceptible to, and victimized by, mystical attack (though this is commonly glossed over in the literature). And while the forms of mystical attack vary (with women being more subject to dramatic episodes of possession by spirits, and men more likely to be afflicted by slow wasting away), the attacks on men and women alike are experienced—and interpreted by others—as testimony to the dilemmas inherent in reciprocity and reproduction. The following case study will serve to illustrate the point.

THE CASE OF RASHID

Rashid was born in Bogang in about 1957. He is a member of the same clan (Lelahmaharaja) and lineage (*darat*) as Mak Shamsiah, and is her sister's son. Rashid's household is without question the wealthiest household in the village. This is largely because of the economic successes of his late father, Haji Yahya, who died in December 1986. Despite his lack of formal education, Haji Yahya was a very clever and resourceful businessman who engaged in various sorts of entrepreneurial activities. He had a hand in the financing and construction of the village mosque, and was involved in other construction both locally and in other states. Perhaps most important, though, is the lumber company he set up and operated, apparently with the help of his wife's brother (a high ranking official in the Ministry of Forests) and some Chinese businessmen. His sons, including Rashid, are involved in the family business and are all doing extremely well financially.

Rashid fell sick about a month after his father died. The first time I saw him during my second period of research was when I encountered him at the local provision shop (*kedai*) that his mother runs. I expected the worst from the stories I had heard, but still was not prepared for what I saw. Rashid was lying in a chaise lounge that had been covered with a blanket and was propped up behind one of the tables placed in the front of the *kedai*. His head appeared freakishly large since the rest of his body was emaciated and withered. He looked all skin and bones, and his feet were covered with flaking skin and a red substance that I initially mistook for blood (it turned out to be medicine). Rashid greeted me by saying that I looked well and fat, and that he was sick and thin. He had been very ill, he explained; this was his fate (*nasib*), so what could be done? He claimed that he was much better now (at least now he had an appetite and could sleep) and not nearly as thin as before. For the longest time he had no appetite, and could only sleep an hour or so a night; and any wind or clothes that touched his skin caused excruciating pain. Though he still could not walk, he was no longer paralyzed and had feeling in his legs, for which he was extremely thankful.

The first account of Rashid's illness comes from Mak Zaini, the relatively poor woman I referred to earlier as having provided one of the accounts (the third) of Mak Shamsiah's misfortune. Her story of Rashid's illness is basically the same as her account of Mak Shamsiah's afflictions: that it reflects mystical retribution for offenses against "ancestral" property that were committed by Datuk Abdul Ghani, the man who was both Mak Shamsiah's mother's brother and Rashid's mother's mother's brother.

The second account of Rashid's illness comes from Datuk Hamzah, who at eighty-nine years of age was one of the oldest residents of Bogang. Datuk Hamzah was sitting at the *kedai* when I spoke with Rashid, and he said that non-Muslim aborigines (*orang asli*) were responsible for Rashid's afflictions. It was not clear if Datuk Hamzah felt that the *orang asli* did this to Rashid "on purpose" or "accidentally." But he implied that it might not have been done with Rashid in mind. On this point Rashid disagreed (see below). According to Datuk Hamzah, the poison entered Rashid's body through his feet, having been spat on the ground by one or more *orang asli*. He explained to me that the saliva or spit of *orang asli* is poisonous (*bisa*) and that any area spat upon by *orang asli* will become poisonous, even if the spit has long since dried up. Hence you can't step or walk on such spots, or on *orang asli* graves. Datuk Hamzah added that Rashid worked with a lumber firm, was always going into the forest, and might have tread on areas, long since overgrown, that had once been spat upon by *orang asli*. This type of work carried certain dangers.

The third account of Rashid's illness comes from Rashid himself and was recounted in bits and fragments as we sat at the *kedai*. Rashid told me that his sickness began about a month after his father died. He was living on the east coast of the Peninsula at the time, working for his family's lumber company. Someone made him ill, he said, and it was intentional. He was fairly certain that it was one of his business friends or associates (*kawan*), someone he worked with, though he didn't know for sure which one. He attributed it to envy (*dengki*) but did not elaborate on any of these points. Rashid also said that he had gone to "forty or fifty" *dukun* for a cure and had undergone all sorts of tests and treatments, but to no avail. He had tried Malay *dukun*, Chinese healers and acupuncturists, Thai ritual specialists, and Western-oriented medical experts, but with no results. At least one *dukun* told Rashid that his illness "isn't in his [the *dukun*'s] book," hence he could not treat him. At the time of our conversation, Rashid's case was in the hands of a Thai healer, who, as Rashid told me, was not a Muslim. But that's okay, he reassured me, adding that he had also spent about two weeks sleeping in a Chinese temple in the Kuantan area, in hopes that that would help cure him.

The three accounts of Rashid's illness that I encountered bear certain similarities, but they also diverge in important respects. The similarities include both the relational interpretations of Rashid's illness, and the belief that Rashid's problems stem ultimately from human malevolence—

or the automatic activation of mystical agency—triggered by Rashid's or his mother's mother's brother's violation of unspoken codes of propriety (concerning the integrity of ancestral property, territorial domains, and relative equality, respectively).

The contrasts are in some ways more significant. One contrast turns on the nature of the agency believed to have caused Rashid's illness: Mak Zaini's account refers to the automatic activation of mystical agency; Datuk Hamzah's account refers to mystical agency controlled by non-Muslim aborigines, which is automatically activated once a taboo (*pantang*) has been violated, and which may cause harm somewhat indiscriminately; Rashid's account makes no reference to notions of taboo, but refers simply to human envy and malevolence, which were focused on Rashid and intentionally caused him harm. Another salient difference involves the source and meaning of danger and the context in which it occurred. In Mak Zaini's account, the source of danger is not clearly specified though the context is without question the handling, transfer, and safekeeping of ancestral property; in Datuk Hamzah's account, the source of danger is the forest and the non-Muslim aborigines who reside there and have long controlled its resources, power, and secrets; the context of danger is also the forest (or an area once cleared that has long since overgrown). In Rashid's account, on the other hand, the danger emanates from his business friends and associates, their social relations with him, and the envy that suffuses these relations owing (presumably) to Rashid's relative economic success. The context of danger, in turn, is the lumber industry and the highly competitive world of modern capitalist business and trade relations, Rashid's involvement in which enabled him to live exceedingly well for a while, but also nearly cost him his life.

Before turning to a discussion of Rashid's case in relation to the illnesses and misfortunes experienced by Mak Shamsiah, Maimunah, and others in Bogang and beyond, I would like to reiterate that Rashid is but one of dozens of men in Bogang who believe themselves (and are thought by others) to have been poisoned or sorcerized. Facts such as these are of considerable significance for, as noted earlier, some of the most insightful and frequently cited literature on Malaysia focuses on women in highly dramatic episodes of spirit possession, and makes little if any mention of the prevalence of men as victims of poisoning and sorcery that involve gradual wasting away as opposed to dramatic possession by spirits. The more general point is that data from Bogang—and elsewhere in Malaysia—indicate that men are just as likely as women to experience mystical attack.[7] I will return to this theme in due course.

COMMENTARY

The case material and other data presented here testify to the prevalence of the ambivalence, alienation, and tension that exist in Bogang and in other Malay communities in Malaysia. The ambivalence, alienation, and tension to which I refer emerge clearly from the comments of *dukun* such as Mak Ijah, who insists that she was sorcerized by her adopted daughter, and who (along with her husband) has decidedly negative views of human nature and local social relations, especially the role of reciprocity in those relations. Her husband, it will be recalled, summed up his experiences and views concerning reciprocity in social relations in the pithy phrase "you give flowers and get shit in return." These ambivalences and tensions surface in other contexts, as well: for example, in villagers' views of Datuk Latiff, who is believed to use his *ilmu* not only to cure people and mend broken or strained relationships, but also to cause illness, other forms of suffering, and death. There is also the amorous *dukun* in Singapore who is widely held to be responsible for the illness and misfortune that have plagued Mak Shamsiah for more than thirty years.

These ambivalences are but one manifestation and condensed expression of the more general and diffuse ambivalence with which villagers view and approach all social ties, including—indeed, especially—those with neighbors and kin. Most relationships in the community are cast in idioms of kinship (particularly siblingship), which continue to have heavy moral and economic entailments, and even when such relationships are not conceptualized in terms of kinship, they come with potentially burdensome moral obligations. The expectations associated with these obligations can be extremely difficult to fulfill; and in many cases, even when they are fulfilled, they are not reciprocated. Further aggravating problems such as these is villagers' heavy reliance on cash-cropping, and their incorporation into the world market economy more generally, which have resulted not only in the erosion and demise of many traditional, reciprocity-based relations of production and proprietorship, but also in the proliferation of individualistic behavior, non-redistributive institutions, and various forms of inequality and socioeconomic stratification. These and other changes have created new (and intensified preexisting) uncertainties and dangers in villages like Bogang, and are partly responsible for the fact that most relationships in the community are conducive to the realization of ambivalence.

This ambivalence is fueled by villagers' suspicions that fellow Malays are frequently motivated by greed, envy, and malice, and are forever try-

ing to get the better of one another through displays of status and prestige, and by attempting to gain control over one another's resources, loyalties, and affections. These suspicions are not expressed openly, however;
nor are personal desires and individual intentions (cf. Weiner 1976:213;
Dentan 1988:859, 869). The formal rules of social interaction prohibit
such behavior, just as they proscribe many forms of direct speech that
could possibly enable people to better read what is on the minds of others.
Villagers are quick to point out that one's inner spirit or soul (*batin, roh*)
is invisible, concealed beneath the physical body (*badan*), and that one's
real intentions, motivations, likes, and dislikes are similarly shielded from
view, and typically unknown. Outward behavior is no indication of what
is on someone's mind or "in one's liver" (*dalam hati*), for outward behavior is not only constrained by generally restricted speech codes, in which
most utterances are "pressed into service to affirm the social order"
(Douglas 1970:22); it also intentionally disguises inner realities. These
themes are highlighted in various local expressions, such as *ya mogun*,
which refers to a "yes" that really means "no"; *janji Melayu* ("a Malay
promise"), which is sometimes used to convey similar meaning; *cakap
manis, tapi hati lain*, which can be translated as "sweet words or talk, but
a different [not-so-sweet] liver"; and *mulut manis, tapi hati busuk*, which
refers to "a sweet mouth but a stinking, rotten liver."

This is the ideal climate for *ilmu* and is, in the local view, where *ilmu*
comes into the picture: Villagers assume—and fear—that many people in
their social universe rely on *ilmu* to achieve what they are prevented by
the formal rules of social interaction from accomplishing (or even setting
out to accomplish). These and attendant assumptions help explain why the
institution of *dukun* continues to flourish despite the decline of traditional
midwifery and most forms of shamanism and spirit cults. In sum, although certain *dukun* (e.g., Mak Ijah, Datuk Latiff) are suspected of trafficking in evil spirits, engaging in sorcery, and otherwise misappropriating
the power of the Word, and although the entire institution has come under increasingly heavy fire from Islamic resurgents (*orang dakwa*) and
critics of disparate persuasion, *dukun* are still very much needed to protect
villagers (and their urban counterparts) from the dangers in their social
universe, including, in particular, the veiled aggression of fellow Malays.

Fellow Malays are not the only source of uncertainty and danger, however. We have seen that non-Muslim aborigines are perceived to be especially threatening. So, too, are various types of spirits in the demonological system, only some of which are controlled by human agency. Of
particular interest in this connection are "epidemics" of spirit possession

("mass hysteria") among young Malay women working in factories in Negeri Sembilan, Selangor, Melaka, Singapore, and elsewhere, which is a recent, much publicized phenomenon that has attracted the attention of anthropologists, among others. Ong (1987, 1988) notes that such cases typically involve spirits that are "wild" or "untamed," as opposed to "domesticated" or "tamed" by human masters. She also demonstrates that epidemics of spirit possession among female factory workers, and "the intensified social and bodily vigilance" with which they are associated, reflect heightened moral concerns and anxieties about the Malay social order, about the dangers of stepping outside it, and about the more encompassing body politic (Ong 1988:32). The contexts in which these epidemics occur—the shop floors of modern factories, especially multinationals in "free trade zones"—provide clear evidence of new (and incipient shifts in) sources of marginality, uncertainty, danger, and power. More generally, such cases (along with material presented earlier) indicate that Malays see themselves as threatened, if not marginalized and victimized, not only by their own neighbors and kin, but also by largely Western-oriented state policies and institutions, and by the state-sponsored nexus of capitalism introduced during the British colonial period, which continues to undermine and otherwise transform rural culture and social relations (cf. Taussig 1980; Zelenietz and Lindenbaum 1981). Evidence of these same shifts appears in the data from Bogang, even though most dangers and tensions still have a decidedly local face; for example, Rashid attributing his illness to the envy and sorcery of a "business friend" from the east coast whom he encountered in the course of his work for a modern capitalist enterprise (as opposed to the sorcery of forest-dwelling non-Muslim aborigines); and Kadir's account of his mother's illness, which focuses on her anxiety concerning her children mixing with, and perhaps mating with and marrying, the "wrong types" in the predominantly Chinese city of Kuala Lumpur (as opposed to sorcery, spirits, or other mystical agency). These cases indicate, among other things, that processes involving the "disenchantment of the world," which Weber analyzed so incisively at times, are far less automatic, mechanical, and uniform than is widely assumed (see Peletz 1988a, 1993a, 1993b).

It is no small irony that the very same historical forces which have exacerbated rural and urban Malays' moral concerns, fears, and anxieties pertaining to poisoning, sorcery, and spirit possession—and which have thus ensured continued demand for certain services of *dukun*—have also rendered superfluous many of the traditional services *dukun* once provided (dealing with fractured and broken bones, other simple physical complaints) and have, at the same time, helped undermine the legitimacy of the institution in its entirety. Most of Bogang's *dukun* are in their sixties or seventies, and to the best of my knowledge there are no young people in the village or outside of it who have expressed strong interest in learning their *ilmu* and replacing them when they retire or die. These and other forms of local knowledge and power obtained through illness, dreams, chanting, trancing, and possession by spirits may thus be lost forever, despite the locally experienced and culturally elaborated need for their deployment. Such a loss may well engender feelings of disempowerment throughout Malay society, even among those who, like Kadir, appear to put relatively little stock in *ilmu* and mystical agency and have yet to experience serious illness or other personal misfortune.

These feelings of loss and disempowerment may well be felt most strongly by women. This is not only because women are increasingly less likely to have other avenues of knowledge and power available to them both in rural and urban contexts (e.g., modern secular education and religious instruction, meaningful on-the-job training and employment opportunities), but also because women have long been more susceptible to spirit possession (which is apparently less responsive to Western medical treatment than other forms of mystical attack), and likewise more dependent on (or at least more inclined to use) *ilmu* to help ensure the affections and loyalties of spouses and children. As growing numbers of village youth turn their backs on the prospective marriage partners their mothers and other female relatives have chosen for them in favor of spouses of their own choosing—which behavior is often taken as a sign of their being under the influence of the latter's *ilmu*—their mothers and other female kin will feel ever more powerless to realize the quintessentially female role of articulating social relations and looking after reproduction in both the social and biological senses. Moreover, as Islamic resurgents, national politicians, and others in largely extralocal quarters place greater emphasis and restrictions on women's attire, sexuality, and bodily functions in their projects to reinvigorate and reconstitute Malay society, rural women will come under intensifying pressure to conform to gender roles of others' choosing. Developments such as these—coupled as they are with the decline of subsistence agriculture (long a female domain) and female labor exchange in the agricultural sector, and various state-sponsored changes in land tenure and inheritance that have undermined many of women's "traditional" prerogatives—will undoubtedly witness the further erosion of women's autonomy and social control, just as they will entail the heightened segregation and dichotomization of male and female spheres.

The most likely result: Women will become increasingly identified with and, to a lesser extent, confined to, the ever more atomized, isolated, and isolating domains of hearth and household, yet will be ritually ill-equipped (except as victims of increasingly delegitimized spirit possession and *latah*) to deal with the vicissitudes of their relational dilemmas and to exercise their more general moral concerns.

Spirits of Resistance Revisited

The analyses presented here build on Aihwa Ong's extremely insightful (1987, 1988, 1990a) work on spirit possession in contemporary Malaysia, but they do so rather selectively. In the interest of encouraging further research and debate on the issues at hand, it may be useful to make explicit some of our areas of disagreement, though I hasten to add that this is not the place to provide an extended discussion of Ong's important contributions to the literature.

Ong argues that prior to the 1970s, spirit possession among Malay women entailed (though is not reducible to) symbolic protest against women's subordinate status vis-à-vis men as well as ritual dramatization of the stresses women experienced in their roles as wives, mothers, and divorcées. With urbanization and industrialization beginning in the 1970s, however, there was a dramatic shift in the locus of possession. In Ong's (1988:29) words: "Before the current wave of industrial employment for young single women, spirit possession was mainly manifested by *married* women, given the particular stresses of being *wives, mothers, widows, and divorcées. . . .* With urbanization and industrialization, spirit possession *became overnight* the affliction of *young unmarried women placed in modern organizations*" (emphasis added). Possession in contemporary contexts such as these, in Ong's view, is best interpreted as both a protest against, and a form of resistance to, capitalist "labor discipline and male control in the modern industrial situation" (Ong 1987:207).

There are, in my view, three problems with these arguments. First, the way in which Ong portrays the purportedly dramatic shift in the locus of possession (at least or especially in her 1987 monograph) makes little provision for the multitudes of rural and urban Malay women—married and unmarried, old and young alike—who have no direct or indirect experience in the modern factory settings on which Ong focuses her discussion.[8] yet who are still subject to possession by spirits.[8] More generally, while possession certainly does occur among some, but by no means the majority of, female factory workers, and, as widely reported both in the media and in the literature, among female dormitory residents and rural-dwelling schoolgirls involved in sports meets, drama programs, and public-sector work projects (Ackerman 1988:218), there is no evidence to suggest—and no reason to believe—that possession is more common among factory workers than among those who have no work experience in factory settings. Thus, it strikes me as rather misleading for Ong to state that possession became "overnight" the affliction of "young unmarried women . . . in modern organizations"—the larger issue being that there are few solid grounds (and not all that many data) on which to base assertions that possession in these or other contexts informed by urban or industrial influences is best interpreted as a protest against, and a form of resistance to, "[capitalist] labor discipline and male control in the modern industrial situation." I certainly agree with Ong, however, that the demise of reciprocity and redistribution brought about in part by transnational capitalism is conducive to the intensification of moral concerns, fears, and anxieties of the sort realized in possession, though I would add that they are likewise conducive to the amplification of moral concerns, fears, and anxieties realized in other (i.e., "male") forms of mystical attack. More broadly, while I concur with Ong that the symbols, idioms, and overall language of spirit possession in capitalist contexts can and frequently do entail critiques of new ways of being for women and men alike, I would attach somewhat more importance to the fact that possession *and* other mystically induced forms of misfortune in more "traditional" settings are equally likely to embody critiques of prevailing or emergent social arrangements and institutions (gendered and otherwise), and, in this sense, have always had strong counter-hegemonic potential.

Second, the purported age shift in the locus of possession to which Ong refers (from "wives, mothers, widows, and divorcées" to "young unmarried women") is more apparent than real, insofar as it is a function of the rise in age at first marriage. Prior to the 1930s, for example, females in Bogang were, on average, about fifteen years old (though in some specific cases much younger) at the time of their first marriage (see also Newbold 1839 I:244; Reid 1988:158–59, 160). Note, however, that the mean age at first marriage for females had increased to about nineteen by the end of the 1960s, and was about twenty-one to twenty-two (or slightly higher) by the end of the 1970s (see Peletz 1988:233, table 15). Similar increases in age at first marriage have been reported for other parts of the Peninsula, including Selangor, where Ong worked (see, e.g., Jones 1980, 1981; Hirschmann 1986). Hence it is not necessarily the case that possession is afflicting *younger* women. The difference is simply that, due to the rise in mean age at first marriage, when women first experience possession they are much less likely to be married (or widowed or divorced) than in times past.

And third, Ong's discussions of mystical affliction focus almost entirely on spirit possession, and effectively ignore those forms of mystical attack (such as poisoning and forms of sorcery that do not involve dramatic episodes of hysteria in which spirits take control of, and otherwise possess, their victims) that predominate among males. This focus follows from the main—and very important—question to which Ong directed her research (how to account for spirit possession among female factory workers), and, as such, is thoroughly justifiable. On the other hand, it gives the erroneous impression that women are far more susceptible to mystical affliction than men, and otherwise entails an unjustifiably dichotomized treatment of the roles and meanings of male and female in both "traditional" and contemporary culture. It also leaves unanswered some very significant questions: Why has poisoning and sorcery since the late 1400s been the "normal assumption in the Malay world when a man [or woman?] died young" (Wheatley 1964:151; cf. Reid 1988:56–57)? And why do fears and anxieties about being poisoned, sorcerized, or otherwise mystically attacked appear to be more or less evenly distributed among men and women?

The analytic framework developed in this chapter is, I believe, more appropriate to the data than Ong's, though I should perhaps reiterate that various commonalities underlie our different perspectives, and that, in any case, many questions and lines of inquiry remain to be pursued. Suffice it to restate my most general position that spirit possession is but one form of mystical attack, and that mystical attack is most profitably approached from a broad perspective which not only deals squarely with femininity *and* masculinity, but which is also attuned to long-term historical developments (e.g., the gendered skewing of ritual activities and women's spiritual disempowerment) over the course of the past few centuries.

In the latter connection we might recall the previously noted point that during the early part of the period 1450–1680, women were extremely active in communal rituals throughout much of Southeast Asia due to the fact that their reproductive and regenerative capacities gave them "magical and ritual powers which it was difficult for men to match" (Reid 1988:146; Andaya and Ishii 1992). This had changed by the latter part of this period, however, owing to the development in Southeast Asia of Islam and other Great Religions (especially Buddhism and Christianity), which provide no textual legitimacy for women's active participation in the highest or most prestigious rituals of the land. Specifically, during the latter part of the period in question, the most prestigious ritual positions in societies under the influence of Great Religions—*ulama*, magistrates, and mosque officials in the case of Islamic societies—came to be reserved for males, who thus found themselves in the historically unprecedented position of presiding over communal rituals. Women's public ritual roles became progressively less apparent, and they were increasingly relegated to shamanism, spirit propitiation, and the like, which, along with *latah*, came to be disassociated from the more universalistic arenas defined in terms of the Great Religions, formal politics, and men (Andaya and Ishii 1992). In the process, the status of shaman (both female and transvestite) declined, and women became the principal practitioners of ritual activities keyed to relatively parochial concerns, such as localized ancestral spirits and healing.

Clear evidence of this gendered encompassment exists in nineteenth- and twentieth-century Malay society. In the late nineteenth century, as Swettenham ([1895] 1984:194) pointed out, the "native doctors" responsible for treating "convulsions, unconsciousness, and delirium" were typically *women*, "usually ... ancient female[s]." [9] Note, though, that the "native doctor's" diagnosis was typically "confirmed by some independent person[s] of authority," namely *pawang* "skilled in dealing with wizards," who were "usually *men*" (Swettenham [1895] 1984:194–95; Skeat [1900] 1967:322–23). Since Swettenham's time, there has been a progressive restriction in women's ritual roles. The eleven healers practicing in Bogang during the period 1978–80, for example, included only one woman (Mak Ijah), and, in a parallel development, the roles of female midwives have been rendered more or less superfluous by male obstetricians. When Mak Ijah dies, the gendered skewing of ritual roles and activities and of professional concentrations of virtues such as *ilmu* may well be complete, assuming, as seems to be justified, that no females step forward to replace her. The more general point is twofold. First, women will find themselves with increasingly delegitimized forms of spirit possession and *latah* as the primary if not sole ritual contexts to dramatize their most basic and pressing moral concerns. And second, the ritual articulation of these concerns will necessarily further reinforce the official/hegemonic view that women have weaker "life force" or *semangat* as well as less "reason" and more "passion" than men. To put the latter point differently, even when women's ritual dramatization of their most basic and pressing moral concerns embodies counter-hegemonic critiques of prevailing social arrangements and institutions, their articulation in the context of possession and *latah* will necessarily have ironic and unintended consequences. To wit, they will bolster the hegemony which legitimizes the gendered distribution of power and prestige in its entirety, and which also defines women as lacking in the moral qualities or virtues that are associated both with maleness and with humanity as a whole.

5   The Person and the Body
Reason, Passion, and Shame

This chapter focuses on cultural constructions of the person and the body, dealing in particular with "reason," "passion," and "shame," which are core (or key) symbolic constructs in many spheres of Malay society and culture in Negeri Sembilan and throughout the Peninsula. The first section of the chapter provides a largely ungendered overview of local ideas about and representations of the person and the body, partly by analyzing the relational nature of personhood (or self) characteristic of Malay culture, along with the relational views informing images of the body and its most significant constituent elements (e.g., the *hati*, or liver, which is the "seat of emotion," and the *semangat*, or animating "life force"). In the second section of the chapter, these issues are pursued through a discussion of gender-specific constructs bearing on conception, pregnancy, and childbirth. The analysis is expanded in the third and fourth sections of the chapter by examining the contextually variable symbols and meanings of "reason," "passion," and "shame," and by assessing the implications of these data for Ortner's seminal but controversial (1974) argument that women in all societies are held to be "closer to nature" and "further from culture" than men. In reevaluating and reworking basic features of this argument, I contend that while it makes inadequate provision for contradictory representations of gender (and has various other limitations), its central logic helps bring into sharp focus critically important aspects of gender, and of society and culture generally, both in Negeri Sembilan and elsewhere in the Peninsula as well.

THE PERSON AND THE BODY: AN INTRODUCTORY SKETCH

Malay concepts of the person or self (*diri*), like those reported for other parts of Southeast Asia and much of the rest of the non-Western world, portray the person in relational terms. This is quite different from what one finds in the West, where the person is conceptualized as a "bounded, unique, more or less integrated motivational and cognitive universe, a dynamic center of awareness, emotion, judgment, and action organized into a distinctive whole and set contrastively against other such wholes and against a social and natural background" (Geertz 1983:59). In Malay culture the person is most fully realized in social relationships, not autonomously or in privacy or isolation, as occurs in Western societies; this basic fact receives expression in various forms of kinship terminology and linguistic etiquette, and in myriad other ways as well.

In many contexts, for example, there is an assiduous avoidance of the term for "I" (*den, aku, saya*), which is thoroughly nonrelational insofar as it makes no provision for the specific relationship(s) between the speaker and the listener(s). In its place, villagers use terms indicating their relationship to their primary audience. Thus, a woman speaking to her child would never say "*I* would like you to do such and such," but rather "*Mother* (or *Your mother*) would like you to do such and such." A boy speaking to his elder brother would likewise refer to himself as *adik* (younger sibling of unspecified gender), rather than by a term for "I" (or by his name); similarly, he would refer to his elder brother by a term indicating either "elder brother" (*abang*) or the elder brother's place in his (and the speaker's) sibling set (see below).

The use of birth-order names and teknonyms further reinforces the relational sense of self characteristic of Malay culture. Birth-order names, which refer to the person's place in his or her sibling set, are quite commonly employed, often with a term indicating relative generation: "elder brother, first born" (*bang lung*), "elder sister, third born" (*kak ngah*), and so on. More often than not, however, especially when speaking to someone of the same relative generation or to an elder, the generational marker is dropped. These conventions have the effect of emphasizing the siblingship tie that obtains between the person spoken to on the one hand, and his or her siblings on the other, and relational orientations more generally. Similarly, teknonymous terms (e.g., "mother [or father] of so and so") are frequently used by married individuals with children when they address and refer to one another. Such terms also promote a relational orientation, though they obviously differ from birth-order names insofar as they emphasize vertical (parent-child) as opposed to horizontal (siblingship) links.[1]

Kinship terminology, like linguistic etiquette as a whole, encodes a variety of mostly implicit moral expectations and constraints. These expectations and constraints tend to be defined relationally, rather than in terms of categorical, absolute standards of behavior or ethics.[2] Indeed, as Read (1955:260, 263) has put it with reference to an otherwise quite different society, moral judgments do not generally "operate from the fixed perspective of universal obligation," since for the most part there are no "common measures of ethical content" relevant to moral agents in all situations in which they find themselves. Moral judgments tend instead to be dependent on, and vary with, social role and position. This is particularly evident in ("traditional") reactions to and sanctions for *sumbang*, which, as noted in chapter 3, refers to incest, related improprieties, and other forms of aesthetically offensive behavior. *Sumbang* involving individuals of the same lineage was a capital offense, but *sumbang* involving distantly related matrikin, though still a crime, was not nearly as reprehensible, punishable by confiscation of the offenders' property and their banishment from the village (if not from the district).[3]

More generally, the person is not construed as "standing apart from and above the world of social relationships and institutions" (Read 1955:250), but as both thoroughly grounded in, and in a very basic sense defined by, the relationships and institutions in which he or she participates. Clan and lineage affiliation figure prominently in the person's identity and sense of self, as do place of birth and current residence. (Most of these variables are encompassed within the concept of *asal* [*asal-usul*], or "origin point," which is central to one's social personality and destiny.) Significant, too, for the person's sense of self and identity are relational roles such as husband and wife. This became especially clear to me in the context of formal interviewing, for when I asked people to talk about the temperaments and personalities of "males" and "females," they almost always responded with answers framed in terms of "husbands" and "wives" (the implications of which are explored in chapters 6 and 7).

Social roles are thus an intrinsic constituent of each person's identity. Indeed, the individual and social role are not clearly separable, which is to say that there is no real dichotomy (though there is a fair degree of diffuse tension) between the individual and society, and that social identity is more important than idiosyncratic individuality. Individuality (and indulgence) of most varieties is in fact strongly discouraged, and the individualist risks criticism that he or she is "different" (*lain*). Discouraged, too, is voicing speculations about other people's motivations, which may be one of the reasons why the vocabulary of emotion (and of social criticism) is relatively undeveloped (cf. Karim 1990).[4]

Local views of the person are grounded in (though by no means derive from) understandings of the human body, for the person is quite literally physically embodied, though constituted of nonphysical (e.g., "psychic") essences such as the "life force" as well. The body is viewed relationally, and is held to be made up of the four basic elements that exist in the universe: earth, wind, fire, and water. Within the body these elements are, ideally, both of "equal weight" (*sama berat*) and in a state of balance and equilibrium. At times, though, one or another predominates. When this occurs, there are telltale signs and potentially serious problems. Such problems may necessitate treatment by a healer (*dukun*), whose primary objectives in the course of treatment include restoration of the appropriate balance among the body's constituent elements and, in some cases, the mediation of relationships between the realms of spirits and nature on the one hand, and that of humans on the other.

Each of the elements of the body is symbolically associated with a particular sensory organ (earth is linked with the mouth, wind with ears, fire with eyes, and water with nose). Each sensory organ is associated, in turn, with one of the four archangels (Mikail, Jabrail, Israfil, Azrail), one of the four spirits that watches over us after we die (Chadi, Wadi, Mani, Manikam), and one of the four Caliphs (Omar, Ali, Osman, Abubakar). Each of these archangels, spirits, and Caliphs is also symbolically keyed to one of the four corners of the world, which is conceptualized as a square plane surrounded by water. There is, in short, a single set of associations which symbolically link the four elements of the human body with human sensory organs, archangels, spirits, and Caliphs, as well as the four corners of the world (cf. Endicott 1970:42–45, 122–24; Laderman 1983).

The parallels between the human body and the universe are also evident in the ways Malays conceptualize human nature, as is the foregoing emphasis on balance and equilibrium. Humans, like other animals, have bodily passions and desires (*nafsu*), but they differ from other members of the animal kingdom in that they have been endowed by God with reason, rationality, and intelligence (*akal*). Within all humans, elements of "passion" and "reason" are forever struggling against one another, as are the forces of good and evil, and those of life and death. The point is often made that an individual's proper actions testify to the dominance, however temporary, of "rationality" over "passion," and that improper actions bespeak an inability or lack of concern to control the baser impulses. Behavior seen as contravening social codes is not merely aesthetically offensive (*tak sedap*), coarse, crass (*kasar*), and unrefined (*kurang halus*), but is also held to reflect faulty or incomplete socialization. Hence, individuals whose comportment is held to be seriously improper are sometimes referred to (out of earshot, never to their faces, for this is a very serious charge) as "less than fully taught" (*kurang ajar*), such that they are accorded an intermediate standing between the world of animals and

nature—where moral codes do not exist and thus need not be learned—
and the rule-governed realm of humanity. Interestingly, while the term
kasar is frequently used in criticism of other people's conduct (albeit not
to their faces), the positive reciprocal of *kasar*, namely *halus* (smooth,
polite, refined) is rarely employed with reference to other people's—or
one's own—behavior. Villagers do not seem to think that there is all that
much *halus* behavior, or that there are all that many *halus* people, in their
social universe(s) or in the world at large. This is in rather sharp contrast
to culturally similar societies such as Java, where both poles of the *halus/
kasar* axis seem to be frequently invoked in people's remarks about themselves and one another (Geertz 1960).

Malays commonly underscore that it is humans' possession of "reason" that separates them from other animals, but they also point out that
"reason" and *hati* (liver, the seat of the emotions) "work together" within
all humans. Some Malays refer to the liver as the "ruler" (*raja*) of the
human body and note that it "governs" or "regulates" (*merintah*) the rest
of the body, much like a ruler or commander governs his army. In other
contexts it is said that *iman* (faith, strong belief or trust in God, sincerity,
resoluteness) is the "ruler" or "magistrate" (*hakim*) within us, and that
one's *iman* "cooperates" with "reason" to "kill" "passion" or at least
"keep it in check." Such views and expressions are of interest in light of
their emphasis both on cooperation, struggle, and killing, and on the roles
of ruler, commander, and magistrate. In particular, they suggest that society and the body politic provide a ready store of symbols and idioms
through which to conceptualize and express ideas about the composition
of the human body as well as human nature.[5] They suggest, in addition,
that the human body is regarded much like a ruler's realm or territory,
and that the health and illness of the body are conceptualized in much
the same terms as sociopolitical order and disorder. Thus the individual
experiences well-being when cooperation and balance prevail among the
elements making up his or her body, a sign that the "ruler" of the body
is in control of its realm. Conversely, the individual experiences illness
when cooperation and balance no longer prevail among the constituent
elements of his or her body, an indication that the ruler has lost control
of its realm. These and related points concerning control and sovereignty
should be kept in mind throughout the ensuing discussion.

While the person is constituted in part by, and literally embodied
within, a physical body, it is also constituted by a "psychic factor." I refer
to the animating *semangat*, which resides in the body but which may
leave the body on occasion (e.g., during dreams, spirit possession, and

various forms of illness) through the fontanelle. *Semangat*, which have been described by Laderman (1983) as "gatekeepers" of the person or self, are spoken of in terms of their relative "strength" or "weakness," with strong *semangat* clearly being the most desirable. A strong *semangat* reduces the likelihood of illness, spirit possession, and the like. Conversely, a weak *semangat* leaves one open to various forms of illness and attacks by spirits. One way of strengthening (or simply preserving the strength of) one's *semangat* is to pray diligently and otherwise behave as a good Muslim. (Others include the wearing of amulets and talismans which, among other things, are thought to help keep evil spirits at bay.) Although women (as we have seen) are invariably believed to have weaker *semangat* than men and thus to be more prone to spirit possession and *latah*, there is no evidence to indicate that women pray (or wear amulets or talismans) more diligently or more often than men, or are otherwise concerned with being "better Muslims."[6]

Various (corporeal) body parts and waste products are also viewed as essential parts of the person. For example, the liver, which, as noted earlier, is viewed as the seat of emotion, is an essential part of the person that must be safeguarded through prayer and other forms of pious and socially valued behavior. Similarly, exuviae, effluvia, and waste products such as excrement, though not accorded the same primacy in discussions of the person as *semangat* or *hati*, should be disposed of properly, lest someone manipulate them (and the person) through sorcery or witchcraft. This is not simply a belief in "contagious magic," but should be viewed instead as an indication of the degree to which an individual's self is seen to reside in various parts or products of his or her body.[7] It is of interest here that when a group of villagers asked me if I would forget them and the rest of the community after I returned to the United States, one wealthy *hajjah* (a woman who has made the pilgrimage to Mecca) remarked drolly that I "couldn't possibly forget" them all, since, as she put it, I had "shit [t]here so many times."

Villagers are relatively comfortable elaborating on the essences of the person and various features of the body, but are rather taciturn when it comes to discussing standards of physical beauty, which, in my experience, are largely implicit and relatively unelaborated. This is even, or especially, true of the ideal physical attributes of prospective spouses. Zainal, the well known bridal attendant (*mak andam*) discussed in chapter 3, mentioned that it would be extremely ill-advised, especially from the point of view of one's "face" or "honor," "to go around saying 'I want a husband or wife with this and that physical quality'—a tall and handsome husband, for example—since what would happen if you didn't get one like that and ended up with a short, fat one?" I heard similar comments from other villagers, some of whom chastised me for the comments I made on one occasion that a particular (male) villager was rather unattractive.[8]

What "really counts" in the marriage market is a prospective spouse's character (*budi bahasa, sopan santun*), knowledge (*ilmu*), descent/ancestry (*keturunan*), wealth (*kekayaan*), and prestige (*pangkat*). It is nonetheless true that, all things being equal, it is more desirable to find a spouse who has smooth, unfreckled, light skin (as opposed to coarse, freckled, dark skin), and straight or curly/wavy hair (as opposed to coarse, frizzy hair). And no one would want a husband or wife who is "too fat," or as another woman put it, someone who is "missing a nose or something." Pronounced splotching or discoloration of the skin, along with other forms of serious skin disease (e.g., *kudis*), are also high on the list of undesirable physical traits, and villagers afflicted with such disorders do in fact have a difficult time finding spouses. One reason for this is that skin afflictions such as these have long been viewed as divine (or other mystical) retribution for violations of incest prohibitions on the part of ancestors. It is of interest, in any case, that one of the two male villagers past the age of thirty who has never been married is afflicted with disfiguring skin disease. (The other is seriously retarded.)

Just as being "incomplete" is an aesthetic (and in some cases a social) liability in local culture, so, too, is being "overcomplete" in the sense of having body parts that are considered "too large." Women with exceptionally large breasts ("bigger than coconuts," as one woman put it) sometimes seek out traditional healers or other medical specialists in the hope that something can be done to reduce their size. And one of the reasons I heard for performing minor clitoridectal surgery on young girls is so that "it won't grow." Aesthetic considerations such as these also figure into the practice of male circumcision (though the fact that such circumcision is seen by Malays as obligatory for all Muslims is obviously important as well).[9]

I have made very little mention thus far of the ways in which local views of the person and the body are refracted in terms of gender. The relatively ungendered discussion is consistent with the fact that many of the basic characteristics of persons and bodies that we have been considering here are relatively unmarked by gender. Subsequent sections of the chapter focusing on conception, pregnancy, and childbirth, and on "reason," "passion," and "shame," will serve to flesh out the material presented here by illustrating the ways in which persons and bodies are construed in gendered terms. Before turning to such topics, however, it will be useful to examine various aspects of local beliefs and practices bearing on death, most of which are ungendered.

Death

At death, the person ceases to exist in the sense of having a distinctive personality, but this does not necessarily mean that it is no longer endowed with agency (the capacity to influence the world of the living). Immediately after an individual dies, the spirit (*roh*) departs the body, though it remains in the vicinity of ("hovers around") the corpse and the house of the deceased for about seven days. It then journeys from the house to the gate of the residential compound. Thereafter it travels to the cemetery (where the body is taken within twenty-four hours of death), though it may journey back and forth between the cemetery and the house of the deceased for about fourteen days. After one hundred days the spirit travels to Medina. It tends to remain there until Judgment Day (at which point God directs it to Heaven or Hell), though it typically returns to the home of the deceased three times a year (on the twentieth day of the fasting month [Ramadan], at the end of Ramadan, and during the festivities commemorating the annual pilgrimage to Mecca [*Hari Raya Haji*]).

Some of the rituals immediately following an individual's death reflect villagers' concerns to sever the emotional ties between the living and the deceased, or at least to minimize the negative impact of death upon the deceased's immediate survivors and help ensure that the spirit of the deceased will not be bothered by the grieving of his or her surviving kin. For example, shortly before the shrouded body of the deceased is taken out of the residential compound, it is held high in the air so that close relatives may walk under it two or three times and thus symbolically break their ties with the deceased and minimize the disturbance created by his or her death and social loss. The burning of incense at the various ritual feasts following death (on the seventh, fourteenth, one hundredth day, etc.) is likewise geared toward pleasing the spirit of the deceased.

Local perceptions of and attitudes toward heaven (*surga*) (and hell [*neraka*]) seem somewhat contradictory, though this may reflect the fact that my data on the subject are not as complete as I would like. On the one hand, heaven is viewed as a place where human "passion" does not exist; on the other hand, it is said that in heaven human "passion" is both easily and thoroughly satisfied (cf. Siegel 1969, 1979). The occasional likening of being in heaven to the situation of "an infant being at the feet of its mother" (*surga anak tepak ibu*) resonates with the latter view of heaven, for what is implied in this expression is that heaven is a place where the person is both thoroughly safe and sated. Interestingly, when children encounter their parents in heaven, they first extend their arms to their mothers so as to help their mothers climb up to and otherwise overcome any obstacles to their reaching their final destination(s). Only after they have aided their mothers in this fashion do they extend such assistance to their fathers. These gendered views of heaven exist elsewhere in Southeast Asia as well, though they are clearly less pronounced than what one finds in Aceh, where, in women's imagery of heaven, men as husbands and fathers are altogether absent (Siegel 1969:177).

Rituals known as *kekah* are geared toward providing children with the transportation they will need when they are in heaven. The *kekah* ritual involves the slaughter of an animal in the name(s) of the child(ren) thus honored, and the holding of a feast to which large numbers of relatives and neighbors are invited.[10] The type of animal slaughtered determines the type of heavenly transportation that will be available to the deceased child(ren) in whose name(s) the *kekah* is performed. A water buffalo, for example, will ensure that seven horses are waiting for the deceased. Sheep and goats may also be slaughtered, as can a two-year-old male chicken, but the sacrifice of such animals is less desirable since the transportation thus guaranteed to the deceased will be less substantial, perhaps a single horse.

Hell (*neraka*), which is the ultimate destination for the souls of persons whose actions are, on balance, sinful, is portrayed as a place of intense heat (fire), suffering, and pain. One male elder mentioned to me that women's souls are more likely to go to hell than men's, though he added that much depends on their comportment while they are living. If they behave "properly," that is, if they aren't consumed by their "passion," their souls aren't necessarily more likely than men's to end up in hell. I never heard this view from other men, or from women, but it is consistent both with the hegemonic (though not uncontested) view that women have more "passion" than men, and with the thoroughly hegemonic (and uncontested) association between "passion" on the one hand, and sin, the devil, and hell on the other. The point to note in any case is that there are no separate resting places for the souls of men and women.

All villagers contend that the actions of the living can either ameliorate or augment the suffering of deceased persons' spirits, but for the most part only elders believe that the spirits of the dead can aid and punish the living. The validity and legitimacy of such beliefs are denied by the younger, educated, and more cosmopolitan members of the community, who view them as contrary to the teachings of Islam. It merits remark, however, that, in sharp contrast to places such as Java and Bali (Geertz 1960, 1973, 1983), there is very little public discussion of contrasting views of this nature; nor, in my experience, is there all that much speculation about the fate of the dead, the Afterlife, or death generally.

In times past, elaborate and highly syncretic funerary ceremonies geared toward honoring the dead were held at various points in the Islamic ritual calendar. At present, however, such rituals are highly attenuated, and in some cases they are no longer performed at all. Many elders regard such ritual shifts and declines—and the underlying cosmological and social changes—with marked disdain, lamenting that village ancestors and guardian spirits have been neglected by the current generation of villagers, much like elders have been neglected and abandoned by their younger, especially urban-dwelling, relatives (see Peletz 1988b). Their more encompassing concern is that the bonds of reciprocity that link both the ancestors and their living descendants, as well as seniors and their junior kin, are no longer ritually or otherwise appropriately acknowledged; and that such failure is not only directly responsible for declining rice yields and other immediate threats to established moral and material orders, but also bodes ill for both the short- and the long-term reproduction of society and culture.

A detailed treatment of the ritual and social changes alluded to here is beyond the scope of the present discussion (see Peletz 1988a, 1988b, 1993a, 1993b; McAllister 1987), but it is noteworthy that these changes have witnessed an incipient cultural shift toward a nonrelational or decontextualized individualism, the social realization of which may not be far behind. Perhaps the best evidence of this incipient shift is that a variety of heinous moral offenses once considered treasonous (such as acts of poisoning, the harboring of vampire-like spirits, and various types of incest) are no longer commonly subsumed under the broadly social rubric of "taboo" (*pantang* [*larang*]), as used to be the case (Parr and Mackray 1910:79, 110, 111). At present, such acts are usually classified as "sins" (*dosa*) and tend not to be discussed in terms of taboo (or treason). This shift is significant in light of villagers' comments that while such transgressions (and all others of a sinful nature) may cause direct harm to specific individuals or groups of people (the objects of poisoning, spirit attack, etc.), they are ultimately of concern to (and best punished by) God alone, and need not concern—*or have any mystical effect on*—the community at large. This is very different from transgressions entailing taboo, which are of broad community concern if only because their mystical effects (which are automatically triggered by violation of taboo, albeit with the sanction and occasional intercession of offended spirits and perhaps God as well) are likely to be visited upon the entire community. Put differently, the "supernatural" consequences of sinful actions tend to be far more narrowly construed than the "supernatural" consequences of actions entailing violation of taboo insofar as they tend to affect only (or primarily) the sinner, rather than the much broader range of people (an entire kin group or community) likely to be affected by violation of taboo. I see in such changes an incipient recasting of personhood and morality; specifically, a tendency to construe the person as less enmeshed in—and certainly less affected by—his or her immediate social universe (household, kin group, community, etc.) and, conversely, as more directly implicated in (responsible for) whatever "supernatural" punishment he or she experiences.

CONCEPTION, PREGNANCY, AND CHILDBIRTH
Conception and Pregnancy

Local views of conception vary somewhat from individual to individual but there is general agreement on many of the basic issues. Some villagers told me that conception is an act of God that occurs in a man's head, and that, after conceiving, a man is pregnant (*hamil, bunting*) for nine days (or longer)—telltale signs of which are "a certain look in the eye," the desire for new or different foods, and so on. If a man in such a condition has sexual intercourse with a fertile woman, the woman will then be pregnant for a period of roughly nine months. These beliefs concerning conception and pregnancy exist among Malays elsewhere in the Peninsula (Laderman 1983:75–76; see also Strange 1981:68–78) and in other Malay-Indonesian societies (Atkinson 1990). Especially significant is that they posit the identity, not simply the complementarity, of male and female in reproduction (see Atkinson 1990).[11]

Other villagers mentioned only that "the seed" (*beneh*) starts off in a man's head, descends through his body to his penis, and comes out when he ejaculates. Still others made no mention of the seed originating in the man's head, and said only that a man's seed, which comes out through the penis, is necessary (but not sufficient) for conception.

There is broad agreement, in any event, that if ejaculation occurs (even once) in the vagina of a fertile woman, conception and pregnancy may result. There is general agreement as well that if a married woman who is presumed to have had sexual relations for more than a few months does not conceive, there is most likely something wrong with her, not with her husband. Thus, when Maimunah (who was twenty-nine when she married) failed to conceive after many months, and finally years, of marriage, it was widely assumed that she, rather than her husband, "had a problem (or disease)." Maimunah and her mother sought out a variety of healers and modern doctors (one of whom reportedly concluded that she had a tipped uterus), but none of their counsel or medicine proved helpful. When her husband was finally asked to submit to examinations or tests, he refused, citing in his defense that he would be embarrassed or ashamed (*malu*) to do so. Some older women with whom I discussed the matter viewed the husband's recalcitrance as unfortunate, but they were pleased in any case that he had remained with Maimunah despite her apparent inability to conceive.

A woman's failure to conceive is commonly regarded as legitimate grounds for her husband to divorce her, or to take a second wife, but villagers, especially women, also express marked ambivalence about such things. This became particularly clear to me when, shortly before leaving the field in May 1980, a number of village women approached Ellen and told her, more or less out of the blue, that they hoped I would never abandon her, and that they had prayed to God so that this would never happen. One woman (my mother) assured Ellen that she would "kill me in her dreams" if I ever left her for another woman. And, as if to impress upon Ellen the nature of the punishment that awaited me in such circumstances, she jumped up and grabbed a large (4 ft. long) machete from its place on the kitchen wall and demonstrated with great dramatic flair and excruciating detail how she would slash and hack me into little pieces. This demonstration was later repeated for my benefit, by which time Ellen and I figured out why village women had been approaching her on the topic: Some ten or eleven months had passed since our wedding and Ellen exhibited no signs of pregnancy. Ergo, Ellen could not conceive and if these problems persisted I would sooner or later abandon her in search of a fertile woman.

Medicines and other aids (e.g., charms, amulets) to encourage conception are viewed in a positive light and are undoubtedly widespread, though I have little concrete information about their specific nature or the extent of their distribution or deployment.[12] So, too, are "love charms" geared toward ensuring that husbands continue to find their wives attractive and sexually desirable (and vice versa). Herbal concoctions and other aids that inhibit or prevent conception, on the other hand, are viewed in negative terms, even though it is widely recognized that frequent pregnancies can endanger some women's health, and that large numbers of children can seriously strain a household's material resources. Generally speaking, contraception is viewed as illogical because it is incompatible with the supremely valued goal of having large numbers of children. It is also seen as sinful (forbidden by God), and as a politically suicidal strategy for Malays, who are ever fearful of being outnumbered by non-Malays, especially Chinese. Villagers assume that non-Malays tend not to practice contraception of any kind, and are otherwise intent on increasing their numbers. On this count alone they feel it is ill-advised to experiment with any forms of contraception, or to engage in any other form of activity (e.g., abortion) that would limit their numbers.[13]

The circumstances of the sexual act, which is said always to occur with "the man on top" (ventral to ventral), may determine both the sex of the child and other features of his or her physical appearance, personality, and fate. Various steps can be taken so as to increase the likelihood that the child will be a particular gender, but according to Pak Zainuddin, a sixty-year-old man with whom I discussed such matters at length, these steps are not widely known.

Pak Zainuddin was clearly embarrassed talking about matters related to sex but he did tell me that if a man thrusts to his right during the act of intercourse, about the time of orgasm in particular, a boy will be conceived. (Thrusting to the left will help produce a girl.) It also helps if a woman pushes to the right (left for a girl) at such a moment. Similarly if a woman sleeps on her right side (left for a girl) after having sex this will enhance the likelihood of conceiving a boy. Men with "much experience" know all about such things, but many men, even old ones, do not.[14]

Pak Zainuddin went on to explain that it is both inadvisable and sinful for a woman to sleep face down after having sex, since "the seed will run out." Overall, however, there seems to be relatively little cultural concern with the amount of (male) seed in a woman's womb—for example, that a single act of intercourse might not be sufficient for conception. Similarly, Pak Zainuddin did not think that the frequency of sex after conception had any bearing on the health of the fetus or the mother. Such things are really up to the woman: If her desire increases, then her husband should respond accordingly; if it decreases or declines, he should also act accordingly.

Datuk Osman, another male elder with whom I discussed such matters, told me that a child's fate (*nasib*) can be affected by the emotional state of one or another of the parents during intercourse. Thus, if one of the parents is worried or upset, the child might turn out "stupid," might not do well in school, or might otherwise have a less than desirable fate. Similarly, if either of the parents has sinned, the parent's seed "won't be good." The example he used to illustrate the latter point involved money obtained in a religiously unacceptable way (i.e., money that wasn't *halal*). If one of the parents has obtained money from the proceeds of *petai* that have been gathered in the forest, but has not paid the government fee that is required to collect *petai*, then the child may have a "bad fate." Ultimately, however, all of this is in the hands of God, as are conception and pregnancy in the first place.

If a woman expresses anger toward someone or otherwise loses control of her emotions during her pregnancy, the child may take on the physical appearance of the object of the woman's anger or emotional outburst. More generally, the emphasis on women controlling themselves, which informs women's behavior in most contexts, is even more pronounced during pregnancy. One woman explained, for example, that her twenty-year-old daughter had facial features that were widely regarded as "Chinese" because during her pregnancy she (the mother) had often gotten extremely angry at the Chinese conductor on the local bus. Another woman told me that her son was distressingly similar in appearance to the village idiot since she had frequently been angry with the idiot's father during her pregnancy.

Overall, however, villagers feel that, in terms of physical appearance, a child is more likely to resemble its father than its mother.[15] This is because a child receives most of its biogenetic substance from its father and, more generally, because men's biogenetic contributions ("seed" and "blood") are "stronger" (*lebih kuat*) than the contributions of women ("flesh," "milk," and "bones"). Agricultural metaphors are sometimes invoked to explain this (e.g., the type of crop that grows in a field is determined largely by the nature of the seed planted there).

The *semangat* of a young child, on the other hand, is more likely to resemble the *semangat* of its mother. This, I was told, is because the mother is "with the child from infancy" and is the "primary caretaker." Presumably relevant as well, though never mentioned to me (or Ellen) in this context, is that the individual's *semangat* develops in utero, during the fourth or fifth month of pregnancy, and is indissolubly linked with that of its mother, much like the developing fetus's "breath" (*nyawa*). I do not have any information on the development of a child's *semangat* subsequent to infancy, but presumably the similarities between the *sem-*

angat of a male child and that of his mother are held to decrease as the young boy matures and is involved in activities that entail his progressive distancing from the influence of his mother and other females. This would begin with formal religious instruction in the Koran, which is under the supervision of the village *imam,* and which begins when children are about five to six years of age, and certainly by the time of circumcision (ten to twelve years of age), which in theory coincides with the completion of Koranic studies.

Pregnancy, which is believed to last nine months, or nine months and two to ten days, is seen as a relatively dangerous time both for the mother and the developing fetus, and is ritually marked off by various food restrictions and other prohibitions. Proper balance of the humors is particularly important at this time and involves (among other things) maintaining and acquiring heat, and avoiding the consumption of "cool" or "cooling" (*sejuk*) foods.[16] So, too, is protection from the ravenous bloodsucking spirits (*pelisit, langsuir,* etc.) that are attracted by the fragrant, sweet blood of the pregnant woman and the fetus growing inside her. Since these spirits dwell in the forest, women are encouraged to avoid the forest throughout their pregnancies. Pregnant women are likewise enjoined to avoid looking at anything strange or freakish (lest they give birth to a strange or freakish child), and to steer clear of funerals (lest they experience dizziness, nausea, shock, and so on). They are also encouraged to refrain from strenuous labor on the grounds that such labor might entail physical harm to them or their fetuses.

Women do not usually formally notify their close kin or intimate friends that they are pregnant, though they are not shy about acknowledging the state of pregnancy when asked about it by close kin or others. Such topics are not talked about in advance, and women are told little if anything about menstruation, which is ritually unmarked, prior to the onset of their first menses. Village girls and women are thus pretty much in the dark about these basic biological processes (as are boys and men). The same is true for sex generally, which is one of the reasons bridal attendants are sometimes asked by brides and grooms about sexual (and related) matters.

The initial signs of pregnancy include a quickening of the pulse, feelings of dizziness (*mabuk*), nausea, fatigue or lethargy, strong desires for new or different foods, or simply missing one's period. Women who are especially irritable during their pregnancies are likened to pregnant tigers (*bunting harimau*).[17]

If a woman is particularly sick or irritable, it is believed that she is pregnant with a boy. One of my neighbors told me that when she was pregnant with her sons, she could not get along with people and was mad at everyone all of the time, especially people who were *bising* (noisy, too talkative). When she was pregnant with her daughter, on the other hand, she got along with everyone. A great deal of movement in the womb (e.g., a fetus that "kicks hard" and "feels strong inside") also suggests a boy. So, too, does a fetus that lies or is positioned on the woman's right side. It merits note as well that giving birth to a male child is felt to be more difficult than giving birth to a female.

Sex during pregnancy is believed improper by some (but not all) villagers. One male elder told me that it is wrong to have sex with a pregnant woman, for the man's penis might "poke" the child and/or "ruin its eyes." The larger theme—that inappropriate sex leads to blindness—occurs both in Indic and Greek mythology, and in many other mythic systems as well (Doniger 1991).

Among the more important rituals traditionally performed during a woman's pregnancy was the "swaying of the abdomen" (*melenggang perut*), which nowadays, if it is done at all, tends to be performed only with the first child (see Lewis 1962:144–45). This ritual occurs during the seventh month of pregnancy and is the occasion for a small feast. The focal point of the ritual is the bathing of the pregnant woman, and the wrapping of her abdomen with seven lengths of white cloth. This is done by a midwife, who recites Yasin (the thirty-sixth *sura* of the Koran [according to the traditional sequence of *sura*]) and gently massages and "sways" the pregnant woman's abdomen to help "open up" the uterus and otherwise facilitate an easy delivery.

Such rituals were, and in many cases still are, overseen by village midwives, known as *bidan* (or "village *bidan*," to distinguish them from "government *bidan*"), the majority of whom are female. Many of their services are still highly regarded, but state restrictions on their activities, coupled with the availability and affordability of modern health care, have seriously undermined their role in village society (see Laderman 1983).

Childbirth

In earlier times, women gave birth in their homes and were attended by village midwives and other female kin who provided medical and ritual assistance as well as emotional support. Men were not usually present at the births of their children; those among them who expressed interest in observing the birth process were told to "go away." According to women in Bogang, most births occurred either in the woman's kitchen or in one of the interior rooms of the house. Midwives oversaw the delivery (which usually occurred with the pregnant woman lying on her back), thus ensuring, among other things, that the appropriate prayers and spells were recited, that the umbilical cord was properly cut, and the afterbirth fully expelled. One of the first things the midwife did after getting the baby out was wash it, put its hands in proper prayer position, and hand it to the mother. Other services provided by midwives during the immediate postpartum period included bathing the mother in water, rubbing her with oil, and tying up her abdomen with a restrictive corset-like garment (*barut*). The fees for such services were between M$10 and 30, though proper compensation also included betel, rice, and other items of food and drink.

At present, however, all children are born in hospitals, and Western-trained doctors assume the role traditionally performed by village midwives, though the latter (or their modern counterparts, "government midwives") frequently attend and assist such births. The first resident of Bogang who was born in a hospital ward is now in his mid-thirties. Because his nickname is Wad—which is a phonetic rendering of the Malay pronunciation of the term "ward"—he is a literal embodiment and ever-present reminder of the timing of the transition to hospital births, as well as the beginnings of the decline of traditional midwifery. And since most doctors are male, Wad also constitutes a clear reminder that the shift to hospital births and the attendant decline of traditional midwifery represent yet another example of women's ritual roles being usurped by men.

Hospital births do not necessarily preclude the performance of traditional postpartum rituals, especially since most hospital stays for childbirth are of relatively short duration. Western-oriented doctors, moreover, frequently encourage women to observe many (but not all) of the traditional restrictions, particularly those related to diet and humoral balance. Doctors are rather ambivalent about the value of some postpartum rituals, however, such as the pan-Southeast Asian practice of "roasting the mother." This ritual (*berselai, salaian*) involves building a small fire and having the postpartum mother stand over it for a few hours each day (for a period of forty-four days) so as to help her restore her heat and "bind up her insides." This practice is still seen by most Malays as highly valued if not indispensable. As one woman put it, if women don't observe this and attendant rituals and restrictions, "their uteruses/wombs will fall, their stomachs will protrude, their faces will look old, and their bones—

along with the rest of their bodies—will start to ache and will feel cold for the remainder of their lives."[18]

One of the most important postpartum rituals performed for the benefit of the newborn child is the "burial (or planting) of the afterbirth" (*taman temuni*), which I have discussed elsewhere (Peletz 1988b:50–51, 53, 348 n.6; cf. Lewis 1962; McKinley 1975). This ritual highlights the social and cultural significance of siblingship (and the relational sense of self generally) by focusing attention on the individual's grounding in his or her sibling set, and on the extent to which the individual's destiny or fate is keyed to that of his or her siblings. The afterbirth (*temuni*) is regarded as the newborn's mystical "elder sibling" ("elder brother" in the case of a male fetus, "elder sister" in the case of a female) since it derives from the placenta, which nourished and protected the fetus in the womb, much like an elder sibling ideally helps sustain and protect his or her younger sibling throughout the latter's life. As such, it must be shown proper respect and otherwise be dealt with in a ceremonial fashion.

In order to properly dispose of the afterbirth, the midwife must first clean it with salt, lime, tamarind, and water, and then bury it in a small hole about two feet deep. Before placing the afterbirth in the hole, the midwife wraps it in silk or other fine cloth, all the while reciting Koranic chants or other incantations. The afterbirth is sometimes wrapped up with pencils and notebooks (in the case of a boy), or sewing needles, cloth, and the like (in the case of a girl). This helps ensure that the child will later attain the requisite skills associated with his or her gender. Other gendered dimensions of this ritual include the location of the hole into which the afterbirth is placed. In the case of a male child, the hole is dug beneath the verandah or out in the garden area; in the case of a female, the hole is beneath the interior of the house. This reinforces the culturally elaborated links between females and interiority on the one hand, and males and exteriority on the other. It also entails both the spatial aggregation of same-sex siblings, and the spatial dispersal of opposite-sex siblings.

Failure to dispose of an afterbirth in this fashion is believed to result in dire consequences for the newborn child. The same is true for failure to light a fire over the hole and keep it burning for a period of forty-four days, this being the period of time that mother and newborn are subject to the most stringent taboos.

The proper disposal of the afterbirth is rendered difficult (though not impossible) when children are born in hospitals. The main reason for this is that doctors and other hospital employees tend to treat afterbirths as "waste products" or "garbage," and to dispose of them in the trash. Hence, villagers must request that the afterbirths be saved, and must also make arrangements to have them brought back to the village for proper burial. The first time I observed the ritual burial of the afterbirth was shortly after I ran into Abang Hamid (an employee at the nearest hospital) coming home from town. I asked him, as villagers are inclined to do, what he had purchased in town, and more specifically, what he had in the clear plastic bag that he was carrying over one arm. His nonchalant reply, "Rokiah's afterbirth," left me feeling that I had intruded where I did not belong and, as such, was somewhat of a conversation stopper (at least temporarily). As we continued walking toward the village, I asked him what he was going to do with it, and upon hearing that he was going to give it to a midwife for burial, I expressed interest in observing the ceremony. He told me that I was welcome at the ceremony (as did the midwife and the others I checked with later on).

I should note, too, that both women and men express a preference for female children. Such preferences do not reflect concerns with the perpetuation of clan or lineage, though social continuity in the form of domestic reproduction—the fact that daughters rather than sons typically inherit and thus maintain houses and house plots—is sometimes mentioned in this regard. Rather, these preferences testify to deeply entrenched convictions (held by women and men alike) that daughters are much more likely than sons to take good care of their parents in their old age and during periods of infirmity and are, more generally, far more responsive to the moral and material obligations associated with kinship and social relations on the whole (even when inducements of inheritance do not figure into the picture). As one female elder put it, "a daughter may have only a bit of anchovy, but she will still give some to her parents; a son, though, may have an entire water buffalo and might not even give them a taste" (cf. Ong 1987:104–5). In light of sentiments such as these, it should come as no surprise to find that while parents and other close kin are extremely distressed at the death of any infant, their sense of grief and loss seems more pronounced in the case of a death involving a female infant. This, at least, is the impression I received from conversations with and observations of women. I have no data from men on this subject, but for reasons noted above I suspect they feel similarly.

The preference for female children does not necessarily translate into longer periods of nursing for female infants, or their being given better (or more) food or medical care. Nor, more generally, are little girls indulged to a greater degree than little boys. On the contrary, male children are treated far more indulgently than female children. Male children are both allowed and expected to play more roughly—and to roam more widely in their play—than female children, and to ignore their parents' and elder siblings' admonitions and requests for assistance with household chores. Behavior such as this is consistent with the widely held view that little boys have more "passion" (and less "shame") than little girls, but is simultaneously out of keeping with the equally pervasive view that, overall, males are less "passionate" than females. The inconsistency in these views is more apparent than real and raises two important issues: First, there is an important developmental dynamic that needs to be considered when assessing local views of male and female (such views are not static over the life cycle). And second, contrasting views of gender keyed to different stages of the life cycle are not equally valorized. These and related matters are the subject of the remainder of the chapter.

THE CONCEPTS OF "REASON," "PASSION," AND "SHAME"

The Concept of Nafsu ("Passion")

Nafsu is an Arabic-origin term (*nafs* in Arabic) that is widely used both among Malays and other Muslims in the Malay-Indonesian archipelago (e.g., Acehnese, Minangkabau, Javanese) and among Muslims (Moroccans, Yemeni, Turks, Bedouin, etc.) elsewhere in the world.[19] It is translated in contemporary Malay dictionaries as "passion," "desire," "lust," "want," "longing," which is in keeping with its uses both in Bogang and in other Muslim communities. In many and perhaps all Muslim communities, the term *nafsu* (hereafter "passion") frequently carries derogatory connotations, especially when it is applied to humans.[20] In many (but not all) Muslim communities, moreover, one finds an entrenched, highly elaborated belief that "passion" is more pronounced among women (and females generally) than among men (males).[21] The latter point will be addressed below. First, however, we need to contextualize such beliefs by examining villagers' basic understandings and representations of "passion" and the ways they relate to local understandings and representations of "reason" (*akal*) and "shame" (*malu*). As will be apparent in due course, "passion" and "reason" (and "shame") are not simply symbols "of" or "about" gender. They also inform village thought about the essence and dynamics of human nature, social relations, and the world at large, all of which is to say that they are central to the local ontology.

In the Malay view of things, God created the universe and all of its features and inhabitants. In accordance with God's will, "passion" is present in humans and other animals, spirits, and all other living creatures. The presence of "passion" in humans, and in the universe generally, dates from the time of Adam, who, after seeing two doves, asked God to make him a companion or mate. God obliged Adam, and made Hawah (Eve) from one of Adam's ribs. God proceeded to instruct Adam and Hawah not to eat the fruit of a certain tree (a pomegranate tree in some local variants of the myth, an unspecified tree in others). But Adam and Hawah were tempted by the devil to eat the fruit, and they did so, which action resulted in their being driven from Heaven. A piece of the fruit lodged in Adam's throat, and to this day men have "Adam's apples" (*halkum*), which serve as embodied reminders of Adam's transgression. Portions of the apple appeared as breasts (*dada, buah dada*) in Hawah, and to this day women have prominent breasts, which, like men's "Adam's apples," signify both Adam and Hawah's sins and humankind's "passion" (cf. Laderman 1983:74).

The moral of this myth of genesis is not only that those who disobey God receive divine punishment, but also—and more relevant here—that sensual and other gratification necessarily entails both the indulgence of desire and ipso facto the absence of restraint. Restraint and control of the inner self are strongly marked moral virtues, the attainment of which brings prestige. Conversely, the absence of restraint indexes a lack of virtue and gives rise to stigma.

This system of moral evaluation helps explain villagers' marked ambivalence about the satisfaction of basic (biophysiological) human requirements. On the one hand, villagers do of course recognize that human beings require food, drink, air, shelter, and the like, if they are to survive and thrive; and they are well aware that sexual activity is necessary for procreation, and for the reproduction of society and culture. On the other hand, villagers view the satisfaction of these basic human requirements with marked ambivalence since their satisfaction is associated with the absence of restraint. People look down upon individuals who are felt to be overly concerned with food, eating, and drinking, although this is one of two domains in which relative indulgence is permitted, even enjoined (the other is illness, real or imagined). (Individuals who fail to fast during the month of Ramadan are especially stigmatized and are liable to criminal prosecution if they break the fast in public.) And they talk about such behavior in terms of the preponderance, if only temporary or context specific, of "passion" relative to "reason," which is seen as unsightly, unbecoming, morally offensive, and, at least in some contexts, as seriously sinful (cf. Newbold 1839 II:353).

More generally, when villagers speak of gossiping, desiring material possessions, being especially (or overly) interested in sex, they often mention "passion"; they are, moreover, quick to link "passion" with the devil and evil spirits and demons of various kinds who tempt them with sinful behavior. As a male elder put it when we were discussing the origins of the universe and related matters: "This 'passion,' it's the devil. You want to eat a lot, drink a lot, that's all the devil, satan. You want to buy clothes, buy a house, make your house all beautiful, that's the same: satan, the devil. These are worldly matters; in the Afterlife they don't exist."

Negative attitudes toward the absence of restraint are well illustrated in widely held views concerning food prohibitions and ethnic groups who appear (to villagers) not to observe any such prohibitions, such as the semi-nomadic non-Muslim aborigines (*orang asli;* literally, "original people") living in the hilly, forested regions behind the village. The aborigines eat the meat of wild boar, which, like all other pork, is forbidden to Muslims, and which is highest on the list of prohibited foods as far as Malays are concerned. The consumption of pork is in fact seen by Malays as thoroughly revolting, far more so than the consumption of snake, dog, lizard, and cockroach, which the aborigines are also said to enjoy.[22] Of greater importance is that because the aborigines eat wild boar, they are assumed not to have any food prohibitions. And because of the perceived lack of food prohibitions, they are thought to "have no religion, only beliefs and superstitions" (*tak ada agama, kepercayaan saja*). More broadly, since the aborigines have no religion, they have no culture (*sopan, kesoponan; budaya, kebudayaan*), which, in the local view, is what distinguishes human beings (*manusia*) from "mere animals" (*binatang saja*). Indeed, when villagers speak of aborigines, they frequently comment that the aborigines are "like animals" (*macam binatang*). Some carry this association even further, suggesting that the aborigines are not simply "like animals," but that they really *are* animals, created from "grime" (*daki*) (cf. Newbold 1839 II:106).

The idea that the aborigines exercise no restraint when it comes to eating pork and are for this reason uncultured and subhuman resonates both with villagers' negative views on other "races" (Chinese, Indians, and "white people" [*orang putih*]), whose behavior—especially with respect to eating, drinking, gambling, and sex—is seen as relatively unrestrained, and with their views of fellow Malays whose behavior is deemed inappropriate and/or aesthetically offensive. The exercise (or absence) of restraint thus serves as an important ethnic/racial marker, which is heavily, albeit never explicitly, gendered (other "races," after all, are accorded the relative lack of restraint that official discourse attributes to and defines as a key feature of [Malay] womanhood), as well as an index of virtue (or its absence) within Malay communities. In cases of seriously offensive behavior on the part of Malays, the offender is sometimes said to be "less than fully taught"—a very serious charge. Violations of incest prohibitions certainly fall into this category, and are sometimes likened to "chickens eating their own flesh" (*macam ayam makan daging sendiri*), which draws a parallel between individuals who mate with their own kind (e.g., members of the same lineage or clan), and domesticated chickens that consume the scraps of cooked food thrown out for them, which frequently include the flesh/meat of their own relatives. The explicit metaphoric link between incest and cannibalism—both of which are construed as quintessentially subhuman—would have certainly delighted Freud ([1913] 1950).[23]

Persons whose comportment is seriously offensive are thus said to be improperly socialized and therefore standing somewhere between the rule-governed realm of humans, where socialization presumes the learning and internalization of moral codes; and the world of animals, which is governed by "passion," not by moral codes or rules. Socialization is in fact seen as a process entailing the gradual curtailment or control of "passion" through the imposition of man-made (but ultimately divinely inspired) codes and rules embodied in Islam and *adat*. The socialization process, and culture generally, thus "work on" the raw material of "passion," which, as noted above, is directly and inextricably associated with the world of animals and nature, and with the relatively if not altogether uncultured ("natural" and in certain respects feminine) behavior of other "races."

Before proceeding to a discussion of "reason," I should stress that there are some crucial differences between Malay understandings and representations of "passion" on the one hand, and those reported for culturally similar groups such as the Acehnese and Javanese on the other. We have already seen that in Malay culture "passion" is experienced and construed in predominantly negative terms, as indexing a lack of restraint, hence weakness, animality, and so on. This is true for Acehnese as well, though Acehnese sometimes remark that "passion," properly guided by "reason," can be and ideally is channeled into Islamic prayer and chanting as well as other forms of pious and morally virtuous behavior (Siegel 1969). I never encountered remarks or views of the latter sort among Malays, even though there are certain contexts (e.g., weddings and funerary rituals) in which Malays, like Acehnese, engage in Sufistic chanting which sometimes eventuates in a kind of frenzied ecstasy. That Acehnese but not

Malays operate with a concept of "passion" that makes explicit provision for the utilization of "passion" in the fulfillment of religious objectives may reflect the fact that, due to the variegated historical development of Islam in Southeast Asia, Acehnese Islam is more thoroughly infused with Sufistic elements than is Malayan Islam. In any event, the more general point about the absence among Malays of Acehnese/Sufistic constructions of the sort at issue here has also been noted by Malay anthropologists such as Wazir Jahan Karim (1990:36), who recently offered the following (understated) observation: "Sufi thinking that passion can be harnessed to a love for religion and ecstasy over God does not permeate Malay thinking, at least amongst the masses."

I might emphasize, too, that, at least in my experience, the conceptual apparatus in terms of which Malays understand and talk about "passion" is less complex and less elaborated than that reported for societies such as Java. Woodward (1989:190–91) notes, for example, that the Javanese he came to know in and around the Sultanate of Yogyakarta commonly speak of there being four different types of "passion" (*nepsu* in Javanese): (1) *aluhama*, or greed, "symbolized by the color black, represented as an animal, and located in the blood"; (2) *amarah*, or anger, "symbolized by the color red, represented as a spirit, [and] located in muscle tissue"; (3) *mutmainah*, or desire for tranquility, "symbolized by the color white, represented as a fish, [and] located in the breath"; and (4) *supiyah*, or the desire to destroy evil, "symbolized by the color yellow, represented as a bird, [and] present in bone marrow." I am not aware of any data suggesting that Malays in Negeri Sembilan or elsewhere view "passion" in terms of this explicit typology, or that they make any of the aforementioned symbolic associations, about which Javanese are, according to Woodward (1989:190), in "nearly universal agreement."[24] Also absent from the Malay landscape, as mentioned earlier, is the idea (found also in Aceh) that certain types of "passion" (*mutmainah* and *supiyah* in the Javanese case) are "the forces directing the individual toward the performance of normative Islamic rituals and the cultivation of the state of *kramat*" (being holy, having the mystical powers of saints [Woodward 1989:191–92, 299]).[25]

The Concepts of Akal ("Reason") and Malu ("Shame")

Akal is an Arabic-origin concept (*'aql* in Arabic) that is of central importance among Malays and other Muslims in Southeast Asia and beyond. The term denotes "reason," "intelligence," and "rationality," the ability to evaluate alternative courses of action (e.g., display perspective and view things from afar) and render informed judgments, and is widely used in Malay culture in connection with "passion" and "shame." As mentioned earlier, it is often said that *akal* (hereafter "reason") distinguishes humans from the rest of the animal world and is our special gift from God; and that "reason" "cooperates" or "works together" both with the *hati* (or liver, the seat of emotions) and with *iman* (faith, strong belief or trust in God, resoluteness, sincerity) to guide the individual along the proper path(s). Villagers also contend that "reason" and "passion" forever struggle against one another within the individual, and that "good behavior" (*budi baik*) is evidence of the preponderance, however temporary or qualified, of "reason" over "passion," just as "bad behavior" (*budi jahat*) reflects the dominance, however short-lived or partial, of "passion" over "reason." "Shame" (*malu*) is relevant here as well, for it, too, acts as a "brake" on "passion" and its expression or realization in social action.

While ("normal," "healthy") human beings are born with the capacity to develop "reason," they do not display or possess "reason" at birth. Rather, in the usual course of things, "reason" "develops" or "expands" (*kembang*) over time, as a consequence of socialization and religious instruction in particular, and is typically manifested in one or another form when a child is seven or eight years old (though this is highly variable), or, as some people put it, when the child begins instruction in the recitation of the Koran (*mengaji*). (Children normally begin such instruction at about the time they commence secular education in the national school system, i.e., when they are about six or seven years old.) It is also true that young children and adolescents are often characterized as lacking "reason," but the point of reference here is adults, not (nonhuman) animals.

Diligent observance of Muslim prayer procedure and other religious strictures is one way to help develop one's "reason." Conversely, the cultivation of "reason" through concentration and various types of mental and spiritual exercises entailing studied restraint facilitates proper prayer and other forms of religiously valued and morally virtuous behavior. Compared to children and adolescents, adults tend to take more seriously their (and to have more extensive) obligations as Muslims. This is one reason why adults are typically regarded as having more "reason" than children and adolescents. Other reasons include their superior abilities (relative to children and adolescents) to make informed judgments based on experience in the world; their demonstrated capacities to perform the myriad tasks and activities associated with domestic maintenance, production, and the like; and, more generally, their greater control over their "passions" and their more systematic internalization of and behavioral adherence to the moral norms of Malay culture; hence (given the explicit link between being Malay and being human), their stronger commitment to being human.

Just as the acquisition or development of "reason" is a gradual process, so, too, in many cases at least, is the dissolution or loss of "reason" in the course of debilitating illness or old age. Individuals afflicted with senility are often said to have "lost" their "reason" and to have reverted to a childlike state in which "reason" is poorly developed or only sporadically manifest. In some instances, senescence seems to be regarded as a "natural" process that is inherent in biological aging, though in others it is attributed to possession by evil spirits harbored by malevolent (human) others.

Various types of severe emotional, psychological, and spiritual disorders (including senility) are sometimes attributed to or regarded as involving debilitated "reason," but for the most part disorders of this sort are conceptualized in terms of livers and/or "life forces" (*semangat*), not "reason." Thus, a person who exhibits what we might take to be symptoms of extreme anxiety, depression, or obsessive behavior is not usually viewed as having something wrong with his or her "reason" or brain (*otak*), but rather to be suffering an affliction of the liver or "life force." Similarly, an individual who is "girl (or boy) crazy" (*gila perimpuan* [*gila laki-laki*]) is commonly believed to be the victim of human malevolence that "worked on" his or her liver or "life force." (Mental retardation and insanity, on the other hand, are seen as disorders of the brain, mind, or "reason.") It is nonetheless true that disturbances of the liver or "life force" can interfere with one's ability to "reason." In this sense, and in many others discussed earlier, Malays view body and mind as integrally related parts of a single and unified whole, and do not operate with a dualistic mind/body dichotomy of the sort informing Western medicine and Western thought generally.

A final point to stress in this brief overview of local understandings and representations of "reason" is that discourses on "reason" are often framed in terms of heavily value-laden spatial metaphors. Thus, certain individuals and classes of people (adult males) are accorded "long," "broad," "high," or "deep" "reason," just as others (adult females, and children and adolescents of both sexes) are held to be endowed with "reason" that is "short," "narrow," "low," or "shallow." Having "reason" that is "long," "broad," and "high" is clearly more valued than having "reason" that is "short," "narrow," and "low"; and the person with "long," "broad" "reason" is accorded more virtue in the hierarchy of prestige (and stigma)—all of which is to say that the allocation of "reason" serves to legitimize the distribution of virtue in the prestige hierarchy, and that "reason" is central to the system of moral evaluation as a whole. I will return to these themes later.

Malu, for its part, is an Austronesian-origin term that is used by Malays to denote feelings or states of "shame" (being "ashamed"), "shyness" (being "shy"), as well as being "self-conscious" and "uncomfortable." *Malu* (hereafter "shame") is, like "reason," a quality or set of qualities that children are believed to be able to acquire, though this, too, requires active intervention on the part of parents, elder siblings, and others. Thus, young children, especially young boys, are frequently taught by negative example that the highly valued state of being "ashamed" and modest necessitates hiding their genitals from view. A favorite pastime of male elders is to ask young boys of toddler age to reveal their genitals. If the young boy turns or moves away shyly or with embarrassment, as typically happens, he is pestered and teased until he pulls down his pants and exposes his genitals. When this occurs there are howls of laughter from onlookers (men and women alike), and squealing on the part of the young boy, who is promptly scolded for having no *malu!* This type of teasing, which was frequently inflicted on my son Zachary (much to his dismay), is not visited upon little girls, who, in any case, are taught and expected to have a "stronger" or "more developed" sense of "shame" than boys of the same age. More generally, as I discuss later, men and women alike contend not only that females have a stronger and more developed sense of "shame" than males, but also that, if they did not, they would be "like wild animals" and the world would be in chaos.

One of the terms for genitals is *kemaluan*, which builds on the root *malu*, and which may be translated literally as a "thing or object of shame or embarrassment." The term is not gender-specific; hence if villagers want to specify male as opposed to female genitals (or vice versa) they simply add the term for male or female (*kemaluan perimpuan*, *kemaluan laki-laki* [female genitals, male genitals]). The term *kemaluan* is sometimes used inadvertently, especially by villagers who lack formal education and who are trying to speak "lettered" Malay. A stock joke of school teachers and other relatively lettered folk concerns the (male) villager who, giving a speech in a large public setting or on the radio, prefaces his comments with a remark to the effect that he is deeply honored and humbled by the opportunity to speak; specifically, he refers to his deep embarrassment or shame, or to being deeply humbled, as "my large *kemaluan*" (*kemaluan besar*), which is typically taken to mean that he has a large penis.

There are other terms for genitals, some of which are gender specific. The penis, for example, is sometimes referred to by a term which also denotes a small bird (*pipit*); alternatively, the term for mosquito (*nyamuk*) is used. Men occasionally make jokes about their "birds biting" or their "mosquitoes stinging." The latter are especially common when men appear at local provision shops to buy mosquito coils, which are referred to as *ubat nyamuk*, a term which can also mean "medicine for a mosquito." "Is your mosquito sick?" "Does it hurt?" "Is it biting a lot?" The fact that testes are referred to by a term (*telor*) that also means "eggs" invites similar types of jokes.

The clitoris is referred to as *kelintit*, which also denotes a cockel, a type of shrub, and a type of creeping, climbing plant. *Kelintit* is said to be a term of abuse that is sometimes used among women, though I never encountered it in this context (neither did Ellen). The related term *puki*, which is an extremely vulgar term similar to the English term "cunt," is rarely used in polite conversation (though I have heard grandmothers use the term in joking references to their infant granddaughters' genitals). The expression *puki muk kau* ("your mother's cunt") is perhaps the most offensive insult that can be hurled at anyone, partly because it entails cursing one's origins but also because it highlights the theme of animality (discussed below).

Breasts, for their part, are referred to as *buah dada* (literally, "chest fruit" or "fruit of the chest"). Like the genitals of people past the age of five or six, the breasts of females over five or six years of age should always be covered (even during bathing). Men's torsos are likewise "good to cover"; indeed, it is thoroughly inappropriate for men to venture beyond their own residential compounds without shirts or a towel (or some such) covering their chests, though exceptions are often made for men performing manual labor, who sometimes strip to the waist when digging ditches or engaging in other arduous physical labor in the heat of the day.

In order to behave in accordance with the moral imperatives of "shame," one must certainly cover one's genitals (even, as noted earlier, while bathing by oneself) and much of the rest of one's body. However, a proper sense of shame also presupposes vigilance in many other social contexts, only some of which entail the spectre of potential cross-sex impropriety. This will be clear from an (edited) excerpt from my field notes and the brief commentary that follows.

> The other day (February 1979), while walking through the village with two (male) friends who were visiting from Kuala Lumpur, I saw Chegu Rokiah, a thirty-eight-year-old school teacher, sitting with her mother and another village woman just outside their kitchen. Chegu Rokiah, who had apparently seen me (us) coming, quickly disappeared into the house as I (we) approached, for she is still an *anak dara*, an unmarried female, maiden, virgin.[26] As she told me later, "It is important to guard one's reputation; it's not that I don't like you; it's just that people would talk a lot and my standing in the community might suffer if I was overly friendly with you, or interacted too freely with any other male [married or single]." She went on to explain that when her brother-in-law comes home, she doesn't talk with him much and generally eschews interacting with him altogether. Particularly if he has brought male friends to the house, she serves them coffee or tea and then disappears into the kitchen. On many such occasions she instructs one of the children of the house to bring them food and drinks, thereby avoiding all contact with them.
>
> Chegu Rokiah explained that this is *adat*, a way of showing respect, and went on to discuss her ideas of friendship, intimacy, social distance, and the like. As a rule, she does not visit fellow villagers unless she has an errand or some business that requires her to go to their home(s). It would be different, of course, if she was married (but even then I suspect she would stick pretty much to her own house and compound, as many married women do, unless subsistence, exchange, or religious activities call for their presence elsewhere in the village or beyond).
>
> Similarly, when she walks through the village on her way to or home from work she usually avoids eye contact with people. More broadly, she seeks to maintain a good deal of distance from everyone in the village. It is important that such distance be maintained, she told me, lest others "lose their respect" for you. She thus implied a positive relationship between social distance and respect, such that the greater the social distance (and formality), the greater the respect. Significantly, she also made an explicit reference to "fear," and to the necessity, or at least the desirability, of having people fear her, so that they would be reluctant to "bother" (*kacau, menggangu*) her.
>
> This particular strategy has earned Chegu Rokiah the reputation of being *sombong* (arrogant, haughty, unresponsive to social expectation) and extremely *garang* ("fierce"). Some younger adult men and women (e.g., her cousins) are indeed afraid of her, though such fear might also reflect their recognition that Chegu Rokiah has a well deserved reputation for having a very sharp tongue and a "bad mouth" (*mulut jehat*).

Though I do not recall Chegu Rokiah making any explicit references to "shame" in her explanation of why she disappeared into the house as I approached, or why she behaves as she does more generally, the gist of her explanation of her behavior fits well with local understandings of "shame." I might note, too, that on previous occasions (e.g., shortly after I first arrived in the village in 1978), she arranged for children to bring me snacks and other food as well as pamphlets on local culture and history, and explained that she couldn't bring me such gifts herself since, if she did so, people would say she had no "shame."[27]

A related and broader point is that behavior in accordance with the moral imperatives of "shame"—and of "reason," "refinement," "style," and "grace"—is not motivated solely or even primarily by concerns that one's conduct be, or appear to others to be, aesthetically pleasing or morally virtuous. Such conduct is also motivated by concerns that might be termed "defensive" inasmuch as the conduct is intended to serve as a defense against being "bothered" or "disturbed" (as the local euphemisms put it) by potentially malevolent others (relatives, neighbors, etc.)—any one of whom may be offended by behavior that hints at impropriety or entails real or imagined threats to one's status, honor or name, and may, as a result, seek retaliation through sorcery or otherwise.[28] That such behavioral strategies can also have "offensive" qualities insofar as they can be geared toward striking fear into the hearts (or livers) of others, is also apparent from some of Chegu Rokiah's remarks. All such strategies are essential to survival in a social and cultural environment in which it is taken for granted that people are motivated by greed, envy, and malice, and are forever trying to get the better of one another through displays of status and prestige, and by attempts to gain control over other people's loyalties, affections, and resources.

These latter points are significant for a variety of reasons, one of which bears on the previously noted theme that women (and females on the whole) are universally believed to be more modest and "ashamed" than men (males). Modest behavior is not merely a constraint imposed on women; it is also a resource that women can and do deploy in the pursuit of their (culturally defined) interests. The same generalizations pertain both to (male and female) children, who are expected to be "ashamed" in the presence of their elders (kinsmen and others), and to subordinates of other varieties, including the (male and female) subjects of "traditional" and modern political as well as religious leaders (see Scott 1985). In sum, deferential and circumspect behavior in accordance with the moral imperatives of "shame" is in many instances a calculated strategy deployed by women, children, political subordinates, and others (e.g., men addressing audiences comprised primarily of status equals and dependents), and thus entails the active exercise of agency, albeit in an environment redolent with real and imagined threats.

Finally, a brief comment on the relationship between "reason" and "shame": To be "ashamed" is, as mentioned earlier, an indication that one is endowed with at least a modicum of "reason," and that one thus stands "above" the world of animals (who know neither "shame" nor "reason" and are governed entirely by "passion"). We have also seen that "reason" and "shame" (along with the liver) "cooperate" and "work together" to "kill," or at least act as brakes on, the expression or realization of "passion" in social action. In the local view of things, however, it does *not* follow from these points that the most modest individuals are also the most "reasonable." Thus, while women are invariably viewed as having more "shame" than men, they are not for this reason (or on any account) held to be more "reasonable" or less "passionate" than men (at least in official discourse). Rather, it is precisely because women have less "reason" and more "passion" than men that they are—and fully need to be— more "ashamed."

NATURE, CULTURE, AND GENDER REVISITED

The concepts of "passion," "reason," and "shame" shed important light on local experiences, understandings, and representations of human nature and sociality. They are of further significance since they are critical markers of contrasts between males and females in a social and cultural environment that places relatively little emphasis on gender or gender difference(s). In this connection we might recall that in most contexts of society and culture there is relatively little concern with gender or gender difference(s); and that compared to many (perhaps most) other societies studied by anthropologists, gender does not constitute an important marker of social activities, spatial domains, or cultural knowledge. There is, for example, a relative deemphasis of gender in forms of address and other features of kinship terminology (which emphasize bilaterality, relative generation, and age); in the sexual division of labor (which emphasizes reciprocity, complementarity, and the interchangeability of men and women); and in most ritual activities. And there are no men's houses, menstrual huts, or other extreme forms of gender seclusion or segregation, though it is true that mosques, prayer houses, and, to a lesser extent, coffee shops are sometimes regarded as essentially male domains. Particularly significant as well, in many contexts villagers contend that males

Figure 16. Women at mosque

Figure 17. Indok Jaliah and niece

and females are essentially the same (*sama*) in terms of their personalities, temperaments, and emotions, and of equal status (*pangkat, taraff*), despite their different, though complementary, roles.

At the same time, there are various contexts in which villagers assert that males and females differ in certain fundamental respects and are of dissimilar status. Recall, for example, that the predominance among women of spirit possession and *latah* is typically explained in terms of females having "weaker" *semangat* or "life force" than men, and being more prone than men to worrying, anxiety, and emotional trauma, such as that associated with poverty or the death of a child. More generally, women are widely held by men and women alike to have less "reason" than men and less status and prestige (though not necessarily less power, or *kuasa* [see below]). And although there is less agreement on this point (as we will see in due course), women tend to be portrayed, particularly in official representations of gender and kinship, as having more "passion" than men, even though villagers are quick to point out that both "passion" and "reason" are present to one degree or another in all humans.

Official interpretations of women having less "reason" and more "passion" than men often focus on the perception (which, like most other local perceptions, is typically stated as "a fact") that women are less controlled and restrained than men insofar as they are more prone to gossiping and desiring material possessions, and are otherwise more closely tied to the "baser" things in life. The arena of sexual relations is the quintessential context, at least (or especially) for men, in which women's stronger "passion" is displayed, for, as some male elders told me, in sexual relations (*hubungan seks*) women "still want more" even after their husbands are thoroughly satisfied (have attained orgasm). The latter point, which may well reflect men's (and women's) limited understandings of the anatomy and physiology of female orgasm, was never conceded (indeed, never came up) in the conversations that I—or Ellen—had with women. Nor did the point made by another male elder, that "women in hotels," by which he meant prostitutes, can have sex ten or twenty times in an evening, or even "all night long," none of which would be possible for a man. I should emphasize, though, that many women *do* espouse the position that women's "passion" is more pronounced than men's. Virtually all women, moreover, hold that women "need to"—and do in fact—have a stronger sense of "shame" than men; significantly, more than a few women (and many men) told me that if they did not, they would be "like wild animals" (*macam haiwan*) and chaos would reign throughout the world.

The extent to which men's views of women's insatiable sexuality are an index of men's sexual anxiety is both exceedingly difficult to gauge and altogether beyond the scope of the present discussion. I would only note that similar types of views have been documented for Malays in the state of Kelantan, and that the "husband's feelings that he cannot handle his wife's demanding sexual expectations" are given (if only by male informants) as one of the major causes of divorce (Nash 1974:38, cited in Spiro 1977:287 n.16). Findings such as these (see also Ong 1990b:273) are not reported for most other societies in Southeast Asia (e.g., Java, Thailand, Burma), and have led Spiro (1977:241 n.14) to comment that while "sexual anxiety is of course widespread in South and Southeast Asia [his main frame of reference], . . . Malay men may represent the extreme case."

Local views of the differences between men and women are of broad comparative and theoretical significance. They are quite similar to the views found among Malays elsewhere in the Peninsula; among Acehnese, Javanese, and other Muslims in Southeast Asia; and among Muslims in other parts of the Islamic world (though there are some important differences as well, which are keyed to variations in systems of production, exchange, prestige, and personhood). Among Malays in Trengganu, for example, "reason" is more strongly associated with men, just as "passion" is more strongly associated with women (Laderman 1982:91, 1983:76). Reports from Pahang indicate, similarly, that "reason" is "a quality that men are supposed to be more generously endowed with" (Massard 1985:72). In Kedah, Selangor, and elsewhere in the Peninsula we see much the same thing (Banks 1983:86–87; Ong 1987:87, 192–93, 1988:31, 1990a:388–90, 1990b:261).

Accounts from other Muslim settings—such as Aceh, Java, Morocco, Yemen, and Egypt—are generally consistent with reports from Malay societies (though there are, as noted earlier, some important contrasts). One of the most comprehensive treatments of such gender imagery comes from Morocco and indicates not only that there is a developmental dynamic that needs to be considered when assessing Moroccan views of males and females (such views are not static over the life cycle), but also, that in what might be termed "private" or "backstage" contexts, some Moroccan women contest certain official representations concerning both their secondary status and the differences between males and females generally (Dwyer 1978). These caveats are relevant to Negeri Sembilan as well. In some respects far more interesting, however, are the ways in which gender imagery in Negeri Sembilan differs from what has been reported for Morocco, other North African societies such as Egyptian Bedouins (Abu-Lughod 1986), and most other societies, including Malays outside of Negeri Sembilan. For in Negeri Sembilan there is a highly elaborated alterna-

Figure 18. Razak

tive discourse, which is in many respects an inversion of the official/hegemonic discourse that I have outlined here, and which clearly transcends "private," "domestic," and "female-dominated" contexts. In short, key features of this very public albeit contextually specific discourse are shared by men and women alike (as discussed further along).

Negeri Sembilan (and other Muslim) gender imagery is of particular theoretical significance in light of Ortner's now classic (1974) argument that women are everywhere held to be "closer to nature" and "further from culture" than men, and that this conceptual linkage explains their universal secondary status (see also Ardener 1972). This incisive and provocative thesis, which builds on the insights of Simone de Beauvoir (1949), Claude Lévi-Strauss (1949), and David Schneider (1968), generated a great deal of additional research, though it did of course meet with much criticism as well (see, e.g., Dwyer 1978; MacCormack and Strathern 1980; Bloch 1987). Many scholars (I am not one of them) tend to regard such criticism as the "final word" on the nature/culture thesis. In the past few years, however, there has been renewed interest in the nature/culture thesis on the part of Southeast Asianists and others (see, e.g., Valeri 1990; Hoskins 1990; see also Shore 1981; Abu-Lughod 1986, chap. 4), some of whom have argued compellingly that much of the initial criticism of the thesis was misguided (and that some of it was in fact spurious), and that key features of the thesis are of considerable analytic value for specific ethnographic cases (such as the Huaulu and Kodi of Eastern Indonesia). I concur with this perspective, as will be apparent in due course.[29]

Key features of Ortner's arguments *do* hold for Negeri Sembilan Malays, and for other Malays, as well as Acehnese and Moroccans, though the latter groups are not my primary concern here. They do so, however, only so long as we (1) limit ourselves to a consideration of official discourse, and (2) specify more precisely than Ortner does which meanings of the polyvalent concept of "nature" are primary both with respect to Malays' understandings and representations of females, and in terms of the world view of the analyst and of Western culture on the whole. In official discourse, as we have seen, women (and females generally) are portrayed as having more "passion" and less "reason" than men (males). We have also seen that there are explicit, culturally elaborated links between "passion" on the one hand, and animality on the other; and that local understandings and representations of animality are encompassed within a larger framework—"the world of nature"—which both governs and is explicitly manifest in (1) internal processes of the human and non-human body (instincts, reproductive processes, etc.), (2) pre-social states, and (3) the ways of "primitives" (see Bloch and Bloch 1980:27–31). The first two manifestations of "nature" constitute the primary meanings of the term for Malays (though the third is by no means irrelevant), which is to say that "nature" is characterized first and foremost by activities and processes that occur "without the agency, or without the voluntary and intentional agency, of humankind" (Mill 1874:8, cf. 12, cited in Valeri 1990:266). This latter sense is, to reiterate, primary in most contexts in which Malays make direct or indirect reference to "nature" (and to women's "passion" and affinities with the world of animals and nature), though it is certainly true that there are other meanings of "nature" as well (some of which are encompassed within Malay variations on the theme of "natural law"; e.g., that numerous aspects of *adat* are consistent with the "laws of nature," such as the downhill flow of water). My culturally informed understanding of "nature" likewise focuses on this meaning of the term (though I sometimes use the term to convey other meanings). I would suggest, more generally, that in most contexts of contemporary Western culture this is the primary referent of the term (though there are obviously many others, some of which are contradictory with respect to that primary referent).

In sum, in the specific sense referred to here, Malay women *are* held to be "closer to nature" than men. In the local view of things this *necessarily* means that women are also "further from culture" than men, for their greater "passion" indexes their lesser "reason," the latter being the specific quality or capacity, which, more than any other, separates humankind from the world of animals and nature.

Official discourse couched in terms of "reason" and "passion"—and, by implication, "culture" and "nature"—does, moreover, serve to legitimize women's exclusion from, or marginal participation in, various domains of privilege and prestige to which they might otherwise have access (e.g., positions of political and religious leadership), and in this sense clearly serves to hinder their prestige standing (and overall "status") vis-à-vis men. It is important to underscore, though, that many Malays view these and most other aspects of gender roles in terms of complementarity, not asymmetry or hierarchy.

None of this, however, should be taken to suggest that all women buy into all facets of the legitimating discourse, or that there is no counter-hegemonic or other alternative discourse. Dwyer (1978), for example, falsely attributes to Ortner the view that the existence of a hegemony necessarily means that the hegemony is thoroughly dominant and absolutely controlling. Nor, as I said earlier, should any of this be taken to suggest that the meanings of "male" and "female" are static over the course of the life cycle.

In Negeri Sembilan (as in Morocco, Aceh, and many, perhaps most, other societies) there is an important developmental dynamic that informs imagery of gender. Earlier on I made brief mention of Negeri Sembilan

Figure 19. Boys at mosque

views that when a woman is pregnant with a boy, the fetus "kicks harder" and is "more difficult to carry," and that, overall, it is "more difficult" to give birth to a boy than to a girl. Such views are consistent with local contentions that young boys are both naughtier (*lebih nakal*) and more of a problem to discipline than young girls, and, more broadly, that they have "more" (or "stronger") "passion," hence less ("weaker") "reason."

Such views pertain only to pre-adolescent children. The attainment of adolescence is believed to entail major changes in the person, the most notable of which are the awakening of sexuality in males and females alike, and the attainment of heightened "reason" on the part of males, which is associated with their circumcision. Sexual awakening has dissimilar implications for males and females insofar as male and female sexualities differ significantly, albeit primarily in terms of their "quantity" or "strength"; for example, male sexuality is inherently "weaker" in the sense of being easier to control and satisfy than the sexuality of females. (Recall that the views discussed here are part of official/hegemonic discourse, and are in some cases inverted in the alternative discourse examined in detail further along.) More specifically, with the awakening of sexuality at adolescence, male and female youth are no longer accorded the proportions of "reason" and "passion" said to characterize their temperaments, personalities, and behavior prior to adolescence. Henceforth,

Figure 20.   Koranic lessons

Figure 21.   Zachary and friends

though partly because of the changes symbolically associated with their circumcision, males are believed to exhibit more "reason" and less "passion" than females.

Boys are usually circumcised (*sunnat, bersunnat*) when they are about twelve years old, the age at which they have ideally completed their les-

Figure 22.   Girls in rice field

sons in Koranic recitation (*mengaji*). In times past, the circumcision ceremony served as the occasion for a large feast and was overseen by a ritual
specialist known as a *modin,* who was responsible for the surgical removal
of the boy's foreskin. At present, however, circumcision is performed by
doctors in hospitals, and the services of *modin* are no longer needed,

though feasts are still held. Prior to the advent of hospital circumcision, boys about to undergo the operation immersed themselves for a few hours in the cold waters of a river or well. The purpose of this (waist-deep) immersion, I was told, was to anesthetize the young boys so that they would feel less pain. But since water has purifying properties and is widely used in healing, exorcism, and life-crisis rituals (birth, marriage, death), it probably served to purify the initiate as well. So, too (albeit in a different way), did (does) the shedding of penile/genital blood in the course of the actual surgery. This blood, along with the removal of the foreskin, symbolizes both the initiate's formal separation from the carefree, "passion"-governed world of childhood, and his formal entry into the more regulated, "reason"-governed world of (male) adolescence and adulthood. Symbolic statements along these lines used to be more emphatic, for in earlier times, prior to the ritual surgery, the initiate had his hands and feet stained with henna and was, more generally, dressed and treated like a bridegroom (e.g., carried about in a sedan chair in a circumambulatory procession). Even at present, the initiate's ritual passage is further dramatized by a series of food prohibitions and other restrictions, which, as many informants emphasized, are very similar to those observed by postpartum women (cf. Laderman 1983:66). More generally, as soon as his wound has healed and he has completed the period of ritual restrictions, he is no longer a "mere child." Now, though still an adolescent, he is conceptually linked with the world of adult men, and with all of the qualities that serve to distinguish them from adult females, such as their greater knowledge of Islam and their stronger "reason" and weaker "passion" (cf. Woodward 1989:161–63).

There is certainly much more that could be said about circumcision, but I will confine my comments to a few basic (and speculative) points, particularly since I was unable to witness what turned out to be the last (village) circumcision in Bogang (I was called away to, and detained at, a wedding in a neighboring community), and thus have rather sketchy information on the subject. Even when performed in hospitals, circumcision might be seen as a symbolic means of inhibiting, restricting, or otherwise controlling young boys' "passion," especially insofar as pre-adolescent boys are viewed as more "passionate" than their female counterparts, but are nonetheless expected to develop into "reasonable" and responsible adult men. This interpretation is broadly compatible with the views of Malays in the neighboring state of Pahang, that circumcision is a prerequisite and otherwise helps prepare males for marriage and sexual experience, and likewise enhances their virility (Wilder 1970). At the same time, since circumcision rituals obviously entail genital bleeding, which occurs naturally among women and is a sign of women's fertility and capacity to give birth, such rituals might also be seen as a symbolic means of transcending or at least minimizing the most salient biological distinction between males and females (see Bettelheim 1962). The previously noted belief that conception occurs in a man's head and that after conception a man is pregnant for nine days (or longer) further strengthens this line of argument. So, too, does the fact that some men are said to experience nausea and other forms of "morning sickness" during their wives' pregnancies. Further speculation along these lines, though potentially fruitful, is beyond the scope of the present discussion, for my main concern here is not with circumcision per se, but rather with the changes that are symbolically associated with this ritual.

Data relevant to circumcision, and to pre-adolescent children generally, are significant for two reasons. First, they demonstrate that from conception to adolescence males and females are on different and opposed developmental trajectories: The male trajectory entails movement or passage from "passion" to "reason" (and "nature" to "culture"), whereas the female trajectory involves movement or passage in the opposite direction, from "reason" to "passion" (and "culture" to "nature"). And second, they indicate that even if we confine ourselves to a consideration of official discourse, Negeri Sembilan gender imagery is far more complex and contradictory than suggested by Ortner's original formulations. The extent to which such data constitute a serious challenge let alone a fatal blow to Ortner's thesis, however, is another matter. Dwyer (1978), for example, invokes Moroccan life-cycle data (which are in many respects quite similar to Negeri Sembilan data) to support her claim that she has refuted the central tenets of Ortner's thesis. In my view, this claim is greatly overblown. Indeed, I would argue that life-cycle data of the sort at issue here are more appropriately seen as confirming many features of Ortner's overall position.

It is obviously important to make provision for contrasting representations of gender (which Dwyer does), but we also need to consider the degree to which such contrasting representations are equally valorized in the culture(s) at hand (which Dwyer does not). In Negeri Sembilan, local understandings and representations bearing on pre-adolescent children do *not* inform official/hegemonic (or other) understandings and representations of "male" and "female" to any significant degree. The latter understandings and representations are informed primarily by images of fully social adults, and, more specifically, by images relevant to adult men and women in the culturally salient kinship roles of husband/father and brother, and wife/mother and sister. The same is true both for Acehnese, for whom there is extensive data on the subject (see Siegel 1969, 1978; Jayawardena 1977a, 1977b), and for Moroccans (as evidenced by Dwyer's data and material presented by Geertz 1979; Rosen 1984; Mernissi 1987). Indeed, I think it is fair to assume that gender imagery in *all* societies is informed primarily by images of fully social adults. Adults, after all, constitute the category of persons most heavily implicated in social and cultural reproduction, and it stands to reason that representations bearing on this category of persons would be hegemonic with respect to representations of gender generally.

In sum, the proportions of "reason" and "passion" said to obtain among adult males and females in Negeri Sembilan, Aceh, and Morocco are hegemonic with respect to overall understandings and representations of "male" and "female." So, too, albeit less directly, are cultural constructions of "culture" and "nature" of the sort addressed in the original formulation of the nature/culture thesis. In the latter regard, it is significant that while Dwyer views her work as a frontal attack on the entire thesis, she nowhere suggests that there are major distortions entailed in viewing Moroccan notions of "reason" and "passion" as metaphoric transformations of Western notions of "culture" and "nature" (or vice versa). It may never have occurred to Dwyer to raise this more radical critique, though this is unlikely. Rather, I think Dwyer chose not to raise the issue because she recognized that these sets of terms share important semantic commonalities.

In this connection it is worth noting that while some scholars, such as Strathern (1980), have suggested that the nature/culture thesis is based on a particularly modern, Western view of things, others, like Valeri (1990:442 n.13), have argued that cultural propositions of the sort analyzed by Ortner predate the modern European period (from the seventeenth and eighteenth centuries onwards), and extend back to at least late premodern times. Such debates are beyond the scope of the present discussion, but it is important to bear in mind that the Malay and other cultures considered here are all Islamic, and that while the key symbols with which we are concerned ("reason" and "passion") are of Arabic (indeed, pre-Islamic) origin, they clearly partake of the early Greek and Christian (i.e., neo-Platonic and more specifically Aristotelian) influences that informed the development of both premodern European *and* Islamic thought and cosmology.[30] Bear in mind, too, that all of the cultures at issue here have been subject to profoundly transforming imperatives and constraints associated with the imposition of European colonialism and state-sponsored capitalism, and have, in these and other ways, undergone broadly homogenizing experiences associated with "modernization" and various forms of institutional and cultural rationalization in particular. In short, it is at least conceivable that the semantic commonalities between "reason" and "passion" on the one hand, and "culture" and "nature" on the other reflect a common intellectual heritage mediated by broadly comparable historical experiences, as opposed to, say, a universal grid, conscious or otherwise, of the sort proposed by Ortner.

The latter discussion has taken us rather far afield from my earlier point concerning the importance of examining the valorization of specific cultural beliefs and practices bearing on gender. I would like to return to this point and its relevance for an understanding of ritual impurity, particularly since the nature/culture argument makes reference to such impurity. Much of what follows thus relates to ritual impurity in Negeri Sembilan, though for reasons to be explained in due course I am especially concerned with some of the conceptual links between menstruation and death.

In Negeri Sembilan, menstrual blood and semen are among the body products capable of causing ritual impurity and pollution (*hadas, najis*). Others include spittle, sweat, urine, fecal matter, hair, and nail clippings, all of which must be handled and disposed of carefully. Failure to dispose of such items properly is extremely dangerous, partly because individuals intent on harming a person can work potentially fatal magic on these (their) body products, or even on a piece of cloth that has their sweat or other bodily grime on it (or on a photograph that contains their image). Dead bodies are also polluting, as is death generally, as will be discussed further along.

Arabic-origin terms for menstruation and menstrual blood (e.g., *haid*) tend not be used much by villagers, though they are common in formal religious and legal discourse—for example, in the Islamic courts and in pamphlets published by religious authorities to instruct young girls on the proper ways to pray. In village discourse, references to menstruation and menstrual blood are usually couched in euphemistic terms. Menstrual blood is said by women and men alike to be "unclean" and "dirty" (*tak suci, kotor*) and is sometimes glossed "dirty blood" (*darah kotor*). Similarly, women sometimes refer to their menstruation as the "arrival of the moon" (*kedatangan bulan*) and, presumably if the menstrual flow is thick, as a "flood" (*banjir*). Since dirt or dirty blood, following Douglas (1966), may be viewed as matter out of place, the conceptual links between

Figure 23.   Village maidens

menstruation, lunar cycles, and flooding argue rather strongly for the association of women with nature and natural threats to established orders.

In Malay culture there is no heavy abhorrence of menstruation or menstrual blood (or women's genitals) such as one finds in many societies in South Asia, Melanesia, and the Amazon. However, these phenomena are clearly devalued and various restrictions surrounding menstruation and menstruating women (and women's genitals) do exist. Women who are menstruating should not touch the Koran, pray, fast, or enter a prayer house, mosque, or graveyard; and they should refrain from having sex (though not all of them do). Sexual relations while menstruating (like sex with a menstruating women) is not simply seen as inappropriate; it is also regarded by some (but not all) villagers as sinful, and is in fact explicitly marked off in Islamic texts, though not in local culture, as "illicit fornication," or *zina*.

To my (and Ellen's) knowledge, however, there are no restrictions on the preparation or other handling of food by menstruating women. Nor are there any prohibitions pertaining to productive labor on the part of such women (e.g., proscriptions barring them from toiling in the rice fields or engaging in other work). Similarly, there is no evidence to indicate that menstrual blood is held to be a powerful substance,[31] though such a view is clearly implied in some of the restrictions cited here (cf. Laderman 1983:74, 242 n.1). And, as noted earlier, there are no menstrual huts or extreme forms of seclusion of the sort one frequently finds in parts of Melanesia, the Amazon, and elsewhere in the world.

Semen (*mani*, or "*mani* water" [*ayer mani*]) is also polluting, and men should not pray (or touch the Koran?) or enter a prayer house or mosque (or a graveyard?) if they have just had sex with a women or ejaculated, unless they have cleansed themselves first. Men, like women, are thus capable of causing pollution and must also be kept separate from the sacred on certain occasions. It is important to emphasize, however, that the pollution associated with menstruating women is in a very basic sense "deeper" or "more profound" than that associated with men who have recently had sex or ejaculated. Men can literally "wash off" their pollution and proceed to enter a mosque and/or pray. But this is not possible for women, for the simple reason that menstrual pollution cannot be "washed off." The issue of agency merits note as well: Ejaculation is a relatively voluntary act over which a man can exert a measure of control, whereas menstruation is an involuntary act or process over which women have no control. More importantly, there is much greater cultural elaboration of restrictions pertaining to menstruation than to ejaculation, and the former loom much larger in the consciousness of men and women alike than do the latter. Indeed, when discussing the issue of menstruation and menstrual blood pollution, I frequently asked if there were any comparable forms of pollution or restrictions pertaining to males. Most people (men and women alike) typically said no and left it at that. It was only when I brought up the issue of semen that villagers of either sex went on to acknowledge the existence of restrictions bearing on men who had recently ejaculated or had sex. This is in sharp contrast to the situation with menstruation, which men and women alike frequently brought up in discussion without any mention of the subject on my part.

The latter points are significant in light of debates in the literature about menstrual blood and women's capacities to pollute, some of which bear directly on the nature/culture thesis. Various scholars, including those who have worked in other Muslim societies, such as Morocco (e.g., Dwyer 1978), have criticized earlier studies of pollution and gender—many of which were carried out by, or informed by the work or research agendas of, male anthropologists—on the grounds that they (1) focus heavily (if not exclusively) on menstrual blood; and (2) fail to consider the larger category of polluting substances and states, thus providing a partial and ultimately distorted view of cultural constructions of gender and women. I agree with this general critique of earlier work on pollution and gender. And I concur with Dwyer on the specific point that Ortner's essay on "nature and culture" overprivileges the importance of essentially negative symbolic constructs pertaining to women that bear on the polluting or defiling features of menstrual blood, insofar as it fails to consider the larger category of polluting and defiling substances, which, in Islamic cultures, certainly includes semen. I disagree with Dwyer (and Ortner),[32] however, on the analytic importance to be attached to the mere *presence* or *absence* of beliefs or symbolic statements pertaining to polluting agents or states.

The key issue, in my view, is how such beliefs and statements are *valorized* in the specific culture(s) at hand. In the Malay case, and in Morocco and other Islamic societies, beliefs and implicit cultural statements that both men and women are able to pollute and thus must be kept from the sacred on certain occasions *do* exist, but they are *not* equally valorized: Beliefs and associated cultural statements pertaining to the polluting and defiling capacities of women are the subject of much greater social and cultural elaboration than those pertaining to men; and they certainly loom more largely in people's thinking about women (and femininity) than those bearing on men (and masculinity). More generally, the importance Ortner attaches to female ritual impurity in her analysis does hold for Negeri Sembilan (and other Islamic societies). So, too, as we have seen, do many other features of her argument.

An important question remains: Why is menstruation negatively marked in Malay and other Islamic cultures, and in so many other contexts throughout the world? Dwyer never addresses the issue and thus leaves the reader wondering what lies "beneath" or "at the root of" Moroccans' heavy devaluation of menstruation (despite the fact that the Moroccan data she presents on the subject are not terribly difficult to decipher). Douglas (1966), Meigs (1978), and many others would have us believe that it is because menstrual blood is simultaneously part of and not part of the human (female) body, and that it thus defies categorization in relation to the body. As such, it is anomalous and calls into question the boundaries that mark off the body from the world beyond, thereby threatening some of the most basic categories through which the world is understood, experienced, and represented. There is some merit to this argument, but as Valeri (1990) and others point out, it begs the question of why menstrual blood is more negatively marked than other bodily products that pose the same conceptual problem(s), such as semen, feces, spittle, sweat, and so on.

I would suggest that menstrual blood is devalued in Malay culture for three interrelated reasons, and that factors such as these also figure into the devaluation of menstrual blood (and menstruation) in Morocco and many other cultures. First, it highlights the cultural ambivalences associated both with women's capacities to give birth (create life) and with the negative antithesis of birth, namely death. Second, it issues from the uterus/womb, which, in Malay culture, is the quintessential symbol both of woman's "passionate" and uncontrollable nature, and of the fundamentally animalistic nature of *all* humankind (male and female alike). And third, it is a type of blood whose release or letting is not under male control and is thus anomalous and (for these and other reasons) viewed ambivalently. I will address each of these issues in turn.

Menstruation and menstrual blood highlight the cultural ambivalences associated both with women's capacities to give birth (create life) and with the negative antithesis of birth, namely death. Conception, pregnancy, and giving birth, like fertility (the capacity to reproduce) generally, are essential for social and cultural reproduction, and are, on these and other accounts, accorded value in local culture. But they are invariably fraught with risks and threats to established orders insofar as they always carry the possibility of failure: failure to conceive, to become pregnant, to carry a pregnancy to term, and to give birth to a healthy child (failed reproduction). Cross-culturally, one common way of dealing with such risks and threats is to surround them with various cultural prescriptions and prohibitions, to ritually mark them off so as to better regulate them and thus minimize their potentially negative (and disastrous) consequences. This need not entail cultural devaluation: In some societies, such as the Rungus of Sarawak (East Malaysia) and the Mbuti of Zaire, menstruation, which symbolizes (among other things) women's capacities to give birth, is marked in relatively positive cultural terms, as are many other features of the Rungus and Mbuti sex/gender systems (see Appell 1988; Turnbull 1961, respectively). In Malay and most other Southeast Asian and Islamic societies, however, the risks and threats entailed in women's capacities to give birth that are symbolized in menstruation are ritually marked in predominantly negative terms. This is partly because of the devaluation in such societies of sexuality—which informs thinking about menstruation, and which is necessary for conception, pregnancy, and birth—and of all things associated with the "baser," uncontrollable side of things. In Malay society in particular, menstruation is a sign of women's awakened sexuality, and of the sexuality and "passion" in *all* humans, a theme to which I will return.

Just as women's primacy in birth and the creation of life is strongly marked in Malay culture, so, too, is the association between women and death. Bloch (1982), among others, has observed that in a good many societies in the world women are accorded key roles in funerary rituals of various kinds, and are in many cases required to engage in heavily ritualized wailing, corpse washing, and the like. To greatly oversimplify, the major part of the reason for this is that women are squarely linked with birth (the creation of life), and that the ritual equating and collapsing of the distinction between birth and its negative antithesis (death), which is achieved through the symbolic vehicles of women and femininity, help symbolically deny and thus overcome death and all that it implies, and simultaneously reaffirm the continuity of established and enduring social and cultural orders. In Negeri Sembilan, women's role in death, though important, is not as pronounced as what one finds in groups such as the Merina (studied by Bloch) or, say, in South Asian or Melanesian societies. However, women in Negeri Sembilan are more centrally involved in the ritual washing of corpses (even though the *imam* oversees the washing of male corpses); and it is generally expected that women, but not men, will wail uncontrollably during funerals (even though all such outpourings of emotion are frowned upon), and that women (and children), but not men, will walk under the shrouded corpse as it is lifted high in the air before being taken out of the deceased's residential compound.

Noteworthy as well are various prohibitions pertaining to women entering the graveyard that are couched in terms of menstruation and female genitalia: for example, women should not enter the graveyard because (a) they may be menstruating and would thus offend the spirits of the dead, and (b) they tend not to wear undergarments and thus inadvertently expose their genitals to and offend the spirits. (No such prohibitions pertain to men.) And although "death pollution" of the sort discussed by Bloch is relatively unelaborated in Malay culture, women attending funerals are much more likely than men to be incapacitated by dizziness and nausea. More generally, women are far more inclined than men to experience the death of others as a threat to their psychological, emotional, and spiritual well-being.

Similar types of conceptual linkages between women, menstruation, and menstrual blood on the one hand, and death on the other, are highlighted in the beliefs and practices associated with the myriad elves, fairies, goblins, vampires, were-tigers, and witches that make up the Malay demonological system. In many respects the demonological system is not heavily marked in terms of gender. For example, people's comments about spirits do not usually incorporate references to the gender of the spirits, their gendered preferences, and so on. However, if the anthropologist raises issues of gender, it turns out that a good many of the spirits are construed as female (e.g., *pontianak, langsuir, nenek kebayan*),[33] while all of the others can assume either male or female form (*orang bunyian, hantu raya, hantu orang mati bunuh, hantu bandan*).[34] Significantly, there are (to my knowledge) hardly any spirits in the demonological system that are invariably male (though of course God, who created the demon world, clearly is, as are His Prophet Mohammad, the primary guardian spirit of the village, Datuk Gelembong, and the spirits of deceased male ancestors). And while many of the malevolent spirits prey on males and females alike, the majority of them—and the most dreaded, the *pelisit*—are more inclined to attack women. They are, moreover, most inclined to prey upon women who are pregnant or postparturient. In the local view of things, such spirits are irresistibly drawn to pregnant and postparturient women by the "fragrant," "sweet" smell of the women's blood, which is their main source of sustenance, and which they consume through sucking, thus draining such women and making them seriously ill, even causing their death (see also Newbold 1839 II:191–93).

In this connection we might recall the mythic origins of the dreaded, vampirish *pelisit,* which frequently assume the form of grasshopper-like creatures with sharp, bloody teeth, and which are the quintessential bloodsuckers. These spirits originated as a result of a primordial act of incest cum cannibalism involving a brother and sister. It was not the act of incest itself, however, that gave direct rise to *pelisit*. Rather, *pelisit* did not come into being (i.e., the brother and sister were not transformed into *pelisit*) until after (1) the sister became pregnant and gave birth, and (2) the offending brother went beneath the house and began lapping up the discharge that flowed from his sister's vagina during the delivery. In this myth, evil and death as represented by the *pelisit* are clearly "of woman born," though they are equally clearly the result of heinous impropriety involving a female *and* a male. The brother's behavior was unequivocally more heinous insofar as he not only engaged in incest, which is metaphorically linked with cannibalism, but also engaged in a more literal form of cannibalism by lapping up his sister's vaginal discharge. What we see in this myth, among other things, is that women's life-sustaining blood and capacities to give birth and ensure social reproduction simultaneously attract and threaten men, and can also entail both their own death (and nonreproduction), and that of intimate others as well.

The conceptual link between dangerous and violent, death-dealing spirits on the one hand, and menstrual blood on the other, is also highlighted in cases of spirit possession that involve young Malay women working on the shop floors of modern factories in "free-trade zones" and elsewhere. Some of the nightmarish visions reported by women involved in epidemics of spirit possession ("mass hysteria") include grisly images of spirits feasting on soiled menstrual pads (Ong 1988, 1990a). Note, too, that the bathrooms of such shops are sometimes littered with used sanitary napkins and are otherwise regarded as extremely dangerous, even life threatening. Ong (1988, 1990a) demonstrates that the recent spate of spirit possession among such women testifies to heightened anxieties concerning bodily vigilance (and the boundaries of one's body in particular), as well as increased tensions and anxieties associated with the integrity of the Malay social body, the dangers of stepping outside traditional moral communities, and the stability of the Malaysian body politic. She also emphasizes the more general theme that concerns about moral borders and boundaries clearly fall more heavily on women than on men.

That women are more heavily implicated in threats to sanctified boundaries is readily apparent from their strong association with embodied and disembodied spirits, which mark such boundaries and throw in sharp relief the consequences of their transgression. Many of the spirits in the demonological system are guardians of boundaries in the two-fold sense that (1) their favored habitats and activities straddle boundaries between village and forest, field and stream, night and day; and (2) they attack people who knowingly or unknowingly transgress such boundaries. And while some such spirits—for example, the flying, bloody head with entrails attached that feasts on human blood and laughs uncontrollably in the graveyard at night—are clearly inverted images of appropriate female (and male) behavior, others relate more directly to the way females *really are*, at least as represented in official discourse. Thus female spirits (*pontianak, langsuir*) that lure men into the forest, cry out for their affection, and then seduce, disorient, and kill them are less an inversion of official discourse than a highly condensed and symbolically exaggerated replication thereof.

The general lines of argument developed here are strengthened both by research among Malays elsewhere in the Peninsula, and by Negeri Sembilan data bearing on women and the mosque on the one hand, and appropriate female attire on the other. Based on research among Malays in Trengganu, Laderman (1983:76) reports that, in the Malay view of things, the womb symbolizes "the dark matrix of our animal nature." Malays in Negeri Sembilan never conveyed this point to me (or Ellen) in explicit terms, but it is certainly both highly consistent with and directly entailed in conceptual linkages of the sort discussed in the preceding pages. In any case, it would seem to follow from this (and from other data presented earlier) that women's genital secretions, including menstrual blood, also represent the "dark matrix" of humankind's animality. As we have seen, this animality is present in all human beings, though official discourse has it that it is more pronounced among women. I would thus suggest that the devaluation of menstrual blood is a function of ambivalences and anxieties not only about women's animality but also about the animality that lurks in all of us (male and female alike). The heavy devaluation of all things sexual, like the marked ambivalences associated with the satisfaction of other basic (biophysiological) human needs, is keyed to these very basic ambivalences and anxieties, especially since their gratification (the indulgence of desire, "passion") is an index of the absence of restraint and "reason," which are quintessentially human but, in the normal course of things, both imperfectly and intermittently realized (fleeting and ephemeral).

Further strengthening this interpretation are the answers some male villagers provided to my questions concerning why women should not go into the mosque while men are praying, and if they do (as often occurs during evening prayers), why they should sit in a segregated area off by themselves, ideally separated from the male congregation by a wall or at least an opaque screen. Rather than being phrased in terms of pollution or the like, these answers focused on the theme that women, if not segregated from men and thus more or less out of their view, would "distract" the men, "ruining" their concentration, prayers, and single-mindedness in the pursuit of religious knowledge and spiritual enlightenment. Similar types of comments were offered in explanation of why women should dress more modestly than men, and why they should ideally wear veils and head gear of various kinds, and otherwise ensure that the only part of their bodies exposed to the view of men (other than husbands, brothers, sons, etc.) is "the portion of the face that is illuminated when the sun shines down"; to wit, that women's beauty, if not covered, will "provoke" men. These types of comments provide compelling evidence of men's views of their own frailties—particularly with respect to the dominant and legitimizing discourse of "reason" and "passion"—when faced by or simply in the company of women, even in extremely public settings.

Menstrual blood is further devalued because it is the product of a process (menstruation) that is anomalous insofar as it involves a regular or routine form of bloodletting that is not under male control (cf. Rosaldo and Atkinson 1975; Buckley and Gottlieb 1988:27). Other forms of routine or ritual bloodletting are effectively monopolized by males: the killing of wild animals, the sacrificial butchering of domestic animals, the circumcision of young boys, and modern warfare. Menstruation is indeed the only form of routine bloodletting that is not controlled by men. (Female circumcision in Negeri Sembilan and other parts of the Peninsula is not controlled by men either, but it is not as routine or regular as menstruation.) The fact that such fundamental processes associated with biological and social reproduction elude men's control, and do so in an environment in which all forms of social control are in theory in the hands of men, cannot help but raise serious questions and doubts about men's basic standing in the world, and their theoretically superordinate status vis-à-vis women in particular. That menstrual blood issues from and clearly symbolizes the wombs of women—"the dark matrix of our animal nature"—renders these questions and doubts all the more serious.

Implicit in much of the discussion in the preceding pages is that menstruation highlights women's conceptual intermediacy between "nature" and "culture." So, too, do the symbols and meanings associated with women's genitals and sexuality, their capacities to give birth, and their central involvement in child rearing and socialization (which is clearly viewed as a transformative, "civilizing" process that works on the raw material of nature). Women's mediating functions are in many respects the ultimate source of the ambiguities and ambivalences associated with local (official) representations of "woman," much as Ortner suggests in her thesis on "nature and culture" (see also March 1984).

As I said before, my main concern here has been to reassess the validity and rework key features of Ortner's nature/culture argument in light of data from Negeri Sembilan (and to a lesser extent other Islamic societies). I have not considered all features of the argument, but I have demonstrated that, if properly reformulated, much of it holds for the specific case(s) at hand. Broadly similar arguments—that the nature/culture thesis, if carefully modified (through greater specificity or otherwise), is relevant to particular ethnographic settings—have been advanced in different ways by Shore (1981), Valeri (1990) and others, who caution against "throwing the baby out with the bathwater" à la Dwyer (1978) and MacCormack and Strathern (1980) simply because the thesis does not appear to fit certain bodies of data. The more moderate and constructive position thus adopted is that appropriately modified variants of the thesis are of considerable value in illuminating some ethnographic cases, even though they may not have universal applicability.

It should be recalled, however, that I registered important caveats toward the beginning of this section, one of which is that central features of the original argument hold only so long as one limits oneself to a consideration of official/hegemonic discourse. In chapters 6 and 7, I focus more squarely on practical discourse, many features of which not only constitute an inversion of the official/hegemonic discourse outlined here but are also shared by men and women alike. In that discussion we will see that practical representations of gender portray men as having *more* (not less) "passion" than women, and as being *less* reasonable and responsible. This is an inversion of the central signs of the hegemonic framework ("reason" and "passion" [and "nature" and "culture"]), not a challenge to the framework itself, and it thus reaffirms rather than undermines the hegemony. To the extent that such representations focus on men in their roles as husbands and fathers, however, they do pose a rather serious problem for one of the a priori, unargued assumptions informing both the nature/culture argument, Ortner's more recent work (e.g., Ortner and Whitehead 1981a), and the work of Simone de Beauvoir (1949), Nancy Chodorow (1978, 1989), and many others. I refer to the assumption that whereas women in all societies are defined "relationally" (e.g., as wife, mother, sister), men in all societies tend to be defined "positionally" (e.g., as chiefs, warriors, and the like, which is to say, by their roles in the public domain or political economy), and not in relational terms of the sort ostensibly reserved for women. This assumption is not borne out either by data concerning Malays in Negeri Sembilan or other parts of the Peninsula, or by data from Aceh (among other societies), but I leave such matters for subsequent discussions.

There are, finally, five broader themes to bear in mind in connection with the data and arguments presented in this chapter, especially those marshalled to support my position that in many respects "reason" is to "passion" as "culture" is to "nature." First, the symbols and idioms associated with the former set of terms in particular are central both to the system of prestige and stigma, and to the system of moral evaluation as a whole. Second, there are a variety of axes along which actors—especially gendered actors—are commonly ranked: the virtues and vices such as "reason" and "passion"; the extent (if any) of the mystical or spiritual knowledge or power (*ilmu*) they have acquired through experience with texts, trance, and/or spirit possession; and the relative strength of their "life force" (*semangat*). Third, generally speaking, the psychological, interactional, and other behavioral or social qualities that are prestigious or stigmatizing with respect to any one of these axes resonate deeply with the qualities that are prestigious or stigmatizing with respect to the others. Fourth, gender is not itself an organizing principle in the most encompassing system of prestige/stigma that is composed of the various axes in terms of which actors are commonly ranked, though it is clearly shaped by its place within that system. The fifth and most general point, which follows directly from the others and which is addressed in more detail in chapter 7, is that our long-range objectives should be to develop comparative and theoretical understandings of expansive systems such as prestige/stigma, rather than of gender "per se."

6 Contrasting Representations of Gender

My husband is good at cruising around, but lazy when it comes to working. When he goes here and there, I don't get angry. If he wants to work, okay; if not, that's okay too. . . . Men aren't as responsible as women.

> Mak Nisah, a female elder from Bogang

Women are more straightforward/honest, they aren't hot-tempered and they don't lie [as much as men]. . . . Men are responsible for most of the problems in marriage and are at fault in most cases of divorce. The basic problem is that too many men like "the good life" and basically expect to "eat for free."

> Pak Haji Adam, a male elder from Bogang

Men, they all lie; you can only believe about one out of ten of them. That's what you see all the time at the *kadi*'s office.

> Mak Su, a female elder from Bogang

Chapter 5 focused on the symbols and meanings of "reason," "passion," and "shame," and the ways they figure into official/hegemonic discourse on gender. This chapter examines official/hegemonic discourse as well, but is more concerned with the fissures, contradictions, and silences in the hegemony, and the ways in which these and other factors have allowed for the development of an alternative (practical) discourse, many features of which constitute an explicitly subversive challenge to (inversion of) the official discourse, and are therefore appropriately characterized as counter-hegemonic.

This chapter is composed primarily of (edited) material obtained from twenty open-ended interviews that were designed to elicit local understandings and representations of similarities and differences between males and females. The interviews were devised and conducted toward the end of the second period of research, after I had already spent some two years in the field. I mention the timing of the interviews partly to underscore that most of the interview questions were framed in terms of concepts and categories that I had long since identified as culturally salient:

"reason," "passion," "shame," livers, and "life forces," or *semangat*. Many of the questions took the following form: "Overall, are males and females basically the same or different with respect to their livers, personalities, and temperaments?" "What about 'reason,' 'passion,' and 'shame'?" "Are these commonalities and contrasts the result of 'natural endowment' or child rearing/socialization?" I also asked about similarities and differences in the roles, responsibilities, and overall statuses of males and females, as well as about various aspects of kinship, social organization, and religion (especially ritual prerogatives and restrictions). Some of these lines of inquiry yielded little of value and, as such, are not pursued here. Others met with looks of bewilderment or the shrugs that often accompanied rejoinders such as "Who knows? That's just the way it is; that's the way it should be according to *adat* and Islam." I should emphasize, in any event, that most of the material presented here is at the level of explicit consciousness, and does not tap into implicit, subconscious, or unconscious meanings or associations. Even so—and despite all the potential problems associated with collecting data via the rather artificial medium of the interview (see, e.g., Femia 1975:44–47; Willis 1977:122; Barth 1987; and Martin 1987:5–9)—the material obtained from interviews is of considerable significance. It not only provides the reader with a sense of the nature of "local voices" (though the questions and underlying research interests were of course mine); it also sheds valuable light on some of the paradoxical and contradictory ways in which particular individuals experience, understand, and represent masculinity and femininity.

The first section of the chapter presents data gathered from the ten men I interviewed. The second presents material collected from ten women. The third section analyzes some of the similarities and differences between men's and women's perspectives on gender(ed) difference and sameness, though my primary concerns are the scope, force, and reproduction of practical representations of masculinity; issues of class; and the variables that have constrained the elaboration of oppositional discourses as a whole. We will see that with respect to a good many issues the men and women interviewed are in strong agreement as to the basic commonalities and differences between males and females, and that the women interviewed appear to accept as accurate and valid much of the official/ hegemonic view of gender, including many features of the hegemony that depict women (and females generally) in predominantly negative terms. We will also see that some men espouse various features of the practical discourse that tends to portray all men in largely negative terms; that this discourse reveals some of the ways in which local perspectives on class are

more or less unmarked in discourse concerning gender and social relations; and that the articulation of variables of gender and class has long
been informed by state policies as well as nationalist and transnational
discourse bearing on the Malay social body and the Malaysian body politic. In sum, gender ideologies are not intelligible as isolates, and are in fact
best understood in light of theoretical perspectives which are conducive to
describing and analyzing gender in relation to other forms of difference
and inequality as well as everyday social process and the broader realities
of prestige, political economy, and historical change.

MALE PERSPECTIVES ON GENDER(ED) DIFFERENCE
AND SAMENESS

The first five interviews presented here provide good examples of the offi-
cial/hegemonic view that men have more "reason" and less "passion" and
"shame" than women. They also illustrate that males and females (masculinity and femininity) alike are conceptualized in relational terms, and
that the most salient components of men's and women's identities are
husband and father, and wife and mother. At the same time, these interviews indicate quite clearly that men do not agree among themselves on
all aspects of gender. That men do not speak with a single voice on matters
related to gender (or anything else) will be even more clear when we
examine the remaining five interviews conducted with men.

(1) Kamaruddin

Twenty-five years of age; single (never married); taps rubber and assisted
me in my research while waiting for the results of an examination taken
upon his completion of two years of training at a technical college in Kuala
Lumpur;[1] comes from one of the poorer households in the village.

"The livers of males and females are more or less the same, but the
behavior of males and females is quite different." Women are gentler
(more *lembut*); males display greater aggressiveness, "like when they
hand something to someone, they do it much less subtly." And women
are more likely than men to resolve the differences that crop up between
them. This may be because they depend on one another more and cannot
let this interdependence be undermined by misunderstandings. Women's
livers are like *kerak nasi*, the hard, crusty rice that forms on the bottom
of the pot that rice is cooked in: "When it comes into contact with water,
it immediately softens up. In other words, though women's livers may at
times be tough, hard, or brittle, they become soft and melt when they hit

water, all of which is to say that women are more easily influenced and more flexible than men."

As for "reason": Males have "broader" (more *luas*) "reason" than females. This is because of training (socialization) as well as natural character (*semula jadi*). Both males and females are born with "reason" and this is among the most important features that distinguish them from the other animal species. It develops as they grow up. To illustrate, Kamaruddin spoke of a mother teaching her daughter not to ask so many questions of her older brother; for example, about where he is going when he leaves the house. He seemed to be saying that mothers (and other socializing agents) constrain young girls, and that this constraint results in their having less "reason" than would otherwise be the case.

As for "passion": "Females have more; for example, they are much more eager than men to become models, singers, and film stars; to wear nice clothes; and to be seen by lots of people [e.g., an audience]. They also have more 'shame.' 'Shame' is what keeps 'passion' in check."

When I asked Kamaruddin how these latter views squared with the local perception that men are more likely than women to squander money and gamble—which behavior might be taken as a sign of their having more "passion" than women—he responded that women, if given the chance, would perhaps be at least as likely as men to spend money, though they would use the money to purchase refrigerators, gas stoves, washing machines, and the like. He didn't make the point (though it did occur to me) that these items would be of benefit to the whole household, whereas this is not necessarily the case with men spending money at coffee shops or in gambling.

As for why women can't become (Islamic) magistrates or mosque officials: Islam gives leadership positions to men; this is because of their natural characteristics, the natural differences between men and women. In response to my questions about menstruation and the restrictions imposed on menstrual women (e.g., why they shouldn't go into the graveyard and so on), Kamaruddin laughed nervously, made a passing, oblique reference to highly syncretic, largely pre-Islamic rituals such as *bayar niat* ("the repayment of vows"), and said that he really didn't know why these rules and taboos exist. He also informed me that people are not supposed to think about or question such things, and that was the end of that.

Kamaruddin went on to remark that children are fonder of and closer to their mothers because mothers are willing to make greater sacrifices for them than are fathers. In response to my question on the subject, he said that he wasn't sure if this is why children are more inclined to give money to their mothers than their fathers. In fact, he wasn't even sure if this is a pattern. (It is.) If it is, it may be because fathers don't need the money as much; perhaps mothers need it more because "they don't work."

I asked Kamaruddin about the origins of the universe, telling him that I had heard the story of Adam and Hawah but forgot the details and wanted him to fill me in. His version was much as others have described it, with God creating Adam and then fashioning Hawah from one of Adam's ribs. They were in heaven, ate the forbidden fruit, and were then sent down to earth for their transgression(s). The forbidden fruit appears as the Adam's apple of men, and as the breasts of women. Kamaruddin also said, in response to my question on the subject, that in one version of the Genesis story Hawah tempted Adam to eat the forbidden fruit; he went on to make clear that he didn't believe this particular version of the story.

On a more general note, Kamaruddin feels that the roles of men and women are equal, though clearly different. He does not feel that these contrasting roles translate into or entail differences in status. They are simply different.

(2) Dato Suleiman

Fifty to fifty-five years of age; married; recently elected to a high-ranking post in the indigenous clan-based polity; served in the armed services for about twenty years (beginning in 1956), much of it in an administrative capacity; currently lives in Lubok Cina (about thirty miles from Bogang) and is probably one of the wealthiest (or at least wealthier) members of that community.

Men certainly have more "reason" than women. They are better at making firm—and correct—decisions, and they are more patient. Women have less "reason"—they vacillate, change their minds, and worry more—and they have more "passion" and "shame." Women are never satisfied, Dato explained, referring to nice dishes and clothes, household conveniences, and the like. And they are all the time insisting that their husbands buy this and that. Husbands are often under tremendous pressure to purchase what their wives and mothers-in-law demand of them, and it is this pressure, stemming from women's "passion," that leads men into corruption. Dato was very firm on this point and reiterated it a few times. He implied as well that petty comparisons and status and prestige games among women are a large part of the problem; for example, "a woman sees her relatives or neighbors with something nice, like an automobile, and she wants her husband to get one, even though he might have barely enough money for a bicycle or a motorcycle. This is 'passion,' and it creates all sorts of problems."

Dato added, in response to my question about "passion" of a sexual nature, that while women also have stronger sexual "passion," they keep it under wraps most of the time because they have more "shame." "When do women approach men and ask them for sex?" he asked rhetorically. "Of course it is men who ask the women, who sometimes whistle at women, not vice versa. If women didn't have more 'shame,' they would be like dogs, and the world would come to an end [*habis dunia*]."

As for the causes of divorce, a major problem is interference from in-laws. It is not the fathers-in-law, however; the problem is mothers-in-law. This is why he advises his junior kin (*anak buah*) to go off and live by themselves when they get married. The recent trend involving couples living on their own has contributed to the decline in the divorce rate because it eliminates some of the problems in marriage. "Not that problems don't arise, but if they do come up, they don't necessarily get much worse, as happens when in-laws begin getting involved." Government servants are less likely to have difficulties on this account since they often live in Kuala Lumpur or elsewhere, away from meddling kin.

We also spoke about managing money and other household resources. In his household, he handles, or, as he put it, "administers" the money, but in most households it is the wife who does so. This is partly because men don't want to be "bothered" all the time with women's requests for money for this or that expense, so they just turn their money over to their wives. I raised the issue of "queen control" (*kwin kontrol*),[2] which refers to women who either dominate their husbands or exert undue influence over them. According to Dato, "queen control" prevails in 20 to 30 percent of all households and typically involves women forcing their husbands to go out and buy things they can't really afford. "This is wrong in terms of Islam. Islam says—indeed, it is stated in the Koran—that men are supposed to be the leaders of the household."

(3) Pakcik Alias

Fifty-five years old; married (never divorced or widowed); has held a clan title since childhood; served in the army for about five years; and currently taps rubber. In terms of income and overall socioeconomic standing, his household is far above the village median[3] and quite wealthy by local standards.

The personalities of males and females "are different, not the same." When men get mad, they really get mad; but with women, the anger doesn't "reach their livers" (*sampai hati*). Men are "harder" (*lebih keras*), more stubborn. And their livers are like stones, whereas women's livers are like the hard crust of rice which forms on the bottom of the cooking pot (*kerak nasi*), but which dissolves when it comes into contact with water. Women's livers, moreover, are cool, while men's are hot. These differences are mainly the result of natural endowment, though the teachings of parents are also relevant.

Men have a bit more "reason" than women; in other words, "if men have ninety, then women have about eighty-five." Women can't calculate as well as men, but, on the other hand, men can't concentrate as well as women. This, too, is because of natural endowment, though teaching is also relevant.

As for "passion": Women have more than men, though of course women feel and say that men have more. The ratio of women's to men's "passion" is "seven to three." Pakcik Alias explained that he was referring not only to sex (sexual "passion"), but also to "passion" in the broadest sense: desires for food, clothes, comfort, and the like. As for women having more sexual "passion" than men: "A woman can have sex with five or six men in one evening; a man could never do that."

Women also have more "shame" than men. "If they didn't, then we men wouldn't be able to walk around; they'd be grabbing us all the time. It is only because of 'shame' and 'laws' that this does not happen." One's "passion" does recede with age, however. In the case of women, it is with menopause. "But if they are still healthy at seventy, then they still like it once or twice a week, and they'll still give in to their husbands if their husbands want it."

On the subject of female roles and responsibilities, Pakcik Alias referred to women as Ministers of the Interior (*Menteri Dalam*), though he clearly meant women in their roles as wives. They are responsible for preparing things brought into the house by the father/husband; for example, taking uncooked rice and turning it into rice that is ready to be eaten. To give a sense of their more general responsibilities, Pakcik Alias recited a *perbilangan:* The mother instills values, teaches right from wrong, the father gives *ilmu*/knowledge (*Buruk baik peribadi anak, tanggung jawab ibu; tinggi rendah pelajaran anak, tanggung jawab bapak*).

Men, in contrast, are the Ministers of Foreign Affairs (*Menteri Luar*).

Their job (by which he meant the job of men in their roles as husbands/ fathers) is to find things that aren't in the house, and to help and support their wives and children. Men are stronger and have "higher thoughts" (*tinggi pikiran*), which is why this particular division of labor exists. It is nonetheless true that women usually look after the money of the house- hold (*jaga duit*). But this doesn't necessarily mean "queen control." It is wrong to jump to the conclusion of "queen control" simply because women keep the money. "There are very good reasons for this: Men burn up money quickly; in the morning they might have M$10 or M$100 in their pocket, and by the end of the day it will be spent if they have gone out. And sometimes men buy things that look interesting or attractive, and then get back to the house and realize that what they bought has no use or value. So it makes sense to let women keep the money at home."

Despite his earlier remarks emphasizing the complementarity, as op- posed to the asymmetry, of male and female (kinship) roles, Pakcik Alias underscored that men have more or higher status (*pangkat*) than women. For example, men get food and drink first, only then do women eat. And women must follow what men say, assuming it's true or appropriate, though, granted, there are two women who serve as ministers in the na- tional government and more than a few women serving as local represen- tatives in parliament (*wakil rayat*). "Overall, women are not satisfied with their status or situation in society; but what can they do?"

I asked Pakcik Alias whether male-female differences of the sort at issue here have always existed, and his response was "Yes, ever since Adam and Hawah, who was made from one of Adam's left ribs." This led into a discussion of the story of Adam and Hawah: for example, their having been told not to eat the *buah kheldi* in heaven, their consumption of the fruit, the subsequent emergence of sexual "passion," and their be- ing thrown out of heaven. When I raised the issue of Adam seeing the two doves and wanting to have a companion or mate, who later became Hawah, he (Pakcik Alias) said that this wasn't for sex, just for companion- ship. The "passion" didn't come until after they'd eaten the forbidden fruit.

We also spoke of menstruation and the restrictions imposed on men- struating women. The latter, according to Pakcik Alias, exist because men- struating women are dirty. "Are there similar restrictions bearing on men?" I asked. "No, men can clean themselves." A bit later Pakcik Alias remarked that the wearing of headgear such as *kain tedung* and other clothes that "cover women up" serve to protect them from kidnap and rape. Women's beauty should only be known to their family.

As for women being in the mosque: "They shouldn't really be allowed in the mosque at all. This is wrong, and if they are let in, then they should be separated from men by walls, not just by the cloth that separates them from men in our village mosque. In Bogang, women are let into the mosque because of the limited space [the interior of the mosque isn't large enough to accommodate a partitioning wall]." Such provisions bearing on women's presence in the mosque exist because of fear of *fitnah* (slander, libel, scandal).

(4) Zaharuddin

Twenty-six years old; single (never married); currently taps rubber and does other odd jobs; comes from one of the poorer households in the village.

The personalities and livers of males and females are basically the same. However, women are more responsible in the performance of their roles/duties (*tugas*), and they are better able to endure life's problems (*masalah hidup*) and make do in difficult life circumstances, such as being married to someone who is poor. These similarities and differences between males and females exist largely because of natural endowment, but one's surroundings and overall environment can be influential as well. Women are more easily influenced by their surroundings.

As for "reason" and "passion": Much depends on one's faith, resoluteness, sincerity (*keimanan*). Women are better at viewing complicated things; men simply make decisions. Overall, though, women have more "passion," men more "reason." Such being the case, though also because of religious law, women are not allowed to serve as Islamic magistrates or mosque officials. More generally, the roles, responsibilities, and overall statuses of men and women are "more or less the same, even though men and women differ in their approaches to life."

(5) Zainal

Forty-two years old; married (never divorced or widowed?); perhaps best known in Bogang for being a bridal attendant and gender crosser (*mak andam* and *pondan*, respectively [see chap. 3]); works in a government office in the state capital and is, by village standards, very well off.

Men's and women's personalities are different, very different: "Women are gentle [*lembah lembut*], loving and quiet; men anger more easily and are more ferocious [*garang*]." These differences exist because of natural endowment. "Boys are rougher, coarser, they jump here and there, and shout. Girls listen. But mothers have more morning sickness with girls, at least this was how it was with my wife."

Concerning "reason" and "passion": Women have more "passion" than men, at least potentially, but it isn't shown or displayed in daily behavior. In day-to-day behavior, men's is more pronounced than women's. And women are much more clever than men when it comes to placing importance on the household. "Women watch over and guard [*jaga*] the money of the household, whereas men squander money, especially if they have high status [*pangkat besar*], for then they have to spend a lot on friends. Despite this, and despite the fact that women think ahead more, men have more 'reason.' All of this is natural endowment, God's will."

Women are also more full of shame, less confident, and of lower status then men. "If women didn't have more 'shame' than men, there would be no peace and families would suffer. They would be out until all hours of the night, walking around like men." God made women weak (*lemah*) and ashamed, hence even if they have lots of education, they can't surpass men.

It is women not men who are possessed by spirits (*kena hantu*) because women have weak natures (*sifat*), unlike men, who are strong, brave, and fearless (*kuat, berani, tak takut*). The fact that it is also women who experience *latah* shows that women are more easily startled, which is a weakness.

The interview material presented thus far suggests that there are many key issues about which men are in basic agreement; most obviously, that men have more "reason" and less "passion" (and "shame") than women. Note, however, that some of the men who espouse these views (e.g., Pakcik Alias, Zaharuddin) also feel that men are quicker to anger than women or, generally speaking, are less responsible than women (especially about managing money and other household resources), or both. Recall, also, Zainal's remark to the effect that while women's "passion" is "innately" stronger than men's "passion," it is less evident than men's on a daily basis. These negative representations of men are particularly noteworthy insofar as they are in many respects out of keeping with official/hegemonic representations of "reason" and "passion" (and masculinity and femininity), but are nonetheless encompassed within or segregated from the hegemonic framework of "reason" and "passion" in such a way as to fail to call it into question. Other evidence of such patterns appears both in the remaining interviews conducted with men, each of which is anomalous with regard to official representations of "reason" and "passion," and in some of the interview material obtained from women, which we will examine in the second section of the chapter.

(6) Pakcik Hamid

Sixty years old; married (never divorced or widowed); served as a member of the Singapore police force for some twenty-five years and currently lives off a moderate pension and income from the rubber land he owns, which is worked (sharecropped) by a fellow villager; belongs to one of the wealthiest households in the community.

Males and females do not really have similar personalities. Women are soft, gentle, not coarse or crass (*lembah, lembut, tak kasar*). "Women's capital is the mouth; this is how they operate and get by, whereas men think before they talk. Also, women like possessions, comfort, conveniences, gold and other jewelry more than men; men are only interested in food and clothes."

Males and females also differ in terms of their livers: Women's livers are gentle, whereas men's are hard/coarse (*keras*). Women can't overcome (*mengatasi*) men; their strength, their *semangat*, is weaker, and they are more easily swayed by sweet talk, kind/refined words (*cakapan baik/halus*), and good manners (*budi bahasa*). Sweet talk is more effective with women, especially as regards inducing them to relinquish their anger.

These differences between males and females are inborn. They don't exist due to external influence. "Women can't surpass/overcome men from any angle; that is why women are underneath when people have sex. Their place is really in the home, but nowadays they compete with men. . . . They also cry more easily, which is a sign of their weakness."

As for "reason" and "passion": Males and females have about the same amount of "reason," there is no real difference here. For instance, there are some things, like sewing, that females just do better than males. This shows that they must have "reason" as well. But females have more "passion," even though men's behavior—their cruising around and spending money—suggests that they have more. Pakcik Hamid had difficulty giving me an example of females' stronger "passion," but finally after I assured him that he needn't be embarrassed, he said, "Okay, like a woman might want to make love two or three times in a single evening, whereas men would only want to once." In general, females also have more "shame." God made it that way. "If they didn't have more 'shame' than men, maybe they'd be like wild animals [*haiwan*]."

The role of females, particularly as wives, is to care for the household and the children, take care of the food, drinks, and clothes, and be the husband's sexual partner. Pakcik Hamid conceded that women often plant rice, but he said, "This is different; this has to do with 'finding food,' making a living." In any case, the husband's role is heavier (*lebih berat*), because he is the one who has to find money, and teach the children, especially religion. Pakcik Hamid acknowledged that, in reality, women do much of the teaching, though he added that ultimately, for example when it comes to religious instruction, it is the father's responsibility.

We also spoke of women wearing veils and other headgear, and I asked Pakcik Hamid why they do. His response: "Some women do, some don't; it's just habit. Actually all women should cover themselves up this way, but many don't. According to Islam, men need only cover themselves from roughly the knees to the navel, but local custom dictates that men should wear shirts if they go out of their compounds. Otherwise, people will think they have no self-respect." He added that the point of covering women up is so that men's "passion" won't be provoked, so that women will be protected from rape. If women are covered up, men won't know if they are attractive or ugly and will thus be less likely to "bother" them.

The subject of men being able to have as many as four wives came up, as did the fact that women can have only one husband. Pakcik Hamid's comment: "Think of the problems that would exist if women could have more than one husband, of how the first husband might react: He might slit his wife's throat. However, if a woman finds out her husband has taken a second wife, she's just mad, 'noisy' [*bising*]."

(7) Pakcik Rashid

Fifty years old; married (never divorced or widowed?); currently works as a security guard in Kuala Lumpur and typically returns home only on weekends and holidays. Pakcik Rashid's household is one of the wealthiest in the village. I might add that Pakcik Rashid is very articulate, clearly enjoys conversation, and is, overall, an excellent informant, especially since, compared to most other Malays, he isn't bashful talking about sexual matters.

In terms of personality, men and women are different. Women are gentle; they are more affectionate and loving toward their children. The way women move, the way they close their eyes, is milder, gentler. Men are tougher, stronger, taller/higher (*tinggi*). Their livers are also different: Women are more sensitive and more easily have their feelings hurt (*singgung, merajjung*).

As for "reason" and "passion": Sometimes twelve-year-old girls have more "reason," more mature "reason," than boys of the same age. In general, however, males and females have the same amount or type of "reason," though much depends on school and "mixing." Women's "passion," however, is "much stronger than men's," in a ratio of "nine to one." (Pakcik Rashid didn't explain where this particular ratio came from, but he was insistent on these numbers.) "Women in hotels [prostitutes], for example, can have sex ten or twenty times in a single night; men could never do this. Even women who aren't in hotels want more sex than their husbands." Pakcik Rashid acknowledged, in response to my question on the subject, that perhaps their husbands don't know how to satisfy them. He went on to say, though, that if you are clever, your wife will be satisfied.

It is because of women's much stronger "passion" that they have much more "shame." "This is written in the Koran. If women didn't have more 'shame' than men, they'd [all] be in hotels, like wild animals."

On female roles and responsibilities: One is to serve their husbands food and drink; the other is sexual intercourse (*hubungan seks*). In theory, if the husband can afford it, he should hire someone to do all of the other work around the house. A wife should get her husband's permission every time she goes out of the house, even if it is to defecate. "I don't make my wife ask my permission each time she goes out, however, for when we got married I told her that she was free to go out whenever she had a legitimate reason to do so; that is, I gave her blanket permission, a 'permanent pass.'" Pakcik Rashid proceeded to recite a short legend, much of which was lost on me, about a woman with a very sick father. The father went to heaven after he died because his daughter had been obedient to her husband.

Pakcik Rashid's comments on female roles and responsibilities centered on the roles and responsibilities of married women. In much the same fashion, his comments on male roles and responsibilities focused on married men: The man's responsibility is to satisfy the basic subsistence and related needs of his wife and family—food, drink, sex, housing, and clothes—and to teach them about religion, the world, and the Afterlife.

On the status (*pangkat*) of men and women: From the point of view of religion, women can't become leaders of men. God made them a little lower in terms of their *pangkat* or *martabak* (rung on ladder, grade in a scale of rank).

As for why women can't pray, among other ritual restrictions, when they are menstruating: This is because they are dirty (*kotor*), in a state of ritual impurity (*berjunub*). There are corresponding restrictions on men, Pakcik Rashid explained, in response to my bringing up the subject and asking about ejaculation. "If you ejaculate and know that you have done so, you must bathe before praying. And if the head of the penis penetrates fully during the sex act, then ablutions are necessary before prayer, even if no ejaculation occurs."

With respect to women wearing veils and other headgear: In theory women should be completely covered up except for the face and the palms of the hands. Men only need to be covered up from just below the knees to the navel. Women must be (more) covered up "because they are like flowers, are a source of *maksiat*" (sin; perhaps temptation in this context). If they aren't covered up, they will arouse men's "passion." To help me understand what he was getting at, Pakcik Rashid pointed with his forefinger to his eyes, and proceeded to gesture from his eyes, to the back of his head, and down his trunk; he then flipped his hand around such that the forefinger stuck straight out, thus indicating an erect penis.

As an aside, I might mention an earlier conversation in which Pakcik Rashid confided to me that most divorce occurs because men masturbate too much prior to marriage; as a result of such activities, their penises become flaccid ("don't work anymore"), and they are thus unable to satisfy their wives' sexual desires. (He also indicated that excessive masturbation changes the hormonal makeup and leads some men to become *mak nyah*, or transvestites.) This explanation of why divorce occurs constitutes a minority view, but it resonates deeply with men's frequently voiced contention that women are insatiable both with respect to sexual gratification and in terms of needs and desires of a nonsexual nature (e.g., creature comforts, consumer goods, and other emblems of modernity and prestige).

(8) Pak Haji Adam

Sixty-six years old; married (never divorced or widowed); has held the highest ranking clan title in the village for over twenty years; has made the pilgrimage to Mecca twice; worked for twenty-five years as a clerk in the local Islamic court and currently lives off his pension and earnings from a number of highly lucrative business ventures with Chinese entrepreneurs; and belongs to one of the wealthiest households in the community.

Men's and women's livers are "different, not the same." Women are "shameful" (his word), weak, have weak thoughts (*pikiran lemah*), and, in response to my question on the subject, are weak with respect to physical strength, as well. If women weren't more "shameful" than men, "that would be the end for men, and this world, I just don't know . . . [*habis kaum laki-laki, ini dunia, tak tahu . . .*]." Women's "reason," moreover, is not as "broad" as men's; this is probably because of education and "mixing," as opposed to inborn differences.

At the same time, women are more *lurus* (straightforward, honest), aren't hot tempered, and don't lie (as much as men). And, while there are many different kinds of "passion," women's "passion" isn't as bad or evil (*jehat*) as men's. Men are "itchier" (more *gatal*) and more flirtatious.

The subject of money came up and Pak Haji mentioned that his wife helped save money and didn't make all sorts of difficult financial demands on him. I used this as an opportunity to ask him if it is usually men or women who "administer" household money; he said that it depends, but that usually it is women. Sometimes men don't even know where in their houses their wives hide the money.

These differences between males and females are due to natural endowment. Men and women are born this way. The differences don't reflect the way they are taught or brought up, although habits can and sometimes do change. The Koran says this.

I should add that in earlier conversations about marriage and divorce, Pak Haji voiced the view that men (as husbands) are not only responsible for most of the problems that couples experience in marriage, but are also at fault in most cases of divorce. The basic problem is that too many men like "the good life," enjoy gambling and alcohol, and basically expect to "eat for free." Pak Haji's views on such matters come from the twenty-five years he spent working as a clerk in the office of the Islamic magistrate, a point to which I will return.

(9) Pakcik Othman

About sixty-seven years old; married (previously divorced?); taps rubber and belongs to one of the poorer households in the village.

Men's and women's livers are different: Women can't assume responsibility, they're weak, not strong, and their husbands take care of them. It is wrong to do otherwise. Indeed, it is forbidden in religion for a man to stay at home and let his wife go out and "find money" (*cari duit*), unless of course he is disabled or sick, or too old to work. This is definitely forbidden from the perspective of religious law.

These differences are due to natural endowment; they are given. And they are already present when the child is in the mother's womb. For example, males (male fetuses) are rougher in the womb, and if a woman is pregnant with a boy, she will always work (*sentiasa kerja*). If she is pregnant with a female, she will want to sleep more and will have less strength.

With respect to "reason" and "passion": Men have more "reason," but they also have more "passion" and can't cover it up, whereas women can conceal theirs. "Passion" doesn't really appear until the age of twelve. It is actually there before that, but it is not born (*lahir*). Women's "passion" recedes with menopause, but there is no such trend with men.

As for "shame": Women have more, and this is because of natural endowment. "If women didn't have more shame, the world would be destroyed [*dunia hangus*]. They would do whatever they want, like water buffalo, wild animals. They'd grab this and grab that; like animals, they would just eat and mate."

We also spoke of the ritual restrictions pertaining to menstruating women and Pakcik Othman mentioned, in response to my question on the subject, that there are similar types of restrictions pertaining to men after they have had sex and/or ejaculated. He noted, too, that men do not have sex with ("eat") their wives while they are menstruating because if they do, their children will be born with "ruined eyes." He related this point partly because I had brought up the issue of sexual restrictions, but also as a warning, a bit of friendly advice, since he wasn't sure if I knew about such things, "being of a different religion and all."

(10) Mustapha

About thirty-two years old; married (never divorced or widowed); works as an electrician in the state capital (and plies his trade in the village as well), and is relatively well off by local standards. Mustapha is also extremely garrulous and has an excellent sense of humor. He speaks on many matters quite freely, and does so with much dramatic flair and intensity. Compared to most other villagers, Mustapha also has a more developed awareness of the dynamics and tensions in local society and culture. For these and other reasons, the interview with Mustapha was very broad ranging and is presented here in some detail.

Toward the very beginning of the interview, Mustapha launched into a discussion of how difficult it is to be married to a Negeri Sembilan, especially a Rembau, woman. My response: "So why did you marry someone from Rembau?" His answer was that he hadn't intended to but that his mother effectively forced him to. He had been engaged to someone from another state and had planned to marry her. But when his mother heard about his plan, she informed him that she didn't want him to bring the girl to the house to meet her, and then hurried down to Rembau (perhaps Bogang specifically) to make arrangements for him to marry a local girl. Mustapha couldn't go against his mother's wishes, for this, according to Islam, would be treason (*derhaka*). He added, in response to my question on the subject, that it is usually women who do the matchmaking and attend to most of the other arrangements for marriage. That his mother did so in this case had nothing to do with the fact that his father had died some years earlier. Even if his father had been alive, he assured me, it would have been his mother who would have made the arrangements. In any case, once the negotiations and preparations had been taken care of, he couldn't go against his mother's wishes; so now he is married to a Rembau woman.

Mustapha expressed intense disdain for local *adat* and said that men lose (*rugi*), they get no property. "What would happen if my wife and I were to argue? Where would I go?" he asked rhetorically. "Back to your sister's house," I suggested. "Hah, but she's married and her husband isn't going to want me there. I could sleep at the mosque for a while, but after a month or so people would want me out. And then what? This is why men married to Rembau women lose out."

In expanding on these views, Mustapha maintained that a great many men here have been made "stupid" (*bodoh*), "like slaves" (*macam hambah*) by their wives. Women do this through *ilmu*, a point he underscored by blowing and chanting like someone practicing sorcery. (These comments were similar to those he made on a previous occasion, when he recounted the story of one of his friends who had tried to hang himself from a coconut tree because of his distressing domestic situation.) Mustapha continued with the following elaboration:

> It is especially bad in Sepri [a parish a few miles away]: All the men who have married there have been rendered stupid and have been made into slaves. Like cows with rings through their noses, they are led here and there by their wives. In some ways it is not so bad when you are young

and able to work, but once you get old, don't have a regular job, or get sick, then you are treated just like trash, kicked about, pushed aside, and made to feel worthless. I've seen this happen many times.

This is why it is important to save up your money and build a house for your family to live in. But it is unwise to build a house on your wife's property, even though many women try to convince their husbands to do so. Because what happens if you get in a quarrel? Then what? Where are you going to go?

This is why I bought a house in Kuala Lumpur for M$30,000. I saved up all my money and put the house in my name. I plan to move there within a few months; then, if my wife and I quarrel, she will be the one who will have to move. At this point I am in the process of discussing all this with my wife; my mother-in-law doesn't know about it yet. Once my wife and I have talked it over and decided that we are going to move, then we will let my mother-in-law know our plans. And if she wants to come visit her grandchildren, that's fine, but it will be on my grounds. And if she has a problem, she can just go back home.

It was about this time that we began discussing divorce. In response to my question on the subject, Mustapha opined that the primary cause of divorce is that "men don't have enough money," and that their wives and mothers-in-law are dissatisfied on that account. He added that the interference of in-laws (especially mothers-in-law) is also a critical factor:

It is always the mother-in-law [who interferes], and rarely the father-in-law, who, in any case, is always a stranger here, having moved in from another village and so on. All of this goes back to the fact that women have more *kuasa* [authority/power] in local affairs to begin with.

Things are backwards here, the reverse of what they should be; for according to Islam, men should be the ones to rule, the ones with the *kuasa*. But here it's not that way. In my own house, my wife has more *kuasa*. [In this connection he referred to the ownership/control of the house, property, etc., and his marginal standing as in-marrying male.] I know many people would be angry with me if they heard me talking this way, but this is the way it is, and I am simply speaking frankly. All of this *adat* rigmarole; what's it for anyway? It is for the women; they are the ones who make everyone do it; the *dodol* [special cakes], being carried around in sedan chairs, circling the house four times, the *menyelang*. This is all a big waste of time, and a big waste of money.

Mustapha implied that if it comes down to it, he will be forced to give his wife an ultimatum: "Do you want your property here or do you want me?" "Do you want your mother or me?" These were phrased as two different (though related) sets of ultimatums (they came up at two different points in the conversation), but they are keyed to the same sets of issues: the choice he may force upon his wife, if he feels it necessary to do so, due to the unbearable pressures and tensions within his household.

On the subject of "reason" and "passion," Mustapha made the point that women have more "reason," an example of which is their having a greater capacity to look at things from afar, to be objective. But don't get them upset, he warned. Here he seemed to have in mind the different sorts of *ilmu* that women use against men when men have jilted them, or tricked, cheated, or otherwise upset them.

He went on to say, in response to my question, that women also have more "passion" and "shame" than men. If they didn't have more "shame" than men, this world would be all over, destroyed (*habis, hancur ini dunia*). Men are lazier, though, or at least potentially so, he said. This is why they aren't given property; for they would be even lazier and would waste it, mortgage it, sell it, who knows. In fact, according to Mustapha, men used to get all the property, but since they were so wasteful and squandered it, the ancestors changed the rules and said from now on women get the property.

The down side, Mustapha complained, is that his own son won't be able to enjoy the yield (*makan hasil*) of the "ancestral" land planted in fruit trees that is or will be put in his sister's name. He himself can do so, but even here there are problems, because his sister's husband wants to keep it all for himself and his own wife and children, and doesn't want Mustapha around. People look askance at him for going back and eating the fruit, and once he is dead there is no way they will tolerate his son going there.

We also spoke of marriage payments and why most such payments are made by grooms rather than brides. The reason is that men pay for/buy (*beli*) this, he explained, pointing to and then grabbing his crotch but referring to vaginas. Mustapha went on to say that much of the expenses for weddings are to impress people, to convey how much money you have spent to marry off your child, but all of this is forbidden in Islam. All that is really necessary is that you pay the *mas kawin,* do the *akad nikah,* and so forth. The rest is for status and prestige and is basically a waste of time.

In much the same fashion, Mustapha complained about the difficulties of having to deal with all of one's neighbors and in-laws, and how upset people get if you don't follow *adat.* "People undoubtedly think I am stubborn and no good for not wanting to put up with all this *adat* and ceremony, but that's not really my concern." In Kuala Lumpur, people mind their own business. "I'm me and you're you, what you do is your business," was the way he put it. This is a real plus, because Malays spend too much time and energy worrying about what other people are doing and saying. It is less of a problem in Kuala Lumpur, though he also acknowledged that in Kuala Lumpur you can't rely on your neighbors the way you can in the village.

Commentary on Male Perspectives

The material contained in interviews 6–10 is anomalous with respect to hegemonic discourse on "reason" and "passion," many features of which appear in interviews 1–5. The anomalies relate either to the contentions that males and females have about the same amount of "reason" (or that women have more) or to those that represent men as having more "passion" than women. The reasons cited for these types of contentions merit brief note. Pakcik Hamid, who feels that women have about the same amount of "reason" as men, cited in support of his position only that women can do some things better than men. Mustapha, who claims that women have more "reason" than men, made mention of the fact that, compared to men, women have greater capacity to look at things from afar, to be objective. This point surfaced in earlier interviews as well (e.g., Zaharuddin, no. 4), but in such cases it was not valorized to the same degree.

What, then, of the bases for the view that men have more "passion" than women, which is espoused by two of the men interviewed? In Pak Haji Adam's case, this view is based on the belief that, compared to women, men are more flirtatious ("itchier"), which is in keeping with his position that men are responsible for most of the troubles that arise in marriage, and for divorce generally. For Pakcik Othman, on the other hand, this view is based on the perception that men's "passion" doesn't recede with age, as occurs with (menopausal or postmenopausal) women. Interestingly, Pak Haji Adam's point was emphasized by some of the other men interviewed (e.g., Pakcik Alias, no. 3) and by many other men I encountered during the course of my fieldwork, even though the majority of such men still maintain that, in the final analysis, men have less "passion" than women. I return to this point further along.

The overall patterns that emerge from the ten interviews with men are as follows. Seventy percent of men feel that men have more "reason" than women, 20 percent claim that men and women have about the same amount of "reason," and 10 percent say that women have more. Eighty percent feel that men have less "passion" than women, whereas 20 percent contend that men have more. All men agree that women have more "shame" than men, and more than a few of them made the point that if they did not, they would be like wild animals and chaos would reign throughout the world. Similarly, although most of the interview material presented here does not address the issue, all men maintain that women have weaker *semangat* than men.

There is of course much more that could be said of male perspectives on gender(ed) difference and sameness. I will address many of the relevant issues in due course. Before doing so, however, I would like to proceed to a consideration of the material obtained from interviews with women.

FEMALE PERSPECTIVES ON GENDER(ED) DIFFERENCE AND SAMENESS

(1) Kamariah

Twenty-four years old; marital status unknown; works in town at the Islamic court as the "women's official" (*pegawai wanita*) and de facto assistant to the Islamic magistrate (*kadi*); has completed some postsecondary education; currently lives about twenty miles from Bogang, and is quite well off by village standards.

Men have more "reason" than women. Women don't think about their decisions as much as men do, which shows that they have less "reason." Women also have more "passion," and they have more "shame" as well. If women didn't have as much "shame," they would go around saying all sorts of things, and of course some women do just that. To illustrate the point, Kamariah cited the example of a woman who had recently come to the magistrate's office and had spoken very inappropriately (*kurang elok*) in the *kadi*'s chambers, in the presence of the *kadi*.

Kamariah added that all of this is natural endowment, and is in the Koran, in religion. She also emphasized that because they have different proportions of "reason" and "passion," men and women complement one another, and "go together."

Note: Kamariah's position on the proportions of "reason" and "passion" among men and women are the most "orthodox" or "conventional" of any of the women I interviewed, and are in fact quite consistent with the general male view. This despite her contention that many (if not the majority) of marital problems that come before the *kadi*'s office are due to men falling short in their duties as husbands and fathers.

(2) Rokiah

About thirty-nine years old; never married; born in a village near Bogang but currently lives in Kuala Lumpur where she is employed as a high-level administrator, educator, and counselor. Rokiah has a bachelor's degree from the University of Malaya and went on to earn a master's degree in the U.S. She speaks fluent English and is among the most articulate and cosmopolitan Malays that I encountered during my research in Malaysia. Rokiah is also very wealthy, which is one of the reasons she has never married.

Although Rokiah was extremely articulate and insightful on most subjects (kinship, local history, religion, *adat*), she was not terribly cooperative or forthcoming when we spoke about gender, and didn't give the questions the attention I would have liked. On the other hand, I'm not sure her comments would have been any more detailed or revealing if she had given my questions more thought (since, for the most part, Malays simply don't think all that much about, or in terms of, gender).

Male and female personalities are different because males and females do different things. For example, men do the physically harder work. Women are, by nature, softer; they use their livers or hearts more than their heads, and are more willing than men to show their emotions. They are more demonstrative, for example, at funerals and weddings, and are more likely to cry. Women don't use their "reason" as much as men; their emotions govern their actions. Men, on the other hand, try to control their emotions more than women; they "go for" "reason." These differences are due primarily to the way parents teach their children, as opposed to natural endowment.

As for "passion": "I don't know if men or women have stronger 'passion'; probably about the same amounts. But men's 'passion' is more uncontrollable than women's. For example, most rapists are men. There has never been a woman caught and convicted of rape. And if I don't wear a scarf [over my head], men will make lewd remarks, even though they may be standing in front of me scantily clad, like with shorts on. Men's 'passion' isn't necessarily stronger, but it is more difficult to tame."

Even so, women have more "shame" than men. If they didn't have as much "shame," you'd have women walking around with little or no clothes on.

We also spoke briefly about status: "Overall, men have higher status; for example, [in jobs] men get promoted first. Men's status isn't necessarily higher in religion, however; it's just that in religion men's role is to protect and lead women. Religion says that men should never be led by women, hence women can't become Islamic magistrates or mosque officials. Actually, women can become *imam*, but only for other women, not for men. They can't lead prayers for men. Women shouldn't have that much more responsibility than they already have [e.g., in terms of raising children, taking care of a husband, a household, etc.], so they can't become *imam* [for men]."

(3) Mak Shamsiah

Fifty-three years old; married (never divorced or widowed); spent much of her married life in Singapore (where her husband Pakcik Hamid [see male interview no. 6] worked as a policeman), but is now living permanently in Bogang; has been subject to possession by spirits for some thirty years but is now relatively healthy (see chap. 4); belongs to one of the wealthiest households in the community.

Our discussion of gender extended over a number of conversations. During a conversation which dealt with marriage and related matters, I asked Mak Shamsiah how her comments on men squared with the local view that women have more or stronger "passion" than men. Her response was that women certainly do have more "passion" than men, that God made them that way; this is why they have a stronger sense of "shame." If they weren't socialized to be shameful, their greater "passion" would be more obvious than it already is.

Men's and women's personalities are the same, as are their livers, although "I am quicker to anger than my husband. Men's and women's 'reason' is also the same. But women's 'passion' is stronger, though they don't show it because they have more 'shame.' God made it this way." Almost as an afterthought, Mak Shamsiah added that she and her husband were "more or less the same."

Women are often more ferocious (*garang*) than their husbands. By way of elaborating, Mak Shamsiah made a loud comment about Abah Ali—the old man who was sweeping up and burning leaves not far from where we were talking—not having had sex with his wife for some seventeen or eighteen years. "Right?" she yelled in his direction. "Yeah, since Azizah was born." I asked Mak Shamsiah why, and she said simply that his wife "won't let him, even though he wants to." Abah Ali then appeared to qualify his story somewhat, by explaining that his wife "won't let me near her when she is menstruating, because it is a sin to have sex then." Mak Shamsiah retorted that this was very different from not having *any* sex for seventeen or eighteen years. Abah Ali laughed but made no further comment on the subject.

Men, though, have higher status (*pangkat*). Here, as an illustration, Mak Shamsiah mentioned that "men have more power [*kuasa*]; wives are supposed to ask them for permission to go out of the house, and not vice versa. Of course not every time you go out of the house," she added, "but if you go out of the village, get on a bus, for example, then certainly you should ask your husband."

We also spoke of women's predominance in spirit possession and *latah*. "This is because women have less/weaker *semangat*. But women aren't the only ones who are *latah*, though it is true that they are more susceptible. Women get more upset and worry more [*susah hati*] than men; they are also more easily startled. But there are always specific reasons. Take Mak Zuraini: She wasn't always *latah*; but after two of her children died, she became *latah*."

On why women can't become Islamic magistrates and mosque officials: "The holy book [*kitab*] says no, but now you see some women who have become judges and lawyers and even drive cars." As for why menstruating women can't touch the Koran: "I don't know, this is just the way it is."

We also talked of her husband (Pakcik Hamid). Mak Shamsiah reiterated what a good husband he is and how he stood by her all the years when she was sick. "Many men would have taken another wife or simply divorced me," she emphasized matter of factly, "and any number of his friends apparently told him to do just that. But he has stayed with me, through all of my difficulties. And he used to have a car, remember? And he could go all around. But still he didn't leave me. He has told me that if anything happens to me, he will get married again, within a month or two at the most, and that is okay. But if he were to take another wife while we were still married, then I would take a *parang* to him and slit his throat!"

(4) Mak Nisah

Seventy-four years old; married (never divorced or widowed); used to plant rice, but is no longer involved in agricultural labor; weaves mats from *mengkuang* (some of which may be sold), but most of the household income derives from her husband's work as a tenant tapper; belongs to one of the poorest households in Bogang.

Mak Nisah misunderstood my question concerning similarities and differences in the personalities and livers of men and women, for she began telling me that she never fights with or gets mad at her husband (Pak Husin). Pak Husin is "good at cruising around, but lazy when it comes to working [*jalan rajin, kerja malas*]. When he goes here and there, I don't get angry. If he wants to work, okay; if not, that's okay too. My mother, though, used to get mad at him all the time because she didn't think he worked hard enough, and one time she even threw all of his clothes and belongings out of the house."

When I asked Mak Nisah about men's and women's livers, she responded that they are basically the same, and reiterated that she never gets mad at her husband, as other women do. She referred to one of her neighbors always screaming at her husband, adding, "Some women tell their husbands to do this and that, to buy this, to buy that; but I don't."

In terms of "reason," "men and women are also the same, but men aren't as responsible as women. Sometimes, if a child shits, the father won't do anything about it; he will just get up and walk away." With respect to "passion," Mak Nisah first claimed that men and women are "the same," though later, in the context of a brief discussion of divorce and marital problems, she revised her position, saying "without a doubt" women have more "passion" than men.

> Women's "passion" is stronger than men's in the sense that women are always wanting to buy things. This is why there is lots of divorce in Negeri Sembilan. Men can't stand women's "passion." Women want a pretty house, this and that; women have all kinds of "passion," and they have more of it.
>
> Husbands don't want to fight with their wives so they end up running up debts here and there. One of my sons left his wife because he couldn't take it anymore. She was always telling him to buy this, buy that, but he didn't make much money, so how could he put up with it?

We also spoke of spirit possession and *latah*, and why it is that women are more likely than men to experience these afflictions:

> Women are the ones who are usually subject to spirit possession because their livers are weak. When I was younger, I would sometimes pound *padi* late at night. My head would get dizzy [*kapala pining*] and I would hear strange, high pitched noises; then I would get possessed. Men have hard livers; they are brave; this is why they aren't usually possessed. These differences are because of natural endowment.
>
> Women are more susceptible than men to *latah* because they worry and always get startled. I became *latah* when I almost stepped on a huge python that had just shed its skin.

Mak Nisah then recounted the death (some years later) of her seven-month-old baby, who was the last (eighth) born, and how upset she had been when the child died. "Women worry more, like when their children are getting married; they worry more about there being enough money for the wedding." She added that sometimes she doesn't go out of the house because people are always teasing her, trying to startle her and thus get her going into a *latah* loop.

Toward the end of the interview Mak Nisah began telling me about her daughter and former son-in-law. The son-in-law was very jealous, and he wouldn't let his wife open the windows of the house for fear that other men would see her and that, as a result, "something would start up." He also beat her, and on at least one occasion he threw her things out on the street. So she went to the *kadi*'s office and filed a petition for a divorce. The husband went as well (though this may have been because he was summoned to do so) but he did not want to divorce his wife. The *kadi* eventually encouraged (more or less forced) him to repudiate her.

I asked Mak Nisah about the major cause(s) of divorce. Her two-word answer, *jantan jehat*, which may be translated as "males are bad, evil," is of particular interest since the term *jantan* is the numeral classifier for male animals, and is never used in polite conversation with reference to males of the human species. To this she added *salah lelaki*, which refers to "male wrongs" (or faults).

> Men can have up to four wives because they are bad, evil [*jehat*]. They see a pretty woman here, a pretty woman there, and they want to get married, even though there isn't enough food for the first wife or family. How can this be?
>
> Divorced or widowed women, on the other hand, often don't want to re-marry because of all the work involved [in being married]. But with men, it is different. If they don't remarry, who is going to care for them? It isn't really a question of "passion"; it is more a concern with who will take care of them if they are sick. Who will give them medicine? Who will wipe their ass? Who will clean up? Being taken care of by children isn't the same as being taken care of by a wife.

Mak Nisah laughed when I brought up the subject of "queen control" and said that sometimes husbands do the cooking, washing, and go back and forth to the *kedai* to get provisions. "It is a sin for men to do women's work, however, so you can't tell your husband to do it." Even so, she has seen lots of "queen control."

(5) Emak (my mother)

Sixty years old; married (never divorced or widowed); used to plant rice but is no longer involved in agricultural work; most of the household income derives from the rubber acreage owned and tapped by her husband (the former village headman), though some comes from his services as a healer (*dukun*); belongs to one of the wealthiest households in the village.

"Male and female personalities and livers aren't very different; my husband and I, for example, are much the same. Women, however, are quick to anger, though quick to get over their anger as well. Not so with men: They are impatient [*kurang sabar*], they stay mad longer, and they are more likely to hit their children."

As for whether these similarities and differences reflect natural endowment or teaching: "I don't know. Sometimes it is the way they are taught. This teaching is the mother's responsibility, not really the father's. What do fathers ever teach their children?

"The father's main job is to get the money. Women's roles and responsibilities are much heavier than men's: washing, cooking, taking care of the household, teaching the children, and watching them; and this is why women age more quickly than men."

Concerning "reason" and "passion": Males and females differ in these regards. Men have "long reason" (*panjang akal*), women don't. Men also have more "passion." For example, women often don't want to remarry after their husbands die, but this is not the case with men. "Take Haji Baharuddin [the sixty-year-old widower whose house Ellen and I were renting]: He wants to remarry, but divorced/widowed women his age don't. I wouldn't remarry if my husband died, but my husband would probably remarry if I died. I don't mind; let him, I would feel sorry for him."

A bit later in our conversation Emak expressed uncertainty about some of her earlier comments. On the subject of males' "passion": "Yes, they have more 'passion,' but this is mainly among the young. It may be that older men are more inclined [than older women] to remarry not because they have more 'passion,' but because they want to eat, to have someone cook for them, do their clothes, laundry, and so on."

Women are more likely than men to be possessed by spirits because they have "weak *semangat*, unlike men's, which is rough/hard [*keras*]. Women also worry more and get upset more easily; they have weak livers and sweeter blood; spirits like to bother them more. Women are also more susceptible to *latah*: sometimes it is descent/ancestry [*keturunan*]; sometimes it is because they worry [*susah*]. Women worry more than men, and are more anxious, or at least quicker to verbalize their worries and anxieties."

The status of men and women is the "same; there's no difference," although she later added that men have "more, a bit more." As regards why women can't become *kadi* or mosque officials: "I don't know. Where are there any women who are *kadi*? Women get *pesaka* [in this context, houses and land]; men don't. This [the privilege of holding offices such as that of *kadi*] is what men get."

On why women face ritual restrictions when they are menstruating: "I don't know; it is forbidden, sinful; they're unclean, dirty. God made it that way."

(6) Mak Zuraini

Fifty-seven years old; widowed; used to plant rice and work as a midwife. Her main source of income at present comes from the sale of roots, herbs, and other local medicines. She belongs to one of the poorest households in Bogang.

The personalities of males and females are different: "Women are soft; men are more clever at speaking [*bijak, lebih pandai perkataan*]. Their livers are also different: Women are gentle, their *semangat* is low, gentle; men are more courageous 'talking high,' and their livers are hard. These differences exist because of natural endowment."

In terms of "reason" and "passion," men and women differ as well. "Reason" depends on the person; there are some women with more "reason" than men, some with less. But in general men have higher "reason." Men also have more "passion." Men's "passion" is more coarse or crass; women's is weak. Even when they are very old, men have crass "passion," but this is not true with women, even after they have had five or six children.

As for "shame": "This, too, depends on the person. Some people don't have any at all. Women tend to have more, though; for example, if they meet someone who is big, they are reluctant to speak [*segan cakap*]. But if they are already married and work, then they aren't as reluctant. These are inborn differences."

With respect to women not being able to become mosque officials and the like: "This is because men have high status [*darjat tinggi*]. Even in the Afterlife, women can't become headmen [*penghulu*]. In Islam, men are the leaders. They have higher status."

Concerning why women can't pray, enter the mosque, and so on when they are menstruating: "because the blood isn't good; it's dirty [*cicir, najis*]. It is also a sin to have sex while you are menstruating, but some people don't care."

On the issue of divorce, Mak Zuraini explained that many divorces occur because of impatience. "The husband talks roughly [*keras*], the wife gets hot, and vice versa. They may disagree and fight because the woman can't bear children, or because the husband has little income and his mother-in-law wants him to be wealthy and hopes to get rich fast." Mak Zuraini also emphasized, in response to my bringing up the issue, that men aren't necessarily the ones who bring on (cause) divorce; there are lots of women with "evil mouths" (*mulut jehat*). "Husbands are sometimes driven away by their wives because the wives are crass, talk too much—and too loudly—and don't know how to take care of them." She elaborated on the importance of speaking nicely to one's husband, smiling sweetly, not embarrassing him in front of other people, knowing one's place, guarding one's reputation, and so on. "Don't blame all divorce on men."

We also discussed remarriage. Mak Zuraini maintained that while men are more likely to remarry than women, this is not because of (their) "passion." The main reason for this is that men don't know how to cook, take care of clothes, do laundry, and so on. Women know how to do everything. As for why she isn't inclined to remarry: "Why bother? Who needs all the extra work? I would have to cook, prepare drinks [tea, coffee], take care of the clothes, ask permission to go here and there, and so on. As it is now, I go where I want and have greater freedom."

(7 and 8) Hajjah Siah and Indok Jaliah

These women, who are very good friends and were interviewed together, are seventy-two and forty-nine years old, respectively. Hajjah Siah, who is widowed, used to plant rice but is no longer involved in agricultural labor. Though she made the pilgrimage to Mecca (in 1976?), her current household income situates her among the poor of the village. Indok Jaliah, who is married (never widowed or divorced) and taps rubber, is also among the village poor.

As with most of the other interviews, my first question concerned whether they felt that the livers of males and females were basically the same or different. They did not understand the question as stated, so I rephrased it and explained with a comment that had been made to me on previous occasions that "men have hard livers, whereas women's are soft." While this may have biased their initial reaction, they went on to say that yes, the livers of males and females are quite different. In response to my question about the origins of these differences, they said that they were inborn, not the result of the ways males and females are socialized. They added that males (male fetuses) kick harder in the womb, that giving birth to a male is much more difficult than giving birth to a female, and that boys play more roughly than girls—all of which is the result of inborn difference.

On the subject of "reason" and "passion": Men (and males in general) have more "reason" than women (females). Males, however, also have more "passion" than females, as evidenced by the fact that men are allowed to marry up to four wives. "Why else would this provision exist if men didn't have more 'passion'?" Hajjah Siah added that men go around "marrying here, marrying there," and then mentioned our landlord, Haji Baharuddin, whose wife died a short while earlier and who is now "looking for a (new) wife." Both Indok Jaliah and Hajjah Siah felt that in general males are "itchier" (more *gatal*).

As to why there are more restrictions on girls' movements and activities, as compared with those on boys: "This is for their protection, to protect them from evil in the form of boys and men who might want to take advantage of them." Hajjah Siah and Indok Jaliah went on to say that if a girl or woman has a brother, even a younger brother, people will be much less likely to bother her because brothers protect their sisters. Indok Jaliah also explained that a younger brother has higher status than his older sister, despite the age difference. Since the issue of status was up for discussion, I asked why it is that women cannot become mosque officials. Their answer: "Because of religion; this is how Prophet Mohammad set things up." They seemed to have no feelings that this was inequitable or somehow unjustified. They did add, though, that if, for whatever reason, the community happened to be all female, then women could officiate in the mosque. This caveat came up in numerous conversations about the exclusion of women (under normal circumstances) from serving as mosque officials, as did the somewhat related point that women may ritually slaughter animals so long as the meat of the animals is eaten entirely by females.

When I asked them if they were concerned or upset about women being accorded a lower status with respect to some of these matters, they replied, "Not at all, things have always been this way." They also made the point that these differences are manifest in religion, but not necessarily elsewhere. The clear implication here is that if one looks at all aspects of social life, women's overall situation is quite good. By way of elaborating they underscored that men have more difficult lives, mainly because of their responsibilities to go out and earn money.

Why can't women go into the graveyard for funerals, and why did they use to go? "Women are not supposed to enter the graveyard because sometimes they don't wear underwear, and this is wrong, sinful. Women used to go in because they were stupid [*bodoh*], because they didn't know that they shouldn't go in." When I asked, "Well, what if they wear underwear?" they said, "Well, then it's okay." The point, though, is that most women don't wear underwear and even if they do, they might be menstruating, and then they couldn't go in no matter what. They added that women should wear underwear into the mosque, and wherever they pray, but that it didn't matter if men wore underwear. And they explained that menstruating women are dirty (*kotor*), no matter how thoroughly they wash themselves with soap. Men, on the other hand, are not like this.

We talked of other matters, such as children giving money to their mothers rather than their fathers, and men paying or not paying child support. As regards the difficulty of getting support from men who are "simply villagers"—that is, no one can "cut [garnish] their wages" (*potong guji*) because they do not earn wages—Hajjah Siah said "Yealah, well, just cut their necks!" (*Yealah, potong leherlah*). In this connection, Indok Jaliah mentioned that it is good that women can earn wages now, because this gives them a more equal footing with their husbands. (Not coincidentally, her soon-to-be-married daughter works full time for the Motorola factory in Seremban, for which she gets about M$300 a month.)

A few weeks after the interview recounted here, I had another conversation with Indok Jaliah during which I asked her why people say that women's *semangat* is weaker than men's. Her answer, "Who knows! I don't know," was not terribly helpful, but she did go on to indicate her agreement with local views that women have weaker *semangat* and that it is usually women who are subject to spirit possession. I asked her why this was so and why some women experience possession whereas other women do not. Her response was that "Women don't think of him/them [the devil, evil spirits], don't pay him/them sufficient respect," and are, in any case, "less able to struggle with ghosts/evil spirits [*lawan dengan hantu*]." She also mentioned that she had been possessed for about three days just before my most recent trip to Kuala Lumpur, but that she didn't

remember anything about it since she wasn't conscious. (Pak Daud tried
to cure her but I don't know if he was successful or not, i.e., whether she
tried another healer as well.) I asked if the spirit was "wild"/"untamed"
(*liar*) or sent by someone (i.e., domesticated, controlled by a human master). She responded evasively that it was a spirit which resides in a certain
(unspecified) place, but which can roam around and "bother" people.

(9) Kak Suzaini

Thirty-seven years old; divorced (three times); rears goats and receives
public assistance; worked briefly in a lumber factory in a nearby town,
and helped us with cooking and chores during the second period of fieldwork; comes from one of the very poorest households in the community
and lives in what is probably the most dilapidated house in the entire
village.

The personalities of males and females are more or less the same. But
women's livers are a bit weak (*lemah sikit*), whereas men's are a bit hard
(*keras sikit*) and they (men) are much quicker to anger, "to get hot."
These differences exist because of the way males and females are taught,
as opposed to natural endowment.

In terms of "reason" and "passion": Women's "reason" is a bit less
when compared with men's; men's is long, high (*panjang, tinggi*). Men
also have more "passion," and here Kak Suzaini emphasized that she disagreed with Mak Shamsiah next door, who a week or two earlier had
stated in her (Kak Suzaini's) presence that women have more "passion."
As an example of men having more "passion," Kak Suzaini said "like
marrying two or three [wives]; one's not enough."

Females also have more "shame"; this is because of the way they are
taught by their parents. But natural endowment is also relevant. Kak Suzaini couldn't answer my question on what would happen, what the world
would be like, if women didn't have more "shame" than men; and she
said she had no idea why women can't pray when they are menstruating.

I should perhaps note that Kak Suzaini had a hard time elaborating on
her answers to my questions; many of her answers were in fact phrased
as questions (e.g., "Women have more, right?") or were heavily qualified.
Thus when Kak Suzaini spoke of status, she first said, "Men and women
have the same; how could it be otherwise?" But she quickly added, "Well,
the same, probably/perhaps [*sama, mungkin*]."

Women are more susceptible than men to spirit possession because of
their weak *semangat*; they are fearful. And maybe they become *latah*
because they have evil mouths (*mulut jehat*). As for why women can't

become mosque officials: "What is the use of women doing this when there are men who can do it? Women don't want to."

This brief conversation was followed by another, during which Kak Suzaini elaborated on her view that men have more "passion" than women, explaining that men are "itchier" than women. When making the point she said, "Look, even old men like Haji Baharuddin want to remarry if they are widowed or divorced." I responded that perhaps in cases like that of Haji Baharuddin it is simply, or mainly, a question of these men wanting to have someone cook for them, do their laundry, and so on, since more than a few people (including some women) have suggested that this is a crucial factor in their wanting to get remarried. No way, she sneered. Haji Baharuddin has a daughter to do these things for him; what more does he need? "Besides, look at the way he takes off his *haji* cap when he rides around on the bus. He does this so he looks younger [more attractive], though he claims it is because he is hot; this shows how 'itchy' he is." Kak Suzaini added somewhat smugly that such strategies don't help much, because no one wants him; for that matter, his daughter won't let him remarry.

Women, in contrast, don't necessarily want to remarry. "My own mother, for example, has received many proposals since my father's death [in 1981]. But she has no interest in any of these proposals. This is very common with previously married women."

Kak Suzaini also spoke at length about her delinquent husbands, especially the second (?) one, who fathered Posah and Lailah. She recounted how they met, and how he had deceived her prior to their (forced) marriage. He had presented himself to her as a widower and had even showed her what he claimed was his wife's death certificate. (It turned out to be his mother's death certificate.) Kak Suzaini had secretly followed him when she figured out that he had lied to her about his marital status, and she later confronted him about the situation. He was eventually forced to admit the truth to her in the face of incontrovertible evidence.

Kak Suzaini's desire to go to the *kadi*'s office in Rembau also came up, as it had on numerous other occasions when we spoke. She really wants to go there to lodge another complaint against her former husband, but she is embarrassed to do so since she has been there several times in the past and would thus have to see all of the clerks again. She said something about going to the *kadi*'s office in Seremban instead, because this way she wouldn't have to interact with the staff at the Rembau office once again.

Interestingly, Kak Suzaini talks very frankly about how terrible Posah and Lailah's father is, even when Lailah is right there listening. She also goes into detail about how much the father likes Posah but doesn't seem to care at all about Lailah. But she does not generalize any of these statements to other men, let alone men as a group.

Note: Kak Suzaini has the most checkered marital history in the entire village and is widely regarded as something of a floozy. All three of her marriages were in fact shotgun marriages, and in the second and third instances she was the second wife (the husbands were already married).

(10) Mak Su

Sixty-seven years old; married (never divorced or widowed); used to plant rice but is no longer involved in any agricultural work. Most of her household income derives from remittances from urban-dwelling children. She belongs to one of the poorest households in the village.

Mak Su spoke for the first fifteen minutes or so about the possibility of her youngest daughter (age thirty-one) getting married in the next month or two. She implied that it would be a tremendous relief since the daughter in question is the only one of her children who isn't (has never been) married, and is also getting on in years.

On the subject of personality:

> Men and women are different. Men's mouths and livers are different; their mouths say one thing, but their livers aren't truthful to what they say [*mulut lain, hati lain; mulut cakap, tapi hati tak betul*]. Women can be trusted more; if they care about or love [*sayang*] someone or something, then they really do care.
>
> Where are there any truthful men? [*Mana ada laki betul?*] Take my former son-in-law: He left Kakak Z. [Mak Su's eldest daughter] when she was five months pregnant. He took up with and married another woman without even telling Kakak Z. Then, after he had been sick and away, he came home to ask Kakak Z. for some money to spend on his new wife, though he didn't say that this was what the money was for. When Kakak Z. confronted him about what he had done, he denied it, so she refused to stay with him. . . . Men, they all lie; you can only believe about one out of ten of them. That's what you see all the time at the *kadi*'s office.

With respect to the issue of men's and women's livers, Mak Su reiterated her contention that women are more affectionate/caring/loving and more straightforward, honest (*lurus*), and that men lie more. "Look at the way Kak Suzaini's husband lied to her, telling her that he wasn't married, when in fact he already had a wife and children." Mak Su added, in response to my question about "faults" in divorce, that it is almost always ("nine times out of ten") the men who are to blame. Their livers are hard; women's are soft.

As for "reason" and "passion": Women's "reason" is less, weak. Men's "passion" is rough compared with women's; and they have more of it. This is stated in the book, in religion (*kitab, agama*). "How do you know this is really true?" I asked.

> Hey, I've lived a long time. But if men are taught well by their parents their "passion" will be a bit less. For example, my son-in-law Hamzah [Maimunah's husband] is very kind, considerate, and gentle with Maimunah; and has promised his mother that he won't look for another wife in order to have children. His mother apparently took him aside and said that it was unfortunate she didn't have any grandchildren, but added that he better not leave Maimunah just because she seems unable to get pregnant. "I promise, I promise I won't," he told her. And when he gets paid, he turns all his money over to Maimunah.

On the issue of "shame": At first Mak Su seemed to misunderstand my question. She insisted that men have more "shame," but I think she meant that they have more to be ashamed about. And she brought up the *kadi's* office again, and the types of cases one frequently sees there, claiming that if men have lots of money, they quickly lose interest in their wives. Later in the interview, Mak Su said that women have more "shame." "If they didn't, men would be inclined to say all sorts of things to them, and they would be like men; the world wouldn't be right."

My questions about similarities and differences in men's and women's status(es) didn't get very far, partly because Mak Su launched into a long tangent before I could explain what I was asking her. She said that nowadays lots of women have high status and look at men like they are trash. "Rokiah is an example of a woman with high status. [See interview no. 2 in this section.] Most men would be afraid of marrying someone like her; and she would probably only be satisfied with a minister. It used to be the case that men always had more status than women. But at present some women go around looking for men; they've become men; things are upside down."

We also discussed spirit possession and *latah:* "Women are more likely to be possessed by spirits because they are weak. Men, on the other hand, have high *semangat,* and they're stubborn, crass, and coarse. Ghosts don't like them as much."

Women become *latah* because they worry. "Like a child dies, then they get startled [*terplanjat*]. Virtually every day I think of my [dead] grandson [Kakak Z.'s first-born], who was run over by a car when he was about four and a half years old. I thought of him a lot when Kassim [her sister's son] got married, because he and Kassim were just seventeen days apart. Men, in contrast, have coarse, crass livers; so they're not likely to go *latah*."

As to why women can't become *kadi:* This is because they have low status (*darjat rendah*); they can only provide assistance, like the "women's official" (*pegawai wanita*) at the *kadi's* office. And as for the reasons menstruating women can't enter the mosque, pray, or fast: "When the bad stuff arrives/appears [*benda kotor datang*], it is wrong, impure [*najis*]. The angels [*malaikat*] don't allow it." Are there any corresponding restrictions for men? "No. Even if they don't bathe, it is okay if they go into the mosque. They aren't dirty, they don't menstruate."

COMMENTARY: PRACTICAL REPRESENTATIONS OF
MASCULINITY, CLASS, AND OPPOSITIONAL DISCOURSES

The Scope, Force, and Reproduction of Practical Representations of Masculinity

The material presented here (and in earlier chapters) indicates that with respect to a wide variety of issues women and men are in general agreement as to the basic similarities and differences between males and females. Particularly noteworthy is that women appear to accept as valid much of the official discourse on gender, including numerous features of the discourse that portray women (and females generally) in culturally devalued terms. Most women, for example, contend that females have less "reason" than males. And virtually all of them claim that women "need to" (and do in fact) have more "shame" than men since, if they did not, they would be "like animals" and the world would be in chaos. Similarly, women invariably view themselves as having weaker *semangat* than men (and thus more likely to be afflicted by spirit possession and *latah*). Noteworthy as well, just as all of the women (and men) with whom I discussed the issue maintained that women are more likely than men to be ritually "dirty" and impure, all of them accepted as appropriate that (under normal circumstances) women not be allowed to serve as mosque officials or religious magistrates, or in other positions of leadership. More broadly, those women who feel that females are accorded secondary status in relation to males (not all of them do) do not seem to feel that this is "unfair" or otherwise inappropriate; nor do any men.

There is less agreement between men and women with regard to the hegemonic view that women have more "passion" than men. The interview material presented here indicates that while most men (8/10 of those interviewed) espouse this view, only about a third (3/10) of the women do. Nearly two-thirds (6/10) claim that men have more "passion" than women, typically citing as evidence that men tend to perform poorly in their roles as husbands and fathers (such that most of the problems in marriage stem from the faults of men); and, more generally, that it is men's greater "passion" that explains why they are far less responsible than women when it comes to taking care of their spouses and children and honoring kinship and other social and moral obligations.

Interestingly, many of the men I spoke with over the course of more than two and a half years of fieldwork also espouse the view of men as irresponsible and at fault in most cases of divorce, even though they still maintain that men are less "passionate" than women. A major difference that emerges from a comparison of these aspects of women's and men's views, then, is that in the case of women—about two-thirds of them at any rate—the theme of men's irresponsibility is used to stand the hegemonic view of "passion" (and "reason" and masculinity) on its head. In the case of men, however, this theme does not usually raise serious questions about the legitimacy of the hegemony. This is either because the theme is encompassed within the hegemony in a way that effectively defines it as a nonissue, or because it is segregated from the hegemony in a way that renders it largely irrelevant thereto (and vice versa).

The limited scope of this discussion precludes analysis of many important issues raised by the interview material presented above, but it is, I think, essential to examine some of the structural factors that have motivated the reproduction of practical representations of masculinity. Such representations—which, as we have seen, include propositions that men are "lazy" and "expect to eat for free," are "at fault" in most cases of divorce, and are, overall, less responsible than women in honoring kinship and other social obligations—are most usefully viewed in relation to colonial and other state strategies which, since the late nineteenth century, have encouraged the development of rural capitalism. These strategies included policies that induced men to acquire commercially valued land (suitable for the cultivation of coffee, rubber, etc.) in their own names, independently of their wives, sisters, and other female kin. They also involved the introduction of strongly individualistic forms of proprietorship and inheritance that contributed to the transformation and demise of many components of the precolonial system of property and social relations. Particularly relevant for our purposes is that these changes undermined the material and moral dimensions of brothers' ties with their sisters and, in the course of doing so, helped shift the burden of (adult male) support for women and children from brothers to husbands. Responsibilities for the creation and accumulation of property, wealth, and prestige for local kin groups thus came to fall ever more heavily on husbands and in-marrying males as a whole (a point to which I will return in due course). More generally, the period since the late 1800s has witnessed spiralling household dependence on male cash-cropping; sharp declines in the predominantly female domain of subsistence rice production; the decreased viability of traditional economic institutions in their entirety; and the emergence of a significant degree of class differentiation and stratification grounded largely in differential access to commercially valued land planted in rubber or other cash crops.

Two ways in which state-sponsored changes motivated the reproduction of practical representations of masculinity merit special emphasis. First, these changes entailed the highly inequitable distribution of land and other productive resources, and are perforce directly implicated in the pronounced disparities that obtain with respect to men's abilities to meet the expectations and demands of their wives and affines. Relatively wealthy men, who constitute a small minority of the adult male population, can rather easily satisfy these expectations and demands, but the overwhelming majority of adult men cannot. This discrepancy both animates and sustains the view that most men are lazy and irresponsible.

A second way in which state-sponsored capitalism contributed to the reproduction of practical representations of masculinity has to do with the historic restructuring of male roles such as brother and husband. I mentioned earlier that since the late 1800s male responsibility for taking care of women and children shifted from brothers to husbands. I noted as well that this shift did not dilute the "elder brother" norms that have long if not always shaped the husband role (i.e., that husbands should support and protect their wives, and otherwise behave toward them much like elder brothers behave toward younger siblings). In point of fact, these norms seem to have become not only more central to the definition of the husband role, but also increasingly idealized (partly because many of the moral and material imperatives of brotherhood are no longer put to the test on a regular basis). Worthy of remark as well is that the quotidian behavior of men in their roles as husbands is evaluated not with reference to standards developed on the basis of the actual behavior of elder brothers

but, rather, in terms of a deeply mythologized set of ideals which constitute the fantasy of the perfect elder brother. If only, or especially, in light
of these idealized standards, there are good reasons to take seriously Althusser's (1969) contention that ideology "expresses a will, a hope, or a
nostalgia, rather than describing a reality" (cited in Eagleton 1991:19;
emphasis added).

I have also suggested that married men have an exceedingly difficult
time living up to the "elder brother" ideals coloring the husband role.
This is due in no small measure to the fact that married men have quite
substantial—and in some ways mutually incompatible—moral and material obligations to their relatives, especially the females among them (e.g.,
their mothers and sisters on the one hand, and their wives and female
affines on the other). Heavy affinal demands on married men's labor
power and productivity can make married life very trying for men (especially men with little or no productive land) and frequently exacerbate
tensions in marriage and affinal relations. Married men who are unable
to deal satisfactorily with expectations and pressures from their wives and
affines commonly divorce or simply desert their wives, along with any
children they might have. Such behavior reinforces practical views that
husbands and fathers cannot be counted on, and it shapes practical views
of masculinity as a whole. These latter, practical views serve simultaneously to offset and vitiate official views of males, and to promote practical
views of females.

It is of comparative interest that the various discourses on gender in
Negeri Sembilan that have been described here and in previous chapters
are in many respects highly congruent with those that exist among ("bilateral") Malays from other parts of the Peninsula, especially in terms of
content. Equally significant in the present context is a point of contrast
related to the fact that the scope and force of counter-hegemonic representation of masculinity (and femininity) are far more elaborated in Negeri
Sembilan than in other areas of the Peninsula.[4]

The latter contrast is keyed to differences in the ways in which husband
(and brother) roles are structured in Negeri Sembilan as compared with
other regions. More specifically, the scope and force of the counter-hegemonic representations of masculinity (and femininity) one finds in Negeri
Sembilan are far more elaborated than their counterparts outside of Negeri Sembilan because husband roles in Negeri Sembilan are in a very
important sense harder to live up to, or at least are seen as such compared
with the corresponding roles outside of Negeri Sembilan. This is partly
because the competing demands on men in their roles as husbands and

fathers on the one hand, and brothers and mothers' brothers on the other, have long been much more intense in Negeri Sembilan. Also contributing to the differences at issue here is the variable relevance of the fantasy of the perfect (elder) brother—generally speaking, men in Negeri Sembilan have long played a more central role in the affairs and reproduction of the households of their sisters and their sisters' children than have men outside of Negeri Sembilan—which clearly sets the standards for Negeri Sembilan men in their roles as husbands, but which is much less relevant and less mythologized (though by no means insignificant or unencumbered by mythic accretions) outside of Negeri Sembilan. Germane as well is the more pronounced tendency toward uxorilocality in Negeri Sembilan,[5] and the related fact that, all things being equal, married men living there not only have to contend with a much larger range of their wives' kin than do married men from outside of Negeri Sembilan but also have to deal with their affines on a far more regular basis. Even if such dealings no longer entail the political asymmetries or the full range of prestige-driven economic expectations that they once did, the fact remains that in Negeri Sembilan married men's affinal loyalties, neighborliness, and myriad social and economic skills are clearly scrutinized and put to the test by their in-laws on a much more frequent basis, and—if only for this reason—are rather more likely to be found wanting.

The more general point in all of this is that masculinity or maleness in Negeri Sembilan (and other parts of the Peninsula) is by no means a singular, undifferentiated, or homogeneous cultural phenomenon; it is, in fact, composed of a number of contradictory representations, many of which are intricately tied up with constructions of adult men's kinship roles. More broadly, data from Negeri Sembilan (and elsewhere in the Peninsula) indicate that in the contexts of everyday life, certain male relational roles—husband/father, elder brother—may well dominate the category of "male," and may also shape the meanings of all other male relational (and "positional") roles.[6] These data reveal, in addition, that it is not merely the meanings of "female" or the social standing of women that may be pulled down by the cultural elaboration of relational roles and their relative hegemony in discourses on gender. This can occur as well in the case of males, even though males may still come out on top in official ideology, and with respect to the overall distribution of power, prestige, and virtue.

The broad comparative and theoretical significance of these data are addressed in chapter 7. We need only note here that such data call into question the validity of an enduring theme which is developed in the work of de Beauvoir (1949) and Chodorow (1974, 1989), and which informs the work of Ortner (1974), Ortner and Whitehead (1981a), and many others who have made important contributions to our understanding of women and gender. To wit, that whereas females in all societies are defined "relationally," men in all societies tend to be defined in "positional" (allegedly "nonrelational") terms. As discussed further along, data from Negeri Sembilan (and Aceh and other societies) suggest that this dichotomy is seriously problematic and has in fact led to a skewed understanding of cross-cultural differences and similarities in structural definitions of males and females.

Masculinity and Class

To summarize and advance the argument one step further, I maintain that Negeri Sembilan masculinity needs to be deconstructed and examined in terms of its component features and their interrelations, and that the data produced by these analytic processes call into question the validity of the "arelational" notion of masculinity that is a central point of reference in the comparative and theoretical literature on gender. It remains to emphasize that in Negeri Sembilan practical representations of masculinity exemplify some of the ways in which perspectives on class are realized and distorted in the context of everyday life; and that the nexus of variables bearing on gender and class has long been shaped both by state policies and by nationalist and transnational discourse concerning the Malay social body and the national body politic.

To appreciate the class dimensions of practical views of masculinity, it is helpful to bear in mind that while divorce is quite common in Negeri Sembilan, it is by no means equally distributed throughout all segments of society. Specifically, divorce is rampant among the poor and relatively rare among the wealthy (see Peletz 1988b, chap. 7). Thus, when villagers speak of the prevalence of divorce, and of the fact that much of divorce is the fault of "lazy," "irresponsible" men, they are referring, albeit usually unwittingly, to householders, and to the behavior of men in particular, at the bottom rungs of the local class hierarchy. These are the men who are least likely to be able to meet the expectations and demands of their wives and affines, and therefore most apt to experience tensions and other problems of the sort that are aired before the local Islamic magistrate or *kadi*, whose primary job is to try to effect reconciliation and/or ensure that women and children receive adequate support from "recalcitrant" husbands.

Further strengthening this interpretation is the fact that the male villager (Pak Haji Adam) who most emphatically expressed the view that the majority of problems in marriage are due to the faults (lying, irresponsibility, etc.) of husbands had served for some twenty-five years as a clerk for the local *kadi*. His experiences in the *kadi's* office have clearly shaped his views of men. So, too, undoubtedly, has his enviable position in the local prestige hierarchy insofar as he implicitly exempted himself from his generalizations about men being lazy and irresponsible and was thus making a statement of distinction between most men—"the rabble"—and wealthy, responsible men like himself. Also noteworthy is Mak Su's remark that "Men . . . all lie. . . . That's what you see all the time at the *kadi's* office." Here, too, we see a blanket generalization pertaining to *all* men which, though not acknowledged as such, is squarely grounded in perceptions that focus on the actions of men at the bottom of the local class hierarchy.

While stereotypes bearing on the behavior of impoverished men—most notably, their "poor showing" as husbands and fathers—provide most of the raw material for (and are unwittingly pressed into service to support) the view that *all* men are lazy, expect to eat for free, and so on, the comportment of other men, including, especially, that of wealthy men, does on occasion fuel practical representations of masculinity as well. For example, my wealthy (recently widowed) landlord, Haji Baharuddin—a retired school teacher and headmaster who draws a handsome pension and undertook the pilgrimage to Mecca in the mid-1970s—was frequently mentioned by women (e.g., Emak, Kak Suzaini) when they were discussing the nature of masculinity and casting about for an example to help illustrate their contentions that men have more "passion" than women. A number of women remarked emphatically and somewhat disdainfully that whereas most divorced or widowed women have little interest in remarrying, "even old men like Haji Baharuddin are keen to remarry if they find themselves divorced or widowed." Some of these women went on to disparage his (unsuccessful) attempts to find a new wife, claiming that his flirtatious and "itchy" (*gatal*) behavior is highly unbecoming. Perhaps most damning in the eyes of women (and men), however, are the tremendous debts he has incurred both in the village and beyond.[7] Haji Baharuddin's debts are viewed as a consequence of his being both consistently irresponsible with money (his own and other people's as well) and overly concerned with splurging at local coffee shops and otherwise attempting to impress upon friends and acquaintances that he is a "man of means." The fact that he has made the *haj* renders these indiscretions and excesses all the more offensive, especially since those who have journeyed to Mecca are expected to behave in a more pious and virtuous fashion than those who have not been fortunate enough to do so.

Class variables impinge upon representations of masculinity in other ways as well, for in terms of the female segment of Bogang's population, practical views of men are most prevalent among the poor (e.g., Kak Suzaini, Mak Su) and least pronounced among the wealthy (e.g., Mak Shamsiah, Emak). This is not all that surprising, for all things being equal, poor women are much more likely to experience divorce or desertion than wealthy women, and thus have more first-hand experience with "irresponsible men" than do women in wealthy households. Thus, Kak Suzaini, who is one of the most impoverished and marginalized of all village women, has extremely uncharitable views of men, which reflect (among other things) her disheartening and overwhelmingly negative experiences in three different marriages, each of which began "inauspiciously" (under scandalous circumstances), was short-lived, and ended in divorce. The fact that Kak Suzaini has been largely unsuccessful in her repeated court-assisted attempts to obtain financial assistance from the fathers of her (three) children further pains and angers her—and further motivates her animosity toward men—the more so since her third ex-husband is a man of some standing who recently made the pilgrimage to Mecca. Mak Su, who also comes from a very poor household, likewise has very negative views of men, as indicated by her previously noted contention that all men (or at least ninety percent of them) lie. Though she herself has never experienced divorce, divorce is by no means a stranger to her household. Her daughter, recall, was deserted by her husband when she was five months pregnant. Making matters worse, he took another (younger) wife without even informing her and proceeded to lie to her about his new relationship when she later confronted him with (circumstantial) evidence of its existence.

Constraints on the Elaboration of Oppositional Discourses

Many practical representations of masculinity are explicitly oppositional and counter-hegemonic in that they constitute subversive challenges to their official (hegemonic) counterparts. To say that practical views of masculinity are most pronounced among poor women and least prevalent among wealthy women is thus to point out that wealthy women tend to "buy into" many official/hegemonic representations of gender in a major way, even though a good number of the latter representations portray all women (and much of femininity in its entirety) in culturally devalued terms.[8] For example, Emak and Mak Shamsiah, who are two of the wealthiest and (in terms of lineage and clan affiliation) highest ranking women in the community—and clearly the wealthiest and highest ranked of all village women interviewed—espouse official views of gender to a much greater degree than any of the other village women I spoke with, even though, as just noted, these views depict them (and females on the whole) in largely negative terms. Neither of these women has been divorced (and neither has any divorced children), and they feel that their husbands do highly commendable jobs supporting them and their children and otherwise providing for their households and ensuring domestic reproduction. Compared to other village women, they have relatively little reason (are not strongly "motivated") to question the official discourse on masculinity (and gender generally), particularly since the alternative/practical discourse on masculinity, grounded as it is in images of men's poor performance in their roles as husbands (and fathers), does not resonate with their own marital experiences or "lived relations to the world." Women such as Emak and Mak Shamsiah also have more at stake in expressing (at least tacit or pragmatic) acceptance of the official discourse, or at least rejecting the practical discourse. This is because their overt acceptance, to say nothing of their public articulation, of practical views of masculinity (the only locally available alternative to official views) would effectively align both them and their husbands and households with the women, men, and households associated with the poorest and least prestigious segments of the community. Concerns with validating and ideally enhancing the enviable prestige standing that they and their households enjoy thus militate against their articulation of practical representations of gender and, in the process, help guarantee that with respect to many aspects of gender, village women do not speak in a single voice.

In this connection we might also recall that the first two women interviewed (Kamariah and Rokiah) do not reside in the village and are in fact members of the new urban middle class. Their views on gender are in many respects congruent with the views of women belonging to the wealthiest and most prestigious segment of the village population, and are, more generally, highly resonant with official Islamic discourse on gender. (Not surprisingly, this is especially so in the case of Kamariah, the "women's official" and de facto assistant to the magistrate at the local Islamic court.) These women are clearly the most highly educated of all women interviewed, and are, in addition, the women most strongly identified with the Islamic resurgence. This suggests (among other things) that, all things being equal, women associated with the resurgence are less likely than other women to espouse oppositional discourses on gender. Ong (1990b) reaches much the same conclusion in her recent study of the contrasting discourses on gender promoted by agents and policies of the (Malaysian) state on the one hand, and (Malaysian) Islamic resurgents on the other. She also makes the more general point that social movements with radical political and religious agendas (e.g., the *dakwa* movement) are often suffused with highly conservative ideologies bearing on sexuality and gender. Marty (1993) takes the argument even further, maintaining that to his knowledge *all* "fundamentalisms" (his term) entail strongly conservative ideologies of sex and gender.

Circumstances such as these raise important comparative and theoretical issues concerning the myriad moral and material variables that constrain—or, alternatively, promote—the development and elaboration of oppositional discourses and strategies of resistance. Since I cannot do justice to all such issues, I will simply offer some very general (and ultimately rather cursory) observations relevant to the theme of resistance, and then proceed with a brief discussion of three sets of variables that have served to constrain the development and elaboration of oppositional discourses within the context(s) of village society and culture.

In light of the material presented earlier, one would expect to find women's oppositional stances and strategies of resistance to be most pronounced among the poorest segments of the female population. This, indeed, is what one finds. In most social and cultural contexts, however, there is very little of what might be termed resistance, let alone actual rebellion. Women occasionally mock and criticize their husbands (and sons-in-law) behind their backs and to their faces, though not men in other kinship or social roles. Such mocking and criticism is usually done in a relatively good-natured way, though it is often peppered with biting sarcasm and black humor. And women sometimes intentionally embarrass their husbands in public or flee from their households (which also causes husbands public embarrassment) to protest what they regard as extremely inappropriate behavior on their husbands' part (e.g., taking a second wife).

Unlike what one finds in some other societies such as Morocco (Dwyer 1978), however, women do not steal money, valuables, or other items (rice, other food) from their husbands or the household larders. They don't really need to engage in such behavior since they control the household larders and administer family finances. The "bad mouthing" of men to young children is also relatively rare, to the best of my (and Ellen's)

Figure 24.   Mak Zaini

knowledge, though I have seen Kak Suzaini make scathing remarks about her second husband in front of her youngest daughter (who the man fathered). Significantly, however, these diatribes were confined to the shortcomings of the second husband and were not generalized to any other men, let alone to men as a whole.

One of the major arenas in which women resist official representations of femininity (and masculinity) is the office of the Islamic magistrate (*kadi*), which, as noted earlier, handles what is often referred to as "family law" (marriage and divorce, failure to provide wives and children with material support). Such resistance occurs in numerous ways, the most overt of which involves direct verbal challenging of husbands and the heaping upon them of insults and other forms of verbal abuse (calling them liars, animals, etc.). While one might assume that the magistrate's office is relatively unreceptive to such forms of resistance, this is not really the case or, in any event, is only partly true. The *kadi* and his staff, including especially the "women's official" (*pegawai wanita*)—who processes and otherwise handles most cases and endeavors to resolve them so that they do not require the *kadi*'s adjudication—operate with many of the same assumptions about male and female livers, temperaments, personalities, and overall "natures" as do villagers themselves. Such officials do, moreover, feel that most of the problems in marriage, and much of the "fault" in divorce, stem from men who are delinquent in their roles as husbands and fathers. Thus, while many women find the relatively formal environment of the *kadi*'s office initially intimidating and otherwise off-putting, once they begin talking with the magistrate's staff they tend both to overcome many of their inhibitions, and to speak and behave in other ways which indicate that they are relatively free of the linguistic and other constraints that normally bear upon women (and to a lesser degree men).

The catch of course is that women's relatively unrestrained behavior in these (and other) contexts can easily reinforce official discourses that portray them as having more "passion" and less "reason" than men. In other words, the very recounting of narratives of male irresponsibility and female virtue sometimes conveys messages which are diametrically opposed to those encoded in the "contents" of the narratives in question, and which are in any event the opposite of those intended. Phrased in broader terms, female resistance of this sort sometimes involves what Denys Turner (1983) refers to as "performative contradictions" inasmuch as it bolsters and helps reproduce the conceptual and other legitimizing structures that undergird the gendered distribution of power and prestige in the first place. The same is true of female predominance in spirit possession, which, as we have seen (chap. 4), has been interpreted by some observers as resistance to one or another form of men's control over women.

There is much more that could be said about issues of the latter sort, but I would like to proceed to a discussion of the three sets of variables that have served to constrain the development and elaboration of oppositional discourses within the context(s) of village society and culture. One such variable (alluded to earlier) is the allocation of prestige in terms of households, which tend to be—and, in the case of the wealthy, almost invariably are—composed of men and women alike. (Prestige is also allocated with respect to lineages [and localized clans], but this is less directly relevant here.) The pooling of household resources (including labor) for the purpose of advancing or at least maintaining the prestige standing of one's household vis-à-vis other households both presupposes and promotes day-to-day economic and other cooperation between husband and wife. It also involves husband and wife conceptualizing their needs and strategies with respect to the satisfaction of subsistence concerns and the attainment of prestige—and their place(s) in the world generally—in relation to their household. Bear in mind, too, that the household is the locus of the individual's most intimate and, in many respects, most sustaining and meaningful social interactions. In sum, the primacy of the household in terms of the allocation of prestige, and with respect to economic matters (production, consumption, and exchange), social identity, and emotional sustenance works against the development and cultural realization of gender-based interest groups, and in these and other ways inhibits the (further) elaboration of oppositional discourses (though it obviously doesn't preclude their existence in the first place).

A second, related variable is the historically specific construction of personhood, social adulthood, and adult womanhood especially. In order to be a full-fledged social adult, one must enter into a legitimate marriage (with a socially approved member of the opposite sex), and bear or father (or adopt) children. For women, this involves not only being defined as a particular man's wife (or ex-wife or widow) and the mother of a particular man's children, but also, as noted earlier, experiencing a potentially extended (but in some cases very brief) period of economic dependence on (though not necessarily co-residence with) a particular man. The relational components of women's identity that focus on women's roles as wives and mothers have become highly salient over the course of the past century as a consequence of the historic restructuring of femininity that occurred as a result of state-sponsored changes of the sort that effected a realignment of the constituent elements of masculinity. In the case of femininity, the changes have entailed the historical deemphasis of women's roles as daughters, (natural and classificatory) sisters, and sisters' daughters, and, as just noted, a foregrounding of their roles as wives and mothers. The factors responsible for such shifts include the economically and politically engendered erosion of a broadly encompassing clanship, and the weakening and contraction of the siblingship undergirding it, as well as the demise of various forms of predominantly female labor exchange associated with the agricultural cycle, which, in former times, drew heavily on women as (natural and classificatory) sisters.

Clearly relevant, too, of course, is the recent resurgence of Islam, which has been animated and sustained in no small measure by ethnic and class tensions and nationalist and transnational discourse. The doctrines of Islam (like those of Buddhism, Christianity, and the other Great Religions) focus on, and, more importantly, are interpreted locally as focusing on, women's roles as wives and mothers rather than as daughters and sisters. More to the point, Malaysia's Islamic resurgence (the *dakwa* movement), which is a largely urban-based, primarily middle-class phenomenon, has highlighted and endeavored to restrict women's sexuality and bodily processes, and has in these and other ways (e.g., through "pro-natalist programs" [Stivens 1987]) emphasized women's roles in biological reproduction along with their other "natural functions." Somewhat paradoxically, the involvement of young Malay women in high-tech factory work in "free trade zones" and elsewhere since the 1970s has had some of the same ideological effects as the Islamic resurgence, for, as mentioned earlier, images of factory women, aside from being exceedingly negative, center on their alleged sexual promiscuity.[9] In short, religious, economic, and attendant developments of the sort noted here have served to define women in relation to men, and as mothers, wives, and sexual (hence "passionate") beings in particular, and have thus effectively promoted official discourses on gender and simultaneously constrained the development and elaboration of oppositional discourses.[10]

A third variable which inhibits the elaboration of oppositional discourses relates to the fact that village men and women alike espouse various features of practical (as well as official) views of masculinity and femininity.[11] This may seem paradoxical and/or tautological, but the paradox and tautology, I would argue, are more apparent than real. It is in certain crucial respects much easier to conceive of and develop an oppositional discourse when those against whom it is arrayed or deployed operate with a seamless, rigid, uncompromising, thoroughly self-congratulatory and Other-despising set of assumptions about the way things—and social relations—are and should be. But this is not the case in Negeri Sembilan (or in other parts of the Peninsula), where men's and women's views of gender difference and sameness are in many respects quite similar: Men and women do, after all, operate with the same overarching framework (of "reason" and "passion") in terms of which gender is experienced, understood, and represented; and even the most extreme contrasts between men's and women's views on gender involve little more than a structural inversion of relationships among the principal signs or signifiers of the framework. More importantly, because many men, especially elite men, espouse views of gender which are far from seamless, uncompromising, thoroughly self-congratulatory or Other-(i.e., female-)despising, they effectively preempt charges and help put to rest women's suspicions that men are trafficking in thoroughly distorting or mystifying discourses. For reasons such as these (and others noted earlier) the discourses of men help constrain the elaboration of oppositional discourses on the part of women, even though they simultaneously provide legitimate moral space for their existence in the first place. Phrased in broader and more abstract terms: Dominant ideological formations both produce and limit the forms, scope, and force of the challenges with which they must invariably contend (see Williams 1977:114; see also Willis 1977; Scott 1985).

Final Remarks

There are, finally, two other sets of issues that merit brief comment. The first relates to Ong's important observations that the sexual promiscuity and dubious morality imputed to young Malay women working in factories in the state of Selangor and elsewhere is, among other things, a register of Malays' profound moral ambivalences about the rapidly changing nature of their "lived relations to the world": most notably, their historically stepped-up involvement in and dependence on the vagaries of the global economy, the transgressions of traditional moral injunctions that such involvement and dependence necessarily entails, and the mystical and other dangers associated with such transgressions (Ong 1988, 1990a, 1990b). To the extent that female factory workers are among the most exploited members of the Malaysian work force, the denigration of such women, and the heaping upon them of blame for threatening the Malay "imagined community" (Anderson 1983), may be seen as yet another ethnographic example of the distressingly widespread ideological phenomenon known as "blaming the victim." A similar type of victim-blaming ideology infuses practical representations of masculinity in Negeri Sembilan, especially those naturalizing, dehistoricizing, and eternalizing representations which attribute to men's "innate" behavior most of the problems in marriage and much of the "fault" in divorce. Interestingly, representations which blame men (male "human nature") in blanket terms for the dissolution of conjugal and familial bonds (and other social ills and threats to the imagined community) are not only thoroughly mute with respect to the specific kinship roles and social classes of men whose behavior (on closer [analytic] inspection) fuels such representations. They are also blind to the material and other conditions of their own (re)production. As such—and regardless of the structural or other variables responsible for their existence—they clearly help divert attention away from the broadly encompassing realities of historical change and contemporary political economy which have engendered land shortages and highly inequitable distributions of wealth, power, and prestige, and which are responsible for a situation in which, as one observer put it (with reference to the state of Kedah), "poverty itself appears to dissolve marriages" (Banks 1983:100).[12] Stated differently, while such representations foreground local cultural views of the indissoluble links between the domains of gender and kinship (and marriage), they simultaneously help bring about (but do not fully effect) a mythical sealing off of such domains from all ravages and other entailments of history and political economy. In these and other ways they serve to define the most serious threats to the imagined community as arising from within the Malay community itself (much like the recently emergent discourses on Malay factory women). This despite the fact that in a good many contexts Malays in Negeri Sembilan and elsewhere are quick to argue that the most fundamental obstacles and dangers to the social and cultural reproduction of the Malay community are posed by non-Malays—Indians and especially Chinese, who, taken together, make up roughly half of Malaysia's population—and the state strategies and policies that are responsible both for their existence in Malaysia in the first place and for their economic prosperity relative to Malays.

The second (and final) issue bears on Lévi-Strauss's insightful, often quoted (1949) remark that "Even before slavery or class domination existed, men built an approach to women that would serve one day to introduce differences among us all."[13] One need not accept this particular (androcentric) formulation of the historical primacy of gender with respect to the development of difference to appreciate that Lévi-Strauss is on to something important here (cf. Bloch 1989:136; Heng and Devan 1992; March 1984). That something is that indeterminacies, paradoxes, and contradictions in representations of gender are, at least potentially, the most profoundly subversive challenges to all ideologies of social order. Such is the case partly because gender differences are among the earliest, least conscious, and most fundamental differences internalized in all societies, though arguably more relevant is that symbols, idioms, and entire ideologies bearing on gender are rarely if ever simply "about" gender. Because they are also "about" kinship, human nature, and sociality—as well as relations of equality/hierarchy, inclusion/exclusion, and the like—challenges to such ideologies necessarily constitute deeply unsettling threats to the most basic categories through which we experience, understand, and represent our selves, intimate (and not so intimate) others, and the universe as a whole. This is perhaps especially so when such ideologies serve to mark and legitimize class and ethnic/racial distinctions, as clearly occurs in many societies, including Negeri Sembilan. (Recall, among other things, that in Negeri Sembilan and for Malays elsewhere in the Peninsula the exercise [or absence] of restraint is an ethnic/racial marker that is heavily [albeit never explicitly] gendered inasmuch as "other races" are quickly characterized in terms of the relative lack of restraint that official discourse attributes to and defines as a key feature of [Malay] womanhood.) In such instances, challenges to ideologies bearing on gender cannot help but raise questions and doubts about the conceptual bases and legitimacy of class and ethnic/racial hierarchies and the state structures and nationalist discourses that help sustain them, though the extent to which such questions and doubts are explicitly articulated or culturally realized is of course contextually specific and otherwise highly variable.

The widely redounding and potentially limitless scope of such ideologies—to say nothing of their psychological, social, and moral force—is more than sufficient reason to strive to ensure that our descriptions and analyses of gender encompass the study of women and men alike, and that they be informed by an understanding of official representations of gender (and kinship) as well as their practical counterparts. More generally, the highly expansive scope and other features of such ideologies should serve as a clear reminder that gender systems are not intelligible as isolated phenomena, and are in fact most usefully examined in terms of theoretical frameworks which analyze gender in relation to other axes of difference and inequality as well as quotidian social process and the encompassing realities of prestige, political economy, and historical change.

7 Conclusion: Negeri Sembilan in Comparative and Theoretical Perspective

A central contention of this study is that gender and kinship in Negeri Sembilan (and elsewhere) are most profitably understood both as mutually determined and in relation to everyday social process and structures of prestige, political economy, and historical change. I have also argued that representations bearing on gender and kinship in Negeri Sembilan are in many respects contradictory, and that one useful way to try to comprehend the contradictions at issue is to view them through the lens of a modified version of Bourdieu's analytic distinction between official and practical kinship. In chapter 2, I delineated the value of such distinctions, pointing out, among other things, that they have deep roots in Marxist contributions to theories of ideology and are intended not to effect an ontological sundering of the world down the middle, but, rather, to highlight the existence and entailments of the different representations, discourses, and registers which invariably comprise any given ideological formation. More broadly, chapter 2 demonstrated that the nineteenth-century system of marriage and affinal relations was embedded within a system of prestige and political organization that placed heavy demands on the labor power and productivity of in-marrying males, and that, with the noteworthy exception of titled males occupying the highest offices in the land, the system of marriage and affinal exchange focused on the exchange of men (transfers of rights over their labor power and productivity). In the course of that discussion I also illustrated that various aspects of practical kinship and gender (especially masculinity) were congruent with and reproduced by these (exchange-of-men) features of the system of marriage and affinal exchange, whereas their official counterparts were keyed to and reproduced by the types of marriages involving local political elites (which centered on the exchange of women not men) and by various aspects of official Islamic discourse on gender. A more general objective of the chapter was to demonstrate that the secondary status (lower prestige ranking) of women was (and is) rooted not in institutions of kinship and marriage but, rather, in a broadly grounded cosmology which has long accorded more spiritual power or potency, along with more "reason" and less "passion," to men.

Chapter 3, which provided perspectives on kinship, gender, and sexuality from the nineteenth century to the present, examined how elements of the nineteenth-century system were reproduced and transformed as a result of the imposition of British colonialism, villagers' involvement in cash-cropping and the global economy as a whole, and various aspects of Islamic nationalism and reform. A central argument of the discussion was that the combined impact of largely exogenous forces did not witness a "breakdown of the system" as much as a highly selective transformation of certain elements of that system; and that key features of these processes are best understood in light of precolonial cultural developments and structural precedents which helped channel and otherwise constrain the dislocating effects of social and cultural change. This is especially apparent in the domain of property and inheritance relations, particularly the continued favoring of women in the inheritance and proprietorship of houses and most categories of land. But it is also clear in the domains of sexuality, mate choice, and marriage on the whole, and with respect to gender crossers (such as *pondan*), who were once held to be sacred mediators but have come to be defined as potentially criminal and, in any case, contaminating mediators who, to paraphrase Stallybrass and White (1986:110), perversely muddle and enmire the increasingly polar terms of the classical gender system.

My analysis of the social drama culminating in Rubiah and Nordin's shotgun wedding underscored many of the same basic themes, as well as historical consistency in the gendered division of labor (ritual and secular), and both continuity and change in the criteria for allocating prestige/ stigma and virtue generally. Perhaps most importantly, we saw that many of the aspects and interrelations of the nineteenth-century system of prestige outlined in chapter 2 remain very much intact, even though they have lost some of their more traditional qualities due to the emergence and spread of new and cross-cutting criteria (in addition to the revalorization of nineteenth-century criteria) that accord prestige to modern education, wealth, and social class, rather than descent. Spiritual power or potency, for example, continues to be not only highly valued but also one of the key symbols in terms of which prestige differentials between males and females are both conceptualized and rationalized. Thus, men are still believed (by men and women alike) to have the stronger *semangat*, and to be more apt to possess mystical knowledge/power (*ilmu*). It is also true, however, that male-female differences such as these are increasingly cast in the symbols and idioms of "reason" and "passion" (and "shame"), and are more firmly entrenched in local society and culture than at any point in times past.

Chapter 4 focused on knowledge, power, and personal misfortune, and addressed the gendered distribution of *ilmu* in local society and culture, some of the ways people go about protecting themselves from the uses of *ilmu* by malevolent others, and the importance of viewing women's involvement in spirit possession within the larger context of mystical attack, which encompasses spirit possession but also includes the various forms of slow wasting away that are more likely to afflict men than women. This broader perspective reveals that women are not necessarily more susceptible to mystical attack than men, despite earlier accounts to the contrary; and, more generally, that men and women appear to be more or less equally vulnerable to many of the social and spiritual dislocations which are associated with the erosion and transformation of indigenous institutions, moral boundaries, and cultural categories, and which are realized in one or another form of mystical attack. We also saw, however, that just as women are viewed as having weaker *semangat* than men, so, too, are they far more likely than men to be adversely affected by future trends bearing on the Malay social body and the Malaysian body politic, particularly since political and religious developments seem destined to (further) undermine the legitimacy of women's mystically articulated relational and overall moral concerns. The larger issue is that men and women alike move about in social fields—and do in fact experience much of their entire lives in a social universe—deeply suffused with ambivalence, alienation, and tension. Taking stock of these themes, especially that of ambivalence, is thus essential if we are to capture something of the texture and quality of social actors' everyday lives and basic social experiences.

Chapter 5 examined various aspects of the person and the body, by moving from a consideration of the relatively ungendered features of persons and bodies (parallels between the human body and the universe; the relational sense of self; the components and essences of persons and bodies; death) to an analysis of gendered themes such as conception, pregnancy, and childbirth. We then proceeded with a discussion of the heavily gendered concepts of "reason," "passion," and "shame," which revealed among other things that Malays are profoundly ambivalent about the satisfaction of basic biophysiological needs associated with eating, sexual relations, and the like. These concepts were also viewed in relation to Ortner's nature/culture thesis, a modified form of which was shown to be of considerable value both for describing and interpreting local experiences, understandings, and representations of gender(ed) difference (and sameness).

Specifically, I argued that the nature/culture thesis is especially valuable in the Malay case so long as we (1) specify more precisely than Ortner did which meanings of the polyvalent concept of "nature" are primary in the Malay scheme of things (and in our own as well), and (2) limit ourselves to a consideration of official discourse on gender. The thesis clearly runs into some difficulties when we expand our purview to include practical, largely counter-hegemonic discourses, for these latter discourses tend to invert the relationship between signifier and signified, such that women (not men) are associated with "reason" and "culture," and men (not women) with "passion" and "nature." In the course of laying out these arguments I also considered data bearing on the life cycle, such as the developmental trajectory according to which males move along a continuum from "passion" to "reason" (and "nature" to "culture"), and females move from "reason" to "passion" (and "culture" to "nature"). Some scholars (e.g., Dwyer 1978) have claimed that life-cycle data such as these force a major rethinking of the nature/culture thesis, and more generally, that no such simple binary contrasts can capture the essence(s) of gender(ed) difference and sameness as they are experienced, understood, or represented in any given society, let alone in *all* societies. I agree with the latter part of this argument, but I also made clear that life-cycle data such as these are more appropriately seen as confirming the basic thrust of Ortner's thesis. The reason for this is that the contrasting representations of gender that one finds distributed over the life cycle are not equally weighted. Put simply, in Malay and other Islamic contexts, and probably in *all* societies, representations bearing on fully social adults are hegemonic with respect to representations pertaining to those who are not fully social adults, namely, children, adolescents, and those who are postreproductive.

A similar argument about the importance of discerning not simply the presence or absence of particular beliefs or practices but the ways in which they are marked in various settings was advanced with respect to pollution associated with bodily fluids such as menstrual blood and semen. Both of these substances are considered polluting in Malay and other Islamic cultures, but they are not valorized in the same way(s). Pollution associated with menstrual blood is by far the more culturally elaborated, partly because it is associated with locally salient ambivalences about women's capacities to give birth (create life), but also because such blood issues from the uterus/womb, which is emblematic of the dark animal matrix of humankind in its entirety. Through a complex chain of symbolic associations, men and women alike appear to view menstrual blood as indexing the limited extent to which humans are able to "rise above" their animal natures and otherwise behave in accordance with the normative imperatives encoded within their systems of prestige/stigma and moral evaluation. I also suggested that menstrual blood, and women generally, represent to men (however consciously) the precarious foundations on which male ascendancy rests.

Chapter 6, also, focused on the ways in which the contextually variable symbols and meanings of "reason," "passion," and "shame" figure into hegemonic constructions of gender; but it was more concerned with the lacunae, elisions, and equivocations in the hegemony and the ways in which these and other factors have allowed for the development of alternative discourses, many of which constitute inversions of the hegemony and are therefore appropriately characterized as counter-hegemonic. The first part of the chapter presented interview material obtained from ten men, some of whom clearly articulated the official/hegemonic view of gender(ed) difference and sameness: for example, that men have more "reason" and less "passion" than women, and that women's greater "passion" is most evident in the context of sexual relations ("They always want more, even after their husbands have collapsed in satisfaction"). We also saw, however, that some men espoused rather "unorthodox" views of gender(ed) difference and sameness, claiming, for example, that while men tend to have more "reason" than women, they also have more "passion," as evidenced by their irresponsible behavior in their roles as husbands and fathers. Interestingly, these assessments of men as irresponsible in the context of marriage did not usually call into question the legitimacy of the hegemony as far as men were concerned, though they clearly did in the case of most women I spoke with. Be that as it may, the material gathered from interviews with men was of additional value in that it pointed up significant variation in male perspectives and thus demonstrated that, at least with regard to gender, village males do not necessarily speak in a single voice.

The data collected in the course of interviews with women indicate that, with respect to a good many issues, women and men are in basic agreement concerning the fundamental similarities and differences between the sexes. In particular, these data reveal that many women "buy into" the official/hegemonic discourse on gender that men espouse, including numerous features of the hegemony that portray women (and femininity in its entirety) in what are ultimately rather negative terms. We also saw the relevance of class variables here: for example, that this tendency to internalize and express, at minimum, tacit acceptance of the hegemony is most pronounced among wealthy (and educated) women and least prevalent among poor (uneducated) women; and that practical representations of masculinity which focus on men being neither reasonable nor responsible are fueled by perceptions bearing on men at the bottom of the local class hierarchy. These latter, practical representations thus serve both to encode and obscure local perspectives on class that are otherwise relatively muted in discourse concerning gender, social relations, and various types of "imagined communities."

The material presented in chapter 6 also illustrates that Negeri Sembilan masculinity (or maleness) is not a singular, straightforward, or internally consistent cultural phenomenon, but is, rather, a protean and hybrid amalgam of a number of contradictory representations, many of which are entangled with the constructions that serve to define adult men's kinship roles. In fact, the category "male" does not have all that much cultural significance (the same holds for the category "female"), though categories such as "brother," "husband," and "father" (and "sister," "wife," and "mother") certainly do. More generally, the data indicate that male relational roles such as husband/father and elder brother may well dominate the category of "male" and, in addition, may color the meanings of all other male relational (and "positional") roles. These data likewise make clear that it is not only the meanings of "female," or the social position of women, that may be negatively affected by the cultural elaboration of relational roles and their relative hegemony in ideologies of gender. The negative dynamics in question can also impinge on the meanings of "male" and the social position of men.

Data of the latter type are of broad relevance partly because they force a revision of earlier thinking concerning the purported existence of cross-cultural universals with respect to differences in structural definitions of males and females. They also demonstrate that Islamic masculinities are not always shaped by rigid, heavily patriarchal discourses. Data of the sort at issue here can therefore help us deconstruct some of the essentialist views of masculinity present in the literature on gender (see, e.g., Gilmore 1990) as well as various types of essentialist perspectives on Islam.[1]

An analytic focus on maleness (which should not be confused with masculine or masculinist perspectives, or a focus thereon) is of value not simply because it yields salient ethnographic data on the internally dissonant and ambivalence-laden construction of masculinity while also augmenting our understanding of the dialectically related domain of femininity. More importantly, such a focus is conducive to the collection of data that remind us of the need to analyze gender in relation to the other axes of difference and inequality (class, race, etc.) that inform the constitution of masculinity and femininity alike. It thus helps underscore that the segregation and compartmentalization of gender as a distinctive subject of study "in its own terms" is highly problematic. To phrase this argument in stronger language: Gender "in and of itself" is a "non-subject" in much the same sense that Schneider (1984) maintains in his critique of conventional studies that treat kinship as an isolable, analytically discrete domain (see also Collier and Yanagisako 1987; Kelly 1993; Peletz 1995).

The merits of this argument become clear when one stops to recall that actors—particularly gendered actors—are commonly ranked along axes or continua defined in terms of virtues and vices such as "reason" and "passion," degrees of mystical or spiritual knowledge or power (*ilmu*), and relative strength of life force (*semangat*); and that, generally speaking, psychological, interactional, and other qualities that give rise to or entail prestige or stigma with regard to any one of these continua are deeply resonant with the qualities that are prestigious or stigmatizing with respect to the others. Gender is neither an organizing principle nor an absolute marker of position in the most encompassing system of prestige/stigma that is composed of the various axes along which actors are commonly ranked, but it is definitely elaborated in terms of and otherwise shaped by its placement within that system. This means, among other things, that as concerns our long-range goals, we should set our comparative and theoretical sights on expansive systems of prestige/stigma, rather than on gender "per se."

To better understand the structure and scope of the expansive system at issue here, we might look more closely at some of the interrelations and entailments of the various axes in terms of which actors are typically ranked. A key question to ask in this context is, "Just how systematically are these axes interrelated?" Phrased differently and in broader terms: "How systematic—and totalistic—is the system?" The short and admittedly rather imprecise and partial answer to these questions is that while there is a fair degree of congruence among axes of the sort noted in the preceding paragraph (and some others addressed in a moment), there is much less internal resonance when one considers all other potential axes of social differentiation and rank. There are, at the same time, various structural contradictions at play here, though the arguably more important point is that neither the main axes nor the system as a whole are totalistic in the sense of embracing or pervading all domains of society and culture.

We might first note that age and birth-order distinctions resonate deeply with axes of the sort noted above inasmuch as the attainment of virtues such as "reason" and *ilmu* are both directly and explicitly linked to age and are strongly associated with adults, especially adult males and the elders among them in particular. Much the same is true of *semangat*. Recall that adults as a group are seen as having more powerful *semangat* than those who have yet to attain adulthood, and that, all things being equal, males of each age group are seen as having stronger *semangat* than their female age-mates. But we need also bear in mind my earlier comment that *ilmu* and *semangat* are not systematically related in local discourse (even though a powerful *semangat* is regarded as a prerequisite [necessary but not sufficient] for strong *ilmu*).

A somewhat different situation obtains with respect to the present-day distinction between membership in gentry and nongentry clans. This distinction is not readily mapped onto axes of the sort noted above and is, generally speaking, more or less ungendered. This despite the fact that one can posit an implicit cultural link between gentry clans or membership therein and "male" virtues such as spiritual potency insofar as gentry clans alone can provide candidates for *Undang*, who is the supreme (terrestrial) repository of spiritual potency as well as the Vice-Regent or Caliph of God (held to be male), and who must, in any case, himself be a male. It merits remark also that members of gentry clans regard themselves (and are viewed by others) as descendants of the original *raja* (rulers) of the region who, according to mythic charters, were among the region's first permanent settlers and who also presided over the first permanent communities. Members of these clans thus tend to see themselves, but are not necessarily seen by others, as heirs to certain psychological, interactional, and other virtues (e.g., "restraint," "refinement," "dignity") associated with rule, particularly when they think of themselves in relation to the lowly nongentry clan (Biduanda Dagang) that is a satellite clan of one of the gentry groups and includes a number of individuals descended from slaves purchased by a gentry luminary during his travels to Mecca in the nineteenth century. The fact remains, however, that one's membership in a particular clan does not necessarily have any implications with respect to the relative strength of one's *semangat* or the ways in which one's overall comportment is defined in relation to one or another set of virtues or vices.

The ranking of racial groups, for its part, is highly congruent with—indeed, builds directly on—axes defined in relation to "reason" and "passion" (and culture and nature), but it simultaneously flies in the face of, and thus undercuts rather than amplifies, the otherwise pervasive conceptual links between "reason" (and culture) and *ilmu* (as well as the links between "passion" [and nature] and the absence of *ilmu*). Remember here that Malays invariably situate themselves at the apex of the racial hierarchy and typically do so on the grounds that, as a race, they are more "refined" and "cultured"—and less "base" ("unrefined," "passionate," "animalistic")—than racial groups such as Chinese, Indians, and forest-dwelling aborigines (*orang asli*), who are denigrated as relatively "uncultured" and, in some cases, altogether subhuman. Recall also that while the marginalized aborigines occupy the lowest rungs of the ladders of culture and humanity, they are also believed to have the most powerful *ilmu* (and *semangat?*). Associations such as these testify to the existence of the "marginality/power/danger" and "bush/power/sorcery" metaphors that continue to animate various domains of Malay culture (and many others).[2] Of more immediate relevance is the following two-fold point: First, as noted above, the latter associations undercut the otherwise highly pervasive conceptual links between "reason" and *ilmu*. And second, they clearly violate the logic of the culturally elaborated but largely implicit view that *ilmu* is a summarizing or master virtue, a metavirtue of sorts in the systems of prestige/stigma and moral hierarchy.

The relatively recent emergence of ranking in terms of social class further complicates matters, partly because it appropriates some of the logic or at least some of the language keyed to distinctions between gentry and nongentry clans but simultaneously crosscuts and thus undermines such distinctions. Members of the "wealthy" class (*orang kaya*) tend to be conceptually linked with (or at least view themselves as having some corner on) various qualities long defined in relation to gentry clans ("restraint," "refinement," etc.), just as those at the other end of the class hierarchy—the "poor" (*orang miskin*)—tend to be accorded (but do not necessarily view themselves as having) qualities such as the relative absence of "restraint," "refinement," and the like long associated with nongentry clans and "the ruled" as a whole. This may make good sense on various counts, including the fact that a disproportionate amount of the wealth in the village is concentrated among the households associated with a particular lineage of one of the gentry clans. On the other hand, a good number of gentry households are far from wealthy, and are in fact among the poorest households in the entire village. More to the point, there are no intrinsic connections between gentry status and wealth (or high class standing) or, conversely, between nongentry status and poverty or lack of wealth (or low class standing). Note, also, that while (as suggested above) there is clearly a heavy resonance between class standing and the distribution of virtues and vices such as "reason" and "passion," there are (to my knowledge) no data suggesting that in the local view of things the possession (or nonpossession) of *ilmu* or the relative strength of one's *semangat* is in any way linked to class standing.

In sum, in the specific contexts in which individuals are ranked in terms of class, the otherwise pervasive albeit largely implicit cultural link between "reason" and *ilmu* (and the possession of a strong "life force") is more or less meaningless, as is the equally pervasive but (again) largely implicit view that the possession of *ilmu* is a summarizing or master virtue in the systems of prestige/stigma and moral evaluation as a whole. In these important respects, the axes of class and racial ranking resonate deeply with one another but are out of keeping with the other axes of differentiation and rank discussed earlier.

There is of course much more to say about relations of congruence and contradiction among the various axes in terms of which Malays differentiate and rank themselves and others in their social universe. And there is clearly a good deal more that could be said about whether, as I believe, the various axes in terms of which actors—especially gendered actors—are commonly ranked are most profitably viewed as constituting a single, broadly encompassing but by no means totalistic system, as opposed to, say, a variety of analytically discrete and obviously less encompassing systems. Rather than pursuing these expansive analytic issues any further, however, I would like to proceed with a more focused discussion that centers on some of the more important implications of Negeri Sembilan masculinity.

The remainder of this chapter provides comparative and theoretical perspectives on Negeri Sembilan masculinity, though I should perhaps make clear at the outset that my main comparative cases are other Islamic societies. The first section of the chapter examines some of the similarities (and differences) between Negeri Sembilan Malays and the "bilateral" Acehnese, partly to point up that the "arelational" notion of masculinity enshrined in the comparative and theoretical literature on gender (e.g., Chodorow 1978, 1989; Ortner and Whitehead 1981a) is also entirely inappropriate to Aceh. In addition to delineating some of the conceptual and analytical problems in this literature, my concerns here are to provide historical perspectives on Aceh so as to help illustrate that Negeri Sembilan and Aceh have much in common, which is to say, among other things, that Negeri Sembilan is by no means anomalous as regards the scope, force, and overall nature of its practical representations of masculinity, or in other ways. The second section of the chapter broadens the comparative perspective by examining data from three other Islamic societies: Minangkabau, Java, and Bedouin. The data of primary interest to me here also bear on practical representations of masculinity, which, as we will see, are in many respects strikingly similar from one case to the next and in relation to those of Negeri Sembilan as well. The third and final section of the chapter (and study) provides some general observations concerning the meanings and entailments of contrasting representations of masculinity on the one hand, and ideology, experience, and ambivalence on the other.

ACEHNÈSE, NEGERI SEMBILAN MALAYS, AND THE "ARELATIONAL" CONCEPT OF MASCULINITY

Nineteenth-century Acehnese society was "not a hierarchical, vertically organized society" but, rather, a society composed of "four encapsulated groups existing side by side" (Siegel 1969:68). These four groups—the sultan and his supporters, the chieftains (*uleebelang*) and their retainers, religious teachers (*ulama*), and peasant villagers—were not all that well integrated in the nineteenth century, which is to say that each existed somewhat independently of the others, or, put differently, was relatively unconstrained (and otherwise uninfluenced) by institutional links emanating from the other groups. Thus, while the sultan, whose office was hereditary and defined in terms of Islamic ideology, stood at the apex of the Acehnese state and claimed jurisdiction over all that occurred within his realm, he was not able to extend substantive control over chieftains (or his other subjects) (Siegel 1969:40, 43, 47), even though chieftains did depend for their (Islamic and overall cultural) legitimacy on official seals (*surat*) issued by the sultan. Similarly, while religious teachers were recruited from village society and trained in local religious schools (*pesantren*), their teachings concerning "reason," "passion," human nature, proper conduct, salvation, and the like, seem not to have been all that influential within the contexts of village society; indeed, in some cases, such teachings were clearly disdained by the rural majority.

The primary revenue of both the sultan and the chieftains came from the taxes they levied on riverine and maritime trade (nineteenth-century Aceh was a world entrepôt), as opposed to, say, the settling of disputes or

the administration of Islamic (or other, e.g., "customary") law. Such revenue was especially important since, for the most part, there were no head
taxes, property taxes, or corvée labor (Siegel 1969:22, but see p. 27) by
means of which sultans or chieftains could augment the revenue they
derived from taxation, or their wealth or prestige more generally. Nor
was the control of irrigation channels in rice-producing areas a significant
source of revenue for chieftains or the sultan, though the former did own
much rice land in such areas and did derive income from leasing out their
fields to villagers (26–27).

Chieftains, who, at the local level, were of far greater cultural salience
than the sultan (Siegel 1979:10), depended for their control of riverine
and maritime trade on retainers and other followers who helped them
police the border regions of their realms (*nanggrou*) and otherwise ensure
their receipt of the taxes they claimed as their due. Chieftains also sought
to promote the production of commercially valued pepper, since the pepper trade was heavily taxed, and to this end were forever encouraging the
expansion of such production. They likewise had a major stake in, and
thus encouraged, successful rice cultivation, for, as expressed in an eighteenth-century epic poem (*Hikayat Potjoet Moehamat*),

> If you farm and get rice, the people of the land thrive.
> If there is no rice from farming, the people all leave.
> If there are no more people in the land, where are we leaders left?
>
> (Siegel:56)

Chieftains' concerns with building up loyal followers and others capable of adding (directly or indirectly) to their coffers, and thus enhancing
their power and prestige, also informed their marriage strategies as well
as those of the subjects within their realms of jurisdiction. Some chieftains
were reported to "marry in every direction" (Siegel 1979:52), presumably
to effect alliances with other chieftains and potential rivals or detractors
(cf. Siegel 1979:46). Nonchiefly villagers, however, were encouraged to
bring in spouses from outside the village, or at least to find spouses within
their villages and remain there, rather than join their spouses in other
communities. But since property codes favored uxorilocal residence, this
typically meant using local women to attract and retain men from outside
the village who would hopefully become loyal *and* productive members
of the community (cf. Jayawardena 1977a:172). This pattern, which is
similar in many respects to what one finds in Negeri Sembilan, other
parts of the Malay Peninsula, and much of Polynesia, probably served to
highlight women's roles as daughters and sisters, as opposed to, say,

mothers and wives (despite countervailing Islamic emphases on women in the latter roles). As such, it would have served to deemphasize their sexuality and reproductive functions, and may account for their relatively high status vis-à-vis women in other societies (e.g., Hindu, Buddhist, Catholic, Mediterranean) (see below).

Nineteenth-century property codes exhibited a strong bias toward females in the inheritance and proprietorship of houses and land. Daughters were given houses and house plots at the time of their marriages, over which they acquired full legal rights once they were ritually separated from their parents, usually one to three years after they were married (Siegel 1969:138–39). They also received plots of rice land, assuming their parents owned and had enough rice land to give to them; this occurred either at the time they were ritually separated from their parents or at the birth of their first child. Sons, for their part, received cash, weapons, and other movable property; they frequently received rice land as well, assuming that the rice land earmarked for their sisters did not deplete their parents' estate of land. It is important to note, however, that men did not acquire rights to rice land until after the death of their parents, and thus typically entered into marriage without access to such land.

In the nineteenth century, males usually got married between the ages of fifteen and twenty. During the first year of marriage they were expected to provide new clothes for their wives and to make periodic gifts of meat to their wives' parents. Similarly, when they slept in their wives' houses (i.e., when they weren't involved in temporary out-migration, or *merantau*), it was generally expected that they would both reimburse their parents-in-law for expenses if their wives had not already been formally separated (officially established in their own homes) and provide for themselves and (to a lesser extent) their children (Siegel 1969:53).

Married men could stay at home and work (plow, harvest, and thresh) their wives' fields or the fields of the rich (the chieftains?). But since Acehnese rice cultivation was not very labor intensive and since women did about half the work (sowing, weeding, and husking), there was not all that much need for male labor in rice cultivation (Siegel 1969:53). Hence, some men marketed cattle or garden produce (Jayawardena 1977b:29), but most had to leave the village and seek work as cultivators, traders, and so on, in the pepper-growing regions of the East in order to fulfill their duties as husbands (Siegel 1969:53–54). The temporary out-migration that this entailed was not so much to satisfy the masculine role, but because men had no other means of earning a livelihood (54) and of acquiring cash in particular, which was necessary if they were to meet their wives' expectations that they provide them with imported cloth and personal adornments. That men were motivated in no small measure by their wives' expectations and demands—and by the structure of prestige generally—is suggested by a local religious teacher who noted early in this century, "Many women embitter the lives of their husbands by demanding more than they can bestow in the matter of clothing and personal adornments. Thus they have themselves to blame if their spouses, weary of domestic strife, go forth to seek happiness in rantos [travels, journeys, foreign settlements]" (183 n.16). More generally, as another observer remarked early in this century, "Achehnese [sic] women ... reproach their husbands for their weak nature.... Their attitude toward Achehnese men seems before all to reveal contempt for their [husbands'] psychical decline which causes them to lose their pride" (96).

There are two points of particular interest about the nineteenth-century Acehnese system. The first is highlighted by Siegel's (1969:68) comment that "[Male] villagers were first of all husbands and fathers." In light of the context of the discussion in which this point is emphasized and the overall thrust of Siegel's arguments, I take this comment to mean that men's primary identities and senses of self—and constructions of masculinity generally—were defined not by men's roles or positions in the political economy or in terms of citizenship, nationality, or religion but, rather, in relational terms of the sort that, according to many of the most influential works in the literature on women and gender, are ostensibly reserved for women. I will return to this point in a moment.

The second point of interest is that "even when men lived up to their material obligations, they had little place in their wives' homes. Women were independent of them, even if men could pay their own way" (Siegel 1969:54). "Although men tried to create a role as husbands and, especially, as fathers, women thought of them as essentially superfluous. They allowed men no part in raising children and tolerated them only so long as they paid their own way and contributed money for goods that a woman could not obtain through her own resources.... A man's role as a husband-father in the nineteenth century was small indeed.... Men [were] like 'guests in the houses of their wives' [as Snouck Hurgronje remarked (1906 I:339; cf. p. 327)]" (55).

Circumstances such as these left men feeling obligated toward and dependent on their wives' families, though these feelings were no doubt alleviated as men contributed to the building of new houses and the purchase of rice land for their daughters (Siegel 1969:55–56). Equally important, these circumstances provided a crucial structural precedent for subsequent religious change, as will be clear in due course.

I noted earlier that religious teachers' (*ulama's*) messages concerning human nature, daily conduct, salvation, and the like, appear not to have been all that well received during most of the nineteenth century. I need to add that this began to change in the latter part of the nineteenth century. Married men, especially, became increasingly receptive to the *ulama's* attempts to provide a new, religiously grounded basis for male identity, which defined men as Muslims not as kinsmen, and which was thus potentially capable of supplanting extant identities framed in terms of particularistic, cross-cutting social roles such as husband and father. The reasons for such changes need not concern us here, though it is important to note that Dutch attempts to "pacify" Aceh beginning in the 1870s—coupled with the devastating Aceh-Dutch war (1873–1913) which effected such pacification—were instrumental in motivating these (and many other) changes. So, too, was the worldwide Depression of the 1930s, which left most Acehnese men without income (Siegel 1969:91, cf. 98, 131). In short, political and economic circumstances of the sort outlined here were crucial both in engendering modernist Islamic movements (such as those headed by Daud Beureueh),[3] and in motivating men's acceptance of the *ulama's* teachings. Especially relevant for our purposes is that these teachings emphasized the conceptualization of male (and female) experience in terms of "reason" and "passion" [*akal* and *hawa nafsu* in Acehnese], and in these and other ways helped guarantee the subsequent cultural salience or "keyness" of these symbols, which, prior to the late nineteenth century, were "culturally present" but not all that significant (183, 196–98; Siegel 1979:234).

Kinship and gender relations in contemporary Aceh are similar in many respects to the situation I have described for the nineteenth century, though there are some important differences. In the village of Pidie, for example, Siegel found that postmarital residence is still predominantly uxorilocal (with about half of all men marrying out of their natal villages) (cf. Jayawardena 1977a:160); and that all married women own their own house and the land on which it stands (no men own houses [or residential acreage?]), provided that they have been separated from their parents (Siegel 1969). In addition, more women own and control rice land than men (even though, overall, more rice land is registered in the names of men than women) (Siegel 1969; cf. Jayawardena 1977b:28). Siegel also discovered that in the absence of their husbands, women manage nearly all land, and that, in any case, income from rice land is controlled by women (Siegel 1969:145; cf. Jayawardena 1977b:29). Women also raise nearly all the secondary crops, such as tobacco, ground nuts, onions, cucumbers, and other vegetables (Siegel 1969:144), the sale of which yields cash income that is used to supplement the subsistence base provided by rice (Siegel 1969:35).

Men, for their part, are mostly traders in the regional distribution systems that the Dutch created when they broke the chieftains' (and sultan's) monopoly over riverine and maritime trade (redefining their jurisdictions to matters of *adat*) and instituted a new system of trade relations that was more conducive to the realization of colonial economic and political objectives (Siegel 1969:137). (Men also help out their wives, work in fruit and vegetable gardens, and tend cattle and buffalo [see Jayawardena 1977a:158–59; 1977b:28].) The temporary out-migration thus entailed provides married men with cash for imported goods (e.g., cloth) that their wives cannot afford.

Interestingly, however, even "wealthy men have little ability to make decisions involving their wives" (Siegel 1969:145) and are said to be "powerless" within their own households. This is much like the situation in the nineteenth century. A key difference, according to Siegel, is that while men are "still unable to make decisions in their families, . . . they [now] feel entitled to do so" and, more generally, now hold "ideas about themselves [that] are no longer defined by their social [i.e., kinship] roles" (Siegel 1969:137).

Siegel explains (i.e., locates) men's "powerlessness" in terms of Acehnese constructions of masculinity (and gender generally) and the ways in which these constructions have been informed by modernist teachings of the sort alluded to earlier. A brief discussion of some of the data marshalled to support his argument may be useful here, especially since the data call into question Siegel's previously noted contention that men now think about themselves in ways that are no longer defined by their kinship or social roles. As will be apparent in due course, my reading of Siegel's data indicates that the latter contention is only partially correct and is, in any case, rather misleading. For while Acehnese men and women alike now have available to them culturally elaborated religious schema that define men in "positional" rather than "relational" terms (e.g., as Muslims, irrespective of their particular kinship affiliations and loyalties), their constructions of masculinity seem to be more thoroughly informed by the "relational" components of men's identities, and by their notions of husbands and fathers specifically. In this respect, twentieth-century Aceh is strikingly similar both to nineteenth-century Aceh and to nineteenth- and twentieth-century Negeri Sembilan.

Siegel's argument concerning men's powerlessness within their wives' households takes as its point of departure a series of null hypotheses. Such powerlessness is not a function of the kinship system (Siegel 1969:138), as might be expected if the Acehnese system included descent units of matrilineal design, in which case men would most likely have formal (but not necessarily all that much substantive) authority over their sisters' households, but not over their wives'. Nor is such powerlessness to be explained either in terms of men's prolonged absences from their wives' households and villages, or in terms of women's appreciable resources or well-honed strategies of resistance (178). Rather, men are powerless and without a place in their wives' families due to "contradiction[s] in what success [currently] means to them" and to the Acehnese generally. On the one hand, men feel that they are due deference and indulgence (and that they have a right to make decisions) in light of their financial contributions to their wives' households. "On the other hand, they feel demeaned when they receive the deference and indulgence they seek" (179). The main reason for this is that, in the wake of modernist teachings concerning the conceptualization of experience in terms of "reason" and "passion," asking for indulgence (gratification of desire) is a sign of their lack of *akal* ("reason") (149), and thus is an index of the predominance of "passion" over "reason."

To understand these dynamics we need to look more closely at the "deference" and "indulgence" to which Siegel refers. Men are deferred to by their wives only so long as they provide cash. In Siegel's words:

> Women feel the husband has a place in the family only for as long as the money he brings home from the East lasts. When it is gone, they no longer want their husbands around. Their understanding of the marriage contract is that men have a place in the home only if they pay for it each day. . . . Their husbands' contributions entitle them to be fed and *deferred to* while they pay for it; but when the money is gone, they should go too. They do not feel that men are entitled to share in the larger decisions of the family. (Siegel 1969:176–77; emphasis added)

Siegel goes on to make the following points:

> To treat a man as a guest is to treat him like a child. Both guests and children are *indulged,* and neither is allowed authority. . . . Without *deference,* men are no longer guests, only children. (181–82; emphasis added; cf. 153–54)

In sum, a man's exertion of power within his household indexes his lack of rationality or "reason," and thus seriously compromises his moral standing as an adult man and as a Muslim generally.

It should come as no surprise to find that conjugal strife is quite common in Aceh and frequently leads to divorce. (In Pidie, some 50% of all marriages end in divorce; the figure for the larger region is slightly lower [39%].) Nor should it come as a surprise to find that Acehnese attribute most divorces to conflicts over money or, more precisely, to conflicts over the fruits of a married man's labor power and productivity (Siegel 1969:174–76). In this connection it is significant that men fear that their wives will demand too much of them, and that of all the qualities that women seek in prospective husbands, generosity ("not being stingy") tops the list (165; see also 174–75). To put the point differently, the ideal husband earns considerable sums of money on the *rantou* (in the course of out-migration) and spends most of it on his wife and children, rather than on himself or on his mother, sisters, or other natal kin. The husband who sends or brings back nothing, by contrast, not only inverts the ideal, but is also subject to divorce (Jayawardena 1977b:29).

The problem for married men, however, is not simply that they feel that their wives and affines expect too much of them (Siegel 1969:165), but also that they have moral and material obligations to their natal households, which are in many respects in conflict with those to their wives. It is not entirely clear from Siegel's data (or from other relevant sources; e.g., Jayawardena 1977a, 1977b) if the husband role is informed by elder brother norms, as occurs in Negeri Sembilan, throughout the Malay Peninsula, and in much of the rest of the Malay-Indonesian world, but this seems to be the case. It is quite apparent, in any event, that conflicts in men's roles as brothers and as husbands/fathers provide much of the raw material for the domestic tensions and strife many men (and women) experience.

Equally obvious are four other, more general, points. First, men's relational roles are the subject of considerable cultural elaboration and are in fact hegemonic with respect to practical representations of masculinity. Second, practical representations of masculinity, which emphasize men's "passion" rather than their "reason," are largely out of keeping with, and are in many respects inversions of, their official counterparts, which emphasize men's "reason" rather than their "passion." Third, these (practical) representations are relatively negative and have this (negative) quality because they reflect appreciable disjunctions between the expectations that married men will generate property rights, wealth, and prestige for their wives' households on the one hand, and married men's actual abilities (and/or willingness) to satisfy these expectations on the other. And fourth, the contrasting representations of masculinity reported for Aceh are quite similar to those I have documented for Negeri Sembilan and are, in addition, motivated and (re)produced by many of the same sets of variables.

Some important questions remain. To what extent are women's views of men shared by men themselves? Is there a class dynamic at work here, as is true of Negeri Sembilan? And finally, what are the comparative and theoretical implications of the cultural elaboration of practical representations of masculinity that focus on men in their roles as husbands and fathers? I will address each of these questions in turn.

The answer to the question concerning the extent to which women's views of men are shared by men themselves is relatively straightforward. Siegel reports that "men cannot withstand their wives' complaints and go back to the East, usually sooner than they had anticipated, because *they share their wives' estimations of themselves*" (Siegel 1969:181; emphasis added). This means, among other things, that we are not dealing with views or representations of masculinity that are part of an exclusively female "counterculture." Note, also, that men sometimes characterize adult males as a whole as "lazy," as do women (Siegel 1969:180);[4] that all such data call into question Siegel's previously cited contention that men now hold "ideas about themselves [that] are no longer defined by their social [i.e., kinship] roles"; and that this situation is very much in keeping with that of Negeri Sembilan.

As for the question regarding class, Siegel remarks only that "men who don't go on *rantou* are noticeably poorer and often have trouble with their wives" (Siegel 1969:166). This might be interpreted to mean that marital strife and divorce are more common among the poor than among the wealthy. It is not clear, however, if views of men as a whole are shaped by stereotypic perceptions bearing on impoverished men (especially their "poor showing" as husbands and fathers), but I suspect that this is the case, as it is in Negeri Sembilan.

The answer to the remaining question, concerning the comparative and theoretical implications of the cultural elaboration of practical representations of masculinity that focus on men in their roles as husbands and fathers, is more complex, particularly since it bears on and calls into question some fundamental assumptions in the anthropological, sociological, and psychoanalytic literature on gender. To sketch out some of the implications of the relevant data from Aceh (and Negeri Sembilan), I provide a quick (highly selective) overview of recent developments in Ortner's thinking about gender, and then turn to a brief discussion of an enduring theme (the "relational/positional" dichotomy) in the work of Nancy Chodorow, which has informed the thinking of Ortner (and Whitehead), among many others, and which has, I believe, led to a skewed understanding of some of the cross-cultural differences and similarities in structural definitions of males and females.

Earlier on we discussed Ortner's (1974) thesis that women are everywhere held to be "closer to nature" and "further from culture" than men, and that this conceptual linkage is what explains their universal cultural devaluation (secondary status). We saw that this insightful and provocative argument stimulated a great deal of additional research, even though it was highly static and did of course produce much controversy. It remains to emphasize that some of the criticism directed at the thesis, along with largely unrelated developments in social and cultural theory, encouraged Ortner to rethink her overall theoretical orientation. This is readily apparent from the 1981 volume *Sexual Meanings: The Cultural Construction of Gender and Sexuality*, which she co-edited with Harriet Whitehead. Both in her essay on "Gender and Sexuality in Hierarchical Societies," and in the introduction to *Sexual Meanings*, which she co-authored with Whitehead, Ortner advocates a processual, dynamic, actor-oriented, practice-theory approach to the study of gender. She suggests, in addition, that the most profitable approach involves examining constructions of gender as inextricably enmeshed both with structures of production and exchange and with the more encompassing systems of prestige to which these structures are keyed.

I am in broad agreement with this position, as many features of the foregoing analysis would suggest. I also find much of value in Ortner and Whitehead's insights into the ways in which the meanings of "female" and the social standing of women may be "pulled down" by the cultural elaboration of certain kinship roles and the relative hegemony of these roles in ideologies of gender. Ortner and Whitehead (1981a:21) point out, for instance, that, cross-culturally, one or another different female relational role—mother, daughter, sister—"tend[s] to dominate the category of 'female' and to color the meanings of all other female relational roles." For example, in most Islamic, Mediterranean, and Catholic cultures, and of course in the United States, the systems of prestige and moral evaluation are such that the category "female" is strongly shaped by local understandings of "mother" and "wife," which, among other things, focus on sexuality and reproduction and thus effectively situate woman and femaleness "closer to nature" in Ortner's 1974 sense. The same is true for Buddhist cultures in Thailand and beyond, as is evident both from the common ground underlying debates between Kirsch (1982, 1985) and Keyes (1984), and from Ledgerwood's recent (1992) work on Khmer women.

This situation contrasts rather sharply with what one finds in Polynesia. In Polynesia, where kinship and political systems tend to be structured by symbols and idioms of cognatic descent, men build up status and prestige by attracting followers, and do this partly by using kinswomen—especially sisters, but also daughters—as "bait" (to use Ortner's term). Consequently, in many Polynesian societies, the category "female" is very much colored by local understandings and values of "sisterhood," and is only minimally informed by local notions of "mother" and "wife." This serves to deemphasize women's sexuality, reproductive capacities, and links with "natural functions," and is partly responsible for the fact that Polynesian women are viewed in a more positive light than women in most Islamic, Mediterranean, Catholic, and Buddhist cultures.

I concur with Ortner and Whitehead on many of these points, and am, more generally, rather heavily indebted to them insofar as their work helped inspire the analytic framework developed in this study. At the same time, there are, I believe, certain features of their approach that limit its explanatory power, two of which merit remark here. First, their perspective on gender ideology (and ideology on the whole) is a rather totalizing one inasmuch as it focuses almost entirely on official discourse and in these and other ways makes insufficient analytic provision for the existence of the contrasting discourses that inevitably make up any given ideological formation. I hasten to add, however, that Ortner now recognizes as much and has gone a long way toward developing an analytic apparatus capable of handling such multiplicity (see Ortner 1989–90).

A second problem with Ortner and Whitehead's approach, one which Ortner does not address in her most recent work, is that it rests on the a priori, unargued assumption that in *all* societies there is a rigid dichotomy between the structural definitions of males and females. (This same assumption also informs Ortner's earlier [1974] work.) More specifically, after Ortner and Whitehead underscore that in all societies females are defined relationally, they go on to claim that there are *no* corresponding patterns in the case of males. In their words, "analogous distinctions among men are *not* critical for masculinity" (Ortner and Whitehead 1981a:21; emphasis added), because men, unlike women, tend to be defined in terms of "positional" ([allegedly] "nonrelational") statuses, such as "hunter," "warrior," "chief," "politician," and so on. Such claims, which seem to derive in large part from the work of Nancy Chodorow, take for granted important issues, such as masculinity, that should be, along with femininity, at the center of analysis, and certainly merit reassessment in light of Negeri Sembilan data, as well as data from Aceh (and elsewhere).

Suffice it to reiterate that, in Negeri Sembilan, the comportment of married men in relation to their wives is judged largely in terms of the behavioral standards that pertain to elder brothers' treatment (nurturance, protection, etc.) of their younger sisters, and that many married men fall short of the "elder brother" ideal due to their inability to produce sufficient property rights, wealth, and prestige for their wives and their wives' kin. Married men who find that they cannot live up to the expectations of, or otherwise cope with pressures from, their wives and affines, frequently divorce or simply desert their wives, along with any children they might have. This course of action not only helps to shape and reproduce local (practical) views that husbands and fathers are both unreliable and untrustworthy; it also colors practical views of masculinity in their entirety. These latter practical views serve, in turn, to offset and vitiate official views of males, just as they effectively substantiate and promote practical views of females. More broadly, data from Negeri Sembilan and Aceh (where similar dynamics prevail) indicate that in the practice of everyday life, certain male relational roles—those of elder brother, husband, and father—may not only dominate the category of "male" but may also inform the meanings of all other male relational (and "positional") roles. As noted earlier, these same data make clear that it is not merely the meanings of "female," or the social standing of women, that may be dragged down by the cultural elaboration of relational roles and their relative hegemony in everyday, practical discourses on gender. This can also occur in the case of masculinity and the social standing of men, even though males may still come out ahead as regards the overall distribution of power, prestige, and virtue.

Ortner and Whitehead's dichotomizing approach to structural definitions of males and females derives largely from Chodorow's feminist reworking of psychoanalytic theory (although it also has deep roots in the pioneering work of Simone de Beauvoir [1949], which also informs Chodorow's thinking on the subject of women). A brief overview of some of the problems with this dichotomy as it is developed in the highly influential work of Chodorow (1978, 1989) may thus be useful here, though I should make clear at the outset that Ortner and Whitehead's position is not burdened with all the cultural and other baggage that Chodorow brings to her analyses.

I cannot do justice to the complexity of Chodorow's extremely insightful arguments concerning the "deep structural" (and other) implications of the fact that females predominate in all societies in the rearing of infants and young children. I am concerned primarily with the way she frames some of her most general conclusions regarding the implications of such facts for the reproduction of gendered difference: for example, that women are, to use the portmanteau concept, "relationally oriented."[5] One problem in this regard is that Chodorow is inconsistent when it comes to specifying whether the particular male-female contrasts with which she is concerned—e.g., conscious and unconscious emotional needs and capacities to relate to others, conscious and unconscious gender-role identifications—involve differences in *degree* versus differences in *kind*. In many places, for example, she argues, quite plausibly in my view, that men have less developed or elaborated relational needs and capacities than women. Elsewhere she states, also quite plausibly, that men often deny such needs and capacities. In still other places, however, Chodorow advances the implausible argument that men do not have any such needs and capacities. The term "arelational masculinity," which Chodorow employs in some of her most recent (e.g., 1989:185) writing, further muddies the issue.

Perhaps most problematic, though, is Chodorow's dubious analytic leap from data concerning conscious and unconscious relational needs and capacities, and conscious and unconscious gender-role identifications, to arguments about formal cultural or ideological constructions of gender. Chodorow contends, for example, that in the capitalist world, in other hierarchical, bureaucratically organized societies (the [former] Soviet Union is cited as an example), and, indeed, in *all* societies, men, unlike women, are defined in formal cultural or ideological terms "positionally" (by their positions or roles in the economy or public domain) rather than relationally (in terms of the domestic domain). But we need to ask the following here: Who is doing the defining, and in what contexts are the definitions at issue relevant to the ways in which people actually experience, understand, and represent one another in the practice of everyday life? It seems quite clear that, from the point of view of state-sponsored nationalist ideologies, men in the United States, the former Soviet Union, Malaysia, and many other places are defined primarily in what Chodorow would refer to as "positional" terms, that is, as members of particular occupational groups, social classes, and ethnic communities (though I should perhaps emphasize the self-evident point that the meaningfulness of such "positional" identifications is thoroughly relational). But if one looks beyond the elitist top-down perspective and examines the situation either from the bottom-up or simply from within the familial contexts, local social fields, and more encompassing (local) communities in which men (and women) act out, experience, and make sense of much of their lives, these types of components and overall definitions of male identity lose much of their salience and are supplanted by relational definitions of the sort ostensibly reserved for women. This is especially true in communities characterized by (1) relatively little racial, ethnic, religious, class, and occupational diversity; (2) structures of kinship that continue to provide hegemonic frameworks for many domains of society and culture; and, more generally, (3) local ideologies that are in critical respects out of synch with state-sponsored ideologies. To put this last point somewhat differently: "Positional" components and overall definitions of male identity lose much of their salience and are supplanted by relational components and definitions bearing on masculinity in communities in which state-sponsored ideologies are not nearly as hegemonic as they are—or are assumed to be—in Western societies, which is to say, in the vast majority of the contexts in which anthropologists have traditionally studied.

The problem as I see it, then, is that Chodorow and others who adopt her "relational-positional" dichotomy not only impose an overly simplistic "either-or" view on Western data concerning similarities and differences in structural definitions of males and females, which is linked to if not derived from an uncritical distinction between domestic and public domains. They also both overvalorize and overgeneralize from culturally and historically specific state-sponsored constructions of maleness, and, in the process, unwittingly offer up selected elements of a particular variant of a heavily motivated native or folkloric model as an analytic model with purportedly universal applicability. Such oversights are especially curious in the case of Chodorow since some of her earliest (e.g., 1974) work not only makes reference to Acehnese material, but does in fact draw on much the same corpus of Siegel's research (e.g., Siegel 1969) that is cited here.

It is interesting, though not surprising, that the "relational-positional" dichotomy has received very little critical analytic attention to date, and has, for this reason, outlived many of the other dichotomies that informed earlier work on gender and women, such as the (originally formulated) distinctions between "public" and "domestic" (or "private") domains and "nature" and "culture." Perhaps the main reason for the undeserved longevity of this dichotomy is that constructions of masculinity continue to suffer from what I referred to earlier on as the "taken-for-granted syndrome."

Although the particular dimensions of Chodorow's framework that I have addressed here have received minimal analytic attention to date, recent years have of course witnessed numerous ethnographically grounded critiques of other psychologically oriented universalistic arguments that claim to lay bare either the "essence(s)" of woman or femininity, or the "essence(s)" of male-female contrasts. Stack's recent (1990) work on African Americans, for example, demonstrates convincingly that hypotheses of the sort developed by Carol Gilligan (1982)—concerning ostensibly universal contrasts between males and females with respect to the development of moral reasoning—suffer from various ethnocentric biases and are for these and other reasons highly problematic. Firmly grounded ethnographic analyses of the sort undertaken by Stack are of critical importance if we are to avoid increasingly free-floating and ethereal psychologistic discussions of purportedly universal contrasts (or similarities) between males and females; or, to put it more positively, if we are to advance our understanding of the myriad complexities and nuances of gender(ed) difference (and sameness).

TRANSFORMATIONS ON ISLAMIC THEMES IN SOUTHEAST ASIA AND BEYOND: MINANGKABAU, NEGERI SEMBILAN MALAYS, JAVANESE, AND BEDOUIN COMPARED

Minangkabau and Negeri Sembilan Malays

The foregoing discussion indicates that the case of Negeri Sembilan is by no means anomalous, and that Negeri Sembilan Malays do in fact have much in common with the ("bilateral") Acehnese of northern Sumatra. Both cases also bear a strong family resemblance to the ("matrilineal") Minangkabau of West Sumatra, who, it will be recalled, are both the southerly neighbors of the Acehnese and the ancestral group from which Negeri Sembilan Malays trace their descent.

Minangkabau systems of prestige, along with many other features of Minangkabau society and culture, are much like those reported for Negeri Sembilan (and Aceh), as will be apparent in due course. One needs to bear in mind, however, that there are also important differences in these two societies, some of which can be attributed to the circumstances of the Minangkabau's migration to and settlement in Negeri Sembilan (beginning around the fourteenth century if not earlier), along with their subsequent interactions (which included occasional intermarriage and various types of trade, political accommodation, and warfare) with both the non-Muslim aborigines as well as the ("bilateral") Malays inhabiting surrounding areas. Other contrasts derive from the rather dissimilar colonial experiences of Minangkabau and Negeri Sembilan Malays (under the Dutch and British, respectively), and their quite different experiences under the postcolonial governments of Indonesia and Malaysia. More generally, there are differences in these societies with respect to political succession, kinship terminology, marriage patterns, postmarital residence, domestic group dynamics (and the role of the mother's brother especially), as well as occupational specialization and entrepreneurial traditions, both of which are far more developed in Minangkabau than in Negeri Sembilan.[6] Additionally, just as the ideological scope and force of Islam appears always to have been more pronounced in Minangkabau than in Negeri Sembilan, so, too, have mosques, prayer houses, and local "coffee shops" always been more efficacious in Minangkabau as regards creating a sense of commonality between in-marrying men and their male affines, and among males as a whole. This despite the fact that the Arabic-origin concepts of "reason" and "passion," which are highly elaborated in many domains of Negeri Sembilan (and Acehnese) society and culture, are culturally "present" though relatively unelaborated among the Minangkabau.[7] Note also that Minangkabau constructions of masculinity, unlike their counterparts in Negeri Sembilan (and Aceh), are informed in important ways by the notion that men both possess and convey to their wives and their wives' households and kin groups highly valued (because biogenetically and spiritually potent) "seed" or "blood"—such that the exchange of men focuses in certain respects on the exchange of such "seed"/"blood" rather than on transactions over men's labor power and productivity (Pak 1986, n.d.). A full treatment of such issues would require a separate volume. My intention here is merely to highlight the existence of such variation, and to caution against the temptation, to which many, unfortunately, succumb, to make across-the-board generalizations embracing the two societies.[8]

Having drawn attention to some of the differences between Minangkabau and Negeri Sembilan, let me turn briefly to some of the commonalities. Perhaps most obvious are the basic values of these societies (encapsulated in notions of *adat, budi, malu*)[9] as well as their matrilineal descent groups, which are similar in many respects both in their structure and operation. Highly relevant as well is that among the Minangkabau, as in Negeri Sembilan (and Aceh), women are strongly favored in the proprietorship and inheritance of houses and most categories of land. Women also manage domestic resources, including the cash incomes of their husbands, and they play an important role in exchange activities associated with the agricultural cycle as well as the cycle of ceremonial feasting. As for other aspects of the sexual division of labor: Minangkabau women do most of the work in the rice fields (subsistence-oriented rice production provides much of the economic base, at least in "traditional" villages), though they also raise cash crops and rear poultry and livestock for sale. Men, for their part, help their wives and sisters during certain stages of the agricultural cycle but are heavily involved in temporary out-migration, which we have seen in Negeri Sembilan (and in Aceh) as well. In earlier times, the yields of men's economic activities were apparently devoted primarily to their mothers, sisters, and other female kin, as opposed to their wives and affines. These activities, like the clearing of previously unclaimed acreage suitable for residential or agricultural purposes, were oriented largely toward the creation of property and wealth for their (natal) kin groups, which could enhance the prestige standing of such groups. Note, too, that, as in Negeri Sembilan (and Aceh), large numbers of followers and substantial wealth were signs of men's spiritual power or potency.

The picture painted thus far is of course highly schematic and "traditional." A good deal has changed in many (but not all) Minangkabau communities. Perhaps most relevant are two changes which closely parallel shifts that occurred in Negeri Sembilan: First, the restructuring of men's roles as brothers (and mothers' brothers) on the one hand, and husbands and fathers on the other; and second, increased socioeconomic differentiation and stratification. Let us take these issues one at a time.

To convey a clear sense of the shifts in men's roles, we need to underscore that, in earlier times, "a husband did not necessarily have to provide a living for his wife and children, or send his children to school, or participate in decisions in their home" (Istutiah Gunawan Mitchell 1969:126). These were the responsibilities of the head of the wife's group or *kaum*, that is, her brother or mother's brother. The husband had responsibilities to the *kaum* into which he was born, which included obligations to his sisters and his sisters' children. Note, also, that a husband "was not necessarily a permanent mate; he might leave his wife over the most minor matter," a fact well captured in the customary saying or aphorism pertaining to men in their roles as husbands, "Like ash on a tree trunk, even a soft wind and it [they] will fly away" (126). Indeed, so minimal was the elaboration of the husband/father role—in contrast to the situation in

Negeri Sembilan (and Aceh), the Minangkabau man was not usually a permanent resident of his wife's house; in many cases he simply "visited" from dusk to dawn—that "reportedly a child sometimes did not recognize its own father on the street" (Hamka 1963:56–57, cited in Istutiah Gunawan Mitchell 1969:128).

Much of this changed over the last 150 years as a result of Dutch colonialism and various economic, political, and religious forces that undermined larger kin groupings (clans, lineages) and key features of the property relations undergirding them, thus effectively guaranteeing the rise to prominence of nuclear families and nuclear family households (see von Benda-Beckmann 1979). Based on research conducted in the 1960s, Tanner (1982:144), for example, reported that "during the past two generations, the husband's financial contributions to his wife have increased." These findings are similar to those of Frederick Errington, who carried out field research in 1975. Errington (1984:68) writes that "the [husband/father] role may have become even more demanding in recent years with the change in the relative importance of a man's affinal and matrilineal obligations." In some communities the father has in fact become economically central to family life to the point that, at least in relation to his wife's brothers, "he is now *entirely* responsible for the support of his wife and children" (Errington 1984:68; emphasis added; see also Istutiah Gunawan Mitchell 1969:130–31).

Changes in the distribution of male responsibilities may have progressed further in the Minangkabau village of Bayur (the site of Errington's research) than in many other Minangkabau communities. "There is currently little mention in Bayur of chronic financial pressures placed on a man by his sisters, evidently still a source of marital tension elsewhere" in the Minangkabau world (Errington 1984:68). Perhaps, opines Errington, this is because "Bayur has long been dependent on the outside world and has, in addition, long been subject to the patriarchal influences of reformist Islam" (68). Worthy of remark in any case is that while the wife's mother and wife's mother's sisters "scrutinize the son-in-law very clearly, they judge him particularly by the amount of his financial contribution to his household" (66). Errington goes on to underscore that "males married to sisters see each other as rivals for the approval of the parents-in-law and feel that their respective economic contributions are always subject to unfavorable comparison" (66).

More generally, as Tanner (1982), among others, has noted, a man "knows that the success of his marriage depends not only on his relationship with his wife but on his relationship to her kin," and that these relationships "are more than a little dependent on his economic contribution to the family" (135). A husband's position in the household of his wife's matrilineal extended family is indeed rather vulnerable, even under the best of circumstances (136). As Errington (1984:67) puts it, men feel they are "welcome only as long as [they are] able to make a strong contribution," but even "their best efforts to provide are often not enough. . . . [and] they never win an entirely secure place in their wife's home" (see also Krier 1994).

At this juncture I might emphasize that the situation described here should not be interpreted as yet another peculiar twist on the famed "matrilineal puzzle," as described either in the pioneering work of Audrey Richards (1951), or in the also classic, but modified and somewhat more sophisticated, version proposed by Schneider (1961). The matrilineal puzzle, in Richards's formulation, turns on how to trace descent through women yet allocate authority to men, and on how such authority is to be divided between matrilineally related males on the one hand and in-marrying males on the other. While Schneider accepts much of Richards's formulation, he suggests that the major tension need not focus on the relationship between the in-marrying male and his wife's brother(s), as Richards assumes, but might be realized instead in the relationship between the in-marrying male and other male members of his wife's kin group (who need not be the wife's actual brother [or mother's brother]). What we see in Minangkabau (and in Negeri Sembilan), however, is not tension arising in connection with contested authority over women and children so much—women in any case exercise far more authority than all formulations of the puzzle imply (Prindiville 1985; Tanner and Thomas 1985; Ng 1987)—as in competing claims over the labor power and productivity of in-marrying males. These are very different sets of issues, as discussed elsewhere (Peletz 1988b).[10]

Consider also that even when competing claims from sisters and other female matrilineal kin do not figure into the picture, as appears to be the case in Bayur, married men are still under tremendous pressure to satisfy the economic expectations and demands of their wives' female kin. These expectations and demands are, at least in part, a reflection of the prestige considerations of women who evaluate and rank one another (including, perhaps especially, their sisters) in terms of what their husbands bring home for them. The expectations and demands at issue also index prestige competition among married men themselves, in a climate in which they are made to feel insecure by their parents-in-law, who are forever judging and ranking the economic contributions of the sons-in-law in relation to one another and, presumably, in relation to other married men as well.[11] Of broader concern here is that status rivalry is particularly intense among the Minangkabau, apparently more so than among Negeri Sembilan Malays, perhaps because socioeconomic differentiation and stratification are both quite pronounced and more elaborated than what one finds in Negeri Sembilan.

The problem for married men, then, is not simply or even primarily that they are subject to competing claims on their labor power and productivity; indeed, in some cases this is not an issue at all: rather, it is the spiralling economic expectations and demands of their wives' female kin, particularly their wives' mothers. But this is only part of it; the other salient issue is that the "rising social expectations have not been proportionately paralleled by new channels being created for realizing these aspirations," one consequence of which is that "the desire to accumulate wealth or professional prestige has become an increasing psychological burden on Minangkabau men" (Istutiah Gunawan Mitchell 1969:131).

Data on divorce and its distribution are especially relevant here and are very much in keeping with data from Negeri Sembilan (and Aceh). Tanner (1982:148 n.9) refers to divorce as "very common" and Errington (1984:66) makes a similar claim—"divorce is frequent"—adding in parentheses that "Naim (1973) calculates divorce to be the highest in Indonesia." While precise figures are hard to come by, Tanner comments that the rate "varies widely" from village to village, and that at the time of her research in 1964 divorce "varied from two to forty-four percent" (Tanner 1982:139). More recent data indicate that the divorce rate among male elders is between 45 and 51 percent, and that the rate for female elders is between 32 and 36 percent (Kato 1982:180–81).

Relatively infrequent divorce, according to Tanner (1982:148 n.10), is due partly to "economic prosperity," though "modernist Islam" is also a factor in lowering the rate. Based partly on the existence of similar patterns in Negeri Sembilan and Aceh, I take the first part of this explanation to mean that divorce is less common among relatively wealthy households because the husbands/fathers in those households are better able to live up to the economic expectations and demands of their wives and female kin than are married men in poor households (though the fact that the adult members of wealthy households also have more to lose in the event of divorce may also be relevant). The second part of the explanation, concerning the influence of modernist Islam, may be interpreted to mean that cultural and institutional factors associated with modernist Islam have effectively discouraged divorce by making it more difficult to effect (as has happened in Negeri Sembilan and other parts of Malaysia), by impressing upon men (and women) their marital and parental responsibilities as Muslims, or by otherwise contributing to the durability (and perhaps the stability) of conjugal bonds. Such factors do not operate in a classless vacuum, however, and, all things being equal, it is probably harder for poor men (and women) to honor their familial commitments as Muslims in the context of marriage. This is significant insofar as the alternative discourse on Minangkabau masculinity that emphasizes men being unreasonable and irresponsible (see below) is undoubtedly fueled by perceptions of husbands/fathers at the bottom of the class hierarchy—as is clearly the case in Negeri Sembilan and Aceh. As in Negeri Sembilan and Aceh, then, our analyses of gender among the Minangkabau must be informed by an understanding of locally salient variables of kinship as well as class.

In light of the overall situation described here, one might reasonably expect to find among the Minangkabau an alternative discourse on masculinity which is in many respects out of keeping with the official line emphasizing male ascendancy,[12] and which is, in addition, highly elaborated. In point of fact, alternative, largely counter-hegemonic representations of masculinity emphasizing male irresponsibility and unreliability and, more generally, the ways in which men's "passion" dominates their "reason" and renders them morally bankrupt, are found in daily discourse and are enshrined in oral and written literature (Postel-Coster 1992:232; Whalley 1993; Blackwood 1995; Krier 1995).[13] But unlike the otherwise similar situations in Negeri Sembilan and Aceh, they do not appear to be highly elaborated. Why this is so is difficult to gauge with any degree of certitude, and it is possible that their minimal presence in the ethnographic literature reflects previous observers' narrow focus on official discourse (or *adat*, matriliny, or women). On the other hand—and this, I think, is more likely—the alternative discourse may exist in relatively unelaborated form due to the fact that Minangkabau masculinity is defined, formally and otherwise, in a much less economically based "performative" fashion than is masculinity in either Negeri Sembilan or Aceh, and is thus less easily called into question by the realities of men's economic performances in their roles as husbands/fathers. Put differently, because Minangkabau constructions of masculinity, unlike their counterparts in Negeri Sembilan and Aceh, are informed in important ways by the notion that men both possess and convey biogenetically and spiritually potent "seed" or "blood" to their wives and their wives' households and lineages (Tanner 1982:137–38; Pak 1986, n.d.; Krier 1994), Minangkabau men are less apt to be defined in negative terms simply because they fall short in a narrow economic sense.[14] The focus on men's contributions conveyed through semen and realized in the production of (ideally) "high quality" children belonging to the wife's household and lineage thus constrains the elaboration of negative discourses on masculinity, though it certainly does not preclude their (relatively unelaborated) existence in the first place.[15]

One corollary of these arguments is that Minangkabau constructions of masculinity are somewhat less vulnerable to the dislocations and other vicissitudes entailed in local communities' heightened integration into state frameworks, global economies, and systems of nationalist and trans-national discourse than is the case with constructions of masculinity found in societies such as Negeri Sembilan and Aceh.[16] But this does not mean that the "relational" components of Minangkabau masculinity are any less significant in an analytic sense. We still see men being defined and judged in critically important ways in terms of what they contribute to their kin (e.g., their wives and children, and their wives' kin), and to re-production in both the biological and social senses of the term: "While [Minangkabau] women are defined as the source of continuity, [Minangkabau] men are essential to the cycle of continuity; they are the agents who are brought in from the outside or who are sent out to create children; the future reproducers of the women's lineages" (Ng 1987:205). Equally noteworthy is that Minangkabau masculinity and femininity alike are deeply suffused with ambivalence, and will undoubtedly continue to be characterized by profoundly mixed emotions as the Minangkabau find themselves forced to negotiate the increasingly slippery terrain of Indonesian modernity. This is all the more likely since the (Javacentric) nationalist, "development"-oriented, and reformist Islamic discourses on Indonesian modernity accord relatively little value to what is uniquely or distinctively Minangkabau, and are thus (further) transforming and erod-ing key features of locally valorized conceptions bearing on personhood and kinship as well as gender(ed) difference and sameness.

Javanese

The earliest accounts bearing on kinship and gender in Java emphasized the formally "bilateral" nature of the Javanese kinship system, its matri-lateral and matrifocal biases, the high rates of divorce, and the prevalence of women both in small-scale trading activities and in the marketplace generally,[17] and in managing domestic resources, including the cash in-comes of their husbands (see, e.g., Geertz [1961] 1989; Jay 1969; Koentjar-aningrat 1960). The authors of these accounts typically took the position that men's relative exclusion from economic activities of the sort at issue here is best explained by Javanese (men's) prestige considerations, most notably men's concerns that their involvement in such domains might undermine their spiritual power or potency (*sakti, kesaktian*) or otherwise sully their status (see also Keeler 1987, 1990). Consistent with such (early) accounts is the assumption that there is in Java a single, seamless, more or less uniform and hegemonic ideology of gender. Brenner (1995), however, has argued convincingly that such explanations and assumptions—along with the attendant line of reasoning emphasizing the "bad" economic decisions that might follow from male economic actors' obsessive concerns with status—only go so far; and that, as such, we need to devote more attention to the limits and silences of this official line on gender. More importantly, she delineates the practical, largely counter-hegemonic view, heretofore effectively ignored in the ethnographic literature, that men do not actively participate in such domains because they are, as Raffles put it early in the nineteenth century, "fools in money concerns" owing to their inabilities to control their desires and "passion" (*nepsu* in Javanese) and thus act in accordance with their rationality or "reason" (*akal* in Javanese). Actually, this point was alluded to some years ago by Hildred Geertz, as evidenced by her remark that men themselves "frequently express the belief that they are incapable of handling money carefully, whereas women are supposed to have thrift and foresight" (Geertz [1961] 1989:123; cf. Jay 1969:92; Smith-Hefner 1988a), though she did not really explore its implications. The precise ways in which these practical views of gender are distributed among Javanese (e.g., in terms of gender, class, etc.) is difficult to discern since the available evidence does not speak to such matters directly or in any detail. However, we do know that the views in question are "not . . . held exclusively by women," and that they do in fact both "underlie key roles that men and women play in the household" and "form the basis for their practices in other spheres of social life" (Brenner 1995:32).

In short, the available literature provides abundant evidence of the existence in Java of alternative representations of masculinity (and femininity), some of which clearly contradict the official hegemony described in earlier works, which was assumed to effectively "sum up" Javanese constructions of gender (and self-control). The question thus becomes, What is the conceptual source of the alternative view of masculinity at issue here? The answer, quite clear from Brenner's data, is men's greater sexual passion: "Most Javanese men and women take as a given that men have an innately greater desire for sex than women, and that this desire is extremely difficult for them to suppress. In relation to economic practices, this view of the "inherent differences between women and men leads people in Solo [Central Java] to conclude that women are naturally better suited to managing household finances, the family firm, or the marketplace" (Brenner 1995:33). As for the connection between controlling money and controlling one's "passions," listen to the words of a Javanese man in his seventies: "Women make better traders and entrepreneurs than men, because men have greater lust (*syahwat*) than women. Men can never hold on to money for long, because if you give them money, they'll spend it on getting women. Give 'em enough money and they'll have more than one wife, either out in the open or on the sly. Men have greater desires than women. It's always men who spend money on women, who 'buy' women. Who ever heard of a woman buying a man?" (cited in Brenner 1995:33).

The perspective articulated by this man resonates deeply with the views of many other Javanese men and women (see, e.g., Geertz [1961] 1989:131). It is also strikingly similar to the perspectives I encountered among men and women in Negeri Sembilan (as is the overall construction of his argument, with the exception of his reference to the term *syahwat*, which, in my experience, is not used by Malays). So, too, ultimately, are the specific contexts or relationships in which such views presumably develop—essentially those of marriage (or extramarital liaisons, which are, by definition, viewed in direct relation to marriage and are, equally clearly, held to be highly threatening to marriage and the economic viability of adulterous men's households). More precisely, it is the cultural understanding and moral evaluation of sexual difference—men's greater or stronger sexual urges as compared with women's—realized in the context of marriage (or adultery) that is the ultimate origin of such views.

The relative importance of the theme of "oversexed" husbands (and men generally) with respect to counter-hegemonic representations of masculinity appears more pronounced in Java than in Negeri Sembilan, Aceh, and Minangkabau, but the reasons for such differences are not altogether clear. The contrasts in question might well be related to the fact that Java is far more stratified than the other societies, and that Javanese, especially Central Javanese, are much more concerned with the maintenance—and transgression—of finely graded social distinctions, speech levels, postural and other bodily regimes, and the like. The scope and force of these concerns presuppose intense, ever vigilant social (especially self-) control and, as such, necessarily foreground forces over and against which self-control is defined—most notably, unbridled sexuality—thus rendering them both more culturally elaborated and more fraught with ambivalence and anxiety than in the other societies we have considered.

Also relevant are differences in variables related to the systems of production and exchange. Women in Java are more strongly associated with marketing, trade, and cash incomes than women in the other societies we have considered, just as Javanese men are less strongly linked with these phenomena than men in the other societies. Partly for this reason—but also because the system of marriage and affinal exchange in Java has never focused on the exchange of men, whereas those of our other societies did and in some cases still do—the economic performance of men in their roles as husbands has long and perhaps always been less of a culturally elaborated concern in Java than in these other societies.

Further information about the Javanese ideology of fault in divorce—whether most marital problems and dissolutions are attributed to the unreasonable and irresponsible behavior of men, as is true in Negeri Sembilan and Aceh—would obviously be useful here, but there is relatively little material on such topics in the relevant studies (e.g., Geertz [1961] 1989; Nakamura 1983). Note, however, that in the late 1950s Hildred Geertz (139–40) found that "sexual infidelity" was the reason for divorce most commonly cited by divorcing couples themselves, and that the sexual infidelity at issue typically involved the husband, not the wife. Significant as well is that divorce among the (then) highest echelons of Javanese society (the *priyayi*) was said to be "rare," and that "shotgun weddings" were more common among the poor (70–71, 138–39). Bear in mind also that, at present, the theme of men's (economic) irresponsibility in their roles as husbands is one that is most often articulated by lower-class women, and that, generally speaking, one of the things that most troubles women about men's sexual infidelities is the threat that such relationships pose to the economic viability of their households (Brenner 1995). The reasons for these overall patterns are undoubtedly quite similar to those we have discussed in connection with Negeri Sembilan and, to a lesser extent, Aceh and Minangkabau. So, too, are many of their theoretical implications; for example, the merits—indeed, the necessity—of describing and analyzing gender in relation to kinship and other forms of difference and inequality (class, race, etc.).

There are two more general points to emphasize. First, while Javanese views bearing on men's ineptness in the marketplace and their mismanagement of funds need not necessarily, but in point of fact do to some degree, focus on men in one or another kinship ("relational") role, stereotypic views of men as ultimately more strongly sexed than women clearly do. All such views, moreover, counterbalance and to some degree negate official representations of men as more reasonable and responsible than women (and offset and vitiate official representations of women), just as they serve to legitimize both the sexual division of labor and exchange, and myriad other features of social and cultural life. It is thus essential to incorporate such views into our discussions of gender (and kinship) in Java. If we fail to do so, we not only find ourselves in the dark as regards the variables many Javanese cite in legitimizing their gendered division of labor and exchange; we also end up with a seriously impoverished analysis of Javanese experiences, understandings, and representations of gender(ed) difference and sameness.

The second point relates to Brenner's important observation (39) that the marketplace as a domain in the control of women is thus also a "place where women cannot be controlled by men." But can or do market women control themselves? The answer, provided in part by ambiguity and ambivalence in the stories of changing female sexual freedoms and embodiments of power that have been appropriated by Indonesian media and national narratives (Brenner 1995; see also Hellwig 1992), would seem to be a resounding, though not altogether unambiguous, no. For according to one view of things, while women are in many contexts possessed of greater self-control and rationality than men, they are ultimately incapable of controlling themselves (sexually and otherwise)—as, in many contexts, are men. According to the competing view, market women can indeed control themselves but are nonetheless prone to sexual exploits outside marriage because of financial need or concerns to get even with womanizing husbands. Both views indicate (among other things) that profound ambivalence permeates some of the most basic categories through which Javanese experience, understand, and represent both their immediate social universe(s) and the world at large. In this respect, Javanese clearly have much in common with people in Negeri Sembilan and Aceh, and, to a lesser extent, Minangkabau.

Bedouin

The Mzeini Bedouin, who inhabit the South Sinai Peninsula (Egypt), provide an especially appropriate ethnographic example with which to conclude this comparative discussion. The Bedouin in this region are heirs to a rich tribal legacy which includes not only segmentary lineage organization built up on a highly elaborated ideology of patrilineal descent, but also a tradition of fiercely independent, nomadic pastoralism. For the past half century or so, however, they have been subject to extreme social and cultural dislocations stemming from the occupation of the region by a succession of foreign armies (British, Egyptian, Israeli, Soviet), the most recent of which—Israelis and Egyptians—also sought to "develop" the region through policies promoting agriculture, sedentarization, and large-scale tourism. For the most part, these policies have precluded the enactment of "traditional" Bedouin cultural identity, and as a result, such identity is nowadays realized primarily in the context of allegorical performances. These performances typically occur when a discussion turns into an argument and one or another creative individual steps up to recount an ostensibly personal story that serves to allegorize his or her experiences for the group as a whole and thus resolve, if only temporarily, both the specific argument which prompted the allegorical performance as well as the paradoxes and contradictions of Bedouin identity at large (Lavie 1990).

Analysis of allegories and other relevant data reveal that in many respects "Mzeini ideas about gender . . . [do] not differ much from the general Muslim ideology of gender—a hierarchical order where women are to be controlled because of their emotional, passionate, and capricious souls, capable of bringing shame (*'eib*) on the whole family, whereas men, with their ability to think and act rationally, acquire religious honor (*sharaf, karāma*) for exerting authority over women" (Lavie 1990:119). Mzeini discourses on gender do in fact build on the concepts of "reason" and "passion" (which, in the Mzeini vernacular, are referred to as *'agl* and *nafs*, respectively), much like the other groups we have considered, though there are of course some characteristically Bedouin twists on these concepts and their social realization that are absent from (or heavily deemphasized in) the other societies discussed thus far. (For example, local understandings of these concepts are tinged with strongly patriarchal overtones and entail the veiling of women, the maintenance of strict *purdah* codes, the favoring of sons in inheritance and many other contexts, and conceptual links underscoring the ways in which masculinity is tied to honor and autonomy [and vice versa] and femininity to modesty and dependency [and vice versa].) Similarly, among the Mzeini we find that official discourses on "reason" and "passion," and on masculinity and femininity, coexist with an analytically distinct, though culturally interlocked, everyday/practical discourse which is highly subversive with respect to—though not, strictly speaking, a wholesale inversion of—the official line(s) on gender.

This discourse focuses on the themes of *ghayii,* or "sexual lust" on the one hand, and *sabr,* or "patience" (endurance, tolerance, and equanimity) on the other. In this latter (quotidian) discourse, men are said to be governed by "sexual lust" (rather than "reason"), women by "patience" (rather than "passion"). This discourse is highly elaborated and is in fact, as already noted, the prevailing discourse in everyday life. Its broad scope and force can be explained in part by the constraints of military occupation and the severe political and economic dislocations associated with it, which make it quite difficult for most men to realize their "rationality" through the economic support of their families. The entailments of wage labor and out-migration are also such that most men are not in a position to exercise daily or other control over their wives or other female kin. One of the few areas in which they can realistically attempt such control is the sexual arena, but for various reasons the sexual advances they make toward their wives are typically rebuffed, and their authority and honor are thus seriously challenged. Repeated episodes involving the contestation of men's control over their wives' sexuality often lead to marital disputes and wife beating, just as they fuel the Mzeini's high rates of divorce. ("On the average, young Mzeinis remarry one to three times" [Lavie 1990:122].) Factors such as these clearly animate and sustain practical, subversive views of masculinity that focus on men's insatiable "sexual lust." So, too, does the fact that many men resort to bestiality (with donkeys) to satisfy their sexual urges (Lavie 1990:123–24), whereas women do not.

Quotidian representations of women are motivated and reinforced by the same sets of circumstances. According to these representations, women are both more "patient" than men and less strongly sexed, and to a certain degree more "reasonable" as well. The theme of women's "patience" (endurance, tolerance, and the like) is encouraged by women's perceived successes in dealing with all that they have to put up with, both from their husbands and in life generally. This includes making do economically in the absence of significant contributions from their husbands, and negotiating various contexts in which, due to the intrusions of occupying forces and gawking tourists, among others, their privacy is invaded and the maintenance of *purdah* codes is rendered extremely difficult.

The prevalence of the idea that women are less strongly sexed than men is due in part to the fact that, as previously noted, they often resist their husbands' sexual advances and in any case are far less likely to initiate sex. The practice of clitoridectomy may be relevant here insofar as it deadens key pleasure zones and tends to make sexual relations very pain-ful.[18] But the more salient issue would seem to be that women are deeply resentful of the authority of their husbands, in particular, their husbands' authority over their own sexualities, and thus resist their sexual and other amorous advances.

Some Mzeini women claim that the cultivation of "patience" can effect qualitative changes in a woman's "passion," such that she evinces a "mas-culine" "rationality," but this seems not to be a majority view either among women or men (Lavie 1990:141). Similarly, while some women assert that men's "sexual lust" is clear evidence of their "passion," others draw no such conclusions and contend that men's greater sexual lust does not call into question the official view that men are more reasonable than women. Circumstances such as these are quite similar to those we encoun-tered in Negeri Sembilan, as are many of their implications. They are also similar, albeit in different ways, to what has been reported for Aceh, Minangkabau, and Java. Equally striking are the ways in which Mzeini data support some of our other very general and by now familiar points: that women and men alike are profoundly ambivalent about gender and sexuality, which is to say, among other things, that femininity and mas-culinity are key sites in the production of contradiction and ambivalence; that masculinities and femininities alike are both highly contingent and fluid, and intensely hybrid; and that even the most intimate discourses on gender, sexuality, and social relations are shaped by their social location(s) within arenas constituted by the intersection of local, national, and trans-national regimes of knowledge and power.

Before concluding this comparative section I should perhaps emphasize that my discussion of practical, largely counter-hegemonic discourses in Islamic societies is not meant to give the impression that alternative dis-courses are found only among Muslims. I focused my comparative discus-sion on Islamic societies partly because this allows for a more controlled comparison, and partly because I feel (along with Abu-Lughod [1986:283–84 n.6], among others) that a systematic comparison of local beliefs about "reason" and "passion" across the Islamic world would make an ex-tremely interesting study. I hope that the material presented here and in preceding chapters will provide some points of reference for such a sys-tematic study and will serve as well as a caution against essentialist as-sumptions that masculinities (and femininities) in Islamic societies are always shaped by rigid, strongly patriarchal discourses. My general posi-tion in any case is that alternative discourses occur to one or another degree in *all* societies, though the precise extent (scope, force, etc.) of their elaboration either publicly or in what Scott (1990) refers to as "hidden transcripts" does of course vary not only from one society to the next, but also within specific societies, in terms of class, race, gender, and the like.

I should perhaps underscore as well that there are subversive discourses in contemporary Western societies that are in some respects highly reminiscent of those we have discussed here. Consider, for example, the American discourses on masculinity which are found in connection with both sides of the reproductive rights debate(s), and which suggest that men, far from being the more rational and responsible of the two sexes, are actually the more lustful, base, and dangerous (Ginsburg 1989:10–11). Key features of these discourses not only undergird various arguments to the effect that women must be protected from men; they are also central to the official rationale for both the origins and continued existence into the present of a wide variety of patriarchal laws and institutions. More importantly for present purposes, they resonate deeply with the Southeast Asian and other Islamic discourses with which we have been concerned (though there are of course crucial differences, an adequate treatment of which would require an altogether separate volume).

IDEOLOGY, EXPERIENCE, AND AMBIVALENCE

The societies considered in the previous sections are of particular interest partly because their dominant discourses on gender are phrased in terms of more or less pan-Islamic concepts of "reason" and "passion," and can thus be described and interpreted in broad comparative perspective. Such a perspective reveals striking commonalities in these societies with respect to constructions of gender(ed) difference and sameness. It also highlights the impressive "staying power" of Islamic ideologies of gender, and of ideologies generally; they are remarkably stable and persistent, especially in terms of content, despite the vast historical and geographic variation that they encounter and must "overcome" in the course of their spread and development (cf. Bloch 1989:131).

Equally striking testimony to the stability and persistence of the official ideologies at issue here is that the main alternative discourses on gender found "alongside" them are not only quite similar to one another but also have much in common with the dominant ideologies in question—with the notable exception that, in many important respects, they entail wholesale inversions of them. Circumstances such as these also attest to the pervasiveness of ideologies inasmuch as they make quite clear the rather remarkable degree to which dissension and subversion are contained within the very frameworks against which they are deployed; put differently, they show how such frameworks severely limit the possibilities of "answering (or arguing) back."

The larger question is this: Do all ideologies necessarily breed their own inversions? Many theorists of ideology (Williams 1977; Willis 1977; Scott 1985; Bloch 1989) contend that they do. Their contentions are frequently based on the position that ideologies are always "about" systems of moral authority, that they necessarily involve processes entailing the legitimization and masking of such systems, and that such processes invariably ground themselves conceptually in the transcendental realm of "nature" so as to naturalize and, in the process, eternalize and dehistoricize authority as well as the differential distribution of power and prestige (see, e.g., Bloch 1982:223–30, 1989:45; but see also Eagleton 1991:58–61, 222). The "value" or "benefit" of such grounding is of course that to one or another degree it can render such phenomena beyond question and challenge. More to the point, such grounding necessarily produces contradictions insofar as nature itself is, and is perceived to be, full of discontinuities and contradictions, or at least paradoxes and enigmas (birth, death, conception, vitality, movement, mutability, permanence), and is invariably experienced, understood, and represented in contradictory terms.[19]

This is not the place to elaborate on the strengths and weaknesses of these types of arguments. Suffice it to say that they help point us in the right direction(s) so long as they are joined with perspectives recognizing that contradictory imperatives are built into the structure and organization of *all* (even "cold") societies, and that the coexistence of such imperatives necessarily gives rise to contradictions that are culturally realized to one or another degree at both the common sense and ideological levels (see Kelly 1977; Giddens 1979; Peletz 1988b; Weigert 1991:5). More generally, recent theoretical developments bearing on contradiction, paradox, double bind, counter-hegemonies, and the like, are, in my view, vital to anthropology and to the study of culture and social life on the whole (see, e.g., Scott 1985, 1990; Ortner 1989, 1989–90; Trawick 1990; Weiner 1992). This is especially so when such contributions advance our understanding not only of the production, reproduction, and transformation of contrasting representations of the social world, but also of the factors that constrain or, alternatively, promote both the development and elaboration of alternative representations and discourses as well as various strategies of resistance (broadly defined).

Bloch (1982, 1986, 1989) is among those who has dealt most directly and extensively with contradictions in systems of kinship and gender, and in political and ideological formations on the whole. His approach builds on a variant of Marxism informed by Lévi-Straussian structuralism and clearly has much to commend it. Somewhat surprisingly, however, most of his discussion of contradiction deals with *conceptual* contradictions, often subsumed under the gloss "ambiguity," which is of course a largely *cognitive* phenomenon. The related but analytically distinct phenomenon of *ambivalence*, which (following Weigert 1991) we have defined as "the experience of commingled contradictory *emotions*," slips through the cracks of Bloch's descriptions and analyses.[20] This may be due in part to Bloch's long-standing interests in indigenous systems of classification and cognition, which prompted him to develop an analytic framework capable of dealing with distinctions between "ordinary cognition" (and knowledge, discourse, and communication) on the one hand, and "ideologized cognition" (and knowledge, discourse, and communication), which is glossed "ideology" on the other. Interests in different types of "cognition" and "thought," in other words, appear to have led Bloch to the study of ideology, and may well be at least partly responsible for his heavily cognitive approach to ideological phenomena.

Whatever the factors figuring into Bloch's relative neglect of ambivalence and other emotional components of ideologies, his oversights are unfortunate for a variety of reasons, two of which merit brief note. First, we know that ideologies must be psychologically compelling if they are to be at all effective, just as we know that the psychologically compelling nature of ideologies has both cognitive *and* emotional dimensions (Althusser 1969), neither one of which dimensions can be privileged analytically. And second, it is increasingly clear that subversive discourses are typically fueled by the disjunctive relationship between hegemonic ideological formations on the one hand, and sentiments and dispositions engendered in everyday, practical experiences, or "lived relations to the world," on the other (Bourdieu 1977; Abu-Lughod 1986). Failure to attend to such sentiments and dispositions—and, more generally, to the "structures of feeling" (Williams 1977) that often entail "the stirring of 'emergent' forms of consciousness" (Eagleton 1991:49)—thus hinders our understanding of some of the key sources of subversive discourses, and likewise leaves us with an overly "muscular" sense of culture's formative (constituting and constitutive) capacities.

This overly muscular sense of culture is by no means confined to the works of Bloch. It is in fact quite—indeed, much more—pronounced both in the writings of Clifford Geertz and others who have been influenced by heavily Parsonian readings of Weber,[21] and in the works of Durk-heimians such as Mary Douglas (1970), who emphasizes the ways in which all cultures simultaneously "strive for consonance" and inscribe such strivings in collective representations and individual psyches alike. Interestingly, it also permeates much of the Marxist-oriented work of Bourdieu, despite the analytic sensitivity he displays in many contexts to the highly distributional nature of culture, particularly in class societies (Bourdieu 1984; cf. Bloch 1989:119). More generally, such views of culture are out of keeping with what we all know, especially from our field-work, of culture's limitations as regards shaping and giving meaning to human experience (see R. Rosaldo 1980; Abu-Lughod 1986; Kleinman 1988; Trawick 1990; Wikan 1990).

If ideologies are invariably fraught with contradiction, and if ideological contradictions typically entail ambivalence, we obviously need to look more closely at the various social sources of ambivalence. This topic is an exceedingly broad one and we have perforce to limit ourselves to a few key points bearing on ideologies of gender and kinship, which provide contrasting but dialectically related languages and ways of talking about the same general "things" (persons, social relations, difference). One point that cannot be overemphasized here is that kinship as a moral system necessarily cuts both ways (see Peletz 1988b, 1995). Kinship's double-edged nature stems partly from the fact that it brings with it heavy moral entailments in the form of expectations and obligations which are in many cases extremely burdensome if not impossible to fulfill. Also relevant is that in most instances the honoring of such expectations and obligations brings little if any guarantee of the diffuse (or other) reciprocity which is so frequently inscribed in kinship as a whole, and which is in any case typically enjoined upon those who benefit most directly from the honoring of the expectations and obligations in question.

Some such points concerning the deeply Janus-faced condition of kinship were noted long ago by Evans-Pritchard (1940) in his disparate and scattered remarks about Nuer ambivalence toward fellow clansmen, although they were not worked into his heavily idealized analysis of Nuer social relations. Consider first the observations presented in the following passage:

> If you wish to live among the Nuer you must do so on their terms, which means you must treat them as a kind of kinsmen and they will then treat you as a kind of kinsman. Rights, privileges, and obligations are determined by kinship. Either a man is a kinsman, actually or by fiction, or he

is a person to whom you have no reciprocal obligations and whom you treat as a potential enemy. Every one in a man's village and district counts in one way or another as a kinsman, if only by linguistic assimilation, so that, except for an occasional homeless and despised wanderer, a Nuer only associates with people whose behavior to him is on a kinship pattern. (183)

So far, so good: Kinship provides an orienting framework for the content and ideology of Nuer social relations, and does in fact supply the hegemonic idiom(s) in terms of which such all encompassing relations are cast. But Evans-Pritchard (183) proceeds to tell us that "Nuer *must* assist one another, and [that] if one has a surplus of a good thing, he *must* share it with his neighbors. Consequently, no Nuer ever has a surplus" (emphasis added). He goes on to underscore that

> Nuer are most tenacious of their rights and possessions. They take easily but give with difficulty. This selfishness arises from their education and from the nature of kinship obligations. A child soon learns that to maintain his equality with his peers he must stand up for himself against any encroachment on his person and property. This means that he must always be prepared to fight, and his willingness and ability to do so are the only protection of his integrity as a free and independent person against the avarice and bullying of his kinsmen. They protect him against outsiders, but he must resist their demands on himself. *The demands made on a man in the name of kinship are incessant and imperious and he resists them to the utmost.* (184; emphasis added)

Many of the same themes can be discerned in a more recent classic, namely, Stack's (1974) study of African American kinship networks in an area around Chicago that she refers to as "the Flats." This despite the fact that Stack's analysis not only plays up the safety-net and Rousseauian features of the system, but also makes too little (analytically) of the fact that, if they are financially able to do so, residents of the Flats commonly endeavor to move out of and far from the Flats, and thus effectively sever ties with their kin who have remained behind.[22]

The larger issue is that we need to deploy a more critical gaze when we try to understand the symbols and meanings implicated in "prescriptive amity," "diffuse, enduring solidarity," and the like, especially those encoded in normative cultural statements such as "Home is the place they have to let you in." It is true that the various sentiments and moral obligations encoded in such expressions may well be very reassuring and heartening to those knocking on the door of a close or long-lost relative, assuming, of course, there is no (or relatively little) "hostile dependence."

But we need to more deeply appreciate that the sentiments and obligations are not necessarily all that comforting, and may indeed be rather disconcerting, to those who feel that they must, or should, answer the door. In much the same vein, we also need to more deeply appreciate the wisdom of Freud's insights that *all* emotional attachments are conducive to the realization of ambivalence, and that intense attachments are in fact thoroughly suffused with mixed emotions.[23]

There is one other major site in the production of ambivalence that merits special emphasis in this context, though there are of course many others—the antinomies of religious experience, the tragedies of humankind's self-consciousness, the sundered selves and myriad double binds and paradoxes of modernity (see Trawick 1990; Weigert 1991). It has to do with the construction of difference and the extremely pervasive tendency to convert difference into hierarchy. As Stallybrass and White (1986:4–5) point out in their fascinating study of the politics and poetics of transgression, in all systems of hierarchy the dependence of the "top" on the "bottom," the "high" on the "low," produces a "mobile, conflictual fusion of power, fear, and desire in the construction of subjectivity," and thus necessarily entails profound ambivalence. Recall here that symbols and idioms of gender and kinship are invariably "about" differentiation and exclusion (as well as commonality and inclusion), and are, more broadly, key components of systems of virtue and morality that encode hierarchically phrased and heavily value-laden difference. Recall, also, that in the case of Malays and others considered here, men are clearly troubled in various ways by the fact that, at least on some levels, they define themselves in (complementary) opposition to females, yet simultaneously see and fear in themselves the very features whose presence or predominance indexes femininity (as well as the moral status of children and decidedly "inferior" [read non-Muslim] racial groups) and whose absence or deemphasis supposedly indexes masculinity. (Malay [and other] women, for their part, are stigmatized and in some instances troubled by the very same ideological framework which they often turn on men to assert their own moral superiority.)

> A recurrent pattern emerges: The 'top' attempts to reject and eliminate the bottom for reasons of prestige and status, only to discover, not only that it is in some ways frequently dependent upon that low-Other (in the classic way that Hegel describes in the master-slave section of the *Phenomenology*), but also that the top *includes* that low symbolically as a primary eroticized constituent of its own fantasy life. The result is a mobile, conflictual fusion of power, fear, and desire in the construction of subjectivity: a psy-

chological dependence upon precisely those Others which are being rigorously opposed at the social level. It is for this reason that what is *socially* peripheral is so frequently *symbolically* central. . . . The low-Other is despised and denied at the level of political organization and social being whilst it is instrumentally constitutive of the shared imaginary repertoires of the dominant culture. (Stallybrass and White 1986:5–6; emphasis in original)

The broader themes are what Stallybrass and White refer to as "the production of identity through negation," and the ways dominant social actors and categories thereof take into themselves as "negative introjections the very categories and domains which surround and threaten them," thus "produc[ing] and reproduc[ing] . . . [their identities] through processes of denial and defiance" (89; see also Gilman 1985). A key dynamic in this process is that what is denied is simultaneously desired. Bear in mind also that by taking "the grotesque" (female) within itself so as to reject it, the latter becomes an "unpalpable and interiorized phobic set of representations associated with avoidance and others" (106, 108). For reasons such as these, "the closure and purity of . . . dominant [entities and essences such as masculinity are] quite illusory"; and members of dominant groups "perpetually rediscover [themselves]— . . . the protean, and the motley, the 'neither/nor,' the double negation of high and the low which was the very precondition for . . . [their] social identit[ies]" (113)— with some sense of shock and inner revulsion.

The recalcitrant Other (female) thus troubles the fantasy of an independent, separate, "proper" (male) identity (148). As Sander Gilman (1985:240) explains, this occurs despite but also partly because of the existence of "crude representations of difference that serve to localize . . . [men's] anxiety, to prove to . . . [them] that what . . . [they] fear does not lie within." Such troubling is effected partly by "calling the bluff of foreclosure, and partly by denying with a laugh the ludicrous pose of autonomy adopted by the [proper male] subject" (Stallybrass and White 1986:183). Clearly relevant, too, of course, are the various disturbing ways in which female Others of one's own race and/or class index stigmatized and undesirable racial and/or class Others, male and female alike.

One of the main points I would add here is that such bluffs, denials, and laughs merit far more attention from anthropologists and others who hope to capture something of how gender and social relations of other varieties are experienced, understood, and represented in specific societies and their myriad contexts. The other more general point is that we need to develop a more robust theory of ambivalence that pays due attention both to the cultural psychology of ambivalence and to the diverse political economies and intrasocietal contexts that give form and meaning to these patterns of mixed emotion. This requires focusing our analytic gazes not simply on official ideologies and/or public contexts, but also on alternative discourses which bear on the seamier side(s) of human nature and social relations, and which are in many cases articulated primarily in relatively private contexts or with reference to personal experience. Such focus may yield certain data and perspectives whose airing strikes some observers as impolitic with respect to the sensitivities of those among whom we work, but it seems to me that we do a far greater disservice to them by producing heavily idealized, one-dimensional, and otherwise ethnographically thin ("anemic") accounts of their social worlds and their lived relations to them. To put this in more positive terms, I would argue that our most important and enduring contributions to the various communities with which we are involved are comprehensive and contextually sensitive accounts of the diverse modalities and representations of human sociality in all their fascinating richness and complexity, warts and all.

Notes

INTRODUCTION

1. The literature to which I refer here includes, among other works, Rubin (1975), Weiner (1976, 1992), Ortner and Whitehead (1981b), Stallybrass and White (1986), Collier and Yanagisako (1987b), Strathern (1987, 1992), Gewertz (1988), Weigert (1991), and Kelly (1993).

2. My usage of the term "hegemony" follows that of Raymond Williams (1977), who has developed and refined some of Gramsci's more enduring insights. In a frequently quoted passage, Williams explains that " 'hegemony' goes beyond 'culture' as previously defined, in its insistence on relating the 'whole social process' to specific distributions of power and influence. . . . It is in [the] recognition of the wholeness of the process that the concept of 'hegemony' [also] goes beyond 'ideology.' What is decisive is not only the conscious system of ideas and beliefs, but the whole lived social process as practically organized by specific and dominant meanings and values" (Williams 1977:108–9). Williams goes on to remind us that "a lived hegemony . . . does not just passively exist as a form of dominance" (112–14). Rather, any given hegemony has "continually to be renewed, recreated, defended, and modified," and is also "continually resisted, limited, altered, and challenged by pressures not all its own." For these and other reasons, Williams develops the concept of an "alternative hegemony," which refers both to norms, values, and beliefs that are simply different from (and in some instances altogether irrelevant to) the hegemony, and to those that are explicitly subversive of it and thus appropriately characterized as "counter-hegemonic." The more general point is that while hegemonies are by definition always dominant, they are never "either total or exclusive"; at any given time, they find themselves up against alternative or directly oppositional political and cultural forms, the scope, force, and overall significance of which are of course highly variable. (See Femia 1975, P. Anderson 1976–77, and Scott 1985 for further discussion of the concept and some of the problems associated with its use by Gramsci and others.)

3. Although the topic of masculinity has clearly received short shrift in the literature on gender, the last decade or so has witnessed some fine studies on the topic. These include works dealing with diverse aspects of masculinity among Spaniards in Andalusia (Brandes 1980, 1981), Greeks in Crete (Herzfeld 1985), and societies in the Amazon and New Guinea (see Gregor 1985 and Herdt 1982, respectively). See also Siegel's pioneering (1969) analysis of constructions of mas-

culinity among the Acehnese of northern Sumatra (discussed in the text, esp. chap. 7).

4. I examine some of the dilemmas associated with the use of these terms later on (esp. in chap. 7), but I should perhaps mention here that Ortner and Whitehead's usage of terms such as "positional" (and "relational") builds on the work of Chodorow (1978), which is informed by the writing of Slater (1961) and Winch (1962). According to Slater (1961:113), who is primarily concerned with distinguishing positional from personal identification, "positional identification [is so designated] because it involves the identification of ego with the *situation* or *role* of the alter; personal identification [on the other hand] involves the identification of ego with the actual person of alter—the adoption of his personality traits, values, and attitudes, even his view of ego" (emphasis added). Note, however, that situations and roles are invariably defined in relation to others around them, and that positional identifications (including those bearing on gender) are thus in key respects thoroughly relational from the start. For these and other reasons, the distinctions between positional and relational identifications (and structural definitions bearing on gender) are far less pronounced than contemporary scholarly usage of the terms might lead one to believe.

5. The term "deconstruction" is used here to refer to analytic processes entailing the opposite or reverse of those involved in construction. The main objective of this "undoing" is to show how relevant concepts and categories (e.g., masculinity) have been socially constructed and historically conditioned.

1. ETHNOGRAPHIC CONTEXT AND FIELDWORK

1. The state of Negeri Sembilan covers an area of 2,566 square miles and has a (1990) population of about 724,000 people (Government of Malaysia 1991).

2. These percentages are broadly comparable to, but should not be confused with, those pertaining to the population of Malaysia as a whole, which amounted to about 17,804,500 in 1990. Malays make up roughly 50 percent of the total population of Malaysia; Chinese account for about 30 percent, and Indians and "Others" make up the other 20 percent (Government of Malaysia 1991).

3. All of the Malay terms presented in this work are spelled in accordance with the conventions of Standard Malay, as set out in Awang Sudjai Hairul and Yusoff Khan's (1977) *Kamus Lengkap*.

4. For important discussions of the concept of *adat*, see Abdul Rahman bin Haji Mohammad (1964), Hooker (1970, 1972), Nordin Selat (1976), Norazit Selat (1990), and Norhalim Haji Ibrahim (1993). Many other relevant references are cited in the bibliography of Peletz (1988b).

5. Some of the material on the 1978–80 fieldwork that is presented in the following pages appears in abbreviated form in the preface to Peletz (1988b).

6. I noted earlier that throughout the present work I employ pseudonyms rather than actual names. I should perhaps add here that I have not tried to be consistent in developing the pseudonyms. In some cases, I simply use birth-order names of the sort that villagers frequently utilize in reference and address. In other cases, I follow other local conventions—for example, kin terms plus first name, as in Pakcik Rosli, which is best translated as "Uncle Rosli." In still other

instances, I use first names, a practice sometimes employed by villagers when dealing with those who are younger than they.

7. Hereafter I refer to my adoptive mother by the more convenient term "mother." I also refer to my adoptive father and adoptive parents as "father" and "parents."

8. We can be somewhat more specific, however. As a well-known Malay anthropologist recently put it, *dakwa* supporters "are mainly middle-level urban workers, student groups or professionals without social status or power, who are marginally involved with modern development processes and generally incapable of acquiring an important platform in decision-making concerned with the government machinery or economy" (Karim 1992:175).

9. One consequence of the resurgence is that the ruling party (more precisely, its dominant clique) has had to work overtime to validate its Islamic credentials—(re)legitimize the state—by going forward with its own far-reaching, though ultimately rather moderate, Islamization program. This program has included the building and refurbishing of prayer houses and mosques, the creation of an Islamic university and an Islamic system of banking and finance, the sponsoring of a plethora of Islamic seminars and conferences, and, last but not least, the passage of myriad legislative measures bearing on members of the Islamic community and on Islam generally. I discuss the details of some such measures elsewhere (Peletz 1993b, n.d.a) and will thus emphasize only two points here. First, while these moves have succeeded in retaining the support of urban middle-class Malays who constitute that segment of the population most responsive to *dakwa* appeals, they have also seriously alienated non-Malays, who, as noted above, make up a full 50 percent of Malaysia's multiethnic population. And second, many such measures have also clearly alienated significant numbers of ordinary, especially rural, Malays. The main reason for this is that they are perceived, and in many cases are intended, as direct attacks on the basic values of ordinary, especially rural, Malays, including, in particular, their prestige considerations and key features of their cultural identities.

10. In some cases, the staking of such claims began long before we made public our specific plans about leaving the village—e.g., the day we bought something!

2. GENDER, PRESTIGE, AND POLITICAL ECONOMY IN THE NINETEENTH CENTURY

1. As will be apparent in due course, the approach that I have developed entails various departures from Ortner and Whitehead's position. My approach to ideology, for example, differs from that of Ortner and Whitehead in that I devote considerable analytic attention to the existence of the contrasting discourses that invariably make up any given ideological formation. I also draw on Kelly's recent (1993) tour de force on inequality among the Etoro, which makes a number of critically important points: that stigma is the negative reciprocal of prestige; that analytic discussions of "prestige systems" would benefit from greater terminological and conceptual precision (see also Yanagisako and Collier 1987:26–28); and that such systems are more accurately characterized as systems or hierarchies of

prestige/stigma. Kelly also distinguishes between systems of the latter sort and systems of moral evaluation:

> The system of moral evaluation can be defined as the component of the value system that delineates virtues and their opposites (such as generosity and self-aggrandizement). The prestige system [for its part] pertains to the achievable virtues or aspects of virtue that differentiate individuals (as opposed to the virtues or aspects of virtue that are ascribed to a categorical social status). The system of moral evaluation thus provides the basis for two different but interrelated foundations of social inequality: a moral hierarchy, and a prestige system or prestige/stigma system. (Kelly 1993:14)

I should point out, in any event, that, like Kelly, I sometimes use the term "system(s) of prestige" as a shorthand for "system(s) of prestige/stigma."

2. I hope the reader will forgive me if this assertion is reminiscent of some of the more free-floating generalizations made by Ruth Benedict (1934, 1946) in her work on what came to be known as "national character." I might simply note here that the assertion in question is well substantiated, at least for the Malay case, by the situational, social-field approach to identities and values adopted throughout the remainder of the book.

3. *Suku* is a polysemic term denoting both the social units herein called "dispersed clans" and the most inclusive (aggregated) components of such units, which I refer to as "localized clans." It also means "one-fourth." The semantic range of the term has been taken as evidence of the quadripartite character of early Minangkabau communities in Sumatra (see de Josselin de Jong 1951:66–71 passim).

The term *perut* also denotes "womb," "abdomen," and "stomach." Members of a single lineage are occasionally spoken of as having originated from the same (ancestral) womb. This sometimes occurs as well in the case of more distantly related persons associated with the same clan, whether localized or dispersed.

Other meanings of the term *pangkal* include "branch," "trunk," "root," "origin," and "starting point."

4. The Sanskrit-origin term *sakti* is translated by nineteenth-century observers such as Skeat ([1900] 1967) as "supernatural power." As such, it has much in common with the Arabic-origin term *ilmu*, which has largely replaced it in common usage. The term *kekayaan* refers to "riches," "wealth," etc., though it can also mean "magic," at least in some parts of the Malay world (broadly defined) (Milner 1982:130, n.95). *Kuasa*, for its part, is translated in contemporary Malay dictionaries as "power," "strength," "ability," "authority."

5. This phrase is Strathern's (1981).

6. For additional information concerning *Yang diPertuan Besar*, see Peletz (1988b:29, 96, 101, 346 n.16) and the sources cited there.

7. "Ancestral" property is defined as property which has been inherited at least once, and which, as such, is subject to various restrictions on its use and transfer. It is usually distinguished from "acquired" property, which has yet to be inherited and which, as such, is not subject to the same types of restrictions. For a detailed discussion of these and related matters bearing on property, see Peletz (1988b).

8. It is not always the case, of course, that female sexuality and reproductive capacities effectively "pull women down." We have already seen that during the early part of the period 1450–1680 Southeast Asian women's reproductive and regenerative capacities "gave them magical and ritual powers which it was difficult for men to match," and thus to some degree "pulled women up" and into complementary relations with males. The positive valorization of female sexuality remains a common theme in numerous societies in eastern Indonesia (see Atkinson and Errington 1990).

9. Cross-cousins include the children of one's mother's brother and father's sister and all others linked by a cross-sex sibling tie in one or another ascending generation. They are usually distinguished from parallel-cousins, who include the children of one's mother's sisters and father's brothers and all others linked through a parallel- or same-sex sibling tie in one or another ascending generation (see Keesing 1975:105–11).

10. Bourdieu's distinction between official and practical kinship is in some ways reminiscent of Firth's ([1951] 1963, 1964) distinction between social structure and social organization, though the similarities are actually rather superficial, especially when one stops to consider the very different theoretical rationales for developing the distinctions and the dissimilar uses to which they are put. Since this is not the place to discuss such matters, I would simply note that incisive critiques of Firth's distinction and theoretical orientation are presented by Kelly (1977:280–82) and Bloch (1989:4–5).

11. In the Negeri Sembilan context, for example, one could conceivably speak instead of "official Islamic discourses" on the one hand, and "everyday discourses" on the other. There is some heuristic value in such a distinction, but to my mind it fosters the erroneous impression that "everyday discourses" are somehow "non-Islamic," when in fact the key signs of such discourses ("reason" and "passion") are "thoroughly Islamic" even though they are frequently mapped onto gender difference(s) in a way that constitutes an inversion of the gender realities depicted in "official Islamic discourses." For these and other reasons I employ the modified version of Bourdieu's distinction discussed in the text.

12. The reconstruction of nineteenth-century marriage and affinal exchange presented in the following paragraphs is based largely on material provided by Newbold (1839 I:254–55, II:123, 249, 281–83, 289, 294–95), Lister (1890:318), Skeat ([1900] 1967:375–77, 383, 389), Parr and Mackray (1910:77–96), Caldecott (1918:40–41), Taylor ([1929] 1970), and Lewis (1962:166–78). I have also drawn on contemporary observations and discussions with selected village elders, clan spokesmen, and other local experts. For an assessment of twentieth-century shifts in affinal exchange and the celebration of marriage, see Peletz (1988b) and below (chap. 3).

13. For additional information on the *wali*'s role in nineteenth- and early twentieth-century marriage ceremonies, see Newbold (1839 I:254) and Parr and Mackray (1910:85, 92–93).

14. Most of the discussion in the following pages is geared toward substantiating my alternative reading of the data, rather than assessing the factual basis of the material presented by de Josselin de Jong in support of his argument about

the exchange of women. The main reason for this is that de Josselin de Jong does not present any such material; that is, he assumes, but makes no effort to demonstrate, that the units allied through marriage and affinal exchange were linked by exchanges of women.

15. Much of this paragraph is taken from my review of Goody (1990). (See Peletz 1992.)

16. For an interesting mythic account of the serious consequences of a man's failure to provide his wife's kin with the requisite marriage payments, see Hervey (1884:253).

17. These and related themes continue to be the subject of considerable cultural elaboration (see Peletz 1988b).

18. This is not the place to assess the implications or relative merits of Pak's claims that "obligations" are more clearly "present in the social philosophy of the [Minangkabau] region" than are "rights." A few points are nonetheless in order, especially since Pak erroneously assumes that all generalizations pertaining to Minangkabau are relevant to Negeri Sembilan and vice versa. First, while an analytic focus on "obligations" has certain advantages in some ethnographic contexts, it also has various limitations—as, of course, does an analytic focus on the flip side of the coin, namely, "rights." Second, the seemingly highly elaborated Minangkabau idea that men are more valued than women because they are the transmitters of biogenetically and spiritually potent "blood" or "seed" is largely irrelevant in the Negeri Sembilan context. The third and more general point is that, despite their obvious similarities (some of which are discussed in chap. 7), Minangkabau and Negeri Sembilan are very distinct societies, each of which has its own unique history and patterns of institutional and cultural expression. Parallels and convergences require sustained analytic scrutiny and cannot be assumed a priori—all of which is to say that facile extrapolations from Minangkabau to Negeri Sembilan (and vice versa) are risky at best (see chap. 7; see also Peletz 1988b:344–45, n.3; Josselin de Jong 1951; Abdul Kahar bin Bador 1963:8–9; and Sweeney 1987:111–12).

19. Unfortunately, however, Douglas's comments do not include any references to the specific African societies characterized by the exchange of men. The societies mentioned in her article include (but are not limited to) the Lele, Plateau Tonga, Lowiili, Bemba, Ndembu, and Ashanti, as well as Akwakim and neighboring groups in southern Ghana, many of which have little in common with the Negeri Sembilan and Minangkabau cases, and appear to be more closely related (structurally) to the Ilongot and other "brideservice societies" described by Collier and Rosaldo (1981) and Collier (1988). It is not my intention here to engage in a critical reappraisal of Douglas's use of the concept of the exchange of men or to explore the very important differences between Negeri Sembilan and similarly constituted societies on the one hand, and brideservice societies on the other. I will simply reiterate my earlier point that Negeri Sembilan is *not* an example of a brideservice society.

20. Kelly's point here is both valid and important, but he may go too far in his criticism of those who argue that brute force can itself engender moral legitimacy. Moral hierarchies and legitimacy can surely be won in conjunction with or in the aftermath of successful projections of force. The existence of hierarchies

involving initial assertions of force of arms which are then followed by the effective mobilization of moral arguments must at least be acknowledged as a possibility.

3. KINSHIP, GENDER, AND SEXUALITY FROM THE NINETEENTH CENTURY TO THE PRESENT

1. See, for example, CRACNS 1874:232–36; CRACNS 1875:8–10, 18–20; CRACNS 1876:193–222; and Gullick 1958:16, 17.

2. For more information on the imposition and consolidation of British colonial rule in Negeri Sembilan, see Peletz (1988b: chaps. 3 and 4) and the sources cited there, and Stivens (1987, 1991).

3. Cited in "Report on the Kuala Pilah District for the Year 1904," p. 4 in Supplement to NSGG 1905 X; see also Peletz (1988b:135).

4. For additional information on the nature of paternal provisioning and its structural significance, see Peletz (1988b:6, 69–70, 84, 86–88, 90, 137, 278–81, 327–28).

5. In earlier times a child resulting from the union would have been claimed and raised by the *Undang* or the *Yang diPertuan Besar*.

6. Which of these alternative views one accepts depends in part on one's assessment of the relevance for the Malay case of the Durkheimian proposition that the ("mere") appearance of a violation of the norm is as reprehensible as an actual violation of the norm.

7. A married man found (or assumed) guilty of *khalwat* is typically forced to take the woman with whom he engaged in *khalwat* as his second wife.

8. Another case of rape which came to my attention through court documents but which did not involve residents of Bogang involved a (Malay) woman in the district of Rembau who was by all accounts "insane" (*gila*), and who had been forcibly impregnated by a married man (also Malay). Though initially classified as a rape, the case was later redefined by officials of the Islamic courts as one of "illicit fornication" (*zina*). The perpetrator was forced to marry his victim, though I don't think he actually lived with her. He later sought a divorce from her, but in the hearings I observed the magistrate was unwilling to grant him one, on the grounds that "he shouldn't get off that easily."

9. Among the relevant studies that come to mind here is Sanday (1990), which suggests that Minangkabau is a "rape-free" society.

10. The term *zina* is not widely used in local communities, but it is commonly used in legal documents and court records issued by the religious authorities. According to an official publication authored by Ramli bin Saad (1978), entitled *Jenayah Zina* [*The Crimes of Fornication*], *zina* includes sex outside of marriage; anal sex among men or among men and women, whether married or not; sex with a dead person; sex with an animal; sex with a child or someone who is insane; sex with a menstruating women, one's wife or not; sex with muhrim (someone you can't marry); and sex among women.

11. Other terms for such phenomena do exist, but they are not widely used. Some such terms are presented in the text, below.

12. His aunt may have accused him of being a *mak nyah* or transsexual, or a eunuch or hermaphrodite.

13. Much of the time we were talking, Zainal was tugging at his crotch, like he was trying to rearrange his penis. I found this rather distracting and offputting.

14. See Keeler (1990) for a similar point concerning local attitudes toward gender crossing in Java.

15. These passages are quoted from *The Star*, August 7 and October 25, 1987, and *The New Straits Times*, October 26, 1987.

16. I should perhaps emphasize that the "official" position articulated here entails various oversimplifications of Islamic textual perspectives on the issues associated with gender crossing. For a fascinating discussion of some of the philosophical, theological, and legal issues involved, see Sanders (1991).

17. At present, persons seeking such operations must go to Singapore or London.

18. The term *bidan terjun* calls to mind the unexpected, and hence hurried, calling of a midwife (*bidan*), as happens when a pregnant woman experiences labor contractions sooner than anticipated.

19. In the account that follows, there are a good many relationships involving informal adoptions (or child transfers). Informal adoption is quite common in Bogang and in Malay communities generally (see Peletz 1988b; McKinley 1975).

20. Muslims are of course forbidden to consume alcohol in any form, and the vast majority of Malays in Bogang and other parts of Malaysia do observe the prohibition. There are, however, a few men in Bogang who drink now and then. Abang is one of them.

21. Marital infidelity in Bogang and Malay communities elsewhere in the Peninsula is not nearly as common as these passages suggest.

22. What she didn't say, perhaps because she didn't know, is that she was indirectly implicated in (though not blamed for) what had happened since Rubiah and Nordin had had sex under her very nose! She was often charged with watching over Rubiah (they slept in the same room, sometimes on the verandah), particularly when Rubiah's parents went out in the evening to visit with friends.

23. Although parents are reluctant for emotional and other reasons to see any of their offspring take up long-term residence outside the local community, they also feel that those who remain in the village and make their lives there do so largely because of their intellectual and educational limitations. For reasons such as these parents are deeply ambivalent about children who remain in the village past adolescence.

4. KNOWLEDGE, POWER, AND PERSONAL MISFORTUNE

1. The phrase is Dato Abdullah's, the modernist *Undang* of Rembau who ruled from 1922 to 1938 (see [Dato] Sedia Raja Abdullah 1925:104).

2. Siegel's (1969, 1978) observations concerning differences in Acehnese men's and women's styles of speaking also resonate with the findings of those who have worked in Java and elsewhere in Southeast Asia (see, e.g., Geertz [1961] 1989; Keeler 1987, 1990; Smith-Hefner 1988a, 1988b), though it should be emphasized

that Siegel's comments on Acehnese women's self-perceptions do not do justice to the complex social constraints that women in Aceh experience in speech. It is also true, as Horvatich (1992) points out, that Siegel's pioneering studies gloss over or otherwise take for granted various other issues that merit detailed analytic treatment. (See Tapper and Tapper 1987 for a discussion of such matters in the context of rural Turkey.)

3. Traditional midwifery has been largely superseded by Western oriented, government-regulated midwifery services provided by modern clinics and hospitals; at present, moreover, most children are born in hospitals (see chap. 5).

4. Ellen never met Mak Ijah, but I am certain that she too would have found her outrageous.

5. I should perhaps add that I have no precise count of the number of women in Bogang who are or ever have been possessed by spirits. My educated guess is that 15–20 percent of women over the age of eighteen have had experiences with spirit possession.

6. A good portion of the literature is reviewed in Winzeler (1984). See also Kenny (1990).

7. Bear in mind, however, that most accounts of mystical attack among Malays do not provide an explicitly gendered breakdown of the cases of mystically induced illness and other forms of personal misfortune that serve as the basis of discussion and analysis. Even so, Laderman's recent (1991) account of Malay shamanism, which is the most exhaustive and sophisticated treatment of the subject to date, gives the impression that men are at least as likely as women to be the targets of mystical attack. One gets the same impression from material presented by Provencher (1979). In a more recent essay, which focuses on a healer known as "Mother Needles," Provencher (1984:143) reports that most of the people who came to her with cases of "bad luck" and "ill fortune" were men, but unfortunately he does not indicate whether the "bad luck" and "ill fortune" in question were held to be mystically induced. (Nor does he provide any other relevant information on gender.) The most comprehensive treatment of Malay poisoning ever to have been published, namely Gimlette's ([1915] 1971) classic treatise on Malay poisons and "charm cures" in Kelantan, suggests that in earlier times men were at least as likely as women to be poisoned.

8. Despite the impression one may get from reading her monograph-length treatment of the subject (Ong 1987), Ong is well aware that spirit possession is still common in rural settings in which capitalism has made relatively few inroads (see Ong 1988:30–32). Similarly, nowhere in her work does she specifically claim that earlier sites of possession have altogether disappeared in the contemporary era, though she does maintain that possession is "more common" among young peasant women who leave the village and work in factories than among married women who have stayed behind (Ong 1988:32). Part of the problem here, as noted in the text above, is the way Ong depicts the purportedly dramatic shift in the locus of possession. The depiction is misleading (as discussed later in the text), particularly for those who are unfamiliar with the Malaysian data.

9. As such, late-nineteenth-century Malay society parallels contemporary Aceh.

5. THE PERSON AND THE BODY

1. For additional information on these and other aspects of kinship terminology, see Peletz (1988b).

2. Many of the points here and in the following two paragraphs were suggested by Read's exemplary (1955) analysis of morality and personhood among the Gahuku-Gama of New Guinea.

3. Similarly, *sumbang* involving political elites and members of gentry clans were regarded as far more serious and reprehensible than *sumbang* involving untitled individuals and members of nongentry clans. For more information on *sumbang*, see Peletz (1988b); cf. Needham (1971).

4. Social criticism usually consists of comments to the effect that an individual is *sombong* (arrogant, haughty, unresponsive to social expectation); *tak ada malu* (without a sense of shame); *leteh* (too talkative); *malas* (lazy); *miang/gatal* (cheeky, itchy, horny); or *nakal/jahat* (naughty/bad). Malay disinclinations to speculate about other people's motivations contrast rather sharply with what one finds in various other parts of Southeast Asia, such as Java, where, according to Geertz (1960, 1973, 1983), speculating about what motivates other people is a culturally elaborated ("national") pastime.

5. The significance of these associations was brought home to me by Kessler (1977); cf. Douglas (1966, 1970).

6. In fact, women appear to pray less often than men.

7. See Read (1955:266) for a similar point with respect to the Gahuku-Gama.

8. Fear of the evil eye might also figure into the muting of a vocabulary of beauty; it is viewed as inappropriate to comment on someone's, especially a child's, beauty for fear of attracting evil spirits ("domesticated" and "wild" alike).

9. Strictly speaking, circumcision is not required of Muslims, though it is meritorious. In the local view of things, however, it is required of—and largely confined to—Muslims. I should note, too, that no Malay woman would knowingly marry an uncircumcised man.

10. Parents (or whoever else performs *kekah* on behalf of children) are expected to eat meat moderately during the feast, and are prohibited from selling the skins, bones, and other by-products of the animal thus sacrificed. The latter should be given away or buried. It is especially important, too, that the meat served up at *kekah* be eaten only by Muslims. Villagers were somewhat ambivalent about inviting us to, and having us attend, ritual feasts involving *kekah*, if only because they were embarrassed about having to explain to us that we couldn't eat the meat of the animal that had been sacrificed for the occasion. We were usually invited anyway and served other meat that had been specially prepared for us.

11. According to one midwife, some men also experience dizziness, nausea, vomiting, and the like, before their wives experience any morning sickness. Apparently such symptoms tend to last for fewer than fifteen days.

12. My data on sex are not as complete as I would like. This is due primarily to (a) the deemphasis of sex and sexuality in local society and culture, along with villagers' reluctance to discuss sexual concerns and other sexual matters both

among themselves and with outsiders; and (b) my own disinclination to broach and delve into topics that are sensitive both in Malay culture and my own.

13. Abortion is held to be sinful and dangerous as well, especially after four months of pregnancy, by which time the mother's and fetus's *nyawas* ("breaths," "spirits") have become intertwined. But preventing conception by eating foods that are either "hot" or "heaty" (*panas*) or allergenic (*gatal/bisa*)—or by resorting to other measures—is not necessarily viewed in a negative light.

14. While Pak Zainuddin's comments focus on the procedure for obtaining a male child, men and women alike express a preference for female children (as discussed later in the text).

15. Even so, villagers feel it is inappropriate to comment on the physical resemblance between father and child.

16. Foods classified as "cool" or "cooling" include juicy fruits and vegetables, sour fruits and vegetables, certain types of bananas, and tea (see Laderman 1983:46–47).

17. Other references from the animal world include the term "pregnant water buffalo" (*bunting kerbau*), which refers to a human pregnancy that extends beyond nine months.

18. I do not have any information bearing on women's attitudes toward hospital births as opposed to home delivery. Generally speaking, Malays have rather dim views of hospitals, even though they embrace many aspects of Western medicine. These negative attitudes reflect their intense dislike of the isolation and confinement of hospitals (and perhaps the discipline as well), and are related to their view that hospitals are places "you go to die." They may also feel loss of both autonomy and social control in the hospital setting, as Martin (1987) reports for various segments of the American population. On the other hand, infant mortality has decreased markedly in recent decades, partly as a result of hospital care, and villagers are well aware of the connection between hospital births and the decline of infant mortality. For this reason, they are far less ambivalent about hospital delivery than might be expected.

19. For discussions of the symbols and meanings of "passion" and "reason" among Malays outside of Negeri Sembilan, see Kessler (1978:220–32), Laderman (1982:91), Banks (1983:86–87), Massard (1985:72), and Ong (1987:87, 192–93; 1988:31; 1990a:388–90; 1990b:261). For relevant material on Muslims elsewhere in Southeast Asia, see Siegel's pioneering (1969) study of Aceh and Woodward's (1989:178–79, 190–98, 272–74 nn.34, 39) material on Java. Also quite relevant is Brenner's (1995) work on Java, which provides an insightful, much needed reassessment of Javanese notions of gender and self-control, and Krier's recent (1994) thesis on Minangkabau. Other pertinent discussions appear in Dwyer (1978) and Rosen (1984), both of which deal with Moroccan material. See also Abu-Lughod (1986) and Lavie (1990) for important perspectives on Bedouins, and Boddy (1989) for an incisive discussion of the Sudanese case.

20. Probably the best known Koranic passages bearing on "passion" are those that emphasize its negative aspects, especially its links to "lusts" or *shahawat* and the doing of evil. See, for example, the *sura* entitled *Joseph*, which includes the celebrated phrase, "In truth, the soul/*nafs* continually incites one to evil." Popular

medieval Koranic commentators such as 'Abd Allāh b. 'Umar al-Baydāwī who are still widely read in many parts of the Muslim world have emphasized (in connection with the story of Joseph) that "In truth, the nafs continually incites one to evil insofar as it is by nature inclined toward al-shahawat (the "passions"/"lusts") and is preoccupied with them, and insofar as it employs one's limbs and bodily forces in pursuing lusts at all times" (David Pinault, personal communication, 1994). Nafs as something to guard against also occurs frequently in the moralizing literature of the Sufis.

21. The "keyness" or centrality of these symbols does of course vary from one Muslim society to the next, as do some of their contextually variable meanings and many of their material referents. These symbols are quite central and highly elaborated among Malays, Acehnese, and Moroccans, less so among Javanese, Minangkabau, and the Turkish villagers studied by Delaney (1991). Among the Sama of the Philippines, these symbols are "present" but not of central significance, and are minimally elaborated (Horvatich 1992).

22. The non-Muslim reader might assume that such aversions to eating pork are uniform throughout the Muslim world. Not so: Some Javanese Muslims do on occasion eat pork; the Muslim Susu of Senegal claim that the prohibition pertains only to those who don't like pork (James Thayer, personal communication, 1983); and the Sudanese Muslim women studied by Boddy (1989:91–92 n.2) were not sure if pork was prohibited to them. The intensity of Malay aversions to the consumption of pork have much to do with ethnic antagonisms between Malays and Chinese, who, as far as Malays are concerned, eat pork—and lots of it—at every meal.

23. So, too, would the basic cultural premise underlying much of the material presented here, namely that sociality and "civilization" generally are only possible because of the constraining influences of society (or culture), which hold in check the individual's instinctive (fundamentally anti-social) impulses. Premises of this sort are enshrined in Freud's later work on religion—for example, The Future of an Illusion ([1927] 1964).

24. The extent of such agreement is actually somewhat in dispute. Some Javanists suggest that the elaborated conceptual apparatus presented here reflects a rather bookish, elite take on Javanese views of "passion" and personhood, and that Woodward's assertions concerning there being "nearly universal agreement" on such matters is valid only with respect to the rather confined universe composed of Javanese mystics and mystical tracts like the Serat Wirid and the Serat Cabolek. It is nonetheless true, as noted later in the text, that most Javanese see "passion" as a potentially constructive force that can be channeled into religious activities and, more specifically, the worship and experience of God (Suzanne Brenner, Robert Hefner, personal communication, 1994).

25. Also thoroughly foreign to Malay culture are Brenner's (1995) findings that Javanese men and women alike subscribe to the view that men's sexual longings are "stronger" or more intense than women's.

26. That she has never been married is partly a function of her high status as both a school teacher and a member of the wealthiest lineage in the village: There are few if any available men of comparable or higher status in Bogang, and those

outside the village who have expressed interest in marrying her have been put off by the exorbitant marriage payments demanded by her mother.

27. I interpreted such gifts as gestures of hospitality (I was renting the house that belonged to her sister and brother-in-law), though they may have also reflected her interest in "getting to know me better."

28. See Wikan (1990) for a similar perspective on Balinese "grace" and "style."

29. Partly in response to some of the early criticism of her work, Ortner has developed a more dynamic, actor-oriented, practice-theory approach to the study of gender, which is far more sophisticated than—and otherwise significantly different from—the early "symbolic/structural" approach that informed the nature/culture argument (see Ortner 1981, 1983, 1989–90; Ortner and Whitehead 1981a). I have already commented on some of the central features of this more recent approach (chapter 2), and will address others in greater detail further along (chapters 6 and 7). My main concern here is simply to reassess key features of the nature/culture thesis in light of data from Negeri Sembilan, not to attempt to establish (or disconfirm) the universal validity of Ortner's arguments. I should also note that I do not consider all of the criticisms or controversies generated by the nature/culture thesis. One reason for this is that some of them strike me as seriously misguided and/or spurious (e.g., MacCormack's [1980:16] claim that the thesis is "biological reductionist"). Another is that some of the criticisms are not relevant to the case at hand (e.g., Strathern's [1980] argument that among Hageners living in the highlands of Papua New Guinea, concepts such as "nature" and "culture" do not exist, even implicitly).

30. For brief discussions of some of the ways in which these influences helped bring about early historical shifts in the semantic domains of "reason" and "passion," see Gibb and Kramers (1953:433–36) and Izutsu (1964:65–68).

31. Data from other parts of the Peninsula, however, indicate that such a view does exist. Some Malay men in Trengganu, for example, claim that sex with a menstruating woman enhances their virility (Laderman 1983:74, 242 n.1). Note, too, that in a Minangkabau (Sumatran) dispute recorded by Krier (1995), a woman who felt herself grievously wronged by an influential male leader lifted her *sarong* in his presence and threatened him with her genitals. Such exposing of the genitals sometimes occurs during episodes of *latah*. For a brief reference to a nineteenth-century occurrence of this phenomenon in the Malay context, see O'Brien (1883).

32. Ortner (1989–90) has since recognized the problems with this view, but I do not want to burden the text with shifts in her position since my main concern here is to reassess her original argument.

33. A *pontianak* is a particularly dangerous type of spirit that typically comes into being when a woman dies during pregnancy or childbirth; that is, it is the ghost of a woman who dies under such circumstances. *Pontianak* are given to flying, climbing trees, screaming, weeping, and laughing, and are especially threatening—sometimes fatally so—to their former husbands, whom they try to lure into forested areas and seduce. *Langsuir* are in some ways similar to *pontianak* insofar as they, too, are the ghosts of women who have died during pregnancy or childbirth, and are also able to fly. *Langsuir* are frequently encountered late at

night along the sides of roads, and have holes about the size of chicken eggs at the base of their necks, which, if plugged up with earth (or various other substances), will enable them to assume the form and behavior of humans. (*Langsuir* are described by some villagers as Chinese variants of *pontianak*.) *Nenek kebayan* are "grandmother spirits" that live alone in the forest (about whom I have little information).

34. *Orang bunyian* are elves or "forest people" who protect and help humans and are invariably "good." Strictly speaking, they are not the "supernatural" manifestations of humans who have died, but rather the transformed essences of humans who have simply gotten lost in the forest or otherwise disappeared. *Hantu orang mati bunuh* are the ghosts of people who have been killed. Such ghosts, which reside in spots where human blood was shed, make groaning, crying noises that are audible to those who pass by. People are likely to incur fever if they pass through or even near such places, which are, in any event, especially dangerous at noon and at night. *Hantu raya*, for their part, may be domesticated or tamed by humans, in which case they will do their masters' bidding for them, and may even reside in their masters' homes. For additional information on these and other spirits, see Skeat ([1900] 1967) and Endicott (1970).

6. CONTRASTING REPRESENTATIONS OF GENDER

1. This interview was conducted before Kamaruddin and I had discussed or otherwise explored aspects of gender in any detail, so I have no reason to believe that Kamaruddin's perspectives on gender were "tainted" by my (analytic) understandings of gender in local society and culture.

2. The term *kwin kontrol* is one of many borrowings from the English language, and most likely originated during the reign of Queen Victoria.

3. The village median is M$240 per month; the mean is M$286 (see Peletz 1988b:187). These figures refer to monthly household income in Bogang during the period 1979–1980 and are based on information obtained from 98 percent (104 of 106) of Bogang's households.

4. In this connection we might consider Banks's (1976: 578, 579) observations for Kedah that informants "suspect that males outside of the sibling group will use marriage as a pretext to get the wealth and preferment from female members," and that "the common wisdom is that a woman who has land will soon let her husband sell it in one lump and pocket all of her wealth." Though this is reminiscent of Negeri Sembilan, there is a crucial difference: In Negeri Sembilan relatively negative views of husbands and in-marrying males inform practical representations to a profound degree; these views are, in effect, hegemonic with respect to the notions of maleness characteristic of everyday discourse. This situation seems not to obtain in Kedah, as indicated by Banks's (1976, 1983:66–69) comments that, despite suspicions and mistrust toward men in the roles of husbands and in-marrying males, *men as a whole are seen as more responsible and trustworthy than women* when it comes to dealing with property, and in most other ways, too. These latter, generally positive perceptions of men appear

to prevail in everyday discourse not only in Kedah but also in other parts of the Peninsula (outside of Negeri Sembilan), even in areas such as Selangor where most of the problems in marriage and much of the "fault" in divorce are seen by Islamic magistrates and others as stemming from men's poor showing in their roles as husbands and fathers, especially their failure to provide for their wives' and children's basic subsistence and other material needs (Ong 1987:131–32).

5. Postmarital residence among "bilateral" Malays is sometimes glossed "patrilocal" or "neolocal" (if only to distinguish it from the uxori- or matrilocal postmarital residence associated with the "matrilineal" Malays of Negeri Sembilan), but research in many regions inhabited by "bilateral" Malays indicates a tendency for married couples to reside with or near the bride's parents after the wedding, if only for a short while, such as a year. (This is sometimes followed [or superseded] by one or another variant of patrilocal or neolocal residence.) The propensity toward uxorilocality has been reported for Pahang (Wilder 1970:239; Massard 1983:106), Kelantan (Nash 1974:35), and Singapore (Djamour 1959:79–80), and is especially pronounced in cases where the bride is the youngest daughter, for youngest daughters often inherit their parents' houses, along with the primary responsibility to care for the parents in sickness and old age (Djamour 1959:40). The larger issue, however, is that the tendency toward uxorilocality noted here is far less pronounced than what one finds in Negeri Sembilan.

6. A similar situation obtains among the Angola Batak (Rodgers 1990) and is probably quite widespread in Southeast Asia (and elsewhere).

7. His creditors include a thoroughly impoverished man with a withered and altogether dysfunctional arm who ekes out a living selling newspapers from an old bicycle.

8. For a similar dynamic in the American context, see Martin (1987).

9. This occurs despite the broad recognition that female factory workers often make critically important economic contributions to their parents' households, thereby enabling their parents to purchase otherwise unobtainable consumer goods and other emblems of modernity and prestige.

10. This continues despite the fact that these same developments have also fostered the emergence of, and have helped sustain, certain types of oppositional discourses (see Ong 1988, 1990a).

11. Contra the impression one might get from reading Gramsci (1971) and his interlocutors, it is not simply or even necessarily primarily in the consciousness of subordinate groups that we often see (to paraphrase Eagleton 1991:36) a contradictory, hybrid amalgam of attitudes and perspectives that reflect values imbibed from, or simply of, the privileged on the one hand, and those which derive more from social actors' practical experiences in (or lived relations to) the world on the other. In the case of Negeri Sembilan, as we have seen, males as a group, and certain elite males in particular, operate with extremely heterogeneous (hybrid) and contradictory views of masculinity and femininity alike.

12. Needless to say, one need not posit the existence of any form of conspiracy (or resort to other functionalist explanations) to appreciate that the representa-

tions of masculinity at issue here have a variety of consequences that are, among other things, both ironic and unintended.

13. Cited in Rich (1979:84) and Chodorow (1989:99).

7. CONCLUSION

1. Essentialist perspectives on gender in the Islamic world are exceedingly widespread. For critical reviews of some of the relevant literature bearing on gender in Middle Eastern Islam, see S. Hale (1989) and Leila Ahmed (1992).

2. See Douglas 1966, Endicott 1970, Zelenietz 1981:12–13, and Zelenietz and Lindenbaum 1981.

3. For information on this and attendant movements in Aceh, see Siegel (1969) and Reid (1979).

4. This is not to suggest, however, that men and women are in absolute agreement with respect to all aspects of masculinity (or femininity). Consider, for example, Acehnese prayer houses (*meunasah*), which, unlike their counterparts in Negeri Sembilan (and Minangkabau and Java), serve both as dormitories for unmarried men and as village meeting halls in which men mull over and resolve political and religious issues. Males move to such houses (which observers describe as "half men's houses, half men's clubs") shortly after attaining adolescence and typically sleep there until they marry. Once they marry, they usually affiliate with one or another of the prayer houses in their wives' villages, though under normal circumstances they do not actually sleep in such houses. These houses provide key sites where men unite as Muslims, and thus overcome, albeit temporarily, the definitions of themselves that are grounded in their roles as husbands, fathers, brothers, and sons. Interestingly, however, women view prayer houses not only as places where men go to pray, chant, and associate with other men, but also as places where men while away the time, gossip, and otherwise act lazy (Siegel 1969). Thus, while prayer houses serve to unite men as Muslims and to highlight, at least for men, official views of masculinity, they have somewhat different meanings for women.

5. For a brief discussion of some of the problems with this term, see Fraser and Nicholson (1990:29–31).

6. Some of the issues relevant to the differential elaboration of entrepreneurial traditions are addressed in Swift (1971) and Peletz (n.d.b).

7. Blackwood (1995), for example, notes that in her recent (1989–90) fieldwork in the Minangkabau village of Taram she never encountered any usage or discussion of the terms "reason" or "passion" in regard to gender. Whalley's fieldwork among Minangkabau in urban contexts, which was carried out from 1986 to 1988, also suggests the relative deemphasis of these concepts, at least in relation to what has been noted for Malays in various parts of the Malay Peninsula (Whalley 1993). Krier (1994), on the other hand, found that the concepts of "reason" and "passion" were central to constructions of gender in the Minangkabau village of Sidie, which she studied from 1990 to 1991. Regional variation among the Minangkabau obviously merits more attention than it has received thus far.

8. For similar cautions, see de Josselin de Jong (1951), Abdul Kahar bin Bador (1963:8–9), and Sweeney (1987:111–12).

9. *Budi,* as noted earlier, refers to "etiquette," "character," "manners," and "breeding." *Malu,* for its part, has a number of meanings; perhaps the most basic of these, as discussed in chapter 5, is "shame."

10. Strictly speaking, moreover, the tensions inherent in the "matrilineal puzzle" are not confined to matrilineal settings: witness the case of Aceh. I would add that there is no empirical or other reason to privilege these aspects of marriage ties as the major source of tension in such systems; siblingship, as argued elsewhere (Peletz 1988b), is equally liable to generate the major lines of cleavage and tension both in matrilineal and other settings.

11. See, for example, Istutiah Gunawan Mitchell's (1969) point about the "extreme sensitivity" of married men in relation to their parents-in-law's, particularly their mothers-in-law's, behavior.

12. The existence of such a line, or, more accurately, its status as hegemonic, is somewhat in dispute as far as certain scholars of the Minangkabau are concerned, though not in my view of things or in the views of most scholars dealing with Minangkabau. Blackwood (personal communication, 1993), for example, sees no evidence to support the argument that cultural assertions of male ascendancy are in any way hegemonic. Similarly, Whalley (1993:295) contends that "there is no fundamental sense in Minangkabau that men are morally superior because of their proclivity to use reason over passion, or because of their guardianship role with regard to women . . . , even though such concepts exist within Islamic doctrine." Pak (1986, n.d.) and Krier (1994), on the other hand, argue that cultural assertions of male ascendancy are indeed hegemonic (though they differ somewhat as to the conceptual bases of such assertions [with Pak stressing men's biogenetically and spiritually potent "blood," and Krier emphasizing men's greater "reason"]). Views of the latter sort are the more widespread in the anthropological literature on Minangkabau.

13. Interestingly, Krier (1994:179–80) points out that most men do in fact fail to live up to the expectations associated with the role of in-marrying male and the role of husband specifically. Aside from not providing adequately for their families ("the obligations that weigh on husbands most heavily"), their most common moral failings include vanity, cattiness, capriciousness, gluttony, and shamelessness. Being "oversexed" is also high up on the list of men's shortcomings, at least as far as women are concerned: "Villagers say that in the first few months after marriage, women are so victimized by their husbands' carnal desires that they become thin, tired, and pale" (101). Not surprisingly, "marriage, and the prospect of sexual relations, causes considerable anxiety among girls" (100).

14. Note here Krier's (1994:144–45) argument that a father's most important contribution is "an invisible substance that Minangkabau usually refer to as 'good seed' or 'white blood.' "

15. Other variables are certainly at work as well (but need not concern us here).

16. This is, of course, a relative point.

17. The prevalence of women in markets, and in local trading generally, contrasts sharply with the situation in Aceh, where all trading is in the hands of men.

18. The Bedouin practice of clitoridectomy entails a major operation; as such, it differs from the practice found in the Malay-Indonesian world, which involves a minor, mostly superficial, incision.

19. These are recurrent themes in Bloch's work; see, for example, Bloch (1982, 1987, 1989) and Bloch and Bloch (1980).

20. Trawick's fascinating (1990) study of love among Tamils does at times conflate the distinction at issue here as well.

21. I discuss some of these issues elsewhere (Peletz 1993b).

22. For additional perspectives on ambivalence in American systems of kinship and gender, see Howell (1972), L. Rubin (1976), Rapp (1982), Ginsburg and Tsing (1990), and Stacey (1991).

23. These themes are developed in different ways by (among others) Coser ([1956] 1964), Goffman (1959), and Weiner (1976).

Bibliography

OFFICIAL RECORDS

Buletin Perangkaan Sosial (Social Statistics Bulletin). Malaysia, 1991. Jabatan Perangkaan Malaysia (Department of Statistics, Malaysia). Kuala Lumpur: Government of Malaysia. 1991.

CRACNS 1874. Correspondence Relating to the Affairs of Certain Native States in the Malay Peninsula in the Neighborhood of the Straits Settlements. (In Continuation of Command Paper [465] of 1872.) Presented to both Houses of Parliament by Command of Her Majesty, July 31, 1874. (Accounts and Papers 1874 [11] XLV, 45.) Public Record Office, London.

CRACNS 1875. Further Correspondence Relating to the Affairs of Certain Native States in the Malay Peninsula in the Neighborhood of the Straits Settlements. (In Continuation of Command Paper [C.1111] of July 1874.) Presented to both Houses of Parliament by Command of Her Majesty, August 6, 1875. (Accounts and Papers 1875 [12] L111, 53.) Public Record Office, London.

CRACNS 1876. Further Correspondence Relating to the Affairs of Certain Native States in the Malay Peninsula in the Neighborhood of the Straits Settlements. (In Continuation of Command Paper [C.1320] of August 1875.) Presented to both Houses of Parliament by Command of Her Majesty, May 25, 1876. (Accounts and Papers 1876 [13] LIV, 54.) Public Record Office, London.

NSAR (Negri Sembilan Annual Report). 1889, 1896. Public Record Office, London.

NSGG (Negri Sembilan Government Gazettes). 1897, 1898, 1905. Public Record Office, London.

BOOKS, ARTICLES, AND THESES

Abdul Kahar bin Bador. 1963. "Kinship and Marriage among the Negri Sembilan Malays." Master's thesis, University of London.

Abdul Rahman bin Haji Mohammad. 1964. *Dasar-Dasar Adat Perpateh*. Kuala Lumpur: Pustaka Antara.

Abu-Lughod, Lila. 1986. *Veiled Sentiments: Honor and Poetry in a Bedouin Society*. Berkeley: University of California Press.

Ackerman, Susan. 1988. "The Phenomenology of Class in Malay Peasant Society." *Peasant Studies* 15(3):206–19.

———. 1991. "Dakwah and Minah Karan: Class Formation and Ideological Conflict in Malay Society." *Bijdragen Tot de Taal-, Land-, en Volkenkunde* 147(2/3):193–215.

Ahmed, Leila. 1992. *Women and Gender in Islam: Historical Roots of a Modern Debate.* New Haven: Yale University Press.

Althusser, Louis. 1969. *For Marx.* London: New Left Books.

Andaya, Barbara, and Yoneo Ishii. 1992. "Religious Developments in Southeast Asia, circa 1500–1800." In *The Cambridge History of Southeast Asia,* edited by Nicholas Tarling, 508–71. Cambridge: Cambridge University Press.

Anderson, Benedict R. O.'G. 1972. "The Idea of Power in Javanese Culture." In *Culture and Politics in Indonesia,* edited by Claire Holt, 1–69. Ithaca: Cornell University Press.

———. 1983. *Imagined Communities: Reflections on the Origin and Spread of Nationalism.* London: Verso.

Anderson, Perry. 1976–77. "The Antinomies of Antonio Gramsci." *New Left Review* 100:5–78.

Appell, Laura W. R. 1988. "Menstruation among the Rungus of Borneo: An Unmarked Category." In *Blood Magic: The Anthropology of Menstruation,* edited by Thomas Buckley and Anna Gottlieb, 94–112. Berkeley: University of California Press.

Ardener, Edwin. 1972. "Belief and the Problem of Women." In *Perceiving Women,* edited by Shirley Ardener, 1–17. New York: Wiley and Sons.

Atkinson, Jane. 1982. "Anthropology: Review Essay." *Signs* 8(2):236–58.

———. 1987. "The Effectiveness of Shamans in an Indonesian Ritual." *American Anthropologist* 89(2):342–55.

———. 1989. *The Art and Politics of Wana Shamanship.* Berkeley: University of California Press.

———. 1990. "How Gender Makes a Difference in Wana Society." In *Power and Difference: Gender in Island Southeast Asia,* edited by Jane Atkinson and Shelly Errington, 59–93. Stanford: Stanford University Press.

Atkinson, Jane, and Shelly Errington, eds. 1990. *Power and Difference: Gender in Island Southeast Asia.* Stanford: Stanford University Press.

A. Wahab Alwee. 1967. *Rembau: A Study in Integration and Conflict in Negri Sembilan, Malaya.* Centre for Asian Studies, Working Papers in Asian Studies, no. 1. Nedlands: University of Western Australia.

Awang Sudjai Hairul and Yusoff Khan. 1977. *Kamus Lengkap.* Petaling Jaya: Pustaka Zaman.

Azizah Kassim. 1969. "Kedudokan Wanita Di-Dalam Masharakat Melayu Beradat Perpateh di-Negeri Sembilan." Master's thesis, University of Malaya.

———. 1988. "Women, Land, and Gender Relations in Negeri Sembilan: Some Preliminary Findings." In *Socio-Economic Change and Cultural Transformation in Rural Malaysia: A Preliminary Research Report,* edited by Tsuyoshi Kato and Shamsul A. B., 132–49. Center for Southeast Asian Studies, Kyoto University.

Bacdayan, Albert S. 1977. "Mechanistic Cooperation and Sexual Equality among the Western Bontoc." In *Sexual Stratification: A Cross-Cultural View,* edited by Alice Schlegel, 270–91. New York: Columbia University Press.

Banks, David. 1976. "Islam and Inheritance in Malaya: Culture Conflict or Islamic Revolution?" *American Ethnologist* 3(4):573–86.

———. 1983. *Malay Kinship*. Philadelphia: ISHI Publications.

Barnett, Steve, and Martin G. Silverman. 1979. *Ideology and Everyday Life: Anthropology, Neomarxist Thought, and the Problem of Ideology and the Social Whole*. Ann Arbor: University of Michigan Press.

Barth, Fredrik. 1987. *Cosmologies in the Making: A Generative Approach to Cultural Variation in Inner New Guinea*. Cambridge: Cambridge University Press.

Benedict, Ruth. 1934. *Patterns of Culture*. New York: Houghton Mifflin.

———. 1946. *The Chrysanthemum and the Sword*. Boston: Houghton Mifflin.

Bettelheim, Bruno. 1962. *Symbolic Wounds: Puberty Rites and the Envious Male*. New York: Collier Books.

Blackwood, Evelyn. 1995. "Senior Women, Model Mothers, and Dutiful Wives: Managing Gender Contradictions in a Minangkabau Village." In *Bewitching Women, Pious Men: Gender and Body Politics in Southeast Asia*, edited by Aihwa Ong and Michael G. Peletz, 124–58. Berkeley: University of California Press.

Bloch, Maurice. 1982. "Death, Women, and Power." In *Death and the Regeneration of Life*, edited by Maurice Bloch and Jonathan Parry, 211–30. Cambridge: Cambridge University Press.

———. 1986. *From Blessing to Violence: History and Ideology in the Circumcision Ritual of the Merina of Madagascar*. Cambridge: Cambridge University Press.

———. 1987. "Descent and Sources of Contradiction in Representations of Women and Kinship." In *Gender and Kinship: Essays toward a Unified Analysis*, edited by Jane Collier and Sylvia Yanagisako, 324–37. Stanford: Stanford University Press.

———. 1989. *Ritual, History and Power: Selected Papers in Anthropology*. London: Athlone Press.

Bloch, Maurice, and Jean H. Bloch. 1980. "Women and the Dialectics of Nature in Eighteenth-Century French Thought." In *Nature, Culture, and Gender*, edited by Carol MacCormack and Marilyn Strathern, 25–41. New York: Cambridge University Press.

Blust, Robert. 1980. "Early Austronesian Social Organization: The Evidence of Language." *Current Anthropology* 21(2):205–47.

Boddy, Janice. 1989. *Wombs and Alien Spirits: Women, Men and the Zar Cults in Northern Sudan*. Madison: University of Wisconsin Press.

Boggs, Carl. 1976. *Gramsci's Marxism*. London: Pluto Press.

Boserup, Ester. 1970. *Women's Role in Economic Development*. New York: St. Martin's Press.

Bourdieu, Pierre. 1977. *Outline of a Theory of Practice*. Cambridge: Cambridge University Press.

———. 1984. *Distinction: A Social Critique of the Judgement of Taste*. Cambridge: Harvard University Press.

Brandes, Stanley. 1980. *Metaphors of Masculinity: Sex and Status in Andalusian Folklore*. Publications of the American Folklore Society, n.s. 1. Philadelphia: University of Pennsylvania Press.

————. 1981. "Like a Wounded Stag: Male Sexual Ideology in an Andalusian Town." In *Sexual Meanings: The Cultural Construction of Gender and Sexuality*, edited by Sherry Ortner and Harriet Whitehead, 216–39. Cambridge: Cambridge University Press.

Brenner, Suzanne. 1995. "Why Women Rule the Roost: Rethinking Javanese Ideologies of Gender and Self-Control." In *Bewitching Women, Pious Men: Gender and Body Politics in Southeast Asia*, edited by Aihwa Ong and Michael G. Peletz, 19–47. Berkeley: University of California Press.

Brown, C. C., trans. 1970. *Sejarah Melayu or "Malay Annals"*. Reprint. Kuala Lumpur: Oxford University Press.

Brown, Judith K. 1975. "Iroquois Women: An Ethnohistoric Note." In *Toward an Anthropology of Women*, edited by Rayna Reiter, 235–51. New York: Monthly Review Press.

Buckley, Thomas, and Alma Gottlieb. 1988. "A Critical Appraisal of Theories of Menstrual Symbolism." In *Blood Magic: The Anthropology of Menstruation*, edited by Thomas Buckley and Alma Gottlieb, 3–50. Berkeley: University of California Press.

Burling, Robbins. 1965. *Hill Farms and Padi Fields: Life in Mainland Southeast Asia*. Englewood Cliffs, N.J.: Prentice-Hall.

Caldecott, Andrew. 1918. "Jelebu Customary Songs and Sayings." *Journal of the Royal Asiatic Society, Straits Branch* 78:3–41.

Chandra Muzaffar. 1987. *Islamic Resurgence in Malaysia*. Kuala Lumpur: Fajar Bakti.

Chodorow, Nancy. 1974. "Family Structure and Feminine Personality." In *Woman, Culture, and Society*, edited by Michelle Rosaldo and Louise Lamphere, 43–66. Stanford: Stanford University Press.

————. 1978. *The Reproduction of Mothering: Psychoanalysis and the Sociology of Gender*. Berkeley: University of California Press.

————. 1989. *Feminism and Psychoanalytic Theory*. New Haven: Yale University Press.

Clifford, James, and George Marcus, eds. 1986. *Writing Culture: The Poetics and Politics of Ethnography*. Berkeley: University of California Press.

Collier, Jane. 1988. *Marriage and Inequality in Classless Societies*. Stanford: Stanford University Press.

Collier, Jane, and Michelle Rosaldo. 1981. "Politics and Gender in Simple Societies." In *Sexual Meanings: The Cultural Construction of Gender and Sexuality*, edited by Sherry Ortner and Harriet Whitehead, 275–329. New York: Cambridge University Press.

Collier, Jane, and Sylvia Yanagisako. 1987a. "Introduction." In *Gender and Kinship: Essays toward a Unified Analysis*, edited by Jane Collier and Sylvia Yanagisako, 1-13. Stanford: Stanford University Press.

Collier, Jane, and Sylvia Yanagisako, eds. 1987b. *Gender and Kinship: Essays toward a Unified Analysis*. Stanford: Stanford University Press.

Comaroff, John. 1980. "Introduction." In *The Meaning of Marriage Payments*, edited by John Comaroff, 1–47. London: Academic.

Comaroff, John, and Simon Roberts. 1981. *Rules and Processes: The Cultural Logic of Dispute in an African Context*. Chicago: University of Chicago Press.

Coser, Lewis. [1956] 1964. *The Functions of Social Conflict.* Reprint. New York: Free Press.

de Beauvoir, Simone. 1949. *The Second Sex.* New York: Random House.

de Certeau, Michel. 1984. *The Practice of Everyday Life.* Berkeley: University of California Press.

de Josselin de Jong, P. E. 1951. *Minangkabau and Negri Sembilan: Socio-Political Structure in Indonesia.* Leiden: Ijdo.

―――. [1956] 1977. "The Participants' View of Their Culture." In *Structural Anthropology in the Netherlands,* edited by P. E. de Josselin de Jong, 233–52. The Hague: Martinus Nijhoff, 1977. (Originally published as "De visie der participanten op hun cultuur.")

―――. 1960. "Islam Versus *Adat* in Negri Sembilan (Malaya)." *Bijdragen tot de Taal-, Land-, en Volkenkunde* 116:158–203.

Delaney, Carol. 1991. *The Seed and the Soil: Gender and Cosmology in Turkish Village Society.* Berkeley: University of California Press.

Dentan, Robert K. 1988. "Ambiguity, Synecdoche, and Affect in Semai Medicine." *Social Science and Medicine* 27(8):857–77.

Dirks, Nicholas, Geoff Eley, and Sherry Ortner. 1994. "Introduction." In *Culture/Power/History: A Reader in Contemporary Social Theory,* edited by Nicholas Dirks, Geoff Eley, and Sherry Ortner, 3–45. Princeton, N.J.: Princeton University Press.

Djamour, Judith. 1959. *Malay Kinship and Marriage in Singapore.* London: Athlone Press.

Doniger, Wendy. 1991. "The Laws of Manus." Paper presented September 16, 1991, at Cornell University.

Douglas, Mary. 1966. *Purity and Danger: An Analysis of the Concepts of Pollution and Taboo.* London: Routledge and Kegan Paul.

―――. 1970. *Natural Symbols: Explorations in Cosmology.* New York: Pantheon.

―――. 1971. "Is Matriliny Doomed in Africa?" In *Man in Africa,* edited by Mary Douglas and Phyllis Kaberry, 123–37. Garden City, N.Y.: Doubleday.

Draper, Patricia. 1975. "!Kung Women: Contrasts in Sexual Egalitarianism in Foraging and Sedentary Contexts." In *Toward an Anthropology of Women,* edited by Rayna Reiter, 77–109. New York: Monthly Review Press.

Dumont, Louis. 1970. *Homo Hierarchicus: The Caste System and Its Implications.* Chicago: University of Chicago Press.

Dwyer, Daisy. 1978. *Images and Self-Images: Male and Female in Morocco.* New York: Columbia University Press.

Eagleton, Terry. 1991. *Ideology: An Introduction.* London: Verso.

Ellen, Roy F. 1983. "Social Theory, Ethnography, and the Understanding of Practical Islam in Southeast Asia." In *Islam in Southeast Asia,* edited by M. B. Hooker, 50–91. Leiden: E. J. Brill.

Endicott, K. M. 1970. *An Analysis of Malay Magic.* Oxford: Clarendon Press.

Errington, Frederick. 1984. *Manners and Meaning in West Sumatra: The Social Context of Consciousness.* New Haven: Yale University Press.

Errington, Shelly. 1990. "Recasting Sex, Gender, and Power: A Theoretical and Regional Overview." In *Power and Difference: Gender in Island Southeast*

Asia, edited by Jane Atkinson and Shelly Errington, 1–58. Stanford: Stanford University Press.

Evans-Pritchard, E. E. 1940. *The Nuer: A Description of the Modes of Livelihood and Political Institutions of a Nilotic People*. New York: Oxford University Press.

Femia, Joseph. 1975. "Hegemony and Consciousness in the Thought of Antonio Gramsci." *Political Studies* 23(1):29–48.

Fett, Ione. 1983. "Land Ownership in Negeri Sembilan, 1900–1977." In *Women's Work and Women's Roles: Economics and Everyday Life in Indonesia, Malaysia, and Singapore*, edited by Lenore Manderson, 73–96. Development Studies Centre Monograph 32. Canberra: Australian National University.

Firth, Raymond. [1951] 1963. *Elements of Social Organization*. Reprint. Boston: Beacon Press.

———. 1964. *Essays on Social Organization and Values*. London: Athlone Press.

Foucault, Michel. 1977. *Discipline and Punish: The Birth of the Prison*. Translated by Alan Sheridan. New York: Vintage.

Fox, Robin. 1967. *Kinship and Marriage: An Anthropological Perspective*. Harmondsworth, England: Penguin Books.

Fraser, Nancy, and Linda J. Nicholson. 1990. "Social Criticism without Philosophy: An Encounter between Feminism and Postmodernism." In *Feminism/Postmodernism*, edited by Linda J. Nicholson, 19–38. Routledge: New York.

Freud, Sigmund. [1913] 1950. *Totem and Taboo*. Reprint. New York: W. W. Norton.

———. [1927] 1964. *The Future of an Illusion*. Reprint. Garden City, N.Y.: Doubleday.

Geertz, Clifford. 1960. *The Religion of Java*. Glencoe, Ill.: Basic Books.

———. 1973. *The Interpretation of Cultures*. New York: Basic Books.

———. 1983. *Local Knowledge: Further Essays in Interpretive Anthropology*. New York: Basic Books.

Geertz, Hildred. [1961] 1989. *The Javanese Family: A Study of Kinship and Socialization*. Reprint. Prospect Heights, Ill.: Waveland Press.

———. 1979. "The Meanings of Family Ties." In *Meaning and Order in Moroccan Society*, Clifford Geertz, Hildred Geertz, Lawrence Rosen, 315–91. New York: Cambridge University Press.

Gewertz, Deborah, ed. 1988. *Myths of Matriarchy Reconsidered*. Oceania Monograph 33. Sydney: University of Sydney.

Gibb, H. A. R., and J. H. Kramers, eds. 1953. *Shorter Encyclopedia of Islam*. Leiden: E. J. Brill.

Giddens, Anthony. 1979. *Central Problems in Social Theory: Action, Structure, and Contradiction in Social Analysis*. Berkeley: University of California Press.

Gilbert, William. [1937] 1955. "Eastern Cherokee Social Organization." In *Social Anthropology of North American Tribes*. 2d ed. Edited by Fred Eggan, 285–338. Chicago: University of Chicago Press.

Gilligan, Carol. 1982. *In a Different Voice: Psychological Theory and Women's Development*. Cambridge: Harvard University Press.

Gilman, Sander L. 1985. *Difference and Pathology: Stereotypes of Sexuality, Race, and Madness.* Ithaca: Cornell University Press.

Gilmore, David. 1990. *Manhood in the Making: Cultural Concepts of Masculinity.* New Haven: Yale University Press.

Gimlette, John D. [1915] 1971. *Malay Poisons and Charm Cures.* Reprint. Kuala Lumpur: Oxford University Press.

Ginsburg, Faye. 1989. *Contested Lives: The Abortion Debate in an American Community.* Berkeley: University of California Press.

Ginsburg, Faye, and Anna Tsing, eds. 1990. *Uncertain Terms: Negotiating Gender in American Culture.* Boston: Beacon Press.

Goffman, Erving. 1959. *The Presentation of Self in Everyday Life.* Garden City, N.Y.: Doubleday.

Goody, Jack. 1990. *The Oriental, the Ancient, and the Primitive: Systems of Marriage and the Family in the Pre-Industrial Societies of Eurasia.* New York: Cambridge University Press.

Gramsci, Antonio. 1971. *Selections from the Prison Notebooks of Antonio Gramsci.* Edited and translated by Quinten Hoare and Geoffrey Nowell Smith. New York: International Publishers.

Gregor, Thomas. 1985. *Anxious Pleasures: The Sexual Lives of an Amazonian People.* Chicago: University of Chicago Press.

Gullick, J. M. 1951. "The Negri Sembilan Economy of the 1890s." *Journal of the Royal Asiatic Society, Malayan Branch* 24(1):38–55.

———. 1958. *Indigenous Political Systems of Western Malaya.* London: Athlone Press.

———. 1987. *Malay Society in the Late Nineteenth Century: The Beginnings of Change.* Singapore: Oxford University Press.

Hale, Andrew. 1898. "Folklore and the Menangkabau Code in Negri Sembilan." *Journal of the Royal Asiatic Society, Straits Branch* 31:43–61.

Hale, Sondra. 1989. "The Politics of Gender in the Middle East." In *Gender and Anthropology: Critical Reviews for Research and Teaching,* edited by Sandra Morgen, 246–67. Washington, D.C.: American Anthropological Association.

Hamka (Haji Abdul Malik Karim Abdullah). 1963. *Adat Minangkabau Menghadapi Revolusi.* Djakarta: Tekad.

Hefner, Robert. 1985. *Hindu Javanese: Tengger Tradition and Islam.* Princeton: Princeton University Press.

Hellwig, Tineke. 1992. "Rape in Two Indonesian Pop Novels: An Analysis of the Female Image." In *Indonesian Women in Focus,* edited by Elsbeth Locher-Scholten and Anke Niehof, 240–54. Leiden: Koninklijk Instituut voor Taal-, Land-, en Volkenkunde.

Heng, Geraldine, and Janadas Devan. 1992. "State Fatherhood: The Politics of Nationalism, Sexuality, and Race in Singapore." In *Nationalisms and Sexualities,* edited by Andrew Parker et al., 343–64. New York: Routledge.

Herdt, Gilbert, ed. 1982. *Rituals of Manhood: Male Initiation in Papua New Guinea.* Berkeley: University of California Press.

Hervey, D. F. A. 1884. "Rembau." *Journal of the Royal Asiatic Society, Straits Branch* 13:241–58.

Herzfeld, Michael. 1985. *The Poetics of Manhood: Contest and Identity in a Cretan Mountain Village*. Princeton: Princeton University Press.

Hirschman, Charles. 1986. "The Recent Rise in Malay Fertility: A New Trend or a Temporary Lull in a Fertility Transition?" *Demography* 23(2):161–84.

Hooker, M. B. 1972. Adat *Laws in Modern Malaya: Land Tenure, Traditional Government, and Religion*. Kuala Lumpur: Oxford University Press.

———, ed. 1970. *Readings in Malay* Adat *Laws*. Singapore: Singapore University Press.

Horvatich, Patricia. 1992. "Toward an Understanding of Gender in Southeast Asia." Paper presented at Conference on the Narrative and Practice of Gender in Southeast Asian Cultures, 9th Annual Berkeley Conference on Southeast Asian Studies, University of California, Berkeley.

Hoskins, Janet. 1990. "Doubling Deities, Descent, and Personhood: An Exploration of Kodi Gender Categories." In *Power and Difference: Gender in Island Southeast Asia*, edited by Jane Atkinson and Shelly Errington, 273–306. Stanford: Stanford University Press.

Howell, Joseph. 1972. *Hard Living on Clay Street*. Garden City, N.Y.: Anchor Books.

Istutiah Gunawan Mitchell. 1969. "The Socio-Cultural Environment and Mental Disturbance: Three Minangkabau Case Histories." *Indonesia* 7:123–37.

Izutsu, Toshihiko. 1964. *God and Man in the Koran: Semantics of the Koranic Weltanschauung*. Tokyo: Keio Institute of Cultural and Linguistic Studies.

Jaspan, M. A. 1969. *Traditional Medical Theory in Southeast Asia*. Hull, England: University of Hull.

Jay, Robert. 1969. *Javanese Villagers: Social Relations in Rural Modjokuto*. Cambridge, Mass.: MIT Press.

Jayawardena, Chandra. 1977a. "Acehnese Marriage Customs." *Indonesia* 23:157–73.

———. 1977b. "Women and Kinship in Acheh Besar, Northern Sumatra." *Ethnology* 16:21–38.

Jones, Gavin. 1980. "Trends in Marriage and Divorce in Peninsular Malaysia." *Population Studies* 34:279–92.

———. 1981. "Malay Marriage and Divorce in Peninsular Malaysia: Three Decades of Change." *Population and Development Review* 7:255–78.

Jordaan, R. E., and P. E. de Josselin de Jong. 1985. "Sickness as a Metaphor in Indonesian Political Myths." *Bijdragen tot de Taal-, Land-, en Volkenkunde* 141(2):253–74.

Karim, Wazir Jahan. 1990. "Prelude to Madness: The Language of Emotion in Courtship and Early Marriage." In *Emotions of Culture: A Malay Perspective*, edited by Wazir Jahan Karim, 21–63. Singapore: Oxford University Press.

———. 1992. *Women and Culture: Between Malay* Adat *and Islam*. Boulder: Westview Press.

Kato, Tsuyoshi. 1982. *Matriliny and Migration: Evolving Minangkabau Tradition in Indonesia*. Ithaca: Cornell University Press.

Keeler, Ward. 1987. *Javanese Shadow Plays, Javanese Selves*. Princeton: Princeton University Press.

———. 1990. "Speaking of Gender in Java." In *Power and Difference: Gender in*

Island Southeast Asia, edited by Jane Atkinson and Shelly Errington, 127–52. Stanford: Stanford University Press.

Keesing, Roger. 1975. *Kin Groups and Social Structure.* New York: Holt, Rinehart, and Winston.

Kelly, Raymond. 1977. *Etoro Social Structure: A Study in Structural Contradiction.* Ann Arbor: University of Michigan Press.

———. 1993. *Constructing Inequality: The Fabrication of a Hierarchy of Virtue among the Etoro.* Ann Arbor: University of Michigan Press.

Kenny, Michael G. 1990. "Latah: The Logic of Fear." In *Emotions of Culture: A Malay Perspective,* edited by Wazir Jahan Karim, 123–41. Singapore: Oxford University Press.

Kessler, Clive S. 1977. "Conflict and Sovereignty in Kelantanese Malay Spirit Seances." In *Case Studies in Spirit Possession,* edited by Vincent Crapanzano and Vivian Garrison, 295–331. New York: Wiley and Sons.

———. 1978. *Islam and Politics in a Malay State: Kelantan, 1838–1969.* Ithaca: Cornell University Press.

Keyes, Charles. 1984. "Mother or Mistress but Never a Monk: Buddhist Notions of Female Gender in Rural Thailand." *American Ethnologist* 11(2):223–41.

———. 1986. "Ambiguous Gender: Male Initiation in a Northern Thai Buddhist Society." In *Gender and Religion: On the Complexity of Symbols,* edited by Caroline Bynum, Stevan Harrell, and Paula Richman, 66–96. Boston: Beacon Press.

Kirsch, Thomas. 1982. "Buddhism, Sex Roles, and the Thai Economy." In *Women of Southeast Asia,* edited by Penny Van Esterik, 16–41. Dekalb, Ill.: Center for Southeast Asian Studies, Northern Illinois University.

———. 1985. "Text and Context: Buddhist Sex Roles/Culture of Gender Revisited." *American Ethnologist* 12(2):302–20.

Kleinman, Arthur. 1988. *Rethinking Psychiatry.* New York: Free Press.

Koentjaraningrat, R. M. 1960. "The Javanese of South Central Java." In *Social Structure in Southeast Asia,* edited by George P. Murdock, 88–115. Chicago: Quadrangle Books.

Krier, Jennifer. 1994. "Displacing Distinction: Political Processes in a Minangkabau Backcountry." Ph.D. dissertation, Harvard University.

———. 1995. "Narrating Herself: Power and Gender in a Minangkabau Woman's Tale of Conflict." In *Bewitching Women, Pious Men: Gender and Body Politics in Southeast Asia,* edited by Aihwa Ong and Michael G. Peletz, 48–75. Berkeley: University of California Press.

Laderman, Carol. 1982. "Putting Malay Women in Their Place." In *Women of Southeast Asia,* edited by Penny Van Esterik, 79–99. Dekalb, Ill.: Center for Southeast Asian Studies, Northern Illinois University.

———. 1983. *Wives and Midwives: Childbirth and Nutrition in Rural Malaysia.* Berkeley: University of California Press.

———. 1991. *Taming the Wind of Desire: Psychology, Medicine, and Aesthetics in Malay Shamanistic Performance.* Berkeley: University of California Press.

Lambek, Michael. 1981. *Human Spirits: A Cultural Account of Trance in Mayotte.* New York: Cambridge University Press.

———. 1988. "Spirit Possession/Spirit Succession: Aspects of Social Continuity among Malagasey Speakers in Mayotte." *American Ethnologist* 15(4):710–31.

Lando, Richard P., and Lynn L. Thomas. 1983. "Hierarchy and Alliance in Two Sumatran Societies." In *Beyond Samosir: Recent Studies of the Batak Peoples of Sumatra*, edited by Rita S. Kipp and Richard D. Kipp, 53–81. Monographs in International Studies, Southeast Asia Series, no. 62. Athens, Ohio: Ohio University Press.

Lavie, Smadar. 1990. *The Poetics of Military Occupation: Mzeina Allegories of Bedouin Identity under Israeli and Egyptian Rule*. Berkeley: University of California Press.

Leach, Edmund. [1954] 1965. *Political Systems of Highland Burma: A Study of Kachin Social Structure*. Reprint. Boston: Beacon Press.

———. [1961] 1966. *Rethinking Anthropology*. Reprint. London: Athlone Press.

Ledgerwood, Judy. 1992. "Khmer Images of the Perfect Woman: Culture Change and Gender Ideals." Paper presented at Conference on the Narrative and Practice of Gender in Southeast Asian Cultures, 9th Annual Conference on Southeast Asian Studies, University of California, Berkeley.

Lévi-Strauss, Claude. [1949] 1969. *The Elementary Structures of Kinship*. Reprint. Boston: Beacon Press.

———. 1953. "Social Structure." In *Anthropology Today*, edited by A. L. Kroeber, 524–53. Chicago: University of Chicago Press.

———. 1956. "The Family." In *Man, Culture, and Society*, edited by Harry L. Shapiro, 261–85. New York: Oxford University Press.

———. 1960. "On Manipulated Sociological Models." *Bijdragen Tot de Taal-, Land-, en Volkenkunde* 116:45–54.

———. 1963. "The Effectiveness of Symbols." In *Structural Anthropology*, 181–201. New York: Basic Books.

———. 1985. *The View from Afar*. New York: Basic Books.

Lewis, Diane K. 1962. "The Minangkabau Malay of Negri Sembilian: A Study of Socio-Cultural Change." Ph.D. dissertation, Cornell University.

Lewis, I. M. 1971. *Ecstatic Religion: An Anthropological Study of Spirit Possession and Shamanism*. Harmondsworth, England: Penguin.

Lister, Martin. 1887. "The Negri Sembilan: Their Origin and Constitution." *Journal of the Royal Asiatic Society, Straits Branch* 19:35–53.

———. 1890. "Malay Law in Negri Sembilan." *Journal of the Royal Asiatic Society, Straits Branch* 22:299–319.

———. 1891. "Pantang Larang of Negri Sembilan." *Journal of the Royal Asiatic Society, Straits Branch* 23:142–44.

Loizos, Peter, and Evthymios Papataxiarchis, eds. 1991. *Contested Identities: Gender and Kinship in Modern Greece*. Princeton: Princeton University Press.

MacCormack, Carol. 1980. "Nature, Culture, and Gender: A Critique." In *Nature, Culture, and Gender*, edited by Carol MacCormack and Marilyn Strathern, 1–25. Cambridge: Cambridge University Press.

MacCormack, Carol, and Marilyn Strathern, eds. 1980. *Nature, Culture, and Gender*. Cambridge: Cambridge University Press.

March, Kathryn. 1984. "Weaving, Writing, and Gender." *Man* 18:729–44.

Marcus, George, and Michael Fischer. 1986. *Anthropology as Cultural Critique:*

An Experimental Moment in the Human Sciences. Chicago: University of Chicago Press.

Martin, Emily. 1987. *The Woman in the Body: A Cultural Analysis of Reproduction.* Boston: Beacon Press.

Marty, Martin. 1993. "Fundamentalisms and the Scholars." *The Key Reporter* 58(3):1–6.

Massard, Josiane. 1983. "Le Don d'Enfants dans la Société Malaise." *L'Homme* 22(3):101–14.

———. 1985. "The New-Born Malay Child: A Multiple Identity Being." *Journal of the Malaysian Branch of the Royal Asiatic Society* 58(2):71–84.

McAllister, Carol. 1987. "Matriliny, Islam, and Capitalism: Combined and Uneven Development in the Lives of Negeri Sembilan Women." Ph.D. dissertation, University of Pittsburgh.

McKinley, Robert. 1975. "A Knife Cutting Water: Child Transfers and Siblingship among Urban Malays." Ph.D. dissertation, University of Michigan.

Mead, Margaret. 1935. *Sex and Temperament in Three Primitive Societies.* New York: William Morrow.

Meigs, Anna. 1978. "A Papuan Perspective on Pollution." *Man* 13:304–18.

Mernissi, Fatima. [1977] 1987. *Beyond the Veil: Male-Female Dynamics in Modern Muslim Society.* Reprint. Bloomington: Indiana University Press.

Mill, John Stuart. 1874. *Nature, the Utility of Religion, and Theism.* London: Longmans, Green, Reeder, and Dyer.

Milner, A. C. 1982. *Kerajaan: Malay Political Culture on the Eve of Colonial Rule.* Tucson: University of Arizona Press.

Moore, Sally Falk. 1986. *Social Facts and Fabrications: "Customary Law" on Kilimanjaro, 1880–1980.* Cambridge: Cambridge University Press.

Naim, Mochtar. 1973. "Merantau: Minangkabau Voluntary Migration." Ph.D. dissertation, University of Singapore.

Nakamura, Hisako. 1983. *Divorce in Java: A Study of the Dissolution of Marriage among Javanese Muslims.* Yogyakarta: Gadjah Mada University Press.

Nash, Manning. 1974. *Peasant Citizens: Politics, Religion, and Modernization in Kelantan, Malaysia.* Monographs in International Studies, Southeast Asia Series, no. 31. Athens, Ohio: Ohio University Press.

———. 1991. "Islamic Resurgence in Malaysia and Indonesia." In *Fundamentalisms Observed,* edited by Martin Marty and R. Scott Appleby, 691–739. Chicago: The University of Chicago Press.

Needham, Rodney. 1962. *Structure and Sentiment: A Test Case in Social Anthropology.* Chicago: University of Chicago Press.

———. 1971. "Remarks on the Analysis of Kinship and Marriage." In *Rethinking Kinship and Marriage,* edited by Rodney Needham, 1–34. London: Tavistock Publications.

Newbold, T. J. 1839. *Political and Statistical Accounts of the British Settlements in the Straits of Malacca.* 2 vols. London: John Murray.

Ng, Cecilia. 1987. "The Weaving of Prestige: Village Women's Representations of the Social Categories of Minangkabau Society." Ph.D. dissertation, Australian National University.

Norazit Selat. 1990. *Negeri Sembilan: Dahulu dan Sekarang*. Kuala Lumpur: Persatuan Muzium Malaysia.

Nordin Selat. 1976. *Sistem Sosial Adat Perpatih*. Kuala Lumpur: Utusan Melayu Berhad.

Norhalim Haji Ibrahim. 1993. *Adat Perpatih: Perbezaan dan Persamaannya dengan Adat Temenggong*. Kuala Lumpur: Fajar Bakti.

Obeyesekere, Gananath. 1969. "The Ritual Drama of the Sanni Demons: Collective Representations of Disease in Ceylon." *Comparative Studies in Society and History* 11(2):174–216.

O'Brien, H. A. 1883. "Latah." *Journal of the Royal Asiatic Society, Straits Branch* 11:143–53.

Ong, Aihwa. 1987. *Spirits of Resistance and Capitalist Discipline: Factory Women in Malaysia*. Albany: State University of New York Press.

———. 1988. "The Production of Possession: Spirits and the Multinational Corporation in Malaysia." *American Ethnologist* 15(1):28–42.

———. 1989. "Center, Periphery, and Hierarchy: Gender in Southeast Asia." In *Gender in Anthropology: Critical Reviews for Research and Teaching*, edited by Sandra Morgen, 294–312. Washington, D.C.: American Anthropological Association.

———. 1990a. "Japanese Factories, Malay Workers: Class and Sexual Metaphors in West Malaysia." In *Power and Difference: Gender in Island Southeast Asia*, edited by Jane Atkinson and Shelly Errington, 385–422. Stanford: Stanford University Press.

———. 1990b. "State Versus Islam: Malay Families, Women's Bodies, and the Body Politic in Malaysia." *American Ethnologist* 17(2):258–76.

Ong, Aihwa, and Michael G. Peletz. 1995a. "Introduction." In *Bewitching Women, Pious Men: Gender and Body Politics in Southeast Asia*, edited by Aihwa Ong and Michael G. Peletz, 1–18. Berkeley: University of California Press.

Ong, Aihwa, and Michael G. Peletz, eds. 1995b. *Bewitching Women, Pious Men: Gender and Body Politics in Southeast Asia*. Berkeley: University of California Press.

Ortner, Sherry. 1973. "On Key Symbols." *American Anthropologist* 75(5):1338–46.

———. 1974. "Is Female to Male as Nature Is to Culture?" In *Woman, Culture, and Society*, edited by Michelle Rosaldo and Louise Lamphere, 67–87. Stanford: Stanford University Press.

———. 1981. "Gender and Sexuality in Hierarchical Societies: The Case of Polynesia and Some Comparative Implications." In *Sexual Meanings: The Cultural Construction of Gender and Sexuality*, edited by Sherry Ortner and Harriet Whitehead, 359–409. Cambridge: Cambridge University Press.

———. 1983. "The Founding of the First Sherpa Nunnery, and the Problem of 'Women' as an Analytic Category." In *Feminist Re-Visions: What Has Been and What Might Be*, edited by Vivian Patraka and Louise Tilly, 98–134. Ann Arbor: Women's Studies Program, University of Michigan.

———. 1984. "Theory in Anthropology since the Sixties." *Comparative Studies in Society and History* 26:126–66.

——. 1989. *High Religion: A Cultural and Political History of Sherpa Buddhism.* Princeton: Princeton University Press.

——. 1989–90. "Gender Hegemonies." *Cultural Critique* 14:35–80.

——. 1995. "Resistance and the Problem of Ethnographic Refusal." *Comparative Studies in Society and History* 37(1):173–93.

Ortner, Sherry, and Harriet Whitehead. 1981a. "Introduction: Accounting for Sexual Meanings." In *Sexual Meanings: The Cultural Construction of Gender and Sexuality,* edited by Sherry Ortner and Harriet Whitehead, 1–27. Cambridge: Cambridge University Press.

Ortner, Sherry, and Harriet Whitehead, eds. 1981b. *Sexual Meanings: The Cultural Construction of Gender and Sexuality.* Cambridge: Cambridge University Press.

Pak, Ok-Kyung. 1986. "Lowering the High, Raising the Low: Gender, Alliance, and Property Relations in a Minangkabau Peasant Community of West Sumatra, Indonesia." Ph.D. dissertation, Laval University.

——. N.d. "Exchange of Men and Ideology of Male Ascendency among the Minangkabau of Sumatra." Typescript.

Parr, C. W. C., and W. H. Mackray. 1910. "Rembau, One of the Nine States: Its History, Constitution, and Customs." *Journal of the Royal Asiatic Society, Straits Branch* 56:1–157.

Peletz, Michael G. 1987a. "The Exchange of Men in Nineteenth-Century Negeri Sembilan (Malaya)." *American Ethnologist* 14(3):449–69.

——. 1987b. "Female Heirship and the Autonomy of Women in Negeri Sembilan, Malaysia." *Research in Economic Anthropology: A Research Annual,* vol. 8, edited by Barry L. Isaac, 61–101. Greenwich, Conn.: JAI Press.

——. 1988a. "Poisoning, Sorcery, and Healing Rituals in Negeri Sembilan." *Bijdragen Tot de Taal-, Land-, en Volkenkunde* 144(1):132–64.

——. 1988b. A Share of the Harvest: Kinship, Property, and Social History among the Malays of Rembau. Berkeley: University of California Press.

——. 1992. Review of *The Oriental, the Ancient, and the Primitive: Systems of Marriage and the Family in the Preindustrial Societies of Eurasia,* by Jack Goody. *American Ethnologist* 19(4):847–49.

——. 1993a. "Knowledge, Power, and Personal Misfortune in a Malay Context." In *Understanding Witchcraft and Sorcery in Southeast Asia,* edited by C. W. Watson and Roy F. Ellen, 149–77. Honolulu: University of Hawaii Press.

——. 1993b. "Sacred Texts and Dangerous Words: The Politics of Law and Cultural Rationalization in Malaysia." *Comparative Studies in Society and History* 35(1):66–109.

——. 1994a. "Comparative Perspectives on Kinship and Cultural Identity in Negeri Sembilan." *Sojourn: Journal of Social Issues in Southeast Asia* 9(1):1–53.

——. 1994b. "Neither Reasonable nor Responsible: Contrasting Representations of Masculinity in a Malay Society." *Cultural Anthropology* 9(2):135–78.

——. 1995. "Kinship Studies in Late Twentieth-Century Anthropology." *Annual Review of Anthropology* 24:343–72.

———. N.d.a. " 'Ordinary Muslims' and Muslim Resurgents in Contemporary Malaysia: Notes on an Ambivalent Relationship." In *Islam in an Era of Nation Building: Politics and Religious Reformation in Muslim Southeast Asia*, edited by Patricia Horavatich and Robert Hefner. Forthcoming.

———. N.d.b. "Comparative and Historical Notes on the 'Great Transformation' among Negeri Sembilan Malays, with Particular Reference to Chinese and Minangkabau." In *Market Cultures: Entrepreneurial Precedents and Ethical Dilemmas in East and Southeast Asia*, edited by Robert Hefner and Hue-Tam Ho-Tai. Forthcoming.

Postel-Coster, Els. 1992. "The Image of Women in Minangkabau Fiction." In *Indonesian Women in Focus*, edited by Elsbeth Locher-Scholten and Anke Niehof, 225–239. Leiden: Koninklijk Instituut voor Taal-, Land-, en Volkenkunde.

Prindiville, Joanne. 1985. "Mother, Mother's Brother, and Modernization: The Problems and Prospects of Minangkabau Matriliny in a Changing World." In *Change and Continuity in Minangkabau: Local, Regional, and Historical Perspectives on West Sumatra*, edited by Lynn L. Thomas and Franz von Benda-Beckmann, 29–43. Monographs in International Studies, Southeast Asia Series, no. 71. Athens, Ohio: Ohio University Press.

Provencher, Ronald. 1979. "Orality as a Pattern of Symbolism in Malay Psychiatry." In *The Imagination of Reality: Essays in Southeast Asian Coherence Systems*, edited by A. L. Becker and Aram A. Yengoyan, 43–53. Norwood, N.J.: Ablex.

———. 1984. " 'Mother Needles': Lessons on Inter-Ethnic Psychiatry in Malaysian Society." *Social Science and Medicine* 18(2)139–46.

Rabinow, Paul. 1977. *Reflections on Fieldwork in Morocco*. Berkeley: University of California Press.

Ramli bin Saad. 1978. *Jenayah Zina*. Kuala Lumpur: Penerbit Kerajaan Malaysia.

Rapp, Rayna. 1982. "Family and Class in Contemporary America: Notes toward an Understanding of Ideology." In *Rethinking the Family: Some Feminist Questions*, edited by Barrie Thorne and Marilyn Yalom, 168–87. New York: Longman.

Raybeck, Douglas. 1986. "The Elastic Rule: Conformity and Deviance in Kelantan Village Life." In *Cultural Identity in Northern Peninsula Malaysia*, edited by Sharon Carstens, 55–74. Monographs in International Studies, Southeast Asia Series, no. 63. Athens, Ohio: Ohio University Press.

Read, Kenneth. 1955. "Morality and the Concept of the Person among the Gahuku-Gama." *Oceania* 25(4):233–82.

Reid, Anthony. 1979. *The Blood of the People: Revolution and the End of Traditional Rule in Northern Sumatra*. Kuala Lumpur: Oxford University Press.

———. 1988. *Southeast Asia in the Age of Commerce, 1450–1680. Vol. 1, The Lands below the Winds*. New Haven: Yale University Press.

Rich, Adrienne. 1979. *On Lies, Secrets, and Silence: Selected Prose 1966–1978*. New York: W. W. Norton.

Richards, A. I. 1951. "Some Types of Family Structure amongst the Central Bantu." In *African Systems of Kinship and Marriage*, edited by A. R. Radcliffe-Brown and Daryll Forde, 207–51. London: Oxford University Press.

Rodgers, Susan. 1990. "The Symbolic Representation of Women in a Changing Batak Culture." In *Power and Difference: Gender in Island Southeast Asia,* edited by Jane Atkinson and Shelly Errington, 307–44. Stanford: Stanford University Press.

Roff, William. 1967. *The Origins of Malay Nationalism.* Kuala Lumpur: University of Malaya Press.

Rogers, Susan. 1975. "Female Forms of Power and the Myth of Male Dominance: A Model of Male/Female Interaction in Peasant Society." *American Ethnologist* 2:727–56.

Rosaldo, Michelle. 1980. "The Use and Abuse of Anthropology: Reflections on Feminism and Cross-Cultural Understanding." *Signs* 5(3):389–417.

———. 1987. "Moral/Analytic Dilemmas Posed by the Intersection of Feminism and Social Science." In *Interpretive Social Science: A Second Look,* edited by Paul Rabinow and William Sullivan, 280–301. Berkeley: University of California Press.

Rosaldo, Michelle, and Jane Atkinson. 1975. "Man the Hunter and Woman: Metaphors for the Sexes in Ilongot Magic Spells." In *The Interpretation of Symbolism,* edited by R. Willis, 43–75. London: Malaby Press.

Rosaldo, Renato. 1980. *Ilongot Headhunting, 1883–1974: A Study in Society and History.* Stanford: Stanford University Press.

Rosen, Lawrence. 1984. *Bargaining for Reality: The Construction of Social Relations in a Muslim Community.* Chicago: University of Chicago Press.

Rubel, Paula, and Abraham Rosman. 1978. *Your Own Pigs You May Not Eat: A Comparative Study of New Guinea Societies.* Chicago: University of Chicago Press.

Rubin, Gayle. 1975. "The Traffic in Women: Notes on the 'Political Economy' of Sex." In *Toward an Anthropology of Women,* edited by Rayna Reiter, 157–210. New York: Monthly Review Press.

Rubin, Lillian. 1976. *Worlds of Pain: Life in the Working-Class Family.* New York: Basic Books.

Sacks, Karen. 1979. *Sisters and Wives: The Past and Future of Sexual Equality.* Westport, Conn.: Greenwood Press.

Sanday, Peggy Reeves. 1981. *Female Power and Male Dominance: On the Origins of Sexual Equality.* Cambridge: Cambridge University Press.

———. 1990. "Androcentric and Matrifocal Gender Representations in Minangkabau Ideology." In *Beyond the Second Sex: New Directions in the Anthropology of Gender,* edited by Peggy Reeves Sanday and Ruth G. Goodenough, 139–68. Philadelphia: University of Pennsylvania Press.

Sanders, Paula. 1991. "Gendering the Ungendered Body: Hermaphrodites in Medieval Islamic Law." In *Women in Middle Eastern History,* edited by Nikkie R. Keddie and Beth Baron, 74–95. New Haven: Yale University Press.

Sangren, Steven. 1988. "Rhetoric and the Authority of Ethnography: 'Postmodernism' and the Social Reproduction of Texts." *Current Anthropology* 29(3):405–35.

Schlegel, Alice. 1972. *Male Dominance and Female Autonomy: Domestic Authority in Matrilineal Societies.* New Haven: Human Relations Area Files Press.

Schneider, David M. 1961. "The Distinctive Features of Matrilineal Descent Groups." In *Matrilineal Kinship*, edited by David M. Schneider and Kathleen Gough, 1–29. Berkeley: University of California Press.

———. 1968. *American Kinship: A Cultural Account*. Englewood Cliffs, N.J.: Prentice-Hall.

———. 1984. *A Critique of the Study of Kinship*. Ann Arbor: University of Michigan Press.

Schneider, David M., and Kathleen Gough, eds. 1961. *Matrilineal Kinship*. Berkeley: University of California Press.

Schwimmer, Erik. 1982. "Structural and Symbolic Anthropology in the Netherlands Today." In *Symbolic Anthropology in the Netherlands*, edited by P. E. de Josselin de Jong and Erik Schwimmer, 1–11. The Hague: Martinus Nijhoff.

Scott, James. 1985. *Weapons of the Weak: Everyday Forms of Peasant Resistance*. New Haven: Yale University Press.

———. 1990. *Domination and the Arts of Resistance: Hidden Transcripts*. New Haven: Yale University Press.

(Dato) Sedia Raja Abdullah. 1925. "The Leading Saints in Rembau." *Journal of the Royal Asiatic Society, Malayan Branch* 3(3):101–4.

Shapiro, Judith. 1979. "Cross-Cultural Perspectives on Sexual Differentiation." In *Human Sexuality: A Comparative and Developmental Perspective*, edited by Herant Katchadourian, 269–308. Berkeley: University of California Press.

Shore, Brad. 1981. "Sexuality and Gender in Samoa: Conceptions and Missed Conceptions." In *Sexual Meanings: The Cultural Construction of Gender and Sexuality*, edited by Sherry Ortner and Harriet Whitehead, 192–215. New York: Cambridge University Press.

Siegel, James. 1969. *The Rope of God*. Berkeley: University of California Press.

———. 1978. "Curing Rites, Dreams, and Domestic Politics in a Sumatran Society." *Glyph* 3:18–31.

———. 1979. *Shadow and Sound: The Historical Thought of a Sumatran People*. Chicago: University of Chicago Press.

Simmel, Georg. [1908] 1971. "The Stranger." Reprinted in *Georg Simmel on Individuality and Social Forms*, edited by Donald N. Levine, 143–49. Chicago: University of Chicago Press.

Siskind, Janet. 1978. "Kinship and Mode of Production." *American Anthropologist* 80:860–72.

Skeat, Walter W. [1900] 1967. *Malay Magic: Being an Introduction to the Folklore and Popular Religion of the Malay Peninsula*. Reprint. New York: Dover Publications.

Slater, Philip. 1961. "Toward a Dualistic Theory of Identification." *Merrill-Palmer Quarterly of Behavior and Development* 7(2):113–26.

Smith, DeVerne Reed. 1983. *Palauan Social Structure*. New Brunswick, N.J.: Rutgers University Press.

Smith-Hefner, Nancy. 1988a. "The Linguistic Socialization of Javanese Children in Two Communities." *Anthropological Linguistics* 30(2):166–98.

———. 1988b. "Women and Politeness: The Javanese Example." *Language in Society* 17(4):535–54.

Snouck Hurgronje, C. 1906. *The Achehnese.* Translated by A. W. S. O'Sullivan. 2 vols. Leiden: E. J. Brill.

Spiro, Melford. 1977. *Kinship and Marriage in Burma: A Cultural and Psychodynamic Analysis.* Berkeley: University of California Press.

Stacey, Judith. 1991. *Brave New Families: Stories of Domestic Upheaval in Late Twentieth-Century America.* New York: Basic Books.

Stack, Carol. 1974. *All Our Kin: Strategies for Survival in a Black Community.* New York: Harper and Row.

———. 1990. "Different Voices, Different Visions: Gender, Culture, and Moral Reasoning." In *Uncertain Terms: Negotiating Gender in American Culture,* edited by Faye Ginsburg and Anna Tsing, 19–27. Boston: Beacon Press.

Stallybrass, Peter, and Allon White. 1986. *The Politics and Poetics of Transgression.* Ithaca: Cornell University Press.

Stivens, Maila. 1985. "The Fate of Women's Land Rights: Gender, Matriliny, and Capitalism in Rembau, Negeri Sembilan, Malaysia." In *Women, Work, and Ideology in the Third World,* edited by Haleh Afshar, 3–36. London: Tavistock Publications.

———. 1987. "Family and State in Malaysian Industrialization: The Case of Rembau, Negeri Sembilan, Malaysia." In *Women, State, and Ideology,* edited by Haleh Afshar, 89–110. Albany: State University of New York Press.

———. 1991. "The Evolution of Kinship Relations in Rembau, Negeri Sembilan, Malaysia." In *Cognation and Social Organization in Southeast Asia,* edited by F. Husken and J. Kemp, 71–88. Leiden: Koninklijk Instituut voor Taal-, Land-, en Volkenkunde.

Stoler, Ann. 1977. "Class Structure and Female Autonomy in Rural Java." *Signs* 3(1):74–89.

Strange, Heather. 1981. *Rural Malay Women in Tradition and Transition.* New York: Praeger.

Strathern, Marilyn. 1980. "No Nature, No Culture: The Hagen Case." In *Nature, Culture, and Gender,* edited by Carol MacCormack and Marilyn Strathern, 174–222. Cambridge: Cambridge University Press.

———. 1981. "Self-Interest and the Social Good: Some Implications of Hagen Gender Imagery." In *Sexual Meanings: The Cultural Construction of Gender and Sexuality,* edited by Sherry Ortner and Harriet Whitehead, 166–91. New York: Cambridge University Press.

———. 1984. "Marriage Exchanges: A Melanesian Comment." *Annual Review of Anthropology* 13:41–73.

———. 1988. *The Gender of the Gift: Problems with Women and Problems with Society in Melanesia.* Berkeley: University of California Press.

———. 1992. *Reproducing the Future: Anthropology, Kinship, and the New Reproductive Technologies.* New York: Routledge.

Strathern, Marilyn, ed. 1987. *Dealing with Inequality: Analyzing Gender Relations in Melanesia and Beyond.* Cambridge: Cambridge University Press.

Sweeney, Amin. 1987. *A Full Hearing: Orality and Literacy in the Malay World.* Berkeley: University of California Press.

Swettenham, Sir Frank. [1895] 1984. *Malay Sketches.* Reprint. Singapore: Graham Brash.

Swift, Michael G. 1965. *Malay Peasant Society in Jelebu*. London: Athlone Press.
————. 1971. "Minangkabau and Modernization." In *Anthropology in Oceania*, edited by L. R. Hiatt and Chandra Jayawardena, 255–67. Sydney: Agus and Robertson.

Tanner, Nancy M. 1974. "Matrifocality in Indonesia and Africa and among Black Americans." In *Woman, Culture, and Society*, edited by Michelle Rosaldo and Louise Lamphere, 129–56. Stanford: Stanford University Press.
————. 1982. "The Nuclear Family in Minangkabau Matriliny: The Mirror of Disputes." *Bijdragen Tot de Taal-, Land-, en Volkenkunde* 138(1):129–51.

Tanner, Nancy M., and Lynn Thomas. 1985. "Rethinking Matriliny: Decision Making and Sex Roles in Minangkabau." In *Change and Continuity in Minangkabau: Local, Regional, and Historical Perspectives on West Sumatra*, edited by Lynn Thomas and Franz von Benda-Beckmann, 45–71. Monographs in International Studies, Southeast Asia Series, no. 71. Athens, Ohio: Ohio University Press.

Tapper, Nancy, and Richard Tapper. 1987. "The Birth of the Prophet: Ritual and Gender in Turkish Islam." *Man* 22:69–92.

Taussig, Michael. 1980. *The Devil and Commodity Fetishism in South America*. Chapel Hill: University of North Carolina Press.

Taylor, E. N. [1929] 1970. "The Customary Law of Rembau." Reprinted in *Readings in Malay Adat Laws*, edited by M. B. Hooker, 109–51. Singapore: Singapore University Press.

Thomas, Lynn. 1985. "Unequal Marriage and Paternity in a Matrilineal Sumatran Society." Paper presented at the 37th Annual Meeting of the Association for Asian Studies.

Trawick, Margaret. 1990. *Notes on Love in a Tamil Family*. Berkeley: University of California Press.

Turnbull, Colin. 1961. *The Forest People*. New York: Simon and Schuster.

Turner, Denys. 1983. *Marxism and Christianity*. Totowa, N.J.: Barnes and Noble.

Umar Junus. 1964. "Some Remarks on Minangkabau Social Structure." *Bijdragen Tot de Taal-, Land-, en Volkenkunde* 120:293–326.

Valeri, Valerio. 1990. "Both Nature and Culture: Reflections on Menstrual and Parturitional Taboos in Huaulu (Seram)." In *Power and Difference: Gender in Island Southeast Asia*, edited by Jane Atkinson and Shelly Errington, 235–72. Stanford: Stanford University Press.

Van Esterik, Penny, ed. 1982. *Women of Southeast Asia*. Dekalb, Ill.: Center for Southeast Asian Studies, Northern Illinois University.

Volkman, Toby. 1985. *Feasts of Honor: Ritual and Change in the Toraja Highlands*. Urbana: University of Illinois Press.

von Benda-Beckmann, Franz. 1979. *Property in Social Continuity: Continuity and Change in the Maintenance of Property Relations through Time in Minangkabau, West Sumatra*. The Hague: Koninklijk Instituut voor Taal-, Land-, en Volkenkunde.

Weigert, Andrew. 1991. *Mixed Emotions: Certain Steps toward Understanding Ambivalence*. Albany: State University of New York Press.

Weiner, Annette. 1976. *Women of Value, Men of Renown: New Perspectives in Trobriand Exchange*. Austin: University of Texas Press.

————. 1992. *Inalienable Possessions: The Paradox of Keeping While Giving*. Berkeley: University of California Press.

Whalley, Lucy. 1993. "Virtuous Women, Productive Citizens: Negotiating Tradition, Islam, and Modernity in Minangkabau, Indonesia." Ph.D. dissertation, University of Illinois.

Wheatley, Paul. 1964. *Impressions of the Malay Peninsula in Ancient Times*. Singapore: Donald Moore.

Whitehead, Harriet. 1986. "The Varieties of Fertility Cultism in New Guinea." *American Ethnologist* 13:80–99, 271–89.

————. 1987. "Fertility and Exchange in New Guinea." In *Gender and Kinship: Essays toward a Unified Analysis*, edited by Jane Collier and Sylvia Yanagisako, 244–70. Stanford: Stanford University Press.

Wikan, Unni. 1990. *Managing Turbulent Hearts: A Balinese Formula for Living*. Chicago: University of Chicago Press.

Wilder, William. 1970. "Socialization and Social Structure in a Malay Village." In *Socialization: The Approach from Social Anthropology*, edited by Philip Mayer, 215–68. London: Tavistock Publications.

Wilkinson, R. J. 1906. *Malay Beliefs*. London: Luzac.

————. [1911] 1970. "Notes on the Negri Sembilan." Reprinted in *Papers on Malay Subjects*, edited by R. J. Wilkinson, 277–321. Kuala Lumpur: Oxford University Press.

Williams, Raymond. 1977. *Marxism and Literature*. Oxford: Oxford University Press.

Willis, Paul. 1977. *Learning to Labor: How Working Class Kids Get Working Class Jobs*. New York: Columbia University Press.

Winch, Robert F. 1962. *Identification and Its Familial Determinants*. New York: Bobbs-Merrill.

Winstedt, Richard O. 1934. "Negri Sembilan: The History, Polity, and Beliefs of the Nine States." *Journal of the Royal Asiatic Society, Malayan Branch* 12(3):35–114.

Winzeler, Robert. 1984. "The Study of Malayan Latah." *Indonesia* 37:77–104.

Wolf, Margery. 1992. *A Thrice-Told Tale: Feminism, Postmodernism, and Ethnographic Responsibility*. Stanford: Stanford University Press.

Wolters, O. W. 1982. *History, Culture, and Region in Southeast Asian Perspectives*. Singapore: Institute of Southeast Asian Studies.

Woodward, Mark. 1989. *Islam in Java: Normative Piety and Mysticism in the Sultanate of Yogyakarta*. Tucson: University of Arizona Press.

Yanagisako, Sylvia, and Jane Collier. 1987. "Toward a Unified Analysis of Gender and Kinship." In *Gender and Kinship: Essays toward a Unified Analysis*, edited by Jane Collier and Sylvia Yanagisako, 14–50. Stanford: Stanford University Press.

Yengoyan, Aram A. 1983. "Transvestitism and the Ideology of Gender: Southeast Asia and Beyond." In *Feminist Re-Visions: What Has Been and What Might Be*, edited by Vivian Patraka and Louise Tilly, 135–48. Ann Arbor: Women's Studies Program, University of Michigan.

Zainah Anwar. 1987. *Islamic Revivalism in Malaysia*. Kuala Lumpur: Pelanduk Publications.

Zelenietz, Marty. 1981. "Sorcery and Social Change: An Introduction." *Social Analysis* 8:3–14.

Zelenietz, Marty, and Shirley Lindenbaum, eds. 1981. *Sorcery and Social Change in Melanesia* (special issue of *Social Analysis,* vol. 8).